CHARLIE MURPHY

The Iconoclastic Showman
behind the Chicago Cubs

JASON CANNON

University of Nebraska Press · Lincoln

The University of Nebraska Press is part of a land-grant institution with campuses and programs on the past, present, and future homelands of the Pawnee, Ponca, Otoe-Missouria, Omaha, Dakota, Lakota, Kaw, Cheyenne, and Arapaho Peoples, as well as those of the relocated Ho-Chunk, Sac and Fox, and Iowa Peoples.

Library of Congress Cataloging-in-Publication Data
Names: Cannon, Jason, author.
Title: Charlie Murphy: the iconoclastic showman behind the Chicago Cubs / Jason Cannon.
Description: Lincoln: University of Nebraska Press, [2022] | Includes bibliographical references and index.
Identifiers: LCCN 2021040675
ISBN 9781496228635 (Hardback)
ISBN 9781496232205 (ePub)
ISBN 9781496232212 (PDF)
Subjects: LCSH: Murphy, Charles Webb. | Baseball team owners—United States—Biography. | Chicago Cubs (Baseball team)—History. | Baseball—Illinois—Chicago—History. | World Series (Baseball) (1918) | Baseball—Corrupt practices—United States—History. | BISAC: SPORTS & RECREATION / Baseball / History | BIOGRAPHY & AUTOBIOGRAPHY / Sports
Classification: LCC GV865.M789 C36 2022 | DDC 796.357092
[B]—dc23/eng/20220201
LC record available at https://lccn.loc.gov/2021040675

Set in Lyon Text by Laura Buis.

For Reagan

For a real wonder-story, the history of Charles W. Murphy outranks anything in baseball records.

—EDWARD MOTT WOOLLEY, *McClure's*

CONTENTS

CHARLIE MURPHY

INTRODUCTION

"He Was a Showman . . ."

On October 16, 1931, Charles Webb Murphy's troubled heart, wracked with the repercussions of a stroke and hypertension, gave out. At sixty-three, Murphy's death returned him—if only momentarily—to the public spotlight after a decade of relative obscurity. In his heyday, primarily the first two decades of the twentieth century, when the team he owned, the Chicago Cubs, won four pennants and two World Series championships from 1905 through 1914, Murphy's activities and comments routinely appeared in America's sports pages. During his years in charge of the Cubs, Murphy upended the typical personality of the baseball magnate. He spoke exuberantly and frequently with newspaper reporters in much the same way as one of the Progressive Era's most powerful figures, Teddy Roosevelt. Unlike his peers, many of whom fought their battles privately, Murphy's relentless public exposure of the underbelly of baseball's business side made him a target of the establishment's wrath.

Hugh Fullerton proved to be an exception. A sportswriter now enshrined in the National Baseball Hall of Fame, Fullerton covered baseball for decades and famously played an important role in uncovering the Black Sox scandal in 1919. Most uniquely, Fullerton proved to be one of the few people around the game of baseball who shared a genuine personal friendship with Murphy. Fullerton met Murphy during their teenage years, before professional baseball made either man famous. They hailed from neighboring Ohio towns: Murphy lived in Wilmington, a small rural community triangulated in the west by

Cincinnati, the north by Dayton, and the northeast by Columbus. Fullerton grew up in Hillsboro, a tiny enclave just over twenty miles to the southeast of Wilmington. They shared a passion for baseball in addition to their roots. "Murph was my friend from boyhood," Fullerton reminisced. "We were friends when he worked in a drug store in Wilmington and spent his meager money to back the Wilmington baseball team against the world."[1] Fullerton's awareness of Murphy's spending habits suggests he knew another reason for his friend's employment that transcended supporting the local nine. Charlie worked at the drug store to support his mother and three younger siblings, who desperately needed money after his father, who suffered an inordinate number of personal tragedies, drank himself into insanity, which forced the oldest son to become a vital financial resource for the family at the age of fifteen. Fullerton knew the fragile, abused Murphy underneath the latter's layers of bluster, hustle, impetuousness, and explosions of creativity. Nearly five decades after meeting Murphy, Fullerton captured the incomparable personality of his old friend and the impact it had on baseball in a eulogy.

> Murphy is dead. The jolly, turbulent little Irishman from Wilmington, who came out of Cincinnati to start more trouble and to make more baseball news than any man in the history of the game, finally lost out in his battle for health and the end came after years of suffering.
>
> Charles Webb Murphy, son of Patrick and Bridget Murphy, was for half a dozen years the central figure of major league baseball and the most hated and upsetting figure in the game.[2]

Yes, Murphy antagonized and annoyed people, including players, fans and, especially, his fellow owners. "Frequently he did foolish things and aroused bitter criticism. Most of his mistakes were made by impetuosity. He did things like a flash, for which he afterwards was sorry, but instead of admitting it, he fought it out," recalled Fullerton. And Fullerton was not immune to Murphy's quirks or impulsivity, but he remained drawn to his friend's ebullient personality. "As I used to tell Murph many times: 'Murphy, I love you but somehow I don't like a darned thing you ever do,'" he wrote.[3] However, history remembers Murphy's faults all too thoroughly while ignorantly belittling his successes as the accidental results of consistently being in the right place at the right time.

Throughout his career, Murphy delighted in stoking the ire of American League president Ban Johnson, much to the chagrin of the other National League owners, who frequently found themselves caught in the crosshairs of the infuriated Johnson's return fire. During one particularly heated squabble in 1911, Johnson fumed over Murphy in a letter to August "Garry" Herrmann, president of the Cincinnati Reds and member of the National Commission, in which he threatened to sever ties between the American and National Leagues. "The American League regards C.W. Murphy as a menace to the integrity and good repute of baseball. If the National League can tolerate such a Club Owner, then we cannot with safety have close affiliation with the organization. The gentlemen who endorsed the resolution love peace and harmony, but it cannot be purchased at a sacrifice of their dignity and honor," Johnson warned.[4]

Several days before Johnson penned his letter to Herrmann, Brooklyn owner Charles Ebbets complained about the impending fallout from the latest of Murphy's transgressions: "I do not think it is fair and just to the other members of this League (I am speaking for myself alone; the balance can speak for themselves) for Mr. Murphy, because he does not agree with Mr. Johnson in some things, to inject his personal differences with Mr. Johnson into the affairs of the League, to the extent that Mr. Johnson retaliates, as any man with red blood in his veins would, and punches the National League."[5]

Murphy routinely responded to the controversy he created by profusely apologizing and using his self-deprecating sense of humor to ratchet down the tension and smooth over any ruffled feathers. Fullerton once described Murphy as "a small, plump man, quick of wit, brilliant in repartee, quick of temper, quick to forgive, even quicker than he is to seek forgiveness."[6] Fullerton recalled an episode that exemplified how Murphy wriggled out of trouble with his peers by applying his traditional wink and a nod. "The entire National League turned against him. At one winter meeting in Chicago the President and the seven club owners were all set to force him out of the game. They were going to call him in, and lay down the law. Murph called me aside, chuckling as he did so, and showed me seven papers, all addressed, one to each rival club owner. Each was a blanket apology for everything he had done. He took those typewritten apologies into the meeting and gravely passed them around—and they forgave him," Fullerton marveled.[7] So it routinely went until the next time he stirred up trouble.

In the midst of Murphy's theatrics, the Cubs proved to be wildly successful on the field, giving him plenty to crow about, which only further infuriated the baseball establishment. Fullerton readily acknowledged Murphy's faults but suggested that they distracted observers from the reality that the wily owner knew what he was doing far more frequently than he was given credit for. According to Fullerton, "Murphy's spectacular success, and his brilliant showmanship naturally made enemies, especially among other club owners. He out-witted them, out-traded them and out-talked them."[8] Murphy forged a close bond with manager Frank Chance after officially taking over as team president following the 1905 season. Together, they successfully deployed the greatest professional baseball team the world had ever seen.

In addition to their shared roots, frequent laughter defined Fullerton's friendship with "Murph." One evening in New York, during the Cubs' heyday, Murphy treated Fullerton, Frank and Edythe Chance, and Secretary Charlie Williams to a night on the town. They went to a play followed by a nice dinner. The bill ran upward of $200, and Murphy paid the check without hesitation. Suddenly, he burst out laughing. Tears squeezed out of the corners of his eyes as his puzzled dinner guests tried to ascertain what had happened. "I just got to thinking how I used to work all day in the drug store, sleep behind the prescription counter to answer the night bell, and got $3 a week," Murphy managed to tell them between chuckles. Fullerton immediately understood that Murphy was thinking about just how far he had come from his modest upbringing. "It was the most magnificent dinner I ever sat down before," Fullerton said.[9]

Murphy's tendency to exaggerate the truth got him in trouble at times, so Fullerton decided to have fun at his friend's expense by using an aggrandized version of the tactic. One day, Fullerton was chopping wood when a large piece of bark flew up, struck him in the face, and gave him a deeply bruised eye. "The color scheme ranged from egg plant to vivid red," Fullerton recalled. Rather than suffer any embarrassment by admitting he had hurt himself, Fullerton put on grave airs and answered an inquirer that Murphy and he were arguing when Murphy threw an inkwell at Fullerton that smashed his face. Two days later Fullerton picked up his ringing telephone and heard the confounded voice of Murphy on the line asking incredulously what had happened, and why were other reporters upset with him. A thoroughly amused Fullerton laughed at his successful prank. "It was a triumph of mendacity," he crowed.[10]

However, as the years wore on, Murphy grew increasingly petulant. The survival reflexes he had developed in his younger days proved to be his undoing when the team's success simply required him to thrive. As the sport skyrocketed in popularity, baseball executives needed to craft a product that met the emerging standards of the Progressive Era. To be more specific, Ban Johnson wanted to root out owners who did not care about the perception of Organized Baseball as a whole. Murphy used the press as a stereotypical Chicago "booster" would have to promote his local team. However, Johnson wanted public attacks on the leagues themselves to cease because they made Organized Baseball appear weak. One of the most well-known anecdotes about Murphy relates how his ill-timed firing of Johnny Evers opened the door for Johnson to get his way and oust the Cubs' owner in 1914. Originally, Murphy had tried to position himself as a champion of the National League, but the other owners suspected otherwise, so he gave up and favored his own franchise. In 1914 Murphy's unwillingness to elevate league loyalty above his interest in the Cubs during Organized Baseball's hostilities with the Federal League threatened the establishment and led to his ouster. The result is that the burned ashes of Murphy's entire career have been thrown to the wind.

This book pieces together the scattered fragments of Murphy's personal and professional life to revisit and reassess his role in baseball and beyond. It examines how Murphy's influence extended outside of Chicago to include his contributions to his hometown of Wilmington, where he built a luxurious theater for his former neighbors to enjoy, but it is mostly about baseball, and one man who set the sport on its ear. In various contexts, historians have called Charles Webb Murphy an "odd duck with a big mouth," an "insufferable blowhard," and "little more than a salaried flunky."[11] Frankly, in moments of time, those assessments hold kernels of accuracy. Murphy made his share of egregious gaffes, but his foundational successes have not been rigorously analyzed. Too frequently, they have been taken for granted or dismissed as inevitable. Murphy has been presented as a poorly written stock character from a bad novel who bumbled his way to the top of the baseball world through comedic luck. Upon closer examination, someone much more complex emerges: a complicated, brilliant human being immersed in the world of Organized Baseball during the Progressive Era. Hugh Fullerton summed up his friend this way: "He was a showman, a baseball fanatic, a quick-thinking, quicker-acting fellow, whose fiery, impulsive temperament kept the entire baseball world bubbling."[12]

WILMINGTON

Beginning in 1845 a deadly microscopic pathogen devastated the lives of Ireland's farmers by infiltrating their primary source of food: potatoes. Fueled by the windy, wet weather of the isle, the organism, *phytophthora infestans*, embedded itself into the leaves of the crops before insidiously working its way through the tubers of the plant en route to the potato itself. Within days, the fungus completely corrupted the integrity of the vegetable and left behind a rotten, inedible mess along with a myriad of hungry onlookers. The disease quickly spread to nearby crops as the spores multiplied and either fell to the ground and invaded the soil or rode the wind to nearby plants to start the cycle anew. This blight wreaked astonishing havoc throughout Ireland. Without potatoes to eat, one million Irish, many of them farmers or laborers, along with their families, died between 1845 and 1851, a tragedy known today as the Great Famine.

As the potato crops rapidly deteriorated, a million and a half starving Irish fled from their homeland before death overtook them too. They scraped together enough money to buy passage across the Atlantic Ocean to America in their desperate race for sustenance. Simultaneously, absentee landlords, many of whom resided in England, exacerbated the laborers' hardship. Scores of property owners foisted tickets to the United States onto their tenants, whether they wanted to relocate or not, because the overseas passage cost them less money than the taxes they were required to pay for having inhabitants on their land. Upon arrival, many of the Irish immigrants decided to begin their lives anew on America's Eastern Seaboard, but a number of them embarked on a westward journey into the interior of the unfamiliar land to find a different environment. They discovered Southern Ohio, a region with ample land and traces of a familiar Irish Catholic population.

A number of immigrants established new homes in and around the city of Cincinnati, a growing trade center on the northern shore of the Ohio River that owed its expansion in no small part to the contributions of several ingenious Irish immigrants. Francis Kennedy, Cincinnati's inaugural Irish settler, arrived in 1788 and created a ferry system that facilitated the transportation of people and goods in and out of the city. James Gamble, born in Enniskillen, Ireland, opened his first store in Cincinnati, and in 1837 he formed a new company with his brother-in-law, Englishman William Procter, that soon bolstered the city's economic reputation. From a cultural perspective, the Catholic Church developed an influential presence in town. The newly arrived Irish families recognized a bit of home and settled in Southern Ohio.[1]

Patrick J. Murphy was born in County Cork, the large coastal region located along the southern edge of Ireland, around the time the devastating potato blight appeared in 1845.[2] Although he was too young to recognize its condition, baby Patrick's community was actually being upended for a second time. Eroding economic conditions in County Cork earlier in the nineteenth century compelled artisans and farmers to immigrate to America. Now, the blight had severely compounded the problems for the Irish working class. Without hope of harvesting a successful crop, a swelling number of local Irish joined the migration to the United States.[3]

Although details remain elusive, young Patrick Murphy sailed west in this immigration wave. It is nearly impossible to pinpoint exactly when. However, he likely boarded a ship in Queenstown, today known as Cobh (pronounced "Cove"), on the south side of the Great Island in Cork Harbour, a port that became known as the "Harbor of Tears" because it was the setting of so many sad separations. Thousands upon thousands of family members said their final goodbyes to one another on that shore, and the weeping Irish aboard the ships tragically watched their loved ones and cherished homeland disappear as they sailed into the gaping waters of the open sea.[4] Census data suggests Patrick was born in either 1845 or 1846, and he very well could have been just a small child when he left Ireland.

Most likely, the ship carrying Patrick initially sailed across the Irish Sea to England, where he transferred to another vessel destined for America. It is uncertain who brought Patrick to the United States, but he was probably too young to travel alone. His crossing was probably difficult. The vast majority of Irish immigrants endured horrific journeys plagued by a lack of provisions, grueling weather, deck fires, icebergs, cruel treatment at the hands of crewmen, and the constant threat of disease, particularly typhus. One former ship's surgeon described the utter misery of their experience. "The torments of hell might, in some degree, resemble the sufferings of the emigrants on board . . . Take all the stews in Liverpool, concentrate in a given space the acts and deeds done in all for one year, and they would scarcely equal in atrocity the amount of crime committed in one emigrant ship during a single voyage," he dejectedly wrote.[5]

Deciphering exactly when Patrick arrived in the United States is equally challenging. What is known is that a fourteen-year-old Patrick Murphy appears in the 1860 census at a Cincinnati boarding house run by a thirty-year-old saloonkeeper of the same name.[6] He is listed among the boarders rather than as a member of the Murphy family, suggesting he was simply living with people who shared the same last name. The census records Patrick's birthplace as Ireland and his vocation as plasterer, two important pieces of corroborating evidence that strongly suggest he is our guy. How he arrived in Cincinnati remains a mystery, yet it is likely that this is the same Patrick Murphy who settled in Wilmington, Ohio, several years later.[7]

Young Murphy developed his plastering skills in Cincinnati, but he decided to strike out on his own and go into business for himself. He relocated to Wilmington, a rural community located fifty miles to the northeast, in 1861. Murphy arrived in Wilmington on the cusp of its population boom. The town more than doubled in size during the 1860s—to just over two thousand residents by 1870—which offered Murphy a robust market for his new enterprise.

Established in 1810, Wilmington was located in the heart of Clinton County, a thickly wooded region in the days before settlers began carving out swaths of trees to construct homes. Wilmington underwent a dramatic transformation over the next fifty years. Winding Indian trails ushered newcomers safely through the forest's thick brush underneath a canopy of tall trees, including the sugar maple, with its sap providing the early settlers with "an almost invaluable article in the economy of their households."[8] Over the next couple of years, surveyors created a series of roads that linked community members to one another, as well as to the outside world. Work on a road that linked Wilmington to Cincinnati received approval from the Ohio state legislature in 1823. Another road, which connected Wilmington to Dayton, was laid in 1835.[9] As early as 1827 local citizens met to strategize on how they could entice a railroad company to include their young town on its travels through the region. It took several decades but, by 1851, locals had approved the allocation of $200,000 from the Clinton County coffers toward building a railroad line. After several delays, the first train arrived in Wilmington on August 11, 1853. The town held a massive celebration, gathering more than ten thousand people together for a community barbecue of epic proportion. On August 15 trains began running their regular daily route between Wilmington and Cincinnati. A one-way fare cost $1.60.[10]

Murphy arrived in town in the midst of Wilmington's dramatic development. Three years later, on September 11, 1864, as Abraham Lincoln pursued reelection, Patrick married Ellen Murray, a local girl who had also immigrated to the United States from Ireland. Father John O'Donoghue performed the ceremony, likely inside Preston's Hall, a local building the parish used for gatherings, after Ellen's father, Michael, gave his legal blessing for his underage daughter to wed the eighteen-year-old Murphy.[11] Although public records do not provide her birthdate, the 1860 census recorded Ellen as being twelve years old, making her either sixteen or seventeen on the day of the wedding.[12]

It is unknown precisely when the Murray family left Ireland, but six-year-old Ellen, along with her parents, Michael and Mary, and her three-year-old sister, Bridget, sailed from Liverpool aboard the

Iowa and arrived in New York on June 1, 1853.[13] Perhaps a key reason the family sailed for America two years after the Famine ended was Michael Murray's vocation as a day laborer. During a period when the cost of passage fares frequently prevented all family members from immigrating together, Michael had saved enough money to purchase transportation for his family of four on the same ship.

Eleven years later, Michael affixed a prominent "X" onto the left side of his daughter's marriage license, indicating his approval of Ellen's union to Patrick while simultaneously revealing his illiteracy. The most logical reason for his consent to the marriage of his young daughter appears to have been Ellen's discovery, earlier in the year, that she was pregnant.[14]

Just over three months later, on Thursday, December 15, 1864, tragedy struck Patrick and the Murray family. Ellen went into labor and delivered a baby boy, but she did not survive childbirth. After experiencing the destruction of lives through famine, and the hardship of migration, Patrick was now faced with the sudden loss of his young wife. The following day, grief-stricken mourners laid Ellen to rest, just west of town, in Sugar Grove Cemetery. The baby boy received the name William, and he split time during his younger years between the homes of his father and maternal grandparents.[15]

Over the next several years, Patrick settled into Wilmington and became a well-known figure about town. He developed his plastering business, and locals took to calling him P. J. In 1866 Murphy married Bridget O'Donnell, an Irish immigrant from County Tipperary. On November 29, Thanksgiving Day, P. J. and Bridget took their vows under the administration of Father O'Donoghue.[16] The couple settled into a home in the heart of town, a house on Mulberry Street, located just one block south of Wilmington's Main Street, that P. J. had purchased for $500.[17] Less than a year later, P. J. acquired an adjacent lot for another $500, notably expanding the footprint of the Murphys' homestead.[18]

As with P. J., a lack of evidence makes tracing Bridget's life before the wedding difficult. We do know that her mother's name was Catherine although her father was unknown.[19] Ship passenger lists do include a mother and daughter of the same names arriving in New York from

Liverpool, aboard the *Columbia*, on December 11, 1863. Bridget would have been eighteen at the time. What little corroborative evidence exists suggests this very well could be P. J.'s second wife and new mother-in-law, but there is no way to know for certain.[20] Regardless, Bridget belonged to a wave of women who immigrated to the United States from Ireland. Historian Janet Nolan contends that "while the Famine affected men and women alike, it had greater impact on women in terms of their social and economic roles in Ireland and their subsequent mass migration abroad."[21] This development compounded the unemployment issues that had already been created, in the decades prior to the Famine, when cheaper British goods entered the Irish market and greatly diminished the size and scope of women's employment in domestic textile manufacturing. Decreasing opportunities to marry during the Famine exacerbated the increasingly woeful outlook for many single Irish women, whose familial and economic roles quickly faded. "As a consequence, hundreds of thousands of young women without prospects at home chose to emigrate permanently," explains Nolan.[22]

Overnight, the newly wed Bridget Murphy established herself as both wife and mother, as young William joined her and P.J. for stretches of time in their home. Additionally, she assumed an important economic role in the family as the Murphys rented rooms to boarders to supplement their income.

Bridget and P. J. immersed themselves in a bustling environment. P. J.'s plastering business expanded, and he hired Webster Ferguson to help him meet the increasingly demanding workload. P. J. and "Webb," as everyone called him, became close friends, and Ferguson, along with six other boarders, quite possibly some of whom worked for P. J., lived together in the tight quarters of the Murphy home.[23] On January 22, 1868, just one week after Ohio rescinded its ratification of the Constitution's Fourteenth Amendment, Bridget and P. J. celebrated the birth of their first child, a boy, whom they named Charles Webb, giving the baby the middle name of P. J.'s best friend.[24] Toward the end of 1868, perhaps with an eye toward building a home with more space for his growing family, P. J. acquired nearly four acres of land, the day after Christmas, for $900.[25] Just over two years later, P. J. and Bridget welcomed another baby boy, Frank, into the world in early 1870.

P. J. Murphy emerged as a reputable businessman, and community members frequently hired his plastering company to work on their buildings. Murphy offered two different plastering services: plain and ornamental. Clients often called upon him to reinforce flat walls, but Murphy handled more creative challenges with aplomb. Wilmington served as the governmental seat of Clinton County, which meant a substantial amount of available work on governmental edifices. He reinforced the walls of buildings on the Wilmington College campus. He also helped forge city hall, an "imposing structure" with features in which residents could take pride. "The clock in the middle tower was, at the time of its erection, the largest of its kind in the United States, outside of the clock on the city hall in Philadelphia," recorded one historical account.[26]

The 1870s began optimistically. P. J.'s business was growing, and so, too, was his family. He had also increased his land holdings. Life appeared to be going smoothly for P. J., but tragedy again crashed the party. His partner and friend, Webb Ferguson, began to lose his grip on reality. Ferguson experienced manic episodes and became "at times dangerous in his delirium."[27] By 1873 he had engendered enough fear in authorities, and presumably the Murphys as well, that he found himself confined inside the Clinton County Infirmary. "Fastened in an iron cage," Ferguson responded by staging a pair of boycotts that transfixed the community. First, he refused to speak with anyone for a year, and then he doubled down by refusing to eat. His abstention from food began eleven months after he ceased speaking. Ferguson aimed to abstain from food longer than Jesus went without sustenance during his forty-day fast in the desert. However, Ferguson miscalculated and ate a tiny morsel for breakfast on July 10, the fortieth day of his fast. He settled for a tie with God.

The medical personnel at the clinic slowly began to nurse Ferguson back to health. He initially received only small bites of food so as not to overload his system. During his fast, Ferguson had only consumed an occasional drink of water. It seemed like a minor miracle he had even survived. He lost about half of his original two hundred pounds. On the day Ferguson broke his fast, he resumed talking. Shortly thereafter, medical authorities declared the twenty-eight-year-old Ferguson insane and admitted him to the Dayton Asylum for the Insane on November 6, 1874, where he, according to one slightly miscalculated account, was "doubtless the only man living who can boast, as he does, of exceeding Jesus Christ in the length of his fasting."[28]

Webb's institutionalization devastated P. J. personally and professionally. Without his right-hand man, Murphy needed to partner with someone new to help him tackle his next building: First National Bank of Wilmington. Murphy hired P. J. O'Leary, and they successfully guided the plastering project to completion. Pleased with the end result, Murphy and O'Leary referred to the bank in their public advertisements that appeared in the fall of 1872 as a "specimen of their work" and boasted that they could "execute all kinds of plain and ornamental plastering at any season of the year, in Clinton and adjoining counties."[29] As Murphy moved about the region where his business took him, Bridget remained at home to keep a close eye on her boys, Charlie, now four, and Frank, two, and tend to the boarders. On April 11, 1872, she gave birth to their third son, James. As his family grew, P. J. diversified his business interests, but he began having a difficult time generating more income.

Despite P. J.'s completing a series of notable jobs throughout the community, several pieces of evidence suggest the family continuously struggled to make ends meet financially. Webb's illness impacted the plastering business, and it's highly likely it adversely affected the boarders living with the Murphys. P. J.'s initial burst of property purchases, which tied up three pieces of land in three years in the late 1860s, had to be unwound beginning in 1871. He had acquired additional pieces of real estate over the years, but those had to be liquidated as well. On September 25, 1871, P. J. and Bridget sold a piece of property they had bought near the Wilmington Turnpike.[30] In the late fall of the following year, they parted with another two lots from their portfolio.[31] Despite the flurry of sales, the family held on to its house on Mulberry Street.

The following spring, debt swallowed Murphy. The probate court of Clinton County ordered him to sell additional pieces of property because he could not pay either his creditors or his taxes. Notices for the sale first appeared in the *Clinton Republican* on March 26, 1874. It read in part, "Lots Nos. Four, Five and Six, in P. J. Murphy's addition to the town of Wilmington, Ohio" would be offered "at Public Sale, at the door of the Court House" on Thursday, April 23, 1874.[32] Officials appraised lots four and five at $200 apiece and lot six at $400, but only the latter garnered a satisfactory bid. In February 1876, nearly two years after the initial offering, lots four and five remained available. The *Wilmington Journal* printed a notice stating that the appraised value of lot four had been lowered to $150 while lot five could be had for even less, at $125.[33] However, the properties did not even fetch those amounts as they sold in April for less than $200 combined.[34] Murphy tried to stay financially afloat. He advertised to school directors in the region that he was "prepared to put on Blackboards in school-houses, which, for excellence and durability, can not be surpassed."[35] In the midst of their money woes, the Murphys welcomed their fourth child, daughter, Katie, born in 1875.

Four years later, on September 9, 1879, the Murphy family nearly suffered an unimaginable loss that nonetheless left nine-year-old Frank seriously injured. The young lad, presumably with his family, visited the local fair and took a particular interest in a group of racehorses being exercised on the track as part of their race preparation. Surrounded by taller onlookers, Frank climbed a fence alongside the track to get a better sight line. Suddenly, someone knocked Frank off the fence directly into the path of an oncoming steed. Without any time to react, the rider could not tug on the horse's reins fast enough to avoid him. The horse trampled Frank. Onlookers gasped in horror as the boy grabbed his leg. The horse crushed Frank's femur just above the knee but miraculously missed the boy's head. A hack rushed Frank home while frantic calls for Dr. A. T. Davis reached him quickly. Dr. Davis hurried to the Murphy home and set the youngster's broken leg. The *Wilmington Journal* reported that, "the little fellow bore it like a hero, seeming more anxious about the time he should miss from school and lest he should receive blame from his parents for an accident which he could not possibly have prevented, than about the pain in his limb."[36]

Like his brothers, Frank loved baseball, and later in life he worked as an umpire in the Western League for a brief spell before the physical toll of the job proved too demanding. The injury Frank suffered as a boy may well have cut short his career in baseball.

Their father's financial hardships did not preclude the Murphy children from successfully immersing themselves in school life. In 1880 the three boys, Charlie, twelve; Frank, ten; and Jim, eight, attended school while five-year-old Katie remained at home.[37] The following spring, Charlie and Jim both received public accolades for their academic achievements. The *Wilmington Journal* reported that Charlie garnered 90 percent in his B Grammar class while Jim also achieved the 90 percent mark in B Primary.

Beyond the classroom, Charlie was developing into a rambunctious adolescent unafraid to put his precocious personality on public display. On March 8, 1881, a crowd of five hundred Wilmingtonians filed into the hall of the public school for a theatrical performance by the grammar school students. Young Charlie stole the show during a musical rendition of *King Lear*. "Charlie Murphy, who manipulated the 'fiddle' in 'His Time for Fiddling,' brought down the house. He furnished his hearers with genuine fun which was highly enjoyed," reported the *Wilmington Journal*.[38] Charlie's performance punctuated the show, one of the highlights of the school year. "The audience went away delighted and in order to get out another big crowd, it is only necessary to announce that another literary performance will take place in School Hall," the *Journal* noted.[39]

Charlie also loved sports, and he wanted to try everything, a perfect combination for a new pastime brought to Wilmington by its enterprising city officials, who transformed city hall into a roller-skating rink. Inquisitive locals showed up in droves to experience it. "Every one that tried it said that roller skating was so fascinating that they could not resist the temptation to visit the Hall every time that an opportunity was afforded them to practice," relayed the *Wilmington Journal*.[40] All members of the community received the opportunity to participate.[41] Thirteen-year-old Charlie jumped at the chance and skated as if his life depended on it. He displayed the same burst of energy at the rink that he had during his musical number the prior week, and everyone couldn't help but notice him. "Charlie Murphy is one of the most active lads on the floor," observed one local reporter.[42]

The Murphy boys received an education on what it meant to be small-town American kids playing baseball, a popular pastime in Wilmington. Together, the three sons of Irish immigrants, Charlie, Frank, and Jim, developed into a "baseball family" on the fields of Clinton County. Charlie found a number of outlets for his copious amounts of energy, but baseball provided him with an escape from the increasing stresses of home life. Charlie impacted the games in which he played with his competitive spirit, which nonetheless had to conform to the rules of the game. Charlie played with an edge, frequently from behind the plate as he "held down the catcher's department." Charlie was a bright kid, who not only wanted to play baseball but learn all he could about its strategies, and he worked hard to do so. Later in life, Charlie's nephew, Tom, described his uncle as a "brilliant student" during his high school years: "As you trace his career, from start to finish, you find him upright, honest and industrious, and at all times a hustler." As Charlie grew older, he played a little baseball with players from the Wilmington College team, although he paid the physical price of several broken fingers as a result. Frank and Jim loved the sport as well. Although Frank's childhood injury curbed his ambitions in baseball, Jim played minor league baseball for a spell before he became a scout for the Chicago Cubs after Charlie bought the team.[43]

Years later, in a piece for *Baseball Magazine*, Charlie identified baseball as an instructive tool for properly developing boys into productive members of American society, an experience shared by the three Murphy brothers. "Baseball has been one of the most tremendous influences in the training of the young which the world has ever known. Nine-tenths of the normal healthy boys in this country dream of the day when they, too, will be big league players. Nine-tenths of the boys in this country set as a model for much of their conduct, the careers of big league stars," he wrote. Charlie praised organizations that utilized baseball to "furnish the boys with the best of physical, moral and mental training."[44] Baseball gave Charlie the chance to exercise, but it also provided him and his brothers with a structured environment through which they could avoid their increasingly tumultuous life at home. Simultaneously, the Murphy boys became "Americanized" as a by-product of playing a sport quickly gaining popularity around the country.

After the ballgames ended, the boys returned home to a growing crisis. P. J. Murphy had endured some traumatic tragedies as a young man. He escaped the horrors of the Great Famine only to watch his young wife Ellen die after delivering their son. In 1880, as financial pressure and the continued insanity of his best friend, Webb, tormented him, P. J. coped by increasingly turning to alcohol.[45] He brooded intensely and lashed out at his wife and children in angry tirades. The already teetering stability within the Murphy home collapsed after P. J. exacerbated his drinking by using opiates. On several occasions, Murphy found himself locked up in the city jail.[46] By 1883 Bridget and the children could no longer rely on P. J. to provide income for their basic needs, so Charlie, now fifteen, took a job working at a local drug store for an annual salary of $100 to help support his mother and younger siblings.[47] P. J. reacted angrily to his son's employment and attempted to swipe Charlie's money from him before he could give it to his mother. But Charlie had learned how to handle his unpredictable father. A determined Charlie skillfully summoned his persuasive powers and deflected P. J.'s antagonism with soothing words. Rather than acquiesce, loquacious Charlie talked his father out of taking his hard-earned money from him. Relying on his remarkable abilities as a wordsmith, Charlie stood firm against his father and refused to relinquish his wages. Later in life, Charlie referred to his verbal skills as his ability to spread "salve."[48] Unable to purloin Charlie's earnings, P. J. changed tactics and threatened to sell the family's remaining property to sabotage his wife's ability to remain solvent. Unable to protect either herself or her children from her husband's increasing hostility, Bridget took P. J. to court for "reasonable alimony" in addition to garnering protection from his intrusions.[49] Bridget received a favorable decision on June 21, and P. J. received the court petition the following day.

As the calendar flipped from 1883 to 1884, P. J.'s vices continued to corrupt his formerly affable personality, with chilling consequences for his family. Two behavioral episodes, or "attacks," late in the year roiled up within Murphy an "inordinate" jealousy of his wife, and his behavior again spiraled out of control. During a ten-day manic episode in October, Murphy threatened suicide and issued warnings of violence against Bridget and the kids. "Yes, Lord I'll do it," P. J. was overheard murmuring to himself as he clutched a large knife in his hand.[50] A terrified Bridget worked with local law enforcement to have P. J. declared insane by the local court.

Persons thought to be insane living in Ohio during the nineteenth century did not have any legal rights against being committed to an asylum. The recommendation of a probate court judge, who relied extensively upon the result of a physician's examination, played an influential role in an individual's fate. After listening to arguments, a judge sent his opinion to the superintendent of the asylum where the patient could be committed. The superintendent then offered the final verdict on committing the individual.[51] The task of evaluating P. J. fell to Dr. George Hill, who assessed Murphy's condition on October 13, 1884. "The said Murphy has for some years been addicted to the use of alcoholic drink + opiates + is now insane from chronic alcoholism," Dr. Hill noted.[52] Bridget signed an affidavit that stated P. J. was insane and a danger to the community. The following day, Murphy was delivered to Joseph Stephens, the superintendent of the county infirmary, who released him, but it wasn't over.

Another episode—this time a seven-day fit during the holidays—led to an additional evaluation of Murphy by Dr. Hill on Christmas Eve. "I hereby certify that from his present condition and from my knowledge of his known history + habits up to the present time am of opinion that he is insane + a dangerous person to be at large," he concluded.[53] In response to the doctor's assessment, Judge John Matthews committed Murphy to the Dayton Asylum for the Insane. However, Dr. C. W. King, the superintendent of the facility, drafted a letter to Judge Matthews, on December 27, to inform his honor that the overcrowded facility did not have space for Murphy. "The male department of this asylum is very full at present, and Clinton County has several more than her quota here now; therefore Murphy cannot be admitted unless some one is removed to make room for him," Dr. King wrote. The superintendent proposed an ironic solution to create room for Murphy. "If you will remove Webster Ferguson, we will admit Murphy if he is provided with clothing as the law requires," he suggested.[54] Judge Matthews must have declined King's offer. The Dayton Asylum for the Insane didn't release Ferguson until May 14.[55]

With P. J.'s manic episodes becoming more dangerous, a separation from her husband emerged as Bridget's best solution to protect herself and the children. On July 8, 1885, the *Wilmington Journal* published a notice announcing a new case in the Common Pleas Court that simply read, "Bridget Murphy vs. Patrick Murphy; divorce," but a lack of documentation suggests that a legal divorce through the courts did not occur.[56] Nevertheless, brave Bridget made her disassociation from P. J. public news, although she continued using her married name throughout her life.

Evidence strongly suggests that P. J. began using an alias: Harvey A. Murphy. He had managed to avoid a commitment to the Dayton Asylum for the Insane, but he could not dodge the law forever. During the early morning hours of March 27, 1886, "Harvey" broke into Zephaniah Underwood's barn and stole two bushels of corn along with several other items, presumably to resell them to generate cash.[57] Murphy was arrested and pleaded not guilty, but a stream of witnesses, including Zephaniah and David Underwood, testified against him. In June, a jury convicted Murphy of burglary and sentenced him to a year in jail.[58] On January 5, 1887, the *Wilmington Journal* published a description of several town lots under their owner's names. Lot numbers 19 and 30 now listed Bridget Murphy as the holder, indicating that she had assumed control of the family's assets from her husband.[59]

The Murphy family adjusted to life without P. J. over the next several years. One month after Charlie turned twenty, he and Frank, now eighteen, decided to go into the food business together. In February 1888 the two brothers bought the Long & Coleman restaurant on Wilmington's Main Street and changed its name to Murphy Brothers with the goal of continuing the eatery's operation.[60] This transaction appears to be the first time Charlie went into business for himself, albeit alongside Frank, the younger brother whom he loved and trusted.

It is at this point that Charlie Murphy's trail goes cold for about two years, until he appears in the 1890 Cincinnati City Directory listed as a drug clerk, a job similar to the one he had held as a fifteen-year-old. In future years, several newspaper writers suggested, without citing evidence, that Murphy moved to Cincinnati to attend pharmacy school. Perhaps he did, but regardless of the reason for his relocation, Murphy's time in the Queen City changed the trajectory of his life forever.

ON TO CINCINNATI

By 1890 Charlie Murphy had uprooted himself from Wilmington and moved to Cincinnati. He landed employment as a drug store clerk and settled into new living quarters just north of downtown, at 140 W. Eighth Street.[1] The flourishing cultural life of Cincinnati inundated Murphy with new and exciting opportunities and experiences, but his exposure to the world of professional baseball dwarfed everything else. Initially formed in 1869, the Cincinnati Red Stockings shone as one of the Queen City's crown jewels. Several unrelated versions of the team, called the Cincinnati Reds, had fielded squads during the ensuing decades, and the latest iteration ushered in a new era, in 1890, as a member of the National League.

Murphy had followed the Reds while he was growing up in Wilmington, and now he desperately wanted to participate in the 1890 Opening Day events but, annoyingly, he had to work. Opening Day was a holiday in Cincinnati. Businesses closed so that workers could attend the afternoon parade that celebrated the beginning of the baseball season. However, drug stores remained open in case patients needed their medications, which left Murphy stuck behind the counter dreaming of baseball. "I wished that I had been anything else save a drug clerk on that day," he recalled. Undeterred, he developed an elaborate scheme to escape the clutches of the pharmacy.

Confessed Murphy:

I visited a friend and told him to call me on the telephone at 2 o'clock. He did and I carried on a conversation with an imaginary customer, for it was my duty to sell to the retail stores as well as to fill prescriptions. Then I went to my employer, an old German, and told him that a druggist in the outskirts of the city wanted to buy a bill of goods and that he had instructed me to come at once.

It worked like a charm and away I went—to the ball park. I had the time of my life, and when I returned I told my employer that the druggist whom I had visited was the worst price shaver I ever saw and that we couldn't get together on anything and that I made no sale.

The old German gave me all the rope I wanted, and when I finished he casually informed me that So and So was in and said I made more noise than anybody at the ball game.

And I was out of a job.[2]

The Cubs defeated the Reds 5–4 that day, but Murphy brushed aside both setbacks. He found work down the street at Keeshan's drug store, although his employment status remained tenuous. He gained a reputation for skipping out on his assigned shifts to watch baseball.[3]

Working at the pharmacies enabled Murphy to meet many folks who lived in the neighborhood, and the young extrovert soon cultivated a social network in the community. He provided good service, and customers knew him for his boisterous nature. Murphy struck up friendships with a number of the city's journalists who frequently shopped in the store.[4] He must have been enthralled by the bustling nature of his new environment. The people, the buildings, the streets, and the busyness of Cincinnati engaged his attention despite its penchant for wandering.

During the following spring, in 1891, Murphy's industry connections paid dividends. The city infirmary needed to replace its druggist, who had recently resigned. Impressed by his credentials, the infirmary's directors selected Murphy, who they called "a competent man for the place, having had a number of years' experience in the capacity of prescription clerk for different prominent druggists." Murphy began his new job at the beginning of April.[5] Murphy's new employer had operated under the supervision of two directors, but that structure underwent changes after Ohio passed a new charter bill that recon-figured the organization. The responsibilities heretofore carried out by the Board of City Infirmary Directors shifted to a newly created four-man committee called the Board of Administration. Cincinnati mayor John Mosby appointed the board's new members, including thirty-one-year-old August "Garry" Herrmann, an up-and-coming member of the city's Republican establishment. Although Murphy did not report directly to Herrmann, his chain of command led to the upstart political figure. Their careers would intertwine for the next twenty-five years.[6]

Just as Murphy joined the city infirmary, John Tomlinson Brush, a retail mogul from Indianapolis, was going through the process of buying the Cincinnati Reds. Born in upstate New York in 1845, Brush grew up on his grandfather's farm after the untimely deaths of his parents. Following the Civil War, in which he served in the First New York Artillery Regiment, Brush took a job with Owen, Pixley & Company, a retail venture. He fastidiously learned the business and, ten years later, his employer sent him to Indianapolis as part of its strategy to expand the company's footprint. Brush moved west and tackled the outfitting of a new, sizable company store. Locals frequently stopped by the site to assess its progress toward completion. Brush had a sign on the building with the date of the store's grand opening. However, construction issues delayed the project and forced Brush to change the date on the sign. Bombarded by inquisitors, Brush finally erased the date from the display board and replaced it with a one-word question: "WHEN?" On March 20, 1875, the newly dubbed When Store at last opened for business.[7]

Brush entered baseball circles in the mid-1880s to promote the When Store. Originally, he bought into the Indianapolis Western League franchise. In 1887 Brush purchased the Indianapolis Hoosiers of the National League, but the league exited the market three years later, and the franchise went defunct. Brush was compensated for losing the Hoosiers, but he no longer owned a local team. Brush wanted to remain active in baseball ownership, so he purchased a minority stake in the New York Giants in 1890. Now fifty-five, Brush had his sights set on obtaining a controlling interest of a team in the Queen City. Brush possessed a clear vision: he wanted to buy a franchise, keep it in the Cincinnati market, and retain a spot in the National League. It was a sure path to profit.

Some of the locals in Cincinnati eyed Brush suspiciously because he was an outsider and, therefore, could not be trusted. Brush's reputation as a businessman also hurt him. Some baseball fans in Cincinnati believed that he had cared more about using the Hoosiers as a vehicle to promote his clothing business in Indianapolis than about winning championships.[8] They weren't necessarily wrong, but Brush also wanted a winning club to keep fans pouring through the turnstiles.

Brush acquired the Reds amid withering criticism from local newspaperman Byron Bancroft "Ban" Johnson, who suspected the new owner of underhanded business practices. Johnson, a bulky blowhard with tightly cropped hair, was a twenty-seven-year-old sportswriter for the *Cincinnati Commercial Gazette*. Johnson was convinced Brush didn't care about running a winning baseball franchise as long as it was a profitable marketing vehicle. "With all regard to Mr. Brush as a gentleman and a clever business man, still he never honestly earned his great reputation as a base ball manager . . . While the local patrons of the game wish Mr. Brush all the success possible in his base ball ventures, still they would prefer that he would confine his speculations to some bailiwick outside of the Queen City," Johnson sniped.[9]

Johnson wanted to sow suspicion among his readers toward Brush, so he created several nicknames for the Indianapolis clothing magnate, including "Mysterious Brush," but, ultimately, he failed to prevent Brush from completing the transaction in February. Johnson questioned the integrity of the sale's process and fumed over Brush's tactics. "John T. Brush was given the Cincinnati franchise by the National League for $10,000 in paper. He watered the stock up to $100,000, and he claimed last night that he had disposed of it all. Sleek Brush. He knows when he has a good thing, and no one is better able to work it," Johnson admitted. Brush's alteration of the franchise's business structure annoyed Johnson to no end. As to Brush incorporating the ball club, Johnson retorted, "Incorporated on what? Wind?"[10]

Charlie Murphy most likely read Johnson's reporting, and therefore familiarized himself with key baseball operatives in Cincinnati and the process of conducting business with other baseball executives. He read Johnson's stories in the *Commercial Gazette* about the orchestrations undertaken by the National League to force its primary competitor, the American Association, to leave the Cincinnati market. However, Murphy also saw how the association refused to allow the National League to monopolize the city's sports sections, which was made possible, in large part, because the association's franchise, the Cincinnati Kelly's Killers, featured Mike "King" Kelly, the most electrifying star in baseball. Kelly's Killers and the Reds shared the Cincinnati market in 1891, but four American Association teams merged with the National League following the season, which effectively ended the American Association's existence as a stand-alone league. Now Brush possessed the Reds with the market to himself.

Murphy's life took a monumental turn in 1892. A naturally gregarious storyteller, Murphy again used his connections, this time with the local scribes, to escape the world of prescription drugs. He found a new vocational calling in journalism as he joined the staff of the *Cincinnati Enquirer* as a reporter.[11] John McLean, a powerful Democrat and city booster, bought the *Enquirer* in 1881 and transformed the paper into a regional media powerhouse, as its circulation increased nearly sixfold under his ownership.[12] In 1869 McLean had played a critical role in organizing the Cincinnati Red Stockings as a tool of civic promotion.[13] Now his paper gave Murphy the opportunity to spin yarns in its pages.

Just as Murphy began his journalism career, the Reds gave Queen City baseball fans a reason to fall in love with their team again. In 1892 Brush hired a new manager, Charlie Comiskey, who had spent nine of the past ten years in the American Association. The Reds' poor performance in recent years had alienated a large portion of their fan base, which retaliated by boycotting games. However, Comiskey's arrival sparked a new excitement in the community for the 1892 season. Fans immediately recognized the team's potential and flocked back to the ballpark. According to the *Enquirer*, "a tremendous gathering of 15,948 fans filled League Park to capacity for the first Sunday home game played by the Reds in two seasons."[14] The crowd enjoyed a robust offensive performance by the Reds as they whacked the St. Louis Browns, 10–2. Comiskey led the Reds to an 82-68 record, good for a fifth-place finish, in his first year at the helm, a distinct improvement over the team's 56-81 mark the previous season. Murphy was not yet covering sports full time, but he took in games at League Park as a fan.

Murphy, Brush, Comiskey, and Johnson mixed together in baseball and media circles in Cincinnati for at least the better part of 1892. Just as Murphy's journalism career was getting underway, Ban Johnson's was coming to a close. Johnson, who had covered the Cincinnati sports scene since 1886, embraced an opportunity beyond journalism. Comiskey and Johnson had developed a close friendship, and Comiskey recommended the newspaperman to Western League executives searching for a new leader the following year.[15] Brush heartily supported Comiskey's recommendation because he wanted to get his foil, Johnson, out of town. Johnson accepted the position and signed a contract in November of 1893 that made him the president of the Western League. Comiskey's and Brush's political machinations changed baseball history forever, as Johnson soon transformed the Western League into the American League and took on the National League for baseball supremacy.

Newly minted as a bona fide journalist Murphy, now twenty-five, upgraded his living situation. In 1893 he moved to 269 Walnut Street, in the heart of downtown, just two blocks north of the Ohio River, where he spent the next several years. Murphy quickly made a name for himself in the newspaper business. How do we know? On June 12, 1893, the *Cincinnati Commercial Gazette* reported, "Mr. Charles W. Murphy, the well known journalist is confined to his apartments ... with a severe attack of inflammation of the bowels."[16] A nod to a good reporter, or a cheap shot at a rival scribe? Either way, the *Commercial Gazette* informed its readers about Murphy of the *Enquirer*, a victory of sorts for the young journalist.

Sadly, in 1894, life again dealt Murphy a staggering blow. One of his close friends in town, Danny Dalton, was stricken with typhoid pneumonia. After convalescing for several weeks, Dalton felt well enough to resume activity, but he experienced a relapse, and his condition quickly deteriorated. On June 4 the twenty-three-year-old Dalton died at his parents' home. The anguished Murphy served as a pallbearer at his friend's funeral.[17]

Covering the police blotter and sports scene around town kept the young *Enquirer* reporter busy during the ensuing months, but not so preoccupied that he did not have time for social engagements. One particular young lady caught his attention, Louise Krumdick, and the two married around 1895 and settled into a new abode on Central Avenue the following year.[18]

A lifelong Cincinnati resident, Marie Louise Krumdick experienced the exciting transformation of the Queen City. Born on August 20, 1871, Louise grew up in a town that emerged as a consequential city in middle America during her lifetime. Louise's familial history mirrored Charlie's in that her parents, Henry Krumdick and his wife, the former Louise Kenker, had both immigrated from Europe. They had joined a large group of German immigrants who settled in Cincinnati after the Civil War years. In 1871, the year of Louise's birth, the Krumdick family lived at 248 Clark while Ernest Kenker occupied the residence at 250 Clark. It is distinctly possible that the Krumdick and Kenker families lived next door to each other. Henry Krumdick supported his family by building carriages, an occupation that became the family business when his sons took up the craft. Ernest, listed as a wheel maker in the *Cincinnati City Directory*, may have also been a part of the enterprise.[19]

While Charlie's life in Cincinnati blossomed, family events back in Wilmington took more sad turns. On August 4, 1896, P. J. Murphy died. An obituary that honored his life appeared the following day in the *Cincinnati Enquirer*. It explained that P. J. had suffered from heat stroke while attending a Reds exhibition game in the community of Washington Court House. The ill Murphy was transported to the house on Mulberry Street in Wilmington, where he passed away the following morning. It seems likely that Charlie composed his father's obituary. That distinct possibility makes it all the more peculiar that the obituary states Cincinnati as P. J.'s birthplace when he was born in Ireland. The narrative goes on to emphasize that P. J. became "one of the prominent plastering contractors" in Clinton County. "He was a lifelong Democrat and leading advocate of the free silver cause. He often had offers of municipal offices, but would never accept . . . He was at one time quite wealthy, but owing to business reverses lost nearly everything he had."[20] The obituary provokes several questions, but it may also answer another one that cropped up later in Charlie Murphy's life. Rumors occasionally circulated that Charlie was Jewish and not Irish.[21] Why would someone suppose Charlie was anything but Irish? The rumors were quickly shot down by those who knew him. Nevertheless, Charlie may have downplayed his father's linkage to Ireland on occasion. If he wrote his father's obituary, this is a piece of evidence that suggests Charlie altered details of his own history at times. He was a storyteller, after all. While the *Enquirer* published P. J.'s obituary the day after his death, the first article about it did not appear in the *Wilmington Journal* until August 12, 1896. It stated that Frank and Jim Murphy had been appointed as administrators of P. J.'s estate.[22]

Frank and Jim focused on resolving their father's estate, but they could not do so for long. Young Katie, not much older than twenty, perhaps afflicted because of the death of her father, suffered a breakdown. In early December she started seeing "strange men" in the house who spoke to her. She also heard the clock implore her to run away from home. Anxious, Bridget took her daughter to be medically evaluated on January 22.[23] Katie was found "to be insane," and she was committed to Athens State Hospital.[24] It was another landed haymaker upon a family that had already endured so many stinging punches.

Amid the cold temperatures of the new year, Katie was transported a hundred miles from home. She arrived at the Athens State Hospital in January 1897. The imposing buildings, which originally opened their doors under the name of the "Athens Lunatic Asylum" in 1874, greeted her from atop an imposing hill that overlooked the Hocking River and Ohio University, nestled within the valley below it. Also known as "The Ridges," the facility was the brainchild of Dr. William Parker Johnson, an Athens native who had served as a physician and hospital administrator during the Civil War.[25] The hospital featured the newly developed "moral treatment" movement spearheaded by Dr. Thomas Kirkbride, who believed mental illness could be treated. The Ridges incorporated a new interior design as part of a holistic approach to lovingly help its patients, born out of the "Victorian impulse" to improve humanitarian care. Sunlight cascaded down upon Katie from high arching windows as she entered the main building. At ground level, colorful flower arrangements enveloped her along with more windows that provided a panoramic view of the surrounding meadow, which doctors hoped would bring Katie, along with the other patients, a bit of comfort.[26]

Baseball provided an outlet for Frank and Jim Murphy in the midst of the further disintegration of their family. In mid-September, Frank's Clinton County team won a pair of games over rival squads, including a 12–11 win over Sabina, for which the winning team received a paltry $10.[27] As the frosty winter warmed into spring, Frank and Jim distracted themselves from their father's death and the commitment of their sister by helping reinstitute the local baseball team for the 1897 season. "The base ball boys in town are getting the fever and have taken steps to reorganize the old Clintons," relayed the *Wilmington Journal*. The group appointed Frank as manager while Jim, who played second base, was named team captain. The positive vibe around the team made observers optimistic for the upcoming campaign. "From the present prospect Wilmington is likely to see some good ball this season," the *Journal* concluded.[28]

Back in Cincinnati, Murphy continued to work the crime beat. He met all the locals during his career as a newspaper reporter, but none was as unique, or loyal, as Bum the Police Dog. Bum did not live with Murphy; he followed newspapermen, police officers, and firefighters around town as they battled bad guys and blazes. Bum scampered after dispatched engines and was frequently sighted at the site of crashes, fires, collapsed buildings, and arrests. Murphy could often be found at the same sites taking notes and talking to sources for his stories. It was not unusual for Bum to leap into the cab carrying Murphy, or another reporter, to the scene of a story. Several origin stories about Bum emerged over the years, but one particular iteration included so many specifics that it seems the most likely scenario. On a cold winter night in 1891, Lieutenant William Krumpe discovered a young puppy shivering under a sidewalk sign and carried him back to Central Station. The officers nicknamed the canine "Bum" and, from that day forward, he never left the force. Bum—thought to be a mix of shepherd, collie, and an unidentified third breed—introduced himself to the city's reporters, who frequently allowed the pup to join them for lunch as they awaited breaking news.

In late September of 1899, Bum could not travel with Murphy to New York when the young journalist covered the return of Admiral George Dewey to the United States following his victory over the Spanish at the Battle of Manila Bay, and the local press took notice. The *Cincinnati Commercial Tribune* reported, "Charley Murphy, the well-known police reporter, will, for the first time in eight years of the existence of 'Bum,' the celebrated police dog, be separated for more than ten hours from that distinguished animal."[29]

Bum grew legendary over the years. Although he began life with a full set of teeth, they went missing during his later years. Some people claimed his habit of biting children who bothered him led to their mysterious "extraction" by an angry parent. Others suspected Bum lost them all during an ill-advised attack on a brewery wagon. No one knew for certain. Over the years, the rambunctious Bum was hit by a bakery wagon and even an automobile, according to one report, but he always recovered. Toothless Bum had an ongoing rivalry with a bulldog named Catholic Dog, who lived at the church across the street from city hall, and they even got into a vicious brawl that became part of local folklore. One year the policemen entered Bum into a local dog show competition. He did not win any ribbons, but everyone loved him, and the myth of the canine grew.

Bum chased around trouble until 1901, when his friend Nell, a dog who occasionally palled around with him, cut him off in front of an oncoming Salvage Corps wagon, which struck him in the middle of Ninth Street. Onlookers assumed Bum would get up as he always did, but they quickly realized he was not moving. "Tenderly they picked him up, and after a few hours' nursing, revived him enough for the old veteran to drag himself out into the street again," reported the *Commercial Tribune*. However, Bum was hit again, this time by a carriage whose driver assumed he would jump out of the way despite the cries of people on the street to watch out. Bum held on for four days, but his internal injuries were too severe to overcome. Bum died on June 16. Murphy joined newspapermen and policemen throughout Cincinnati who intensely mourned his death.[30]

By 1900 Louise Murphy, now twenty-eight, along with Murphy's in-laws, the Krumdick family, had left Cincinnati for Lake, Illinois, a neighborhood in south Chicago.[31] Perhaps the family moved to work in the booming carriage business in Chicago, but that still does not fully explain why Louise left Charlie and joined them. It remains a mystery.

Over the years, Murphy added sports reporting duties to his police beat, and he became the *Enquirer*'s sporting editor following the death of the highly respected Harry Weldon on January 28, 1902. For over twenty years, Weldon, one of America's premier sportswriters, had written for the *Enquirer* and worked, in various capacities, for baseball teams in Cincinnati.[32]

Readers could not reasonably expect Murphy to maintain Weldon's level of excellence, but Murphy had a strategy to keep them engaged. "When I was sporting editor of the *Cincinnati Enquirer* I held the view that baseball was bigger and better than all other sp(o)rts combined and at times on a Sunday I would devote more than a page to baseball," Murphy explained. He fed the readers' interest by, as he called it, "publishing baseball 'dope,'" and they couldn't get enough of it. Murphy filled the section with off-season news, rumors, and gossip to keep the public reading. *Enquirer* owner John McLean did not fully understand the local public's obsession with baseball, but he let the new sporting editor publish what he thought best. "'The people want it . . . and what I think about it does not count,'" McLean told Murphy.[33]

Murphy could not have timed his sports writing career much better. Newspaper coverage of baseball exploded during the 1890s, and the public voraciously consumed it. Increased baseball coverage was a boost for daily papers, because they published more recent scores, news, and statistics than their weekly counterparts. "Glance over any great daily during the season and observe how the affairs of the nation, the most interesting local events, the vast field of music and drama, and very often even the editorial columns, shrink into comparative insignificance contrasted with the space and attention given to baseball," Francis Richter, founder of the popular *Sporting Life*, observed in 1889.[34] Savvy pockets of the newspaper industry picked up on the trend. "In every well-regulated paper of the first-class a competent sporting editor and baseball reporter is an important and indispensable adjunct of the editorial staff," Richter noted.[35]

Murphy took his role very seriously, and he was at the forefront of being a local beat writer who made covering baseball a year-round pursuit. He wrote about Reds games during the summer, and during the off-season, he traveled to the winter meeting at the Fifth Avenue Hotel in New York, where he reported on the National League's organizational and labor issues in addition to player movement. Murphy embraced holding baseball executives accountable, an emerging component of the new wave of baseball writers' work in the late nineteenth century, when rowdyism severely damaged the game's reputation among fans. When owners addressed the financial losses that occurred during the 1900 season, in part due to "dirty ball on the field," Murphy lambasted the National League magnates as hypocrites for undercutting their own discipline chief, President Nick Young. "Young is merely a scapegoat if he is forced to withdraw," an exasperated Murphy griped. "The magnates themselves, as THE ENQUIRER has pointed out many times in the past, are the real ones to blame, for they have refrained from disciplining kicking players, and also have abused and protested even the best umpires in the country. When such first-class officials as Tom Lynch and Tim Hurst are made objects of the fault finding magnates . . . what can a more aggressive successor to Nick Young accomplish?"[36]

During one particularly long meeting held by the owners, Murphy gathered all the bored writers together inside the hotel bar and held court. He declared himself the president of the group and informed its newly christened members that the National League's minutes were adopted, the pennant awarded, and the constitution amended. Murphy then marched to the parlor room containing the huddled owners and banged on the door. It opened, and Murphy announced that their proceedings were over. "Tell the magnates we have held a meeting in the bar room at our own expense and we are going home. It is a waste of our employers' money to stay here any longer. We have the news," Murphy said loudly enough for all inside the room to hear.[37]

National League president Nick Young heard Murphy and called him inside the room. I need some good stories for my newspaper, Murphy told everyone, and you're holding out. Young called for the other writers to follow Murphy inside and concluded the owners' session so interviews could be conducted. Murphy's performance amused one magnate in particular, his acquaintance from Cincinnati, John T. Brush.

Although he made friends in the sport, Murphy had no problem teasing owners and ballplayers for their misdeeds. He wrote about the cheating system used by the Philadelphia Phillies that featured binoculars in center field and a corresponding buzzer device that allowed the team to steal signs. Murphy dubbed Petie Chiles of Philadelphia the "'Human Pin Cushion'" after a sounding board was dug up from the first base coaching box.[38] He also antagonized Barney Dreyfuss, owner of the Pittsburgh Pirates, by calling him a "'buzzer' man" for a similar system that used a trick screen embedded in his home park's center-field fence that allowed signs to be stolen and conveyed through said device to coaches on the field. For every criticism Murphy directed at someone, he received praise from those who agreed with him, presumably the people who had told him the story in the first place. Murphy found it delicious fun, and his coverage increased in popularity.

In 1902 Charles Phelps Taft lured Murphy away from the *Enquirer* to work as a reporter for his paper, the *Cincinnati Times-Star*. The move proved to be another life-changing event for Murphy in the years ahead, but it had to be difficult to relinquish his role as sports editor at the *Enquirer*. Initially, Murphy worked as a reporter for the *Times-Star*, but the following year, he ascended to assistant city editor.[39]

Taft knew of Murphy's journalistic talents, but baseball scribe Hugh Fullerton gave an interview to the *Sporting Life*, several years later, in which he described another of Charlie's characteristics that may have drawn the interest of the *Times-Star*'s owner. Fullerton called Murphy a "hustler," who demonstrated his knack for business sense when he created a souvenir program for an Ohio Grand Army of the Republic encampment meeting. According to Fullerton, Murphy made a fortune, as he sold $18,000 worth of the souvenirs.[40] While the dollar amount seems highly exaggerated, Murphy's plan displayed ingenuity and hard work, which netted him a notable profit.

Politics were not a motivating factor for Murphy in deciding to leave the Democratic-leaning *Enquirer* for the Conservative *Times-Star*, but the papers' owners make the topic impossible to ignore. With very few exceptions, the *Times-Star* served as the mouthpiece of the Tafts, a staunchly Republican family. Over time, Murphy developed a deeply rooted patriotism that he publicly expressed later in life, but his primary focus centered on developing his journalism career and making connections with influential Cincinnatians. He happily engaged baseball fans, a demographic that included Democrats and Republicans alike.

Charles Taft established himself as an important presence in Murphy's life. Taft's powerful family had emerged as a national dynasty following the Civil War. Taft's father, Alphonso, was born in Vermont on November 5, 1810. He studied law at Yale but, prior to sitting for the bar exam, he decided that moving west best suited his future endeavors. Initially, in 1838, Alphonso went to New York, but the city made a poor impression on him, and he couldn't get away fast enough. In a letter to his future wife, Fanny Phelps, Alphonso wrote, "The notorious selfishness, or dishonesty of the great mass of the men you find in New York is in my mind a serious objection to settling there."[41] He decided to move to Cincinnati, a bustling town tucked in among rolling hillsides along the Ohio River. Upon arrival, he found work at a law firm run by Nathaniel Wright, a fellow Vermont native. Within months, Alphonso passed the Ohio bar exam, successfully asked Fanny to marry him, and became a partner in the firm.

On August 29, 1841, Alphonso and Fanny married, and they welcomed their first child, Charles, on December 21, 1843. Another son, Peter, was born in 1846. Sadly, Charles and Peter were the only two of Alphonso and Fanny's five children to survive, and both boys were considered feeble. In 1852, following a difficult childbirth that resulted in the death of the newborn, Fanny's health quickly spiraled downward. A woman with a strong spiritual faith, Fanny did not fear death, but she nevertheless expressed hope that her boys, Charles and Peter, would remember her.[42] On June 2, 1852, Fanny Taft died. Charles was eight years old.

Less than eighteen months later, Alphonso married Louise Torrey, the daughter of a prominent New England family. Alphonso and Louise had five children together, four of whom reached adulthood, including William Howard Taft, who would become the twenty-seventh president of the United States. The Taft brand, along with Alphonso's political influence around town, had grown rapidly, but Charles's frailty concerned his new stepmother. Any physical concerns had no effect on his enjoyment of sports, however. As youngsters, the Taft brothers played baseball on local sandlots with other boys from nearby neighborhoods.[43]

Gifted with an exceptionally bright mind that he augmented with an admirable work ethic, Charles graduated from Yale in 1864 before completing law school at Columbia. He continued his formal education in Europe, where he earned a degree from the University of Heidelberg that established him as an expert in both canon and civil law.[44] Finally, he concluded his formal education with a degree from the College de France. Simultaneously, he immersed himself in the music and arts of the continent while he honed his French and German.[45] Charles Taft returned to Cincinnati in 1870 and formed a partnership with fellow lawyer, and future Ohio governor, Edward Noyes.

The 1870s were an important decade for the Taft family. On December 4, 1873, Charles married Anna Sinton, known as Annie, the daughter of David Sinton, a pig-iron magnate whose fortune made him the

wealthiest man in Ohio. The wedding, which instantly created one of
the most dynamic young power couples in the state, was "the great
social event of 1873 in Cincinnati," according to one historian.[46] In
addition to making social waves, the political influence of the Taft family grew exponentially. In 1876 Pres. Ulysses S. Grant tapped Alphonso
Taft as his secretary of war before making him the attorney general of
the United States shortly thereafter.

The law firm partnership between Alphonso and his sons, which
had been formed after Noyes was elected Ohio's governor in 1872, did
not sustain the loss of the family patriarch to the nation's capital, and
Charles in particular began thinking seriously about leaving behind
his law career for a new enterprise in journalism. Drawing upon his
extensive experience studying languages in Europe, Charles and his
father-in-law purchased a significant number of shares in one of Cincinnati's most popular German newspapers, *Volksblatt*.

Charles continued his foray into newspaper ownership when he
acquired the *Cincinnati Chronicle* in 1879. The following year, he and
Sinton purchased the *Star*, a standout afternoon paper, and they merged
both papers to create the *Cincinnati Times-Star*, a Republican-leaning
evening paper that reflected the political positions held by the family.
Sinton led the first official meeting of the newly formed *Times-Star*,
where he was elected to the board of directors, which in turn elected
Charles as president of the company.[47] The first edition of the *Times-Star*
appeared on Monday, June 27, 1880. It proved to be popular with both
readers and employees.[48] Twelve years later, Taft hired Charlie Murphy.

Murphy's journalism career made him a well-known figure throughout baseball. His work demonstrated keen knowledge of the game on
the field as well as a growing understanding of the business side of
the sport, particularly its political machinations. Embattled National
League president Nick Young decided to resign in 1902. He had served
the league in a variety of capacities from its inception in 1876, the last
seven years as its lead executive. The National League needed a new
president, secretary, and treasurer, and Murphy emerged as a candidate. The *New York Times* reported that National League officials
considered bringing the "well-known" Murphy aboard as secretary

and treasurer.[49] Other newspapers substantiated the rumor. "Charley Murphy looks to be the man," claimed the *Cincinnati Enquirer*.[50] However, instead of hiring Murphy, National League officials selected Harry Pulliam, a former Kentucky assemblyman and secretary of the Pittsburgh Pirates, to fill all three roles. The local Cincinnati press believed Murphy "doubtless would have been chosen if the Executive Committee . . . had remained in office."[51]

While covering the Reds for the *Times-Star*, Murphy's friendship with the team's owner, John T. Brush, continued to grow. As Murphy familiarized himself with the Reds, first as a fan and then as a reporter, his growing admiration for Brush burgeoned into something closer to reverence. Murphy closely observed how Brush ran his franchise, and he absorbed the owner's business philosophies. Unlike Ban Johnson, Murphy heartily endorsed Brush's acumen at every turn. Years later, Murphy wrote an article expressing his appreciation for all that Brush had taught him. "If anything I may say in praise of Mr. Brush seems too extreme, it must be overlooked because I am a great admirer of the President of the New York National Baseball Club," Murphy wrote. "I have a special interest in him since he, more than any other one man except the Hon. Charles P. Taft, brother of our beloved President, was responsible for my present position in Organized Baseball."[52]

In 1902 Brush purchased enough additional shares in the New York Giants to make him its majority shareholder. His dual stakes in the Reds and Giants made him an influential syndicate owner, and his tactics antagonized some. For example, he initiated transfers of players to bolster one team's roster at the expense of the other. Brush's Reds acquired Christy Mathewson following the nineteen-year-old's disappointing six-game audition for the Giants during the 1900 season, but then Cincinnati dealt him back to New York on December 15 for Amos Rusie.[53] Mathewson pitched 336 innings and won twenty games for the Giants in 1901. Brush's actions did nothing to belie Ban Johnson's original suspicions about Brush's intentions for the Cincinnati club. Other writers publicly criticized Brush's approach. "Chicanery is the ozone which keeps his old frame from snapping and dark-lantern methods the food which vitalizes his bodily tissues," wrote one reporter.[54]

Brush's takeover of the Giants proved to be serendipitous for Charlie Murphy. On January 25, 1905, Brush hired Murphy as assistant
secretary of the New York National League Baseball Club in charge
of public relations. Murphy would work alongside Fred Knowles, a
longtime Giants executive who led its business affairs department,
in the front office.[55]

The *Cincinnati Commercial Tribune* lauded Brush for hiring "so capable a man as Mr. Murphy, whose appointment is regarded as a deserved
compliment to the newspaper profession." Murphy's popular baseball
coverage left an indelible mark on fans of the sports page everywhere.
"His literary contributions on baseball and kindred outdoor sports were
widely copied and commented on throughout the country," raved the
Commercial Tribune. The newspaper published Murphy's photo next
to its article, which ran on January 26, 1905, four days after Murphy's
thirty-seventh birthday. His heavy eyebrows and small ears frame his
round, mustached face. He sports a dark suit coat, with a light-colored
weskit, layered over a dark shirt with a white collar. Murphy dressed
well.[56] His alert eyes twinkle knowingly.

Murphy's rise from drug clerk to assistant secretary of the New York
Giants had taken fifteen years to materialize. He had found incredible
opportunities and met remarkably influential people in Cincinnati. He
had cultivated them both, and he now found himself immersed in the
day-to-day operations of one of baseball's most powerful franchises.
In 1905 he could count the likes of John McGraw, Christy Mathewson, and Roger Bresnahan as his coworkers, although even the great
yarn-spinning Murphy could not possibly have predicted the future in
pop culture for the Giants' little-known outfielder named Archie Graham, who joined the team in May. Murphy must have felt exuberant
when he arrived in chilly New York on February 2, 1905. He reported
to work at the St. James Building, just north of Madison Square Park,
the following day.[57]

"A REAL WONDER-STORY"

Before he left for New York, Charlie Murphy said goodbye to his friends whom he had known for years, including Garry Herrmann, the now-established member of the Republican political machine in Cincinnati. Herrmann, along with George Cox and brothers Max and Julius Fleischmann, had purchased the Reds from John T. Brush, who in turn acquired the New York Giants, in 1902. Immediately, the ownership group had installed Herrmann as the team's president. The following year, Herrmann gained a seat on the newly established National Commission, a three-man oversight panel in charge of running the National and American Leagues. Murphy and Herrmann displayed big personalities in a town full of them. Herrmann, however, had a political sense about him that Murphy never cared to nurture. While they both knew how to use the press to gain leverage, Herrmann only did so out of necessity. Unlike Murphy, Herrmann successfully developed close-knit political relationships that enabled him to maintain a place within the city's elite. The two men shared a genuine fondness for one another, but their comradery would soon be tested.

In the meantime, Murphy strongly believed that naming Herrmann as team president was one of the smartest decisions the Reds franchise had ever made. For his part, Herrmann publicly praised Murphy, a few years later, after the Giants hired him as assistant secretary. A mutual friend, Alfred Henderson, relayed Herrmann's "send-off" to Murphy, who relished Herrmann's kind words. "You may be sure that I was pleased beyond expression," Murphy wrote in a thank-you letter to Herrmann. "In the first place I knew that Mr. Henderson—the soul of honor—spoke the truth and was handing me that which I am often charged with spreading indiscriminately—salve. In the second place I knew it was sincere coming from you, because if you had not felt that way, you would have remained silent."[1]

Newspapermen across the country had a vested interest in the ex-reporter Murphy's success. Murphy's hiring followed a trend in which baseball owners installed former sportswriters in influential positions in the business. The *Buffalo Times* counted thirteen examples of writers who had been hired by leagues and clubs, including Murphy, Ban Johnson, and Harry Pulliam.[2] If the former journalists continued to perform well, the pipeline from the newspaper office to the ballpark would remain a viable source of talent acquisition for clubs.

Murphy's primary responsibility as assistant secretary was to serve as the Giants' press agent. Murphy promoted the team to the New York media, and, more importantly, he facilitated newspaper coverage in cities where the Giants played on the road. Theoretically, the stories would generate the fans' interest by relaying to them the high-flying exploits of the great Giants roster which, in turn, would motivate them to attend a ballgame in the series. The Giants stood to profit from higher road attendance, because visiting clubs received a percentage of the gate receipts.

Murphy had a compelling team to promote. The New York Giants entered the 1905 season as the defending National League champions as well as one of the most disliked outfits in the game. Led by their tenacious manager, John McGraw, the Giants won 106 games in 1904, and then, out of defiance, refused to play the Boston Americans in the World Series. The team featured talent throughout the diamond, including star pitcher Christy Mathewson, who would go on to have the best season of his young career.

Murphy left New York to join the team on its spring exhibition tour in late March. The Giants were pinging around the South playing a series of games as they worked their way north for the start of the season. One evening in Memphis, John T. Brush and Murphy organized a ten-cent poker night at the team hotel. Several players, including Mathewson and Bill Dahlen, writers, and team trainer Harry Tuthill showed up.

Cigars were passed around, and the card game commenced. As the night wore on, Murphy and Brush gleefully took the players' money.

Brush had just won another hand, with three sevens over kings up, when a loud pounding on the door silenced the room and sent panic down the card players' spines. Tuthill ran for the fire escape, but two policemen busted through the door before he could reach it. "Hands up!" they cried. The room froze. "In a raid last week two detectives were killed, but we are prepared to-night!" yelled one of the officers. Suddenly, the room broke into a myriad of shouts, and the card players offered everything in their pockets to the cops, but they refused to be tempted by the bribes.

Murphy jumped in and claimed that they were merely playing hearts. In a strategy that only succeeded in muddying the water, Brush said that, actually, they were playing pinochle.

"The stall won't go; there are cards and chips, and that is all we need," claimed one of the officers. They informed the group that they needed to call for the hurry-up wagon, and they left the room. As soon as they were gone, Brush dashed out of the room and back to his suite. He shut the door and locked it behind him. The cops soon returned and flushed Brush out of his quarters.

Suddenly, a voice rang out in the hallway. "Murphy!" screamed John McGraw. Murphy slumped into the hallway and joined McGraw and the officers, who were already negotiating. In the end, the cops agreed to take $100 to walk away from the incident. Murphy scrambled around to get the cash and handed it over. He returned to the scene of the crime, where Tuthill and the players remained on high alert. "Everybody get to your rooms and say nothing," Murphy whispered. "We have squared it."

The sun rose later that morning, but it did not shine brightly on the disgruntled gamblers. They sniped all day about losing their money to the cops. Murphy ripped into "Southern police forces." They complained so loudly that they could not hear McGraw laughing. McGraw reveled in playing pranks—he once convinced a rookie catcher aboard a night train to "stand on the rear platform of the sleeper and wave a lantern to prevent a locomotive from coming up too fast" and causing a collision—and he had set up the poker players beautifully.[3] Several of McGraw's horse-racing friends were in town for the Montgomery Handicap, and he, along with Giants catcher Roger Bresnahan and horse trainer Mike Shannon, schemed to terrorize the new guy, Murphy. Scaring the other card players would just be enjoyable collateral damage. McGraw, Bresnahan, and Shannon recruited a local brewery agent and a bookmaker to disguise themselves as police officers and break up the card game. The "officers" performed their roles to perfection. The following day, with no game scheduled, the Giants enjoyed a day of boating on the Mississippi River, and the topic du jour among the "sailors" was the poker "raid."[4]

Murphy learned the hard way that McGraw cleverly executed practical jokes with the same attention to detail that made him a master tactician as a baseball manager, and he took advantage of his unique opportunity to learn from baseball's best field general. As a youth, Murphy loved playing baseball, and a significant angle to his passion for the game stemmed from his desire to learn about its strategical inner workings. "From my boyhood I wanted to know—not guess—why some clubs won flags and others did not. I found there were many reasons," Murphy recalled. McGraw became a willing resource for Murphy, and the latter wisely took advantage of the opportunity to pick the former's brain. One of McGraw's most influential opinions centered on a club's ideal balance. He impressed upon Murphy the importance of having a lineup with four right-handed batters offset by four left-handed hitters, excluding the pitcher. The combination made it more challenging for opposing pitchers to have an advantage. "They should be about evenly balanced, Charley. Nearly all the really great clubs were put together in that manner," McGraw told him. "I never forgot that," Murphy said.[5]

As the regular season approached, the Giants organization developed grand plans to celebrate winning the National League pennant the previous year, and Murphy's fingerprints were all over them. Brush, Knowles, and Murphy designed a pregame parade through the streets of New York, featuring players and team personnel from both the Giants and their Opening Day opponents, the Boston Beaneaters, riding in automobiles down Fifth Avenue to the Polo Grounds. The *New York Times* called the parade an "impromptu affair" and a "novel innovation," strongly suggesting that Murphy, who had witnessed Opening Day parades for over a decade in Cincinnati, was behind it. Large yellow bunting with "Champion Giants" written in black letters adorned the cars carrying New York's players. Fans lined the streets and waved excitedly at the players, but many more people waited at the Polo Grounds, in a huge throng, tingling with anticipation at raising the pennant flag.[6]

The excitement of celebrating New York's first pennant since 1889 infused the fan base with a palpable enthusiasm. Thousands upon thousands of fans accumulated outside the ballpark's gates in hopes of getting a good seat. The "Paul Kelly Gang" hung out next to the gate on Eighth Avenue as its members angled for fifty-cent bleacher seats. The "Five Pointers" and "Cherry Hill Boys" set aside their differences as they purchased twenty-five-cent tickets. Meanwhile, New York's aristocracy turned out to celebrate as well. "The gowns, the jewels, the breathing, bulging prosperity were overwhelming," reported Allen Sangree of the *New York World*. "No royal pageant ever called forth more beauty and wealth."

The massive crowd of forty thousand fans gasped at the sight of the sparkling field as they streamed into the Polo Grounds. A large blue pennant that would soon be raised greeted them. The initial of each infielder's last name had been written in the dirt behind his defensive position. The setting for the celebration was perfect, and Giants fans showered their team with praise. "New York liked them because they had brought honor to her doors—had captured the nation's athletic prize," Sangree explained.[7] The Giants added to their fans' excitement by drubbing the Beaneaters, 10-1, behind "Iron" Joe McGinnity's pitching and Mike Donlin's three-hit performance, including his first home run of the season.

Murphy paid attention to every detail. The successes of the parade, pennant raising ceremony, and convincing victory must have made him incredibly happy, but his joy with the sell-out crowd overshadowed all of it. The Giants' promotional strategies paid off in a big way as they convinced all the segments of New York society to attend the game, and it became a story unto itself. The *New York Tribune* marveled at the demographics of the crowd in its game story the following day. "When the gathering was completed it was one of the most cosmopolitan possible of production in this most cosmopolitan of cities. Here was 'pa,' who thought Willie would enjoy the game, and there was the man who but yesterday completed his last six months 'on the island.'

"Here was the broker, there was the office boy, all intent on watching eighteen men chase a little leather covered sphere over two acres of more or less green lawn. But how they enjoyed it!"[8]

However, despite his best efforts, Murphy struggled to gain traction with the local reporters. He pushed and prodded them to cover the Giants more aggressively. He fired off pages of promotional material about the team to all the New York papers as quickly as he could write them. Miffed reporters rolled their eyes when a delivery from Murphy landed in their hands, and then they threw it in the nearest trash can. No one, especially a youngster from Cincinnati in the Giants' employ, could tell them how to cover the team. Nevertheless, Murphy remained undaunted and continued to type away vigorously. He did have a few successes, among them a *New York Times* story, written by Edwin Tracey, in its Sunday edition during the opening weekend of the season, headlined "At a Dress Rehearsal of the Champion Giants," that gave readers an inside look at the team's preparation routines, but his efforts largely went unrewarded. One writer wrote a poem about Murphy's time as the Giants' press agent:

> When Murphy came to Gotham town
> He wore a smile and not a frown,
> But when C. Murph was here awhile,
> He wore a frown and lost the smile.[9]

Contrary to his difficulty with reporters, Murphy's influence on the Giants' promotional department flourished. The Giants bravely displayed their championship pedigree for their opening road game. The players actually rode in carriages draped with orange blankets

that boasted of their championship status, through the streets of Philadelphia, from their hotel to the Baker Bowl. This display went over
about as well as one might expect. The Phillies fans hurled objects at
them as the victorious Giants, who won twenty-five out of their first
thirty-one games on their way to another pennant, left the stadium.

On June 11 the Giants were scheduled to begin a three-game set in
Chicago, and Murphy, whose in-laws lived in the Windy City, arrived
ahead of the team to visit as well as to promote the upcoming series.
Murphy met up with Jim Hart, president of the Chicago club, at the
West Side Grounds. As the two conversed in the stands, Hart began
talking about the very real possibility of putting the Cubs franchise
up for sale. Murphy and Hart had known each other for a while, and
Murphy had expressed to the Cubs president his dream of one day
acquiring a minor league team. Murphy had admitted that capital
remained his primary obstacle, but he had told Hart the previous year
that he would willingly invest every penny in his savings account into
a ball club if one went on sale for a reasonable price.[10] Murphy asked
Hart how much the Cubs would cost, and the latter stunned him by
replying that the team could be had for $100,000. Murphy's extensive
working knowledge of the business of baseball allowed him to immediately recognize that, if Hart was indeed serious, he had stumbled
upon the deal of a lifetime. Three years prior, Brush had sold the Cincinnati Reds to Garry Herrmann's investment group for $150,000, a
significantly larger financial transaction for a team in a smaller market.[11] Now, Hart was not only telling Murphy that the Chicago Cubs
franchise of the National League could be bought for a sale price, but
that it was on clearance.

As team president, Hart served as the public face of the ownership
group, but John Walsh, a banking power in the city, held heavy sway
over the franchise's financial direction behind the scenes. In 1905
Walsh found himself in the midst of a shifting political landscape that
left his banks vulnerable to federal government regulation, a terrifying
proposition for Walsh, who had used the bank's liquid assets to finance
his personal business ventures, a risky, not to mention illegal, use of

the funds. Several of Walsh's businesses were losing money, and he needed to raise capital to replenish lost dollars. Selling the team was one easy way for Walsh to acquire a few quick bucks.

Murphy's mind churned quickly. He knew that a successful National League franchise could profit close to $50,000 in a single season.[12] Murphy's awareness of how much revenue a franchise could generate gave him the confidence that he could repay any loan needed to buy the Chicago outfit. Murphy had also been a diligent saver of his money over the years, and he was willing to put every penny of it toward buying the team. He just needed to figure out how he could borrow the remaining amount. Murphy knew that if anyone with the means to buy the team found out about its sale price, his opportunity would vanish instantly. Therefore, an exclusive window emerged as his most logical move. He asked Hart for an option on the team at the stated price that would expire after a few days if he failed to obtain funding. Hart agreed. It was perhaps Murphy's savviest move of all, as Harry Pulliam also wanted to buy the team, but he had not yet arrived in Chicago. Rumors later circulated that Ban Johnson was also interested in the Cubs. Murphy knew the news wouldn't stay quiet for long. He raced out of the ballpark to catch a train for Cincinnati.

Charles Taft was a bit surprised to hear from him, but he warmly greeted Charlie Murphy, his former star writer at the *Times-Star*. Murphy explained to him that unique circumstances had made the Chicago Cubs available for an extraordinarily cheap price. John T. Brush had taught Murphy that winning mattered more than anything in terms of successfully running a team, and Murphy explained to Taft that Chicago possessed a nucleus of young talent that boded well for its prospects on the field and, most importantly, in the standings. Undoubtedly, Murphy contended that buying the team would be one of the best investments Taft could ever make.

A very soft-spoken and practical man, Taft kindly declined to jump at Murphy's initial pitch. Taft enjoyed baseball; he could be found at the ballpark watching the Reds at various points throughout the season, but he was not initially swayed to buy a team. Murphy expressed his willingness to risk everything he had to make a deal. The bold gesture had its intended effect. Taft agreed to send one of his emissaries to Chicago to verify the situation. Taft promptly received a positive report, and he agreed to lend Murphy the money. Taft recalled some time later, "I always enjoyed watching a game, but had never had the slightest idea of becoming interested in a financial way. But I liked Murphy and had some confidence in his judgment. When I found that he was willing to invest every cent of his savings in the deal I concluded that it might be a pretty good thing and went in with him."[13]

Charles and his wife, Annie, who had inherited a twenty-million-dollar fortune from her father, David Sinton, a pig-iron mogul, agreed to join Murphy as business partners. In addition to being generous with their family and friends, the Tafts benevolently supported the arts in Cincinnati, playing crucial roles as benefactors of the local opera house and symphony. Annie loved the arts, especially the theater, a passion Murphy shared. During his time in the Queen City, Murphy enjoyed not only attending live performances but creating them as well. Upon his hiring by the Giants, the *Brooklyn Daily Eagle* relayed to its readers that Murphy "has some reputation as a playwright, having written several successful vaudeville sketches."[14] Murphy actively participated in the Pen and Pencil Club, a local group of journalists who met monthly at the Grand Opera House in Cincinnati. They wrote vaudeville plays for a special performance that frequently took place at the Lyric Theater. The group received Charles Taft and his brother William Howard Taft, then secretary of war, in 1907.[15] Murphy was gone by then, but it's highly likely that Annie knew Murphy through their joint membership in Cincinnati's theater community.

Murphy's proposal reached the Tafts' ears while they were in the midst of an incredible buying spree in which they added a number of significant paintings to their art collection. Eventually, the Tafts bequeathed the pieces to the city of Cincinnati, along with their home, which today stands as the Taft Museum. In terms of being caretakers of public cultural entities, buying a baseball team made some sense for the Tafts, although they did not buy the Reds from Brush in 1902, suggesting Murphy's involvement made all the difference. Murphy, along with the Tafts, contacted Hart and exercised their option to buy the Cubs.

On July 15, after he had resigned his position as the assistant secretary of the Giants, the Chicago National League club announced that Charles W. Murphy would be installed as the team's new vice president, and he would be taking over a significant portion of President Jim Hart's duties. The public was told that Hart wanted to soon retire because of his desire to dedicate more time to several of his successful business ventures outside baseball. The press reports also mentioned the fact that Hart had been in the game for twenty-five years and "this has been sufficient to wear off much of the enthusiasm with which, as original baseball fan, he had embarked into the business."[16]

Strange rumblings regarding Murphy and the Cubs reached the interested ears of Garry Herrmann in Cincinnati during the first week of July. Stunned, he reached out to Murphy to ascertain what was really happening. Murphy remained silent. "The matter upon which you seek information is a private one and a discussion of the details among those whose interests are inimical cannot possibly redound to the benefit of those concerned," Murphy replied. To pacify Herrmann, Murphy added his regret at not being able to go into further detail with his "friend of so many years."[17] It isn't personal, Murphy was saying; it's business. Nor were Murphy's actions political. He refused to risk alienating Taft over engaging in political gossip, an uncharacteristic move for a baseball magnate. However, the day the sale of the Cubs was announced in the press, Murphy wrote Herrmann a lengthy letter in which he revealed the truth. He knew that the press would incorrectly surmise that Brush, or Giants minority owner Andrew Freedman, had financed him. Murphy still wanted to keep the identity of Taft, who was currently out of the country, confidential and requested that Herrmann keep the information to himself. In the meantime, Murphy expressed his desire to have a great working relationship with Herrmann in his new role. However, Murphy hinted that he would not hesitate to rebel against commonly held ideas if they hurt his business. "I shall be independent in my actions but anything you want is yours now. By that I mean that if I can aid you in any reasonable way you have only to ask me," he said.[18]

A buoyant Murphy did his best to reassure everyone about the sudden and shocking rise of this young man from Cincinnati. He knew the sport of baseball and, perhaps more importantly, the business of baseball. He also would be reunited with his wife, Louise. Murphy sought to quell any doubts about his motivations and abilities with his first comment as vice president. "I am not speaking from motives of policy in saying I am a great admirer of Chicago. I believe there is a fine opportunity in connecting myself with the National league club in this city, and only hope I shall perform my duties in a way satisfactory to those who support the game in this city. I am well acquainted with President Johnson of the American league and also with President Comiskey of the local American league club, and am sure my relations with them will be most pleasant."[19]

By the end of July, the sale was made official, and Murphy was elected vice president of the Chicago National League franchise. Writing for *McClure's*, Edward Mott Woolley captured Murphy's stunning rise to power. "For a real wonder-story, the history of Charles W. Murphy outranks anything in baseball records."[20] The truth is it was a "wonder-story." Murphy went from writing about the Reds in Cincinnati to promoting the Giants in New York to working in Chicago's front office within six months.

Although Jim Hart still ran the franchise as team president, a role he maintained for the rest of the 1905 season, he willingly gave Murphy the opportunity to contribute to the direction of the organization. Murphy spent time familiarizing himself with the work of team secretary Charlie Williams, who had started his career with the organization as a fourteen-year-old youngster operating the scoreboard in 1885. Williams's stepfather, John Brown, worked as the team's treasurer for twenty-five years, and in 1898 Charlie was asked to assist him. The following year, Hart became team president and elevated Williams to the full-time role of secretary-treasurer. *Sporting Life* reported: "When Mr. Murphy secured control of the club during the 1905 season he,

recognizing Mr. Williams' value to the club by reason of his long service, experience and fidelity, at once continued Mr. Williams in his
office, then retaining a strong link in the great club which now stands
at the head of the National League columns."[21] In his youth, Charlie
Williams tallied the runs produced by the prodigious home runs and
searing line drives off the bats of "King" Kelly and Cap Anson on the
scoreboard, and now he served the team's next generation of stars in
a much more complex capacity.[22]

Murphy hired a familiar face to work in the Cubs' scouting department: his brother Jim. The youngest Murphy brother possessed enough
talent to play semi-pro ball for a while, but his career stalled out. Nevertheless, Jim developed a reputation as a heady player on teams that
featured professional talent. In 1898 he played shortstop for Mattoon,
a small town in central Illinois, alongside future National Leaguers
Luther "Dummy" Taylor, Bob Wicker, and Del Howard. According
to a local legend, it was there that Jim Murphy helped develop the
suicide squeeze play. One afternoon, Mattoon found itself tied with
Springfield and its ace, and future New York Giant, Joe McGinnity. As
Jim Murphy told it, the story went this way. Mattoon's Pug Bennett
tripled with one out in the ninth inning of a tied game. Murphy, who
was coaching at third base, approached the batter, Jack Wilkinson, and
instructed him to take the first pitch and then bunt McGinnity's next
offering. "He was puzzled," Jim remembered. "After letting the first
one cut the plate he called me off third and inquired about the play
again. I told him to bunt the next one, because Bennett was going to
sprint for the plate as soon as McGinnity wound up.

"Wilkinson did as told and sent a dinky grounder straight at Joe.
Bennett came tearing for the plate and beat the throw in. Our new
catcher, reaching first in safety, danced up and down, yelling, 'Gee, I
see it now.'"[23]

Charlie wanted Jim to scour the playing fields of America for talented
players who thirsted to know more about the intricacies of game strategy, or "inside baseball," as it used to be called, as much as they had
in their younger years. Jim accepted his brother's offer and remained
with the organization for the next eight years.

After solidifying the front office, Murphy established his promoter credentials less than two months into his tenure as Cubs vice president. He wanted to generate headlines to galvanize fans and establish his brand as an executive but, most importantly, Murphy owed Taft nearly a hundred grand, and he wanted to whittle away at his debt. On July 26 Murphy challenged his old friend Charlie Comiskey, now owner of the crosstown White Sox, to a local interleague series of games for bragging rights, which served all of his purposes. Jim Hart had not pursued a postseason series the previous year, and Murphy happily put it back on the front burner for 1905. "I hope my friend Commy will be able to strengthen his team in order to give us a fight," goaded Murphy.

Comiskey accepted the challenge and said the teams wouldn't have to wait as long as the Sox weren't in the World Series. "Mr. Murphy will doubtless find use for all the minor league stars he can pick up when the Sox get busy with the Cubs," he needled.[24]

With Murphy moving to town, Comiskey got reacquainted with the newspaper writer who used to cover him. They had spent three years around the ballpark in Cincinnati, but that had ended when Comiskey retired as the Reds player/manager after the 1894 season. Comiskey invited Murphy over to the South Side to watch the Sox while the Cubs were on a road trip.[25] They must have recalled many memories made over a decade ago. Little did either man know what awaited them in October of 1906.

Within forty-eight hours of the inner-city challenge, all the newly infused enthusiasm brought to the organization by Murphy vanished as manager Frank Selee asked Hart for a leave of absence on July 28. Selee had been out since July 1, having initially suffered what was publicly called an "acute attack of intestinal indigestion."[26] He heeded his doctor's advice to take time off, but the pain did not ease. Selee's doctor wanted him to rest in Colorado and New Mexico for the next several months with the hope of recovering in time for the 1906 campaign. The stunning development shocked and saddened the entire organization. The press constantly referred to the team not only as the "Cubs" but as "Selee's Men," indicating his leadership qualities and the players' admiration for him.

Selee, forty-five, had arrived in Chicago prior to the 1902 season, after twelve incredibly successful seasons managing the Boston Beaneaters, with whom he won five pennants during the 1890s. Selee immediately provided the young Orphans, so nicknamed after longtime manager Cap Anson left the organization following the 1897 season, with their true north leader. He reshuffled the team's defensive alignment and installed youngsters Joe Tinker at shortstop, Johnny Evers at second base, and Frank Chance at first base. He then nurtured his young talent. Selee's leadership was unparalleled in the game, and the success of his personnel work could be seen everywhere on the diamond. The Orphans finished one game under .500 in 1902, but the freshly branded Cubs won eighty-two games the following year and upped that total to 93 in 1904. They sat in fourth place with a record of 52-38 on the day of Selee's announcement.

Hart tried to capture in words all that Selee meant to the franchise. "I believe he stands as premier in the most difficult position of team manager, second to no person living or dead, who ever has occupied a similar position. That we shall miss him and his ability decidedly goes without saying," said Hart. Outsiders may not have noticed anything amiss with the Cubs manager, but Hart knew Selee had been toughing it out. "I do not think any one realizes how sick a man Selee has been. He has been sick ever since he came to Chicago this spring, but stuck to his team until compelled to retire," Hart disclosed.[27]

Leaving his team in the middle of the season cut Selee to the core, but his decision revealed the true extent of his debilitation. Still, he grieved. In a note to Hart, Selee wrote, "It is with sincere regret, as it is hard for me to sever myself from the pleasant associations I have enjoyed under you. The Chicago League Ball club is today not only a grand ball club as far as playing ability goes but is composed of manly young men of whom I am proud. I wish you and the boys success, and hope to be with the club again in the spring."[28]

Compassionately moved to aid their former skipper, Hart, Murphy, Chance, and Williams went to work rebranding a late-season game between Chicago and Boston, the two clubs Selee had managed, as a "testimonial game." All the proceeds of the September 28 contest at West Side Ball Park would be donated to Selee to help pay for his care. Boston readily agreed, and the Cubs front office got to work. They contacted people throughout the sport to let them know what they were doing, and the response was overwhelming. Owners and writers from around the country poured in contributions. "President Hart and Vice President Murphy of the Chicago club have worked unremittingly for the success of the testimonial, which promises to exceed in realization their hopes when the movement was started," read an update in the *Chicago Tribune*.[29]

A group of a hundred members of the Oshkosh, Wisconsin, community bought tickets and arranged travel to Chicago to show their appreciation for Selee, who had managed their team to a pennant in the Wisconsin State League in 1887.[30] However, no one showed the manager more love than Chicagoans, who heeded the call of the *Chicago Tribune*:

> The testimonial to Frank G. Selee which is set for that date was originated with the idea of making it largely a Chicago affair, but the former manager has made himself so well known and generally respected wherever baseball is known that the idea was taken up with enthusiasm all over the country and rapidly assumed a national affair . . . But Chicago owes him a heavier debt than does the rest of the country for what he has done since he took charge of the local club. All that it is today, a distinct credit to any city, is due to his efforts almost without reservation. To show that, it is only necessary to pick out the players on Chance's team the men who were members of it when he undertook its management. From the wreck left by the war raids of 1900, 1901, and 1902, Mr. Selee has built up the present strong team.[31]

An enthusiastic crowd of five thousand fans happily paid their way into the stadium on September 28 for the fundraiser. Cap Anson was there. National League president Harry Pulliam made an appearance. Admirably, Charlie Comiskey also walked into West Side Ball Park to pay his respects to Selee. Comiskey's White Sox were playing a critical series in Philadelphia against the A's with the pennant on the line. The Pale Hose and A's were tied for the American League lead with only eleven games to play. Yet Comiskey made sure to support the testimonial. He made a brief appearance before retreating behind the scenes to follow his team on the ticker. Hart and Murphy knew that Comiskey would not be the only one in the park interested in results from the Sox game in Philadelphia, so they decided to post the score, inning by inning, to keep fans abreast of developments in the game. Beat writers took notice of the crowd's overwhelmingly positive reaction to the novel out-of-town scoreboard. "This is an act highly appreciated by the fans, and proved so popular yesterday that it may become a permanent practice at both local grounds in the future," read one report.[32]

The Cubs delighted their home fans by knocking off Boston, 7–4, but that seemed to be a footnote to the overwhelming acts of charity. Murphy tabulated all the gate receipts and donations, which totaled an astonishing $3,640.25. Hart sent Selee a check for $640.25 and put the remaining $3,000 in a trust so it would earn interest. The fund issued Selee a monthly check for $125 until he received all the money in the account.[33] Selee wrote a letter to Hart and Murphy from Colorado Springs thanking them for their hard work on the fundraiser. He also expressed his sincere appreciation for the people throughout baseball who generously contributed to his care.[34]

As the weeks passed without Selee, reality began to set in for Hart and Murphy. Sadly, Selee's ailment was not going to allow the manager to return, not in 1906 or any other year. Frank Chance managed the Cubs on an interim basis during Selee's leave, and now the organization faced a critical decision about how to move forward. The twenty-eight-year-old Chance proved to be an effective manager, who could potentially lead the Cubs to great heights. Chance's teammates deeply respected him, and the fans adored him. Chance had joined the organization as a young catcher in 1898. He was a talented prospect but struggled defensively. It was Selee who had permanently installed Chance at first base, strengthening the team at that position, as well as behind the plate, where Johnny Kling took over as the Cubs' catcher. The fans watched as Chance grew into his stardom, a homegrown talent who developed into one of the elite players in the National League. When Chance stepped into the batter's box for the first time after being named the interim manager, the crowd roared its approval. Everyone knew Chance was stepping into a very difficult situation in replacing the team's beloved skipper under gut-wrenching circumstances. Harry Ford captured Chance's daunting task in a game story he wrote for the *Inter Ocean* following Selee's departure at the end of July. "As was mentioned a moment ago, they are the adopted Cubs. For twenty-four hours they were orphans after Frank Selee turned them adrift. But President Hart had compassion on them and yesterday he asked Captain Frank Chance to step into Selee's place and adopt the whole zoo. Frank bravely accepted the hardships offered him, and it was not long before he realized fully the task he had undertaken."[35] A story out of Louisville that suggested fans could expect to see Cap Anson reinstalled as Chicago's manager earned a wry smirk out of Hart. "We have two managers now," Hart retorted. "I don't think we want three."[36]

In the middle of September, Charles Comiskey visited Jim Hart and Charlie Murphy to reach an agreement on the postseason series between the Cubs and the White Sox should the latter not win the American League pennant and advance to the World Series. Murphy's prodding had paid off as the series, if played, would undoubtedly be popular with local fans. They agreed on the details in short order and only needed to select which stadium would host Game One. Murphy tossed a coin, and Comiskey correctly chose the flip's outcome.[37] The Sox would host the opener of the best of seven series. Despite a valiant push by the White Sox, the Philadelphia Athletics held off Chicago and won the American League pennant by two games, setting up the cross-city battle.

The Cubs easily dispatched the White Sox in five games, clinching the series with a 10–5 win on the South Side. Exultant Cubs fans rushed the field clutching and grabbing at Frank Chance before lifting him upon their shoulders and carrying him off to his waiting carriage on Thirty-Ninth Street. Jimmy Slagle, Johnny Evers, and Mordecai Brown, among others, also received a shower of affectionate cheers, handshakes, and a few slaps on the back that struck them just a little too hard. The players made it to their hacks, but they were hopelessly stuck in a sea of screaming humanity. A reporter for the Chicago *Inter Ocean* hyperbolically compared the chaotic scene to sights seen during the French Revolution. "The carriages were surrounded by a mob that would make the more famous revolts of history fade into insignificance."[38] Cubs fans roared through the streets as they returned home.

The Cubs' victory put others on notice that the franchise was ready to take the next step. They had been notable underdogs to the White Sox in the series. Their win demonstrated that the youthful roster was ready to contend in 1906. "We won because we played the better baseball," Chance remarked after the fans set him down. "We feel all the better over our victory because of the adverse criticism that has been made of us at one time or another, especially contrasts made to our disadvantage in the matter of so-called 'fine points' of the game. In this series we demonstrated that we could play not only better baseball than our rivals, but better 'inside ball.' We did it through the series."[39] By the end of the following season, exceling at playing "inside ball" would become the trademark characteristic of Chance's Cubs.

The series victory proved to be a smashing success for the young National Leaguers. Each Cub took home an additional $414.81 for beating their crosstown opponents. Several players, including Chance and Evers, hung around the office after receiving their money to talk about the games.[40] The delighted fans soaked in the victory. They turned out in droves to watch the games and celebrated the Cubs win as a consequential outcome. Murphy accomplished several goals on and off the field. His team won, which generated additional money for the players and goodwill with the fan base. He also succeeded in generating more revenue to pay down additional debt. Taking full advantage, he was not shy about using the victory to market the Cubs. It was a strong return for having his team play five additional games.

The official changing of the guard for the West Siders took place in October. Frank Chance signed a three-year contract that officially added managing the Cubs to his job title. Murphy was thrilled to get the deal done. He believed Chance to be the right man for the job because "he is not only a great all around player but undoubtedly a manager of tact, ability, and rare skill."[41] As part of the deal, Chance was allowed to buy into ownership of the club. He received access to a hundred shares of Chicago National League Ball Club capital stock on November 1, 1905, from Charles and Annie Taft, at the price of $105.76 per share. The following year, Chance paid for the stock in seven installments, from July through October, with interest.[42] It was a nice perk. Chance could now directly benefit if the franchise performed well financially, a pretty sure bet with their young nucleus of talent. With his contract done, Chance left for his home in California on October 23, where he would spend the winter scouting all the talented ballplayers on the West Coast for reinforcements. "Of course our club at present is in great condition, and we haven't got a single kick, but we want none but the best stick handlers; consequently there is a scouting expedition on all the time," Chance said before boarding his train.[43] With the interim tag gone, Chance headed out of the smoky city toward the Pacific Ocean with personnel decisions on his mind.

Murphy, too, left Chicago for a few days in late October, with his first season in professional ball complete. He traveled to Ohio, where he spent several days visiting his mother, Bridget, in Wilmington before he stopped in Cincinnati to say hello to some old friends. News of Jim Hart's impending retirement had gone public earlier in the summer, and on November 1, 1905, Murphy officially replaced him as the president of the Cubs organization. Murphy sent his inaugural communication as president to Garry Herrmann. "The enclosed letter bears the first signature which I have attached to a letter as President of the Chicago League ball club. The transfer of stock was made on November 1st without any friction whatsoever. Mr. Hart and myself arranged everything in a satisfactory and harmonious manner, and it had always been my intention that my first official communication should be sent to you."[44]

Hart's retirement was the end of an important chapter for the organization. He had led the Chicago National League Ball Club for fourteen years after taking over as team president, for Al Spalding, in 1891.[45] Hart had been in baseball for well over two decades—he managed prior to becoming an executive, including leading the Boston Beaneaters in 1889, before Frank Selee replaced him the following year. Hart spearheaded the effort to build the team a new ballpark on the property that was located on Polk Street just across the road from Cook County Hospital.[46] That stadium, the West Side Grounds, opened on Sunday, May 14, 1893, to rave reviews. Over thirteen thousand fans cheered loudly, yet amicably, for Chicago, but the Reds spoiled the day a bit by eking out a 13–12 win. During his later years with the club, Hart navigated the end of Cap Anson's tenure as manager and, after several false starts, landed Frank Selee in 1902. After Taft and Murphy purchased the club, Murphy was to be Hart's understudy for the rest of the season before taking over as the club's president the following year. However, Murphy welcomed Hart's counsel and wanted him to continue providing input after the transition. He invited Hart to join him at the National League meeting that winter.

In December, rumors abounded throughout baseball that Frank Selee wanted to manage again. Western League president Tip O'Neill sought to land the big fish. He successfully convinced Selee to manage the team in Pueblo, which would allow him to establish a home in Colorado throughout the calendar year. Selee piloted the team for the next several seasons. Simultaneously, in a twist of fate, the Cubs, a group of players he played an instrumental role in assembling and developing, reeled off three consecutive World Series appearances eleven hundred miles to the east. Sadly, in 1909 consumption overtook Selee's body, and he was placed in hospice care. Selee died of tuberculosis on July 5. The following day, the *Chicago Tribune* published Selee's photograph next to his obituary on its sports page. The picture captured the regal nature of the noble, placid man, in a crisp pinstriped suit and tie, in his healthier days. Selee's younger face featured his instantly recognizable thick, vigorous mustache.[47] Now he was gone, much too young, at the age of forty-nine.

"HE IS ONE OF US"

Personally and professionally, the second half of 1905 was a whirlwind for Charlie Murphy. After he arrived in the Chicago area from New York in July, Murphy reconnected with his wife, Louise, in Austin, a small enclave just west of the Windy City.[1] Initially, it made for both an easy transition and a short commute to the office, but the Murphys, nevertheless, decided to move about a month later.[2] They selected Oak Park, a thriving community next to Austin. They chose a house at 242 Marion Street, located about eight and a half miles west of West Side Grounds.

Oak Park residents enjoyed residing in their region as its distance from Chicago kept out many of the city's vices and influences. Family life and church participation dominated its culture. Additionally, social clubs played a crucial role in building relationships with neighbors. The arts figured prominently in the everyday life of the village. Music performances throughout the year entertained the community, although the minstrel shows were incredibly racist. Most Oak Parkers held staunchly Republican views, although their conservatism gave way to progressivism on certain issues.[3] For example, *Oak Leaves*, the local paper, published a letter whose author questioned the morality of child labor.[4] Murphy's own political views remain somewhat elusive, but he effusively praised his acquaintance William Howard Taft and enthusiastically supported his run for the presidency in 1908. For the most part, Oak Parkers concentrated on local issues like streetlights and water system safety more intensely than national concerns.[5]

The Murphys settled into their new home on Marion Street and began building relationships. They met a doctor, Clarence Hemingway, who ran the local Agassiz Club. Dr. Hemingway's seven-year-old son, Ernest, played baseball and followed the exploits of the local stars Frank Chance and Eddie Cicotte. Dr. Hemingway treated Murphy throughout his time in Chicago. Louise Murphy passionately followed baseball, and she could frequently be spotted at ballgames. At home, she played with her dog, Cub.[6] The baseball season kept Charlie Murphy away from most social events, but he made an exception for attending theater performances.

The newly minted partnership of President Charlie Murphy and manager Frank Chance created a new era for Chicago's National League baseball club. Murphy's in-season work began to earn Chance's trust, while the young skipper's approach so impressed Murphy that the latter began referring to the manager as the Cubs' "Peerless Leader," a nickname created by reporter Charles Dryden.[7] Underneath the fresh-faced skipper's exterior burned the fire of an intense competitor, and Murphy's engagement in helping the team add talent to its young roster won Chance over in short order in spite of the team president's inexperience. Frank Selee and Jim Hart had assembled the core of the Cubs roster, but Murphy played an instrumental role in acquiring Harry Steinfeldt, Pat Moran, and Jimmy Sheckard, in separate deals, to augment the 1906 team's nucleus. Murphy and Chance operated harmoniously together early on. They believed that the strong blend of holdovers and new acquisitions would be talented enough to compete for the National League pennant.

Garry Herrmann had approached Murphy, in late July of 1905, to gauge his interest in acquiring Harry Steinfeldt, Cincinnati's third baseman. Steinfeldt was only two years removed from an excellent 1903 campaign, during which he batted .312 and tied for the National League lead with thirty-two doubles. Murphy had seen plenty of Steinfeldt's quality play in Cincinnati, but he initially expressed skepticism that the player's skill set would mesh with Frank Selee's preferences. Murphy wrote to Herrmann from French Lick, Indiana, where he was relaxing with some friends. "I note carefully what you say about Steinfeldt, but doubt if he would fit in our team, as Selee wants fast men on the bases."[8]

However, Murphy and Jim Hart reconsidered their position after Selee went out on leave. They opened negotiations with the idea that a deal with the Reds could be agreed upon, but the players would not be officially exchanged until after the season ended. After serious deliberations, on September 10, Hart and Murphy agreed to send left-handed pitcher Jake Weimer to Cincinnati in exchange for Steinfeldt and Jimmy Sebring, a fast outfielder who had left the Reds in midseason to care for his ill wife, Elizabeth. After they reached the agreement, Murphy amended its terms to ensure no word of it would be given to the press until after the Cubs postseason series with the White Sox concluded, because the Cubs fully expected Weimer to pitch against their intercity rival. However, news of the deal leaked in Cincinnati and prematurely found its way into the Chicago papers on September 29.

Murphy racked his brain to figure out how the news could have gotten into the paper. The Reds had recently been in Chicago and, on the evening of September 19, Murphy had run into several players from both teams at the theater, including Chance and Steinfeldt. Now, ten days later, Murphy asked Chance if he told Steinfeldt about the trade that night. "I didn't have to tell him," Chance replied. "He knows it." Meanwhile, Cubs fans fumed over the subtraction of Weimer, who had pitched well during his three seasons in Chicago. They hooted derision at Hart, Murphy, and Chance whenever they saw them around the West Side Ball Park. Weimer instantly became a martyred hero, and the fans cheered his every move at the ballpark. The leak frustrated Murphy, who did not want the impending acquisitions to distract the current Cub players from finishing the 1905 season strong and beating the White Sox in the postseason City Series. Murphy lodged his complaints with Herrmann. "The management of the Chicago Club regrets exceedingly the premature publication on your end of the line of our deal of September 10," Murphy pointedly told him. "Mr. Hart and myself have been as mum as clams," he added. Murphy softened his tone as his letter concluded. He referred to Herrmann as the "soul of honor" whose "word is as good as your bond." Murphy also expressed his hope that Herrmann would be successful in an upcoming election.[9]

Murphy would have to wait until next season for Steinfeldt to prove his worth to the disgruntled fan base.

What changed Murphy's mind about Steinfeldt after his initial aversion to acquiring him? Johnny Evers believed Frank Chance heavily influenced the front office's thinking. In his memoir, *Touching Second*, Evers explained that Chance wanted the team to upgrade at third base.

> He knew the man he wanted, Harry Steinfeldt, who was playing indifferent ball in Cincinnati . . . Chance knew Steinfeldt, had played with him two winters, in California, and knew also that internal dissentions were causing the trouble in the Cincinnati ranks. The Cincinnati club was anxious to trade Steinfeldt, but gossip among his enemies in Cincinnati had kept other clubs from bidding for the player. Chance asked Murphy to make a trade. Murphy went to Cincinnati, but the stories whispered to him sent him flying back to Chicago without the player. A few days later Murphy asked Chance: "What third baseman can we get?"
>
> "Steinfeldt," said Chance.
>
> Murphy argued, but went to Cincinnati and again returned without the player, but with even more startling stories to tell Chance. "Who shall we get," he asked.
>
> "Steinfeldt," replied Chance, unmoved.
>
> So Murphy, still unconvinced, went to Cincinnati and traded Weimer, a left-handed pitcher for Steinfeldt.[10]

Evers did not expound on the "startling stories" Murphy heard about Steinfeldt, which left his readers hanging, but it was clear that Harry was unhappy in Cincinnati and intended to force his way out of town. Evers's account of the trade differs from the correspondence between Murphy and Herrmann, but his description of Chance's influence on the situation rings true. If anything, Murphy discovered through his trade discussions that Steinfeldt's knee was in much better condition than he had previously been led to believe.[11] Chance molded the team as he saw fit, and his firsthand knowledge of Steinfeldt's situation paid dividends. Chance's personal relationships with players throughout baseball gave the Cubs an incredible advantage in trade talks. Jake Weimer won two games for the Cubs in their series win over the White Sox, and then he went west for Steinfeldt and Sebring.

The talented, but frequently injured, Jimmy Sebring never played for Chicago. The mercurial Sebring began the season in Cincinnati before suiting up for an outlaw team in Williamsport, Pennsylvania. During his wife's illness, he had spent money lavishly and desperately needed a financial boost. Murphy met with Sebring in Williamsport, and they came to terms on a three-year contract. Sebring signed the deal, but he ultimately decided to remain in Williamsport.[12] Accused of "jumping," or ignoring his contract, Sebring was banished, but three years later he convinced the National Commission to reinstate him. He appeared in twenty-five games for the Brooklyn Superbas in 1909. On December 20 a seizure struck down Sebring, and he was hospitalized. He died two days later of kidney disease. Sebring was twenty-seven.[13]

In December Murphy set out with Hart for the National League meeting in New York a few days early to give him a head start in further trade negotiations before the official events of the gathering got underway. Murphy had already added lefty pitcher Jack Pfiester to replace Weimer, and he eagerly anticipated adding a few more pieces.

Jim Hart took center stage when the meeting officially opened at the sparkling Victoria Hotel in Manhattan. Hart informed the owners that he had sold his shares in the Chicago franchise and announced his retirement. He then graciously introduced Murphy to the group. One year after covering the meeting as a reporter, Murphy addressed the group as president of the Cubs:

Mr. President and fellow members of the National League: I am naturally gratified over the eulogistic introduction of myself as a club president by Mr. Hart and I take this opportunity to pledge my loyalty to the time-honored National League, which has been linked by some to that august and ultra-exclusive body of statesmen, the United States Senate.

Incidentally I shall recall the reputed statement of a once new member of the Senate and let you judge whether it is apropos in connection with my debut here. An Ohio man, who had never shown the ability of a Gladstone or Disraeli, was elected to the Senate. Many regarded his election as a huge joke and after he had been in Washington a week or so, he met a constituent, who asked: "Well, how does it feel to be a Senator?"

"During the first day," replied the new Senator, "I employed most of my time wondering how I really got there. After I had been there for a few days longer, however, had listened attentively to measures introduced and the accompanying speeches, I began to wonder how the other fellows got there."

Seriously, gentlemen, I wish to add that the National League is doubtless the greatest association for the promotion of athletics ever organized and I shall always strive in my humble way to uplift and foster it.[14]

A measure of discontent with National League President Harry Pulliam developed into something larger for several owners during the meeting, specifically Herrmann and John T. Brush. They disagreed with Pulliam's handling of a disciplinary measure taken against Giants manager John McGraw the previous season. Quiet questions persisted about whether Pulliam's sensitive temperament could withstand the rigors of the job. Herrmann and Brush did not have the votes to oust Pulliam, so they tried to sway other owners. Most likely, Herrmann recruited Murphy to replace Pulliam during a meeting they had in Cincinnati in August, but the new Chicago president felt uneasy about it. Murphy expressed his reservations to Herrmann directly. "When I got back to Chicago I started to tell Mr. Hart about the matter which you called me to Cincinnati to discuss. I had not proceeded far when he began to smile and told me more about the proposed change than I had learned from you. Mr. Hart says he has given the matter some thought and from what he has been told doubts the practicability of the plan as you outlined it to me," he said. Prior to leaving for the winter meeting, Murphy decided that he would vote to reelect Pulliam.[15]

Herrmann and Brush did not have the votes to remove Pulliam from office, but they held a surprising wild card that shook up the gathering.

Herrmann and Brush decided to use the well-respected Hart's presence to their advantage. Rather than simply voting against Pulliam, they decided to nominate Hart for the presidency. Hart thought they were doing it as a sign of respect, a sort of swan song farewell to thank him for his contributions to the National League. Hart was shocked and angered when Herrmann and Brush actually cast votes for him. It wasn't enough, however, to oust Pulliam, who was reelected by a 6–2 margin.

Before leaving for the winter meeting, Murphy had sat down with Chance to map out their off-season plans for the roster. "I want to go out after something bigger than the Chicago championship next season. I want to win the biggest prize in baseball," Murphy told him.

"Well, you don't want to do it any worse than I do," Chance replied. The manager told the president he believed two specific players would put the Cubs over the top in the National League: Boston catcher Pat Moran and Brooklyn outfielder Jimmy Sheckard.

Upon arriving in New York, Murphy contacted Boston officials about Moran's availability. He learned that the Pirates were also sniffing around Moran, but Murphy pounced after Chance sent him a telegram urging him to get a trade completed.[16] On December 13 he sent catcher Jack O'Neill and pitcher Jeff Pfeffer to the Beaneaters in exchange for Moran. Murphy was thrilled. "If Moran had not been dissatisfied in Boston we never would have secured him, as he is regarded by Clarke, Duffy, Tenney, and others as not only a finished catcher but a hitter of the 'clean up' kind, who is liable to slam the ball against the fence at any stage of the game," Murphy said.[17]

Jimmy Sheckard possessed star qualities despite his inconsistent play for the Brooklyn Superbas. He broke into the National League, as an eighteen-year-old, with the Brooklyn Bridegrooms in 1897. He took the league by storm in 1899 after Brooklyn assigned him to the Baltimore Orioles. Manager John McGraw installed the twenty-year-old Sheckard in right field, and the youngster exceled. He batted .295 and led the league with seventy-seven stolen bases before being assigned back to Brooklyn at the end of the season. In 1902 McGraw joined the Giants, and following the 1903 season, he tried to trade for Sheckard, who wanted to reunite with his former skipper. However, Brooklyn president Charlie Ebbets rebuffed McGraw's overtures and kept his star attraction.

With one item on his to-do list checked off, Murphy turned his attention to the more complex task of acquiring Sheckard, who was also drawing trade interest from Pittsburgh. Coming off a season in which they posted the worst record in the National League, the Superbas needed to make changes. Only the Beaneaters scored fewer runs than the Superbas in 1905. Ebbets had already started remaking the club by letting go of manager Ned Hanlon and replacing him with Patsy Donovan. He then pondered his options with Sheckard. Ebbets desperately wanted to keep him, but there were no guarantees Sheckard wanted to regain his old form while wearing a Brooklyn uniform. Disappointed at not being traded to New York, Sheckard played badly in 1904, hitting just .239, amid accusations from Hanlon that he was playing badly because the Superbas hadn't traded him to the Giants. Sheckard's bounce-back season in 1905 rekindled the Giants' interest in trading for him. Other organizations heard rumors of Sheckard's malcontent behavior and weighed the cost of getting into the bidding. The Pirates placed a lot of value on his skill set and put together a trade package for Ebbets to consider.

Murphy recognized the unique opportunity in front of him. He could acquire Sheckard while simultaneously preventing the Giants and Pirates from getting him. Just after Murphy arrived in New York and started talking to Brooklyn about the outfielder, the Giants caught wind of the Cubs' efforts to secure Sheckard, and they immediately offered Ebbets $10,000 for him. Ebbets, however, wanted an infusion of talented players to help him rebuild the team. The Giants reworked their proposal to include three players as well as cash. Murphy contacted Chance to apprise him of the situation. Chance knew Sheckard would play outstanding defense in the difficult sun field at West Side Ball Park and provide more speed at the top of the lineup. He encouraged Murphy to add a fourth player. In the end, Murphy's trade offer to Ebbets included center fielder Billy Maloney, left fielder Jack McCarthy, third baseman Doc Casey, pitcher Buttons Briggs, and $2,000 for Sheckard. It was a stunning proposition, and Ebbets accepted.

Following several days of drama, during which he declared he would not play for Chicago, Sheckard informed Murphy he intended to report to the team. Relayed the *Inter Ocean*: "James T. Sheckard wrote to Murphy yesterday and took occasion to deny all the stories which said he would not be seen with the Cubs during the coming season. He also said he would be on hand and be a hard fighter in the race for the championship."[18]

Murphy blamed the owner of an outlaw team in Sheckard's hometown for feeding the press what he believed were bogus stories about his intentions. "Sheckard will be in left field when we open the season, barring accidents," Murphy cheerfully declared. With Sheckard in left, Jimmy Slagle would slide over to center field. Frank Schulte retained his customary spot in right. Chicago's outfield was set.

Cubs players excitedly praised Murphy's trades. After the National League meeting ended, Murphy traveled upstate to visit one of the team's most important players, in his hometown of Troy. "I met Johnny Evers in New York, and after he had heard that we were to be re(i)nforced by Sheckard and Moran, said: 'I've got the batting order made out in my mind, and with the lineup we can present we will make a few pitchers look sick. We'll make 'em all go some.'"[19] Harry Steinfeldt, who was all set to join Chicago in the spring, wrote Murphy a letter praising his personnel work. A recuperating Frank Selee checked in from New Mexico, where he had been keeping up with off-season news. He stamped both winter trades with his approval.[20] On their way back to Chicago, Murphy and Hart took stock of the newly augmented roster. "Ex-President Hart told me on the train coming home from New York that our team as at present constituted was by far the strongest, in his opinion, that ever has represented Chicago," boasted Murphy.[21]

Any doubts Chance had about his new boss vanished after the winter meeting. Not only did Murphy add Moran and Sheckard on the heels of Steinfeldt, but he gave all the credit to the young manager entering his first full season on the job. Murphy told the local media, "Not only were the deals for players at New York made with the sanction of Manager Chance, but they were made at his suggestion."[22] At this stage, Chance and Murphy partnered together beautifully. They were simultaneously young and trying to establish themselves in the shadows of Frank Selee and Jim Hart. Chance knew how to improve the team and had excellent relationships with players throughout the game. Murphy already knew the principal baseball executives from his reporting days, and he challenged Chance by proposing any idea imaginable—outrageous trade proposals were a frequent brainstorming pastime—to improve the club, even incrementally. As an outsider, Murphy needed to establish trust with Chance, and the combination of the trades and his public praise of Chance did the job. Chance was thrilled and ready to make Murphy look good for showing faith in him.

> "I'll wager that there is no one in base ball any closer to his players than President Murphy, of our team," Chance said. "There is not a man on the team who does not like him and you will see this bunch pulling together this season as hard as any team ever did. Mr. Murphy, like most of us, has youth and enthusiasm and knows how to treat ball players. He is one of us. He takes an active interest in everything that affects the men in any way and is always ready to give good advice and counsel when anything goes wrong. It is a pleasure to be associated with him. Every deal that has been made this winter has helped Chicago. It is true that I mapped them out, but someone had to put them over the plate and he delivered the goods. Many a manager has told the club president what he wanted to add strength to his team, but the chief executive didn't always get what the manager asked for. Some persons may doubt the wisdom of our deals, but I guess time will show that we knew what we were doing."[23]

As for Murphy, he had found the perfect manager for his team in Frank Chance. Physically strong and incredibly intelligent, Chance could hit, field and, most importantly, lead men. During the era in which Teddy Roosevelt promoted the strenuous life, Chance—who boxed in the off-season—idealized the president's vision of masculinity. The Cubs' exciting roster was full of dynamic players with big personalities, who frequently clashed with each other, yet Chance began his first full season as manager by instilling the culture he wanted in the club. Evers, the prickliest of ballplayers, described Chance's methodology to sportswriter Grantland Rice. "'Frank Chance was a great builder of fighting spirit. We were taught in that school to suffer in silence—no alibis, no complaints, no squawking. Later on in my career, when 'don't rub' was the slogan of the team, I once slid into second base and broke a leg. The ball bounded several yards away. 'Don't rub,' was the call from the bench. If I hadn't been brought up in the Chance school I would have stayed there at second nursing a broken leg. As it was I got up and ran to third. That was Frank Chance's idea of what baseball should be."[24] Just as Murphy had pacified Chance's skepticism, the manager won over Murphy for the same reason: the singular purpose of winning.

Murphy delighted in the trades but also in the amount of off-season news coverage they generated. Local newspapers and national publications not only reported the transactions but gossiped about their impact. Murphy's trade for Moran garnered little notice nationally, but the Sheckard trade stunned everyone. "This is his first deal since he has been president, and it is a sensational one," reported one New York paper.[25] The Superbas received credit for picking up four new players in one transaction, and their new manager, Patsy Donovan, told the press that he had encouraged ownership to make the deal. Around the country, Murphy got torn to shreds. "The consensus of opinion is that Donovan made a grand trade when he got rid of Sheckard, while the first outburst in Chicago was that President Murphy must have taken leave of his senses when he parted with four good men to get one. The murder has been done and the outburst has been hushed considerably," wrote Pittsburgh columnist J. C. Morse.[26] "Had the meeting lasted much longer, somebody would probably have traded an umpire and a bat bag for Evers," Bill Phelon wailed in *Sporting Life*. "It is well that Charlie came home when he did."[27] A note in the *Decatur Herald* was more direct. "Some Chicago fans are 'cussing' President Murphy for letting four good players go for Jim Sheckard whom no one seems to rate as a valuable player any longer," its baseball reporter charged.[28]

Undaunted, Murphy reveled in the attention being paid to the Cubs. He had outfoxed McGraw for both Sheckard and the headline. Murphy had learned about the importance of newspaper coverage from John T. Brush. In 1894 the *Cincinnati Commercial Gazette* praised the then Reds owner for understanding the value of filling its pages with baseball news: "Mr. Brush recognizes the fact that the editors of those papers keep up the interest in base ball in their towns, and that they help the club a great deal during the season."[29] Murphy embraced Brush's philosophy, which was made easier by his background as a journalist. Murphy not only swiped a good outfielder from under the nose of the New York Giants but a story as well. Murphy provided a follow-up quote for the writers with his retort to criticism of how the Sheckard trade would pan out on the field. "I figured that if this outfielder was strong enough to strengthen both Pittsburgh and New York, which finished ahead of us in the race, he would look pretty well to west side fans in a Chicago uniform," he acutely surmised.[30] The trade signaled the arrival of a rising threat to the Giants' superiority.

Having put the finishing touches on the roster, Murphy turned his attention to finding ways to create new revenue streams to offset the organization's increasing payroll and, most importantly, to pay down his debt to Charles Taft. Murphy began by reconfiguring the pricing structure of West Side Ball Park. He restricted the number of twenty-five-cent bleacher seats to 2,500 and doubled the price of tickets in the main body of the bleachers to fifty cents. He also began selling the more desirable seats at the West Side Ball Park at the team's new downtown office near the Masonic Temple. *Sporting Life*'s Bill Phelon reported on the eve of the 1906 season that fans did not make so much as a "peep of displeasure" at Murphy's price increases, because those paying twenty-five cents to watch the competitive Cubs "had been getting more for their money here than anywhere in the league."[31] The immensely popular Cubs played in front of large crowds throughout 1905, and yet, according to Phelon, who claimed he had knowledge of the official National League figures, the New York Giants generated more revenue despite drawing fewer patrons.[32] Cubs fans had seen Chicago finish third on the heels of a second-place season in 1904.

The flurry of player acquisitions by the new ownership group signaled to them that Murphy wanted to win, so the fans willingly shelled out more of their hard-earned income for tickets in hopes of seeing their team ascend to the top of the National League.

To compliment developing the business side of the franchise's operation, Murphy endeavored to creatively market the club. He borrowed his first idea from his brief time in New York. Murphy ordered horse blankets that read "Chicago Champions: 1906," to be utilized by the Cubs transports when they played on the road, for winning the City Series. The plan infuriated Brush, whose Giants had just won the World Series over Philadelphia. Brush complained to the National Commission that Murphy's inscription misled the public into thinking a team other than the Giants had won the title. The committee forced Murphy to give up his phrasing, in the name of false advertising, but allowed a tamer inscription that reflected the Cubs' postseason exhibition victory over the crosstown White Sox: "Champions of the City of Chicago—1906."[33]

The first two months of the 1906 season realized every Cubs fans most optimistic expectations, and the city responded enthusiastically. "Chicago is base ball crazy, and I cannot remember in years seeing the public so worked up over base ball as is the case to-day," Phelon wrote. "The new, reorganized team has everything. It can hit . . . It can run bases like a streak . . . The fielding is wonderful, catlike in speed and agility, and the team has fought its way up to first in spite of the fact that the pitchers have not been in their proper form. When all the slabmen get going, what can be anticipated?" Huge crowds turned out to see the talented roster, including the reengaged Harry Steinfeldt and reinvigorated Jimmy Sheckard, perform a "new sensational stunt every day."

"What on earth have you done to Sheckard?" the curious Reds manager, Ned Hanlon, inquired of Murphy during a series in early June.

"Nothing," Murphy riposted, "Except to treat him like a man."[34]

Buoyed by the enthusiastic throngs that streamed into the West Side Grounds to witness the Cubs' early-season success, Murphy packed the place as tightly as he could. An early example occurred during the Cubs' first meeting of the season against the Giants. Out of either ignorance or disregard, Murphy maximized attendance by allowing fans to spill into the aisles of a Sunday game, on May 20, that drew a bulging-capacity crowd of twenty-five thousand, setting a new attendance record at the West Side Ball Park. Several thousand fans roamed around outside the stadium but could not find tickets. Another 1,500 supporters watched the game from rooftops of buildings across the street. It was a chaotic scene. Ignoring police instructions, fans spilled onto the playing field and scuffed out the chalked baselines, which had to be redone before the first pitch. They shimmied up flagpoles for better views and pocketed loose baseballs bounding around the field. Murphy called the police in for assistance and petitioned the fans to move. Finally, at twenty minutes past three, umpire Hank O'Day decided enough of the playing field was unimpeded to play baseball, but any ball hit into the crowd would only be worth two bases.[35]

The fans went home happy after the Cubs whipped the Giants 10–4, but city officials were not amused at Murphy's manipulation of the citizens' enthusiasm. Disgusted by what he had witnessed, fire marshal John Campion tried to revoke the ballpark's amusement license only to discover none existed. Deputy building commissioner A. F. Hughes sent Murphy a letter demanding that the Cubs pay $300 for the required license and promise to restrict the overcrowding of the aisles or risk the closure of the stadium.[36] A repentant Murphy profusely apologized and blamed the oversight on his being new to town. He would not let it happen again (wink).[37]

Early in the season Chance had declared to the press that Murphy "is one of us." Certainly, the new president's commitment to winning won over the clubhouse, but he ingratiated himself further by continuing to pick fights with the New York Giants, the Cubs' intensifying rival. At first, Murphy needled New York in small ways, with horse blankets and by allowing crowds beyond capacity into the ballpark when Chicago hosted the Giants. Murphy's badgering intensified significantly with the Sheckard trade, and he delivered another message when he refused to honor the Giants' pass requests for games at the West Side Ball Park.

It annoyed Murphy to hand out free passes to ballgames. Murphy believed seats should be sold, particularly in light of the quality product the Cubs provided. He made a few exceptions for individuals who would bring prestige to the ballpark but, generally speaking, Murphy put an end to the steady stream of nonpaying customers. He targeted the Giants as a gross offender of the system. Three days after their jam-packed Sunday matchup earned him a scolding from city officials, the Giants refused to take the field after Murphy ignored the organization's request to provide passes to several of their guests, presumably to keep seats open for paying patrons. The furious Giants promised to retaliate when the Cubs visited the Polo Grounds.[38] He didn't care.

The Giants roared back after losing the series opener and won the final three games of the late May set, to pull into a first-place tie with the Cubs. Chance's pitchers allowed twenty runs in the three losses, and he realized the club needed to acquire more pitching to fend off New York.

The Cubs fashioned a six-game winning streak during the first week of June, capped off with a 19-0 bludgeoning of Christy Mathewson, which boosted Chicago's record to 34-15 and pushed their lead over the second-place Giants to three and a half games. Behind the scenes, Chance and Murphy discussed improvements they could make to the pitching staff. Chance had a pair of hurlers in mind. He had met the first pitcher as a teenager when he played for the Fresno Republicans. The Republicans played games throughout Central California, including against Visalia, a town fifty miles to the south. In 1897 the Visalia team featured Orval Overall, a strapping prospect whose size and versatility on the diamond caught everyone's attention. The Republicans recruited Overall, but he turned down their offer and stayed with Visalia. Chance kept tabs on Overall as he blossomed into a tremendous pitcher over the years, initially at U. C. Berkeley, then in his first year of professional baseball in Tacoma. The Reds had signed Overall in 1904, but things had not panned out as either side had hoped. Joe Kelley, Cincinnati's manager, overused Overall during his rookie year to the tune of 318 innings, and in 1906 the young right-hander continued to struggle under the heavy workload. Both Frank Selee and John

McGraw had looked into acquiring Overall in the past, but neither had completed a trade.

Chance saw an opportunity to buy low on a quality arm he completely trusted, and Murphy got to work on pursuing a deal with Garry Herrmann. Murphy agreed to ship Bob Wicker, a pitcher of some repute, to Cincinnati in exchange for Overall and $2,000. On its surface, the trade appeared risky for the Cubs, because Wicker had been a mainstay in the Cubs' rotation for three seasons, but Chance viewed the physically declining pitcher as expendable, correctly as it turned out. Wicker only made seventeen starts for Cincinnati before the Reds sold his contract at the end of the season. Upon arriving in Chicago, Overall received orders from Chance to rest his arm. The Cubs' skipper designed a plan to give Overall's body a break and rebuild his confidence before easing him into the rotation.

Murphy and Chance completed another shocking trade on July 1. Murphy dealt Fred Beebe, Pete Noonan, and cash to the St. Louis Cardinals for Jack Taylor, a veteran right-handed pitcher who had previously pitched for the Cubs, before accusations of throwing games in the 1903 postseason series against the White Sox nearly got him banished from the sport by the National Commission. Jim Hart had unloaded Taylor onto the St. Louis Cardinals for Mordecai Brown, a trade of genius. Hart declined to pursue charges against Taylor, but Herrmann accused the pitcher of throwing games. By acquiring Taylor, Murphy was tacitly asking Cubs fans to let go of any lingering resentment they felt toward him. It was a bold and stunning ask, and *Sporting News* editor Joe Flanner pointed out the risks of the deal, particularly for a marketer like Murphy who promoted baseball as a clean game. Flanner predicted the move would backfire on Murphy. He told Ban Johnson, "The Taylor scandal will not help Murphy's popularity with patrons. He should never have been permitted to again play with that team. I do not think he has sold games, but he is a bad actor and the Chicago regular patrons regard him as dishonest."[39]

Taylor's train arrived in Chicago on the morning of July 2, and he immediately set off for the Victoria Hotel, where he reunited with Chance for a lengthy discussion. Then Taylor sat down with Murphy for another meeting before signing his contract. While the contents of the discussion remained private, the topic of conversation can be reasonably surmised. Murphy did not have to make such a risky trade, especially with things going so well in his first season at the helm, but he believed it would put his team over the top and that the fans wanted to experience winning a pennant. He believed Taylor was worth the risk.

Sporting Life routinely included a section in each issue titled "Wise Sayings of Great Men." In its May 26 edition, *Sporting Life* published a quote it attributed to Charles W. Murphy. "Flattery is simply praise of other people," he allegedly said.[40] Neither Murphy nor Chance cared what others said about them. Winning drove every move Murphy and Chance made. What criticism they bore they did so together, and both men knew that a World Series championship would quiet all the naysayers permanently. Murphy also believed that a winning team would fill his stadium with capacity crowds, which would generate higher dividend payments for shareholders and allow him to pay down his debt.

Overall and Taylor pitched exceedingly well for Chicago in 1906. They each went 12–3. Overall, who had arrived nearly a month earlier than Taylor, had an earned run average of 1.88, and Taylor bettered that number with his 1.83 mark. Taylor's sixteen starts and one relief appearance were valued at 1.8 wins above replacement. Overall's fourteen starts and four appearances out of the bullpen racked up 1.7 wins above replacement. The acquisitions created incredible rotation depth in support of Mordecai Brown, Ed Reulbach, and Jack Pfiester.

Murphy and Chance had assembled the greatest collection of talent the game had ever seen. The Cubs led the Pirates by two and a half games and the Giants by four on July 1, the day they acquired Taylor. It proved to be the slimmest margin between Chicago and second place for the rest of the season. A five-game winning streak to close out July put them six games clear of both Pittsburgh and New York. Then the Cubs reeled off an inconceivable twenty-five wins in twenty-six games from early August through September 1, which enriched their record to 93–31. Chicago had ripped away National League supremacy from New York with still over a month of the season remaining. The Cubs won sixty out of their seventy-two games during the second half of the season. They beat up on both the Giants and Pirates, defeating them a combined thirty-one times in forty-three games. Chicago clinched the pennant with a 3–1 win over Boston on September 19, but the players hardly shrugged after they recorded the final out of the game. "Chance and his men gave little heed to the fact that their victory today, together with New York's defeat, put the pennant beyond possible doubt. They have considered the pennant won for so long that they are now thinking of setting a big 'game won' record," the *Chicago Tribune* nonchalantly reported on page six.[41] It was the Cubs' first pennant since Cap Anson led them to the National League title in 1886.

Murphy's gambits paid off in ways even he could not have imagined. His marketing wizardry boosted attendance early in the season, before the Cubs' dominance on the field took the baton as the season moved into the summer. The team's acquisitions jelled beautifully with their new organization. The Cubs set a new National League record with win number 116, on October 4, against the Pirates, a 4–0 shutout victory pitched by Jack Pfiester. Record crowds responded to the Cubs' success by turning out in droves throughout the late summer and into the early fall. A mid-August series against New York drew over seventy thousand fans. With increasing frequency, one average Cubs home game generated more revenue than an average theater show did in a week. "There is so much interest in baseball here and now that at a game played by either of the two big teams more money is taken in at the gate than any race meeting, theatrical performance, or circus ever played to," reported the *Chicago Tribune*.[42] The Cubs' growing prosperity enabled Murphy to repay Taft quickly. Murphy and Chance also saw their personal incomes rise due to increased dividend payments they received as shareholders in the club.

In addition to realizing short-term success in 1906, Murphy's contributions successfully completed the reshaping of the Chicago Cubs brand that lasted for the duration of his ownership tenure. The team fought hard to win and did everything necessary off the field to ensure it could compete with its rivals once ballgames started, even if it was unconventional. Murphy provided the newspapers with tidbits to meet the gnawing appetites of baseball fans who craved more information. He also gleefully stirred the pot with rivals and the National Commission to create news where none existed beforehand. Charlie Murphy helped the Cubs fortify their status as one of America's premiere sports franchises, and Chicagoans responded to his efforts. As the Cubs prepared for their first World Series, the *Chicago Tribune* outlined the intensifying love locals expressed for baseball: "More money now is being spent in Chicago upon baseball than ever was spent before. Baseball is talked about more than it ever was before. More people are interested in it. More people are acquainted with the minutiae of the game, the biographies of the players, and the fortunes of war, as they are exemplified in the activities of the two baseball teams upon the uniforms which appear 'C-H-I-C-A-G-O.'"

The White Sox captured headlines of their own as the Cubs crosstown rival staged a remarkable comeback in the standings, fueled by a nineteen-game winning streak, and chased down their foes from seven and a half games out of first place. They edged out the New York Highlanders for the American League pennant. The White Sox would face the heavily favored Cubs in the World Series. Chicago went crazy with excitement. "The baseball talk is incessant in the stores, the factories, and the office buildings," according to the *Tribune*. "Everyone seems to be interested in it. Knowledge of it is the passport to many a conversation . . . Knowledge of batting and fielding averages has come to be looked upon as a part of a liberal education. The man that knows nothing about baseball is lonesome."[43]

On October 9, 1906, on the morning of Game One of the World Series, the Chicago *Inter Ocean* published a cartoon on its front page featuring two older gentlemen sitting on a bench staring at each other icily, one a Cubs supporter and the other a White Sox fan. The Cubs, or "Giant Killers," as they had been dubbed by members of the local media at Murphy's encouragement, were all set to host the series opener at the West Side Grounds. The excitement had been palpable for days, and baseball lovers in the Windy City could hardly wait for the series to begin. The Chicago City Council closed city hall and all its affiliated offices to allow public employees to attend Game One.

According to the *Inter Ocean*, "The faithful fans, who have waited for months and some for years, will be rewarded, and the reward is so great that many of them will pinch themselves to make sure that they are not day dreaming."[44]

During the previous several weeks, the National Commission and Murphy had negotiated plans for the World Series, just the third in baseball history. Murphy read the commission's rule book in hopes of obtaining an edge over his old friend Comiskey. The commission's guidelines stipulated that the World Series was a best-of-seven contest, although Murphy objected to a guideline that stated a potential seventh game would be played in a city selected by the National Commission. Murphy argued that the rule should refer to a ballpark rather than to a city. He wanted to ensure that any winner-take-all affairs would be played at the West Side Ball Park and, in general, everyone agreed with him. Murphy also voiced his concern over a plan to utilize two umpire crews throughout the series. National League president Harry Pulliam supported Murphy's case, so only Silk O'Loughlin and Jim Johnstone received World Series umpiring assignments. In 1906 only two umpires worked the field, so O'Loughlin and Johnstone rotated duties. Murphy may have won these battles, but he made a mistake by claiming that the Cubs wanted diamond-studded cuff buttons for winning the championship. Regardless of whether he wanted the request to become public or not, Murphy's comments "created quite a stir," one that White Sox manager Fielder Jones and his players undoubtedly noticed.[45] In addition to preparing for the series administratively, Murphy mulled over different ways in which he could promote it. He kicked around the idea of hiring a camera crew to film one of the games and show it around the country. "I am looking up some of these concerns about taking such a picture. For I believe there would be as much interest in such a show as there is in a prize fight picture," he said.[46]

Murphy was an object of interest for the press in the weeks leading up to the series. Here he was—one of them, for all intents and purposes—in the World Series as Cubs president. Murphy happily chatted with all the writers and tried to deflect credit for the team's success. "It is the biggest kind of luck that I secured the Chicago Club when I did. I feel like a man who has accidentally fallen overboard, and on being fished out of the river finds his pockets filled with gold, with a diamond necklace or two around his throat and his fingers loaded with valuable rings. I don't consider myself any shrewder than the ordinary mortal—only luckier," he loquaciously opined.[47]

The World Series opened at the West Side Grounds on October 9 with the record-setting Cubs as notable favorites over the White Sox. The dismantling of the South Siders by the Cubs in 1905 was fresh in the minds of the local fans, but that did not prevent a significant number of White Sox supporters from attending the game in spite of the frigid temperatures. A section of Pale Hose fans kept warm by serenading Murphy with their own version of a popular musical hit, "So Long, Mary" from *Forty-Five Minutes from Broadway*.

So long, Murphy
How we hate to see you lose
So long, Murphy
We know you will have the blues
We'll all feel sorry for you, Murphy
While we cheer
So long, Murphy
Maybe you will win next year.[48]

Mordecai Brown, who led the National League with nine shutouts and a minuscule 1.06 ERA, started the opener for the Cubs against Nick Altrock, an underrated, if slightly eccentric, left-hander who finished second on the White Sox pitching staff with twenty wins. On a cold Windy City fall afternoon, the two pitchers posted zeros through the first four innings, before George Rohe, the fill-in for the White Sox's regular third baseman, George Davis, opened the fifth inning with a triple. Brown then struck out Jiggs Donahue, which brought Patsy Dougherty to the plate. Dougherty hit a dribbler out in front of the plate, which Brown dashed toward as Rohe broke from third. Brown scooped up the ball and flipped it to Johnny Kling, but the Cubs' excellent defensive catcher surprisingly could not handle the throw, and Rohe scored to give the White Sox a 1–0 advantage. In the sixth inning, the White Sox doubled their lead on Frank Isbell's RBI single, which drove in Chicago's center fielder and manager Fielder Jones. The Cubs got a run back in the bottom of the frame when Altrock uncorked a wild pitch which allowed Kling to score from third base, but that was as close as they would get. Altrock rebounded by retiring Jimmy Sheckard and Frank Schulte to end the threat. He cruised from there as the Sox took Game One, 2–1.

The Cubs bounced back in Game Two behind Ed Reulbach, who tossed a complete game one-hitter in the West Siders' 7–1 win. The teams split the next two contests to set up a pivotal Game Five. Following his brilliant performance in the Cubs' first win of the series, Reulbach again got the start. However, in Game Five, the Sox inflicted as much offensive damage against him in three batters as they had in all of Game Two. Ed Hahn led off with a single to center. Jones sacrificed him to second. Then Isbell plated Hahn with a scorching double into right to give the White Sox a 1–0 lead. The Cubs counterpunched in the bottom of the first with a three-run rally helped in large part by two misplays by White Sox infielders. Back-to-back doubles by Isbell and Davis in the third knocked Reulbach out of the game and narrowed the Sox deficit to 3–2. Davis, who had reached third, stole home to tie the game.

The tide of the series turned in favor of the White Sox in the top of the fourth inning. Tied 3–3, the American League champions scored four times, highlighted by Davis's two-run double, en route to an 8–6 win. The following day, the White Sox unleashed an early offensive onslaught against Mordecai Brown. They scored three runs in the first and tallied four more in the second to give their talented lefty, Doc White, all the support he needed as the Sox went on to win, 8–3, and captured the World Series title. White Sox players whooped joyfully while their fans poured onto the field to celebrate with the team.

Murphy graciously accepted defeat. A large group of White Sox fans noticed Murphy still in his box along with fellow Cubs shareholder Charles Schmalstig, Charles Taft's personal secretary, following the game's final out. The crowd gathered around Murphy and teasingly demanded that he give a speech to honor the White Sox. In spite of his disappointment, Murphy good-naturedly obliged. A *Chicago Tribune* writer captured his words. Murphy stood and addressed the crowd thusly, "The White Sox played better ball and deserved to win. (Cheers.) I am for Chicago, and will say that Chicago has the two best ball teams in the world. (More cheers.) The contests have been well contested, and Chicago people should be proud of both their clubs. (Add to cheers.) If we had to lose I would rather lose to Comiskey's club than any other club in the world," he said. Upon the completion of his short address, a woman in the box next to Murphy held out a White Sox banner and requested that he wave it. He did, and the crowd erupted in applause and laughter. Murphy then exhorted the fans to give three cheers for the White Sox. "These contests have been made possible by the excellent patronage which Chicago has given its two ball clubs, thus enabling the management to go out and secure good players. The games of this series have been fought fairly and squarely, and we accept defeat gracefully," he said with good cheer. The fans gave the Cubs owner another ovation and several of them hollered, "Murphy, you're all right."[49]

While Murphy held court, the angry Cubs struggled to wrap their minds around what had just happened. "I can't understand it, but probably I will in two or three days," muttered a stunned Johnny Evers.

Johnny Kling glumly, but aptly, assessed the series. "They outplayed us and we have to give it to them," he said.

"They beat us all right, and by great ball playing, too," admitted Joe Tinker.

A dejected, yet still defiant, Frank Chance praised the White Sox's work while lamenting the lost opportunity. "It was the greatest series ever played, and we have got to give it to Comiskey's champions. The Sox played grand, game baseball, and outclassed us in this series just ended. But there is one thing I never will believe, and that is that the White Sox are a better ball club than the Cubs. We did not play our game, and that's all there is to it. The Sox, on the contrary, were fighting us in the gamest kind of way. They fought so hard that they made us like it and like it well."[50]

As the players changed, Murphy made his way to Comiskey's office, where he congratulated the victorious owner in the midst of a celebratory party. Murphy grasped Comiskey's hand and said, "Commy, I want to shake hands and congratulate you. If I had to lose, there's no one I would rather lose to than you."

Touched, Comiskey replied, "Well, Charley, I'd rather beat any other club in the country than yours. Maybe we'll get another whack at each other next year. I've only evened up for last fall, you know."[51] After White Sox players joined him, Comiskey presented manager Fielder Jones a check for $15,000 to be distributed among the players for their victory, in addition to the $25,401.70 from gate receipts earmarked for the winning team. Each Sox player took home just over $1,900, no small sum.[52]

Charlie Comiskey celebrated his team's victory late into the night inside the luxurious Pompeian Room at the Auditorium Annex. He gratuitously handed out bills that he peeled from a thick roll of cash and ensured that the alcohol flowed, but Comiskey, out of his deep respect for Frank Chance, paused when his guests implored him to give a victory speech. Comiskey spoke seriously as the noise in the room dimmed. "All I can say, boys, is that I'd rather [have] beaten any team on earth than Chance's. He's got a fine lot of fellows, and I wish I could find him tonight, for he's game enough to help me celebrate"[53] Far from the clinking glasses and celebratory cigars of the Sox's lively party, the steely Chance had already turned his attention to fishing back home in California, "But we are coming back next year, remember," he warned.[54]

5

CHAMPIONS

The Cubs' pennant-winning season raised Charlie Murphy's profile. Some of his neighbors in Oak Park did not even realize he lived in their midst, but that changed when *Oak Leaves*, the village paper, published his picture on its front page in late August, along with an accompanying story. "It is not generally known that Oak Park numbers among her prominent citizens one who is perhaps more in the public eye just now than any other individual in the United States. He lives at 242 Marion street and his name is Charles W. Murphy, president of the west side baseball club. Mr. Murphy has lived in Oak Park about twelve months and is an enthusiastic admirer of its people and its homes."[1] The story praised Murphy for his work in making the Cubs a pennant winner and described his wife, Louise, as a passionate baseball fan.

The Cubs' appearance in the World Series provided a platform for Murphy's intriguing personal journey to readily appear in print throughout the country. In overseeing the Cubs to a record-setting 116 regular season wins in his first full season as president, writers around the league were drawn to the youthful, loquacious owner with a flashy business sense taking the National League by storm. Just before the World Series opened, *Sporting Life* published a note, written by Jack Ryder of the *Cincinnati Enquirer*, that explained to fans just how extraordinary a season it had been for Murphy from a financial standpoint. "By the end of this season the club will have earned approximately $80,000, or almost paid for itself in one year, and at the same time vastly increased its value," an astonished Ryder relayed to readers. "Millionaire sportsmen will today give $300,000 for the Chicago Club and not take possession until the close of the season. Quite a sudden rise in value, and the value is there, too."[2] The same issue of *Sporting Life* reprinted an article taken from the *New York Globe* that marveled at the thirty-eight-year-old Murphy's success. "Murphy frankly admits that he is the victim of extreme good luck, and thinks he is the especial charge of the kindly fates. It is seldom a young man is able to buy a controlling interest in so fine a club as Chicago and then have the team win the pennant the first year of his presidency.

"Some persons are inclined to attribute great business shrewdness to Murphy, but he says it was pure luck," wrote the *Globe* reporter.[3]

Ren Mulford, who knew Murphy well from the days when they both reported on baseball in Cincinnati, praised his former colleague in his *Sporting Life* column:

> Those Chicago Cubs have not only put up a world's record, but I think Captain Frank Chance has made a new managerial mark when he went on record with the declaration: "The Chicago Club would not have won the pennant this year if it had not been for President Charles W. Murphy." Once in a while you'll hear some fellow say: "That Murphy is a lucky duck." Possibly, but kindly run in a large capital "P" as a prefix and you've got it.[4]

Despite having suffered a pair of defections during his reelection vote the previous December, Harry Pulliam oversaw a remarkable operating year for the business of National League clubs, and Murphy was an indisputable cog in its success. All eight National League franchises turned a profit during the 1906 regular season for the first time in thirty years.[5] The *New York Times* reviewed payouts to road teams to analyze the financial health of the game. Visiting clubs earned 50 percent of the paid gate, and the *Times* concluded that just over 5.7 million fans attended National and American League games in 1906. The top draw in the game: the Chicago Cubs, which drew 654,300 fans, an average of 8,497 per game. Both marks led baseball. The Chicago White Sox were the second highest draw in baseball with 585,202 spectators, which trailed the Cubs by 69,000, a wide margin. Baseball fans in the

Windy City experienced a magical year, and they flocked to games to participate in the groundswell of excitement.[6]

Business could not have been better for Murphy, as he had eagerly sought to use his revenue to pay off the loan from Charles and Annie Taft. Murphy boosted his stake in the team on October 24 when he purchased 279 shares for $100 apiece.[7] Following the World Series, a rumor attributed to Pirates owner Barney Dreyfuss hinted that Taft was going to "make Murphy a present of the club at Christmas."[8] Writers who covered baseball believed that the financial boost of appearing in the World Series pushed the Cubs' profit into the six-figure range. In other words, Murphy had the cash to extinguish the loan and, simultaneously, bolster his stake in the club. Murphy saw it coming. In September, he had taken a trip to Wilmington and excitedly told his family and friends about the franchise's incredible success. "I will say that the Chicago club is absolutely in my control, and that I will be the principal owner before long," he predicted. "I would not sell the club for a million dollars."[9]

At the National League meeting in New York, the board of directors unanimously reelected Pulliam as president and demonstrated its support for him by boosting his salary to $10,000, a 40 percent increase. To further empower Pulliam, the directors created a new position of secretary-treasurer and filled it with John Heydler, thereby lightening Pulliam's responsibilities. Murphy supported these measures, but he vehemently disagreed with a proposed plan to eliminate the practice of parading players in carriages from their hotel to the ballpark. Murphy loved his horse blankets. "It is a great advertisement for the game and should be encouraged," he pleaded. "I am opposed to the boys riding to the park in trolleys, because they would be a target for the chance cheap wit who might be aboard with them. After losing a close game baseball players are in no mood to hear the petty twitterings of the bugs."[10]

Murphy's first year had gone incredibly well, too smoothly for some people in the game. In the small circle of baseball owners and executives, personal alliances and rivalries developed, fell apart and, on occasion, reestablished themselves. Murphy's personality of largesse dominated most rooms, but he was now competing against owners with bigger egos, if quieter constitutions. Murphy's immediate success stoked a measure of jealousy in his peers, powerful men not accustomed to being bested by extraordinarily ambitious members of the working class. Murphy loved every second of it and, instead of receding in the face of their annoyance, he doubled down in his pursuit of success. After all, that's what the other owners did. However, unlike many of his corporate peers, Murphy welcomed the limelight and spoke openly with the press, revealing inside information about the business side of baseball, too nonchalantly for their liking. Murphy never understood why baseball surrendered winter headlines to football.

Murphy's garrulousness hurt matters at times. As it had done to the New York sportswriters in 1905, Murphy's overbearing style could grate on his peers, who made fun of him for it. Perhaps born out of spite for his team's success, they perceived him at times as too creative, too intense, too disruptive for their liking, and that dissonance began to emerge after the 1906 season. Pirates owner Barney Dreyfuss wired Murphy a congratulatory note following the Cubs' pennant-clinching win, to which Murphy ornately responded, "Let me say without hesitation of self evasion of mind in me whatever, that among the many hearty communications which have reached us since our recent triumph, none have melted our hearts with more fervor than the sentiment now at my elbow." *Sporting Life* published a portion of Murphy's letter under the satirical headline, "A Work of Art." It called Murphy's note "a master piece of the rotund boss in his best art." The fledgling Murphy's excessive flattery irritated his older peers at times, but ironically, his deference to them ingratiated him to them as well.[11]

Charlie Murphy continued concentrating on improving the club for another pennant chase. Murphy wanted to acquire Reds starting pitcher Chick Fraser to bolster Chicago's rotation. At the National League winter meeting, Murphy and Garry Herrmann discussed Fraser's availability. Herrmann was open to dealing Fraser to Chicago, but only if Murphy met his price: $1,500. Herrmann didn't care if Murphy wrote him a check or sent him a player he could sell to another team for the same amount of money. At some point during the conversation, Herrmann asked Murphy, how about swapping Fraser for Doc Gessler?

Gessler seemed like a reasonable target. The backup outfielder only played in thirty-four games for Chicago in 1906, and he didn't appear to fit into the Cubs' long-term plan. However, complicating matters was Gessler's other ambition: medicine. He had received his medical degree from Baltimore Medical College, raising the possibility that he wanted to walk away from baseball and start a new career.[12] Herrmann had no interest in having Gessler play for the Reds; nevertheless, Herrmann was open to acquiring him because the outfielder's rights could be sold to Columbus of the American Association for $1,500, the same amount the Reds wanted for Fraser. According to Herrmann, Murphy balked at dealing the outfielder, and their trade talks in New York fizzled. Several weeks later, Murphy visited Cincinnati and called upon Herrmann to revisit the trade conversation. Herrmann held firm on his price and, ultimately, Murphy agreed to swap $1,500 for Fraser.

Imagine Herrmann's surprise when he opened a letter from Murphy, dated January 12, 1907, in which the Cubs president accepted the Reds' offer of Chick Fraser for Doc Gessler. Herrmann was stupefied. He immediately dispatched a note to Murphy disputing the terms of the deal. Murphy responded on January 14 with a sheepish letter in which he recognized Herrmann's irritation. "I regret exceedingly that this misunderstanding has arisen, because each club doubtless wishes to be fair. Perhaps I can refresh your memory." Murphy then relayed their trade conversations from his perspective. He alleged Herrmann had told him in New York that the Cubs could name their price for Chick Fraser. According to Murphy, Herrmann said, "Whatever you make it will be satisfactory to me."[13] Next, Murphy contacted Frank Chance to get the manager's perspective on Fraser's value. The Cubs skipper thought an offer of $1,000 ought to get the deal done. However, Herrmann declined that low offer. At a follow-up meeting, Murphy contended that he inserted Gessler into the discussion, which prompted Herrmann to declare, "It is all the same to us whether we get Gessler or $1,500.00. We don't want him for our club, but we can sell him to Columbus for that amount." When Murphy stopped by Herrmann's

Cincinnati office in early January to close the deal, he claimed Herrmann told him, "It is Randall and $500 or $1,500." Murphy agreed to the terms and, upon arriving back in Chicago, promptly sent Gessler to the Reds under the pretense that he could stand in for the money. "That was, I supposed, fully understood," claimed Murphy.[14]

Herrmann fumed as he read Murphy's letter. Hadn't they agreed on an exchange of $1,500 for Fraser? Herrmann was dumbstruck not only that Murphy was now substituting Gessler for the cash, but that including Gessler in the trade was even an option. Herrmann replied to Murphy that he expected to receive a check for $1,500.

For his part, Murphy's blood pressure rose the following day as he read Herrmann's letter and quotes from the Reds' president in the newspaper. Herrmann accused Murphy of attempting to fool him into taking Gessler. He believed that Murphy had discovered that Gessler was all set to retire from baseball and begin his medical practice, and he was trying to pry Fraser away for a "gold-brick," a player who appeared serviceable but, in truth, held no value. "It looks to me like an attempt at false practices on the part of Murphy," said Herrmann. "I have an idea that when he got back to Chicago he found out that Gessler had decided not to play professional baseball any longer, but to retire from the game to practice dentistry at his home in Pennsylvania. Thereupon he attempted to hand me a dead one in exchange for Fraser." Herrmann then issued a not-so-subtle threat to the new kid. "Such methods of doing business will not go in the National League."[15]

Murphy didn't want Herrmann to take the matter to the commission so, reluctantly, he wrote a check for $1,500 and mailed it. Herrmann got his money, but he also received something more: a piece of Murphy's mind. When Herrmann's mail arrived, it included three separate letters from Murphy. The first note was brief and acknowledged the inclusion of the check written for Fraser, as well as the recalling of Gessler to Chicago. The other two letters were a pair of extraordinary rants in which Murphy disputed Herrmann's account of events and vehemently defended himself against any charges of dubious dealings. Murphy's fiery binges, spread over twelve pages, accused Herrmann of lying— "We talked the matter over in the office of the Havlin hotel and you said to me that Gessler would be the same to you as $1,500, because you could sell him to Columbus for that amount. This statement you re-peated to me. THERE WERE NO WITNESSES"—and defended his integrity. "It was not my intention to deceive anyone," wrote Murphy indignantly. "The principal trouble seems to be that there is more or less envy at the success or luck of the Chicago Club under the present management. This manifests itself in your office almost daily, or whenever the club is mentioned."

Murphy admitted to Herrmann that the latter had warned him about losing his temper; however, whether driven by genuine hurt, feigning ignorance, or some combination of the two, Murphy intensely defended himself.

> If I had any knowledge of any sort that Gessler intends to retire from the game and then tried to trade him to you I would consider myself a common THIEF. From your interviews you seem to proceed along the theory that I am totally devoid of any sense of honor or integrity.
>
> There may be reason for this and that is that your experience with baseball men has not been satisfactory, especially when it came to trades.
>
> But I had counted myself a friend of yours.
>
> Did I ever take advantage of you?

Murphy used capital letters and then underlined them to express his frustrations with the baseball establishment.

"PLEASE BEAR IN MIND THAT YOU ARE CONSTANTLY SURROUNDED BY PERSONS, WHO ARE MORE OR LESS ENVIOUS *of what little success I may* have achieved in baseball. I have always believed that you are personally too broad to include in that class, but there are OTHERS."

Murphy ended the letter by assuring Herrmann that he had written it in a "perfectly calm and dispassionate" frame of mind, a questionable claim considering the content of his message.[16]

In the end, the Cubs got Fraser, the player Murphy had been after all along, in exchange for the price Herrmann wanted. Chicago even retained Gessler, who signed his contract, although Murphy, likely based on intel he gleaned from Herrmann, shipped him to Columbus for cash before the season. Both parties should have been pleased, but a sense of bitterness seeped into the relationship. Additionally, Murphy's letters had exposed his anger, even slight paranoia, in a new way. He had put them in writing for a member of the National Commission to see.

With Fraser in the fold, Murphy felt content about the roster and turned his attention to promoting it. Murphy toyed with the idea of placing numbers on the jerseys of Cubs players, so that fans could more easily identify them from the stands. Generally speaking, the earliest conception of numbering uniforms is attributed to Alfred Lawson, manager of the Reading ball club in the Atlantic League. However, Murphy, inspired by a conversation he had with *Sporting Life* editor Francis Richter about ways to improve the sport, gave the matter serious consideration during the 1906 off-season. Struck by the numbering systems used for jockeys in horse racing and contestants in track and field competitions, Murphy envisioned creating a similar arrangement for baseball players. However, Murphy never got around to officially asking permission to implement a numbering process. "I intended to bring the matter before the National League, but I forgot it," he admitted. "I did, however, discuss it informally with some of the club owners and they think well of it." Murphy believed that creating a number system as an evolution of uniform design would not only make the experience of attending a baseball game more enjoyable for the fans but also establish the National League as a progressive trendsetter.

> The idea is to enlighten the public as to the identity of players before them without making it necessary to ask questions. The club roster can be printed in the score book, with the names and numbers of the players. Then numbers to correspond with those printed can be sewed on the shirt or cap of the player in a neat manner, so that a person having a score card can tell who is playing without yelling to the ushers, umpires or the players themselves. We shall probably do it at the West Side park regardless of what

any other team does. As the National League has been a purveyor of base ball for thirty years, I see no reason why we should not take the initiative in this manner.[17]

Too bad Murphy forgot about it; otherwise, he might be known today as the pioneer of the practice.[18]

The train carrying Frank and Edythe Chance from the West Coast pulled into chilly Chicago in late February. Ready to put the disappointing World Series loss behind him, Chance declared his ball club would be ready to compete for another pennant in 1907. "Although all the teams have gone out to strengthen up in the hope of beating us in the race, we had done a little strengthening ourselves and will be there when the struggle begins," he said assuredly. "It looks like a harder battle than that of last year, but I am confident the boys will let every team that meets them know they have been in a ball game."[19] Although upbeat, Chance acknowledged that predicting the outcome of the upcoming season was a fool's game. "I have been in the business long enough to learn the folly of claiming pennants in the winter, however, and know how many things there are which may throw every bit of dope out of line."[20]

Murphy returned to Chicago from New York, where he had attended to league business and met with Jimmy Sheckard, who had not yet signed his contract for the upcoming season. Sheckard ran a furniture store in Pennsylvania during the offseason, and he was busily preparing its spring sale. As the players readied themselves for their treks to West Baden, Indiana, for spring training, Murphy took a moment to assess his team's prospects for the season. "But I look for a closer race than last year's. There will be four, yes five, clubs in it, I think. Besides Chicago, New York, Pittsburg, Philadelphia, and Brooklyn will have to be counted in the running."[21]

On Wednesday night, three days before his planned departure for Indiana, a gnawing pain in his side started bothering shortstop Joe Tinker. He assumed it was due to his being out of shape, but the discomfort intensified the following day. On Friday Tinker was rushed to

Chicago's St. Anthony de Padua Hospital with an inflamed appendix. Surgery revealed that pus had built up around Tinker's appendix but, fortunately, it had remained intact. Dr. H. M. Everett, the Cubs' team doctor, successfully removed it but suggested that waiting another day could have had dire consequences for Tinker. Murphy visited Tinker in the hospital. He still had a slight fever, but the doctors anticipated he would fully recover.

Trainer Jack McCormick greeted the players with a rigorous workout regimen when they arrived in West Baden. Charles Dryden of the *Tribune* reported that McCormick, whom he dubbed "the demon trainer," "introduced a training schedule based on scientific calculation" that commenced at six o'clock in the morning. He incorporated several of West Baden's numbered hot springs into their routine. "They make three trips to No. 7 and two to No. 1 with sprints around the bicycle track in the interval," Dryden relayed. In their downtime, the players spent time relaxing in quiet contemplation and hiking along the Lost River.[22]

The Cubs' preseason tour worked its way north over the next several weeks. Their preparation went smoothly. However, the team received an unexpected surprise in Memphis when a residence next to its hotel burst into flames. A group of Cubs followed several firemen into the house "(w)ith visions of rescuing millionaire's daughters" dancing in their heads. The players hustled out of the house with a variety of saved objects. Chance, who had wrapped his head with a wet blanket, emerged from the front door of the crisped house with a mattress. Orval Overall discovered four pairs of, well, overalls, naturally. Other items were retrieved as well, including chairs and mirrors. Unbeknownst to the rushing players, the firemen had already put out the small fire, and the danger had passed. After everyone calmed down back at the hotel, they noticed that Frank Schulte, old "Wildfire" himself, had gone missing. Spooked, a group of them hurried back to the burnt house in search of him. They found Schulte inside intensely searching underneath rugs for loose hairpins, which he believed would bring him luck during the season. Found one! He discovered it beneath a Smyrna carpet in the drawing room. Schulte finished second on the team with a .287 batting average.[23]

The Cubs opened the 1907 season at home on April 11. Snow pestered the city, limiting the Cubs and St. Louis Cardinals to only two games, both of which Chicago won behind a pair of marvelous pitching performances by Orval Overall and Carl Lundgren. Following the series, Cardinals players squawked about the lowly condition of the visitors' clubhouse at West Side Ball Park. Murphy dismissed their complaints as ridiculous and took a public shot at their manager, John McCloskey. "I spent over $600 fitting up quarters for visiting teams on the west side, and Mr. McCloskey and the other Cardinal crabs will find them better than the visiting teams' quarters in other cities. The St. Louis club has provided no quarters whatever for visitors at its grounds, and is liable to a fine of $25 a day for not doing it."

The players agreed with Murphy. Jack Taylor, who had played for both teams, thought the Cubs' visiting clubhouse was a better setup than what the Cardinals experienced in their own facility at home. The Cardinals' complaints miffed Chance. "The Cardinals were sore over not getting a game out of us, and had to kick on something."[24]

The Cubs burst out of the gate by winning twenty-nine of their first thirty-eight games in April and May, bolstered, in part, by the play of Artie "Solly" Hofman, the Cubs' indispensable utility man, who performed magnificently at shortstop as Joe Tinker recovered from his appendectomy. After a tremendous performance in the season opener, beat writer Frank Hutchinson promulgated the utility man's excellence: "Wherever two or more fans got together the main topic of discussion was the star work of Artie Hofman. Circus Solly was in every play and scored four times, and the fans will not tire of discussing his wonderful work."[25] After being limited to a single pinch-hitting appearance on April 18, Tinker resumed his spot in the lineup on May 11. It wasn't an issue for Hofman; he happily moved around. In May alone, Chance deployed the versatile utility knife at six different positions. Hofman hit .318 during the first two months of the season and provided his customary steady glove work throughout the diamond. His contribution was an important reason the Cubs compiled a gaudy 29-9 record. However, Chicago entered June in first place by the slimmest of margins. They led the equally hot Giants by only one game.

The first week of June proved to be a decisive moment in the race for the National League pennant. Not only did the Cubs host the Pirates and Giants in a pair of interesting series, but the Sunday, June 2, edition of the *Chicago Tribune* blared a headline that announced it would be providing fans with more sports coverage.[26] The *Tribune*'s baseball coverage exceled as it featured Charles Dryden, Sy Sanborn, and Hugh Fullerton, as good a trio of sportswriters as any paper in the country employed.

The Cubs opened up a bit of breathing room in the standings after sweeping their short series against the Pirates by scores of 4–3 and 3–2. Meanwhile, the Giants arrived in Chicago having lost their last two games to the Brooklyn Superbas. The morning of the series opener, the *Tribune* published a cartoon, drawn by Clare Briggs, featuring a large, lumbering uniformed Giant walking determinedly toward West Side Park while clutching a bat over his right shoulder. Surrounding him is a large crowd of jeering Cubs fans. Young and old, mustached and clean-shaven, the diverse group is united in their vitriolic hostility and glares at the Giant menacingly. "We've waited long for this," reads one quote bubble. "Say your farewells," hollers another, above a police officer, no less. A large sign shouting, "Welcome Giants," sits atop the "Insane Dept." next to Cook County Hospital. So was the mood of the fan base on the cusp of the series. Frank Chance slated Mordecai Brown to pitch the opener, while John McGraw countered with his ace, Christy Mathewson. The stage was set, and the frothing city of Chicago was ready to unleash its fury upon its rival from New York.

Fans swarmed into the West Side Grounds by the thousands. Super fan Ed Heeman marched in with two hundred of his closest friends from the Chicago Board of Trade. A noisy band provided music for the parody songs written by Heeman's group, specifically aimed at McGraw. The throng took over the area designated as the Giants' bench and forced New York's players to move. The compacted horde suffocated the outfield and forced any ball struck into the crowd to be worth only two bases. Dryden described the noisy scene, "Much flub dub caused the doings to listen like a riot in a boiler factory, but the noise was all of the glad kind."[27] Some lemons were thrown. A few particularly unruly fans were kicked out.

The game began with a blur. No sooner had rain begun to emanate from the clouds overhead than the Giants put together a run-scoring rally against Mordecai Brown in the top of the first inning. As fans reached for their hats to keep their heads dry, Art Devlin struck a two-run double to give the Giants a 2-0 lead. The rapidity with which New York scored momentarily stunned the crowd, but the Cubs got a run back, in the bottom of the first, against Mathewson. Brown settled in and kept the Giants off the scoreboard while his teammates tied the game in the bottom of the fifth on Jimmy Sheckard's sacrifice fly.

The tenor of the game changed in the bottom of the sixth inning. Mathewson tweaked his ankle while attempting to field a ground ball off the bat of Johnny Evers. He managed to record the third out, but the joint stiffened up on him as the Giants batted in the top of the seventh, and he lost his effectiveness when he returned to the mound. The Cubs' relentless lineup broke the game open against the hobbled Mathewson by scoring four runs against him on their way to an 8-2 win.[28]

Chicago won all three games played against New York and opened up a four-and-a-half-game lead over the Giants in the National League standings. It was a memorable week full of images that many fans wouldn't soon forget. Before each game, a group of fans presented a bouquet of roses to Chance who, upon receiving them, bowed. Someone sitting among the group of stock market traders flew a kite overhead with a stuffed McGraw dangling from it as the real version sat stoically, refusing to acquiesce and flash his trademark temper. The series thrilled the packed crowds. The Cubs drew sixty thousand spectators for the three games to set a new attendance mark.[29] It was as exciting and fulfilling as a series can be in June.

Murphy reveled in the Cubs' sweep for several reasons. First, the wins firmly established the Cubs as the team to beat for the pennant. Second, he recognized that the team possessed a truly devastating weapon. Following the series, the *Sporting Life* noted that "President Murphy, of the Cubs, is credited with saying that the weakest man of his pitching staff is a match for the strongest man New York can present."[30] If Murphy did indeed say it—and he very well could have, in the midst of a joyful celebration—his hyperbole sounded preposterous on its surface, because only Brown could even be considered the equal of Mathewson in 1907. However, Murphy's opinion spoke to a significant development: the dominance of the Cubs' pitching staff.

As the Cubs continued to pile up victories in June, Murphy busied himself with preparations to celebrate the previous season. He wanted a grand occasion to raise the pennant flag, so he had selected the Fourth of July. The Cubs had a doubleheader scheduled that day, against Cincinnati, with the first game set to begin at 10:30 a.m., so Murphy put together a program beginning an hour earlier. He ordered a large pennant and hired a band. Somehow, someone procured a shipment of two bear cubs. They arrived a day early and were introduced to the players at the ballpark but, ultimately, they did not appear at the ceremony. Leading up to the event, Murphy begged the fans to refrain from lighting fireworks or shooting their pistols inside the stadium, a more than reasonable request that, nonetheless, went unheeded by some of the attendees.[31] The National Commission—made up of chairman Garry Herrmann, National League president Harry Pulliam, and American League president Ban Johnson—was invited and scheduled to participate in the flag-raising ceremony. The organization asked Mayor Fred Busse to throw out the ceremonial "first new ball."

The crowd cheered as the band struck up its initial note, on Murphy's order, and began marching to the clubhouse to escort the parade of players onto the field. They looped around the field as the cranks roared. "Then with bared heads the players watched the big blue and white banner, emblematic of the leadership of the National league, hoisted in its place, where it unfurled its legend to the gaze of the rooters, who let loose all the pent up enthusiasm of three months' waiting for the occasion," Sy Sanborn reported.[32] The din of loud cheers accelerated into a cacophony of yelling, pierced by the sharp pops of fireworks and cracking shots fired from revolvers. One of the Cubs' turnstile workers, with the last name of Roach, heard something whiz by him followed by a single short clicking noise. He looked down to discover a button had been sheared from his vest by a stray bullet. After a brief search, Roach found both the button and the bullet.[33] Although the members of the commission arrived late, at least they showed up. Mayor Busse skipped the event entirely, forcing Herrmann to throw out the first pitch.

Following the ceremony, the Cubs went out and swept the Cincinnati Reds. Mordecai Brown dominated the Reds, 5–1, in the opener, and Orval Overall, who had purchased a car for $4,000 earlier in the week because he was tired of paying for train fare to and from California, pitched a complete game shutout to beat his former club, 2–0, in the nightcap.[34] The Cubs, and their 52-16 record, hustled to the station with their hoard of packed trunks and bags to board a train to begin a sixteen-game road trip.

Chicago continued its torrid play throughout July and early August, while the Giants and Pirates simply could not accumulate wins at the same pace. Chicago's huge lead benefited their ailing Peerless Leader.

In August, Frank Chance's body ached in agony, and his condition deteriorated. He had contracted the grippe, and the virus sapped him of his strength. Additionally, Chance suffered from intermittent flashes of neuralgia in his face, a terribly painful condition caused by an inflamed or damaged nerve.[35] The determined Chance tried gutting his way through the maladies, but he had to insert Del Howard at first base in his stead numerous times in August.

By the time the Cubs arrived in New York on August 17, to begin a series at the Polo Grounds, Chicago comfortably sat atop the National League standings, a full 14.5 games clear of both the Giants and Pirates. Chance may have already been considering taking a leave of absence from the club to heal, but a letter waiting for him in New York boiled his blood. The ominous note, written by a notorious Mafia-related extortion outfit, was addressed to Chance and threatened the Cubs with physical harm if they continued their winning ways.

Manager Chance (Chicago National League of the Baseball Club):

Dear Sir: Your club must not get again Pennant this year 1907 from the New York and you will let New York Club will have Pennant championship of the year 1907 from your club. Your club are too coward, but "Poor Giants."

If you not let the Giants from the first place this year, Gang of Black Hands will see you after, wil [*sic*] help you for your life. Look out for danger life. We will use bomb on your players team on train wreck and we will follow your team traveling.

No fear to tell Policeman, but my powerful than them.

New York Club must have the Pennant this year from your club. "We are cranky on Giants."

> Yours truly,
> "BLACK HAND."[36]

That afternoon, with the Giants leading 2–0 in the ninth inning, the Cubs rallied against Christy Mathewson. Solly Hofman singled to center and, after Mathewson retired Sheckard on a ground ball to second, Frank Schulte doubled the utility man home to make it a 2–1 game. Up to the plate stepped the ailing and threatened Frank Chance. Attempts to terrorize the man were futile. Chance rocketed a line drive over the head of Giants first baseman Frank Bowerman and down the right-field line. Schulte trotted home as the fans groaned, while Chance lumbered into second base. The unfazed Peerless Leader's double gave the Black Hand the finger and tied the game at two. Jimmy Kling's home run, a solo shot into the left-field bleachers off Mathewson, won the game for Chicago in the twelfth inning. Make that a 15.5-game lead over New York.

Despite the excitement of the victory, and the intensity of the rivalry, Chance's aching body would not let him continue playing. On August 21, Chance left the team for the remainder of its road trip. He would meet up with the guys on September 1st in Chicago. He hoped stepping away from the daily grind of the season would help his body recover, but he wouldn't just be lying in bed. With the National League race well in hand, Chance aimed to spend a few days scouting potential World Series opponents as well as watching a few young players the organization might be interested in signing to future contracts. Chance and Murphy worried that the ease with which the Cubs had won the pennant in 1906 had hurt them against the White Sox, and they didn't want to repeat the mistake.[37] When Chance asked Jimmy Sheckard to manage the team in his absence, he urged the outfielder to hold his teammates accountable to the team's high standard of play. With that, the Cubs left for Boston without their Peerless Leader.

Chicago continued to grind its way toward a pennant that was all but certain as the dog days of summer came to a close. On September 1 the Cubs' lead over the Giants and Pirates had swelled to 17.5 games after they went 22-8 in August. An amusing photograph appeared in the *Chicago Tribune* that same morning featuring a suited Frank Chance sitting on the Detroit Tigers' bench next to their manager, Hughie Jennings. Chance had traveled to Detroit to scout its ball club when Jennings noticed him in the stands and beckoned him to watch the game next to him. A nearby photographer snapped their photo. Jennings is completely at ease while Chance's stiffened back and arched eyebrows convey an element of surprise at the unwanted attention that belie his wide smile. He rejoined the Cubs in Chicago feeling much better and ready for the stretch run.

The Cubs thrilled their soaked fans when they clinched their second consecutive pennant with a rain-shortened 4–1 win over the Philadelphia Phillies on September 23. In the game, Johnny Evers stole home and Del Howard combined with Evers to turn a triple play, two extraordinary feats executed by a team with both talent and flair. Evers's play brought a smile to the face of his former manager, Frank Selee, who sat in the stands and proudly watched his former team repeat as National League champions. Chicago had taken sole possession of first place on May 30 and never looked back.

A thrilled Murphy momentarily celebrated the pennant and then quickly got to work on making preparations for the World Series. He first met with a contractor to expand the stadium's seating capacity to best meet the anticipated demand for tickets. Ever the optimist, Murphy sent President Teddy Roosevelt an invitation to the World Series. Perhaps Murphy genuinely did not know that the commander-in-chief despised the sport. The Cubs would meet the surprising Detroit Tigers in the World Series. The Tigers, led by their immensely talented and combustible young star, Ty Cobb, captured the American League flag following a bruising pennant battle with the favored Philadelphia Athletics in the season's final days.

Pundits agreed that Chicago's outstanding pitching staff gave it an advantage over Detroit heading into the series. Mordecai Brown, Orval Overall, Carl Lundgren, Jack Pfiester, and Ed Reulbach made at least twenty-two starts for the Cubs in 1907. Remarkably, all five pitchers posted earned run averages that finished in the top six of the National League. Pfiester led the league with a 1.15 ERA, followed by Lundgren and Brown. Pittsburgh's Sam Leever snuck into fourth place with a 1.66 mark as Overall and Reulbach nipped at his heels. Brown's 0.944 WHIP (walks plus hits allowed on average per inning pitched) led the league. Chick Fraser, the player that had created so much consternation between Murphy and Herrmann, pitched 138.1 innings and finished the season with a 2.28 earned run average. The magnitude of the staff's depth and the mastery with which Chance deployed them resulted in the absence of all the Cubs' pitchers from the National League leaderboard for innings pitched. None of their hurlers finished in the top ten. With the exception of Brown, who was bothered by some soreness late in the year, each hurler's pitching arm remained strong deep into the season. The Cubs' pitchers allowed a paltry 2.5 runs per game, nearly three-quarters of a run lower than the next closest National League staffs, Pittsburgh and Philadelphia. Catchers Johnny Kling and Pat Moran masterfully aided and abetted their pitchers' dominance of hitters from behind the plate. However, the Cubs were well aware of the frailty that advantages on paper held, and the focused group refused to give credence to any analysis of the series after losing to the White Sox the previous year.

An expansive crowd of more than twenty-four thousand fans squeezed into the West Side Grounds on Tuesday, October 8, for Game One of the World Series. Chance tabbed twenty-three-game winner Orval Overall as his starting pitcher, opposed by Detroit's ace, "Wild" Bill Donovan. Johnny Kling's RBI single in the fourth inning drew first blood, and Overall kept the Tigers scoreless until he ran into trouble in the eighth. With the aid of three errors by the Cubs, Detroit put together a 3-run rally to turn its 1-run deficit into a 3–1 lead. With Chicago on the ropes, a contingent of disheartened fans got up and left while the remaining spectators slumped in their seats. However, the Cubs stunned Detroit by scoring twice against Donovan in the ninth inning to force extra innings. Incredibly, Harry Steinfeldt tied the game at three when catcher Boss Schmidt could not smother a swinging strike three with Del Howard in the batter's box. Steinfeldt sprinted home from third base while Howard reached first as Schmidt tried in vain to chase down the ball.

In a bit of a letdown, the game finished in a tie as darkness descended over the ballpark and forced the teams to stop playing. The game would not count toward the series standings, and Game Two would be reset as Game One redux. Schmidt's error proved costly for Detroit. The opportunity to put pressure on the Cubs by reminding them of their failure in their previous World Series didn't slip through Schmidt's fingers as much as sail past his glove, and Chicago made the Tigers pay dearly. The Cubs won the next three games behind stellar pitching performances by Pfiester, Reulbach, and Overall.

Mordecai Brown, hampered by a sore arm, had yet to appear in the series, but he was available for Game Five, and Frank Chance eagerly deployed his valuable pitching weapon with an eye toward finishing the series immediately. So many Tiger fans were curious about seeing "Three-Finger" Brown pitch that they looked for him at the Cubs' team hotel in Detroit. Brown, who had lost parts of two fingers in a farming accident as a child, obliged their curiosity by demonstrating his pitching grips on an apple.[38] Now they would get to see the Cubs' living legend pitch in the flesh.

Saturday, October 12, was a cold day at Bennett Park, and the fans tried earnestly to layer themselves to keep out the chill. Murphy sat in the stands next to the hot dog counter, a snack and wafts of warm steam within reach, wrapped in his beloved horse blanket. George Mullin, a talented right-hander plagued by an occasional loss of control, took the mound for Detroit. The Cubs looked to beat him again, having already defeated him in Game Two, 3–1.

Chicago jumped out to a quick lead, which settled any nerves Murphy may have been entertaining. Jimmy Slagle drew a base on balls to lead off the game and then promptly stole second base on the first pitch Mullin delivered to Jimmy Sheckard. Mullin bounced back to retire Sheckard and Del Howard. Harry Steinfeldt, Chicago's most prolific run producer throughout the season, collected an RBI with a single to center that scored Slagle, who—with two outs—had been off running with the crack of the bat. Chicago tacked on another run in the second inning with an RBI groundout off the bat of Slagle that scored Evers from third base. A 2–0 lead proved to be more than sufficient for Brown on this day.

Murphy's emotions fluctuated intensely throughout the game. In the eighth inning, the Chicago newspapermen sent Cubs secretary Charlie Williams to ask Murphy if the ball club would be playing an exhibition game the following day, at the West Side Grounds, to give the fans the chance to celebrate the team's championship, but the president brushed him aside. "I refuse to answer until this contest ends. Remember the Maine and the cuff buttons," Murphy warned Williams.[39] Murphy's reference to the Cubs' selection of a gift for winning the 1906 World Series had only motivated the underdog White Sox. Murphy wasn't about to take winning for granted again. He needn't have worried. Brown cruised into the ninth inning with his shutout intact. He bamboozled Ty Cobb, striking him out to open the frame. Claude Rossman singled to bring the tying run to the plate. The Tigers had one last chance, but Brown smothered the rally like a candle snuffer. Coughlin popped out to Joe Tinker; then pinch hitter Boss Schmidt repeated the feat. Schmidt's pop fly settled into Tinker's glove with a soft thwack, and the Cubs' shortstop triumphantly raised his arms in the air. The Chicago Cubs were World Series champions.

Rather than burst from the seams with excitement, the team took its accomplishment in stride. "All of the Cubs took their victory quietly," noted one observer. "Tinker threw his arms in the air when he caught the fly that ended the game, but the remainder of the team walked quietly to the bench, took the congratulations that were showered on them modestly, rode to their hotels, and remained indoors most of the evening until their train left."[40] Once safely outside of Detroit, however, they let loose on the ride home. "Cap Chance wore a grin a barber could not remove with the sharpest razor," noted Charles Dryden.[41] Murphy announced that the team would play the exhibition game for the fans the following day and that the players could keep all the proceeds from the event as an additional bonus for winning the series.

The Cubs won the World Series because their starting pitchers allowed only three runs in the four Chicago victories, in large part because they limited Detroit's star outfielders, Cobb and Sam Crawford, to a combined nine hits in forty-one at bats, eight of which were singles. The pitching staff was supported by the outstanding work of catcher Johnny Kling, who limited the Tigers' running game. The pitching staff was so dominant that even the loss of Frank Chance to a dislocated middle finger in Game Three could not derail the team. The Cubs were the best team in baseball, and now they had the title they had longed for to prove it.

Charlie Murphy was ecstatic. He praised his team's effort and enjoyed taking a little dig at American League president Ban Johnson. "We have given the American League the worst drubbing it ever got at the hands of the National, and I believe all will agree with me when I say that this is a vindication of our defeat last fall. The Cubs did not go into this fight overconfident and consequently put up a good fight. They never know when they are beaten, and when they get a lead no club can overtake them. I think they are the greatest ball club ever known," Murphy crowed.[42] For his part, Johnson credited Chicago for playing better in the series, but he simultaneously blamed Detroit's subpar play on its pennant chase that lasted into the season's final days. Johnson also took umbrage with some of the strategy used by Tigers manager Hughie Jennings. Part of Johnson's post-series comments to the press included a stupefying suggestion. "I must say that I do not think Manager Jennings followed the generally well-defined rules of baseball entirely in handling his team during the series but there is no criticism of him for that. It was his managing which brought them to the head of the American League. But today, for instance, with Crawford at second base and none out he sent Cobb up to hit the ball, when I should have thought the play was to sacrifice Crawford to third," Johnson lamented.[43] Bunt Ty Cobb with a man in scoring position, with nobody out, while down two runs in an elimination game? Seriously?

Murphy celebrated the Cubs' stylish victory, the first sweep in the young history of the World Series. "By winning the championship the Cubs proved themselves the best team in the world. I expected they would do it, but to tell the truth, I felt that the element of luck would prevent us from capturing four in a row. Saturday's victory for Chicago proved more than anything else could the honesty of base ball. A Sunday game in Chicago would have meant thousands of dollars for the clubs, and I am glad no one can say gate receipts were ever held above the integrity of the pastime," Murphy said. "I am delighted that the world's championship pennant will stay in Chicago."[44]

Frank Chance had projected the utmost confidence that his players were going to find a way to get the job done, but even he had to admit that a series sweep had surprised him. "After the first game I never had any doubt about the outcome of the series. We played our game and won. Every man on the Chicago Club did his duty. After the first game we played at about the speed we showed during the race for the pennant. I am happy, of course, I expected Detroit to make a better showing, however, I hardly thought at the start that we could take four straight games. The Cub pitchers worked wonderfully well. Overall was in good form, and so were the remainder."[45]

Even without the Sunday game, the Cubs players received a substantial financial payout for winning the series. The receipts added up to $101,728.50, of which the National Commission received the first 10 percent. The players got 60 percent of the remaining dollars, while the rest was split between the two clubs. The victorious Cubs earned an additional bonus beyond the World Series money. Murphy chipped in an additional $10,000 to the Cubs' pool, so that, after the proceeds from the exhibition were added, each player, along with trainer Jack McCormick and Secretary Charlie Williams, earned $2,250.[46]

Murphy worked hard to cultivate an inviting environment at the West Side Grounds during the World Series to attract large crowds. He had successfully created an atmosphere of comfort for all fans, who had behaved cordially. However, the Tigers had failed to draw well.

Poor weather was largely blamed for the low attendance, but whispers about ticket scalping could also be heard if one listened carefully enough. But none of that could overshadow the triumph the World Series was for Murphy and the Cubs. "You've got to give it to Charlie Murphy when it comes to handling crowds and arranging boxes—that little man knows as much about fixing up an army of people as he does about choosing ball players who can win a flag," Bill Phelon confessed in his *Sporting Life* column.[47]

A gaudy banquet honoring the victorious Cubs was held at the Auditorium Annex at the end of the week. Dignitaries, players, and fans mingled while enveloped in live music. A series of speeches ensued that praised the team for its accomplishment. John Black, a leading member of the fans' committee, announced the creation of a trophy cup that would be crafted over the winter and presented to the organization in the spring. Black expressed his hope that the award would be given out annually as baseball's answer to the America's cup to the yachting community. Following speeches from several dignitaries, Murphy delivered a short address in which he thanked everyone for attending and commended the organizers of such a wonderful event. Then he effusively praised the Cubs' former executives and players for earning the team's World Series title. He emphasized to the attentive crowd the crucial roles played by former team president Jim Hart and former manager and star player Cap Anson in laying the foundation for the franchise's current success. He also praised the players for their hard work and remarkable baseball skills. Murphy showered Frank Chance with accolades for deftly leading the club.[48] It was a magnanimous and well-received speech.

6

SUPREMACY AGAIN

After his team conquered the baseball world, Charlie Murphy focused on commemorating the feat. In 1906 Murphy had wanted cuff links if the Cubs won, but he decided against revisiting anything that reminded him of that loss. Here was an opportunity to turn the page for good. The organization selected watch fob medals as the symbol of its World Series victory, and Murphy enthusiastically set about designing one worthy of his team's accomplishment to be distributed to the players.

Following several postseason exhibition games, the Cubs dispersed for the winter. A small group of players, including Jimmy Sheckard and Joe Tinker, headed for Wisconsin to unwind on a fishing trip. Frank Chance had intended to join them, but he remained afflicted by the aftereffects of his illness as well as his newly fractured finger, suffered in Game Three. He decided on the most prudent course of action and returned home to California for rest.[1] Johnny Evers left for New York to check in on his shoe store in Troy. Evers wrote Murphy a letter, several days later, to tell his boss that he was working on a newspaper article that would soon be published.[2] The old scribe, Murphy, assuredly beamed with pride. Catcher Pat Moran underwent an operation to reset his broken nose. Orval Overall got engaged.[3]

Several writers gave Murphy accolades for his team's performance. Ren Mulford penned a flattering piece in *Sporting Life*. "Cincinnati is willing to let Wilmington share the distinction of claiming 'Murph' as a citizen, but let it be known he came to Cincinnati and got his peck of diamonds before he ever dreamed of going to Chicago and showing James A. Hart how easy it is to equip a championship team,"

Mulford quipped.[4] The Cubs certainly enjoyed winning, but the hand slap Murphy and the club had received from the White Sox the previous season had trimmed their egos a bit. One sensed they were as relieved as excited about winning. Speaking requests arrived in Murphy's office, and the affable president agreed to squeeze in a number of events throughout Chicagoland. Murphy spoke at a banquet at St. Martin's Church in Austin. Later in the fall, he appeared at the Grace Church Men's Club in Oak Park for a talk titled, "How We Won the World's Championship."[5]

In late October, William Jennings Bryan, the political heavyweight from Nebraska and the soon-to-be Democratic presidential nominee for a third time, authored a short article on the World Series in his newspaper, *The Commoner*. Titled "An Honest Game," Bryan's commentary reflected how the recently completed series exemplified the moral nature of baseball.

> Baseball maintains its hold on the American public because it is not only a manly sport but an honest sport. How honest it is has been demonstrated by the championship games between the champion teams of the two great baseball organizations. The Chicago "Cubs," champions in their league, contested with the Detroit "Tigers," champions in their league. Seven games were to be played, and the gate receipts were to be divided among the players. Had the seven games been played probably $125,000 would have thus been furnished for division. Other sports might have been "fixed" so as to keep the public in suspense and thus get its money, but baseball is not "fixed." There were but four games, for the "Cubs" won four straight games and the world's championship. Nothing would prove more conclusively the honesty of the great national pastime. And that is one reason why the people love it and support it royally. Managers of other sports who look to the public for support might ponder over this fact with benefit to themselves.[6]

Although Bryan's description of the revenue distribution was not quite accurate, he, nonetheless, captured the essence of why a sweep in the World Series was consequential for reasons beyond the Cubs' dominance.[7] It made a compelling argument for the integrity of baseball games, particularly those played in its championship series. The performance of Murphy's team elevated the credibility of the sport, in the eyes of the public, to new heights. In general, baseball fans throughout America replaced their disdain of rowdyism with praise for the game's cleanliness. Chicago had not intentionally lost any games to extend the series for financial gain. The Cubs' sweep helped shift the conversation about the sport away from any notion of moral debauchery and toward mythological virtue.

Bryan's piece crossed Murphy's desk, and he read it with great interest. Murphy's father, P. J., had been a silver man in his day, a loyal Catholic Democrat, who most likely supported Bryan's run for the presidency in 1896 in spite of the opponent, Ohio's own governor, William McKinley. Bryan delivered his captivating "Cross of Gold" speech, which heavily criticized the gold standard, at the Democratic National Convention on July 9, 1896, three and a half weeks before P. J. died. An emotional Murphy read the article, and he immediately reached out to Bryan. Murphy sent him a season pass to the West Side Grounds as a thank you for his kind words about the game of baseball.[8] He then packed his bags and left for Ohio, where he spent the next several weeks with his family.

It was a good thing Murphy had taken two weeks off while he could, because he jumped back into the fray when he returned to Chicago on November 8. He coordinated a slate of spring exhibition games, with stops in towns throughout the South, for the 1908 team. He also finalized the details for the championship fob design. Additionally, Murphy excitedly plotted to expand the West Side Grounds to meet the spiking demand for tickets. His plans were complicated when a financial crisis, triggered in mid-October by a failed attempt to corner the copper market, caused a run on banks and bankruptcies throughout the country. The panic also crushed the value of stocks. Undaunted, Murphy pushed ahead with his plan to renovate the ballpark. Murphy aimed to increase the seating capacity of the ballpark to upward of thirty thousand. He planned to extend the grandstands to add more fifty-cent seats. Additionally, Murphy poured his focus into cultivating a better experience for his higher paying customers. During the just-completed season, the high demand for reserved seats had forced some fans to put in their requests a week in advance, which was simply unacceptable to Murphy. He wanted more tickets available for spontaneous buyers. Lengthening the grandstands also provided additional space to add box seats. The renovation plans satisfied Murphy, but they needed a touch of luxury. A thought struck him: telephones. What better way to keep his most exclusive clientele in their seats for all nine innings than to give them a mechanism to avoid leaving? He decided to install telephones, replete with secure connections, in the first row of boxes. Additionally, Murphy decided that the team would hold a Ladies' Day promotion once a week.[9] He also hired local sculptor Osborne Olsen to create several statues for the grounds that would add a new level of gravitas.

With the National League's winter meeting on the horizon, Murphy spent time channeling his creativity into ways to improve baseball. He concluded that the World Series ought to be expanded to a best-of-nine series. In order to make the change palatable for the players, Murphy wanted to expand their financial cut to include the fifth game. He looked forward to presenting his idea to the owners. In the meantime, he planned a banquet for the gathering in New York to celebrate the Cubs' championship. White Sox owner Charles Comiskey had thrown a party at the American League meeting the previous year, and Murphy would not be outdone.

Once again, the owners gathered at the Waldorf Astoria in Manhattan during the first full week of December. Murphy arrived in the evening. He was the last official to show up, but he didn't miss anything of consequence. Trade rumors bounced around the hallways of the hotel as writers tried to induce the executives to give them inside "dope" on any potential deals between the clubs. Murphy was quiet on the personnel front for once. He wanted to leave the roster alone and let the players have the opportunity to defend their title.

The juiciest trade rumor involved the Boston Doves and the fate of their manager/first baseman, Fred Tenney, a fourteen-year veteran and one of the premiere players in the National League, who had fallen out of favor with several of his players. John McGraw was looking for ways to upgrade his infield—he was even considering returning to playing himself—particularly given the Giants' first base situation, and Tenney drew his interest. McGraw had competed against Tenney for years, dating back to his playing days with Baltimore, and according to Boston president George Dovey, the Doves' star could be acquired for the right price. McGraw played coy with the media, and he could do so with a straight face because of a young, talented player the Giants already had on the roster. When asked if the Giants could use Tenney, McGraw responded, "Well, I don't know. I think pretty well of my new man, Merkle. Still, you never can tell how these newcomers will turn out. Tenney is an experienced player."[10]

Rumors of a Tenney trade intensified after Joe Kelley, a veteran baseball man, arrived at the hotel. The following day, the Doves announced a stunning piece of news: Kelley had signed a two-year contract to manage the club. Tenney, who handled the news professionally, and even met with Kelley, was officially on the trading block.[11] McGraw pounced. He sent five players to Boston for Tenney, infielder Al Bridwell, and catcher Tom Needham. The deal generated headlines in sports pages around the country. It was the biggest trade of the off-season, and one that would impact the 1908 season, and baseball history, forever. Murphy, who always slept with one eye open watching the Giants, was impressed by the swap. "With Tenney, McGraw, Bridwell, and Devlin for an infield, and Donlin, Seymour, and Shannon for an outfield, the Giants are going to be mighty strong," he conceded.[12]

Murphy hosted his banquet on Thursday night. The festive affair featured magnates, players, newspapermen, and managers. They cavorted for over three hours. The highlight of the evening was an award presented to Honus Wagner, the Pirates' exemplary shortstop, for winning his fifth National League batting title during the 1907 season. "It was the biggest surprise his bashful nature ever encountered when the presentation took place," one report observed. Murphy made sure that the Cubs were well represented. He feted the throng with a speech while Johnny Evers made an appearance.[13]

Inside the owners' meeting, Murphy presented his idea of an expanded World Series format. He argued that more fans could attend games, which made the series more accessible to the general public. There is no question the outcome of the 1906 series still gnawed at Murphy. He maintained that a longer series would prevent fluky outcomes. Murphy's peers agreed with him, and they voted to change the format. The majority of American League owners already supported the measure. Ultimately, however, Murphy's idea was nullified after Charles Comiskey convinced the American League executives that a longer series format worked in favor of the National League. Comiskey contended that the American League pennant race was frequently closely contested, while the National League winner often rested during the season's final weeks, after cruising through the regular season. The other American League magnates reconsidered their positions and sided with Comiskey, and Murphy's proposal was shot down.[14] Murphy framed his disappointment in the measure's failure as a loss for baseball's workforce. "Well, there is one thing sure. The players of both organizations will regret it if the number of games is not increased, as it will deprive them from sharing in the receipts of five instead of four games," he said. But Murphy decided against butting heads with his longtime friend over the issue. "I understand Comiskey is responsible for the action of the American league. Well, Commy is a pretty shrewd man in baseball," Murphy admitted.[15]

During the meeting, Murphy again supported Harry Pulliam, who was reelected as National League president despite the opposition of Giants owner John T. Brush, the lone holdout. The New York organization continued to harbor resentment over Pulliam's discipline of John McGraw, in 1905, for the "Hey Barney" incident, a screaming match instigated by McGraw with Pirates owner Barney Dreyfuss, as well as a $1,000 fine the Giants incurred for breaking a contract to play spring exhibition games against a minor league team in New Orleans. When business concluded, Murphy returned to Chicago and refocused his energies on the stadium renovation project.

The Cubs opened the 1908 season with a six-game road trip, starting in Cincinnati, on April 14. Murphy joined the team for its first series of the year. He took along a guest of honor, Osborne Olsen, the young Chicago artist who had created several magnificent pieces for the new West Side Grounds, including a sculpture of Frank Chance. Murphy and Olsen excitedly talked about art, and Murphy took advantage of being in Cincinnati by taking Olsen to Charles and Annie Taft's house to view their breathtaking collection of European art, which was valued at over a million dollars.[16]

Hampered by rain, Chicago's Opening Day starter, Orval Overall, struggled to effectively grip his pitches during the bottom of the first inning and allowed Cincinnati to score five runs, but the Cubs battled back to tie the game. Overall did not surrender another run before giving way to Heinie Zimmerman, who pinch hit for him in the ninth inning. Zimmerman drove in the go-ahead run, and the Cubs went on to win, 6-5, in front of nearly 20,000 disappointed Reds supporters. The Cubs swept Cincinnati and won two out of three games in St. Louis before returning to Chicago for their home opener on April 22.

Fifteen thousand excited fans, as well as a cast of baseball luminaries such as Ban Johnson, Garry Herrmann, and Jim Hart, poured into the renovated West Side Grounds to celebrate the raising of the National League flag; then they watched the Cubs play the Reds. Dozens of fans chose to watch the game from a set of bleachers atop a building across the street, where they had a panoramic view of the field. Local journalists effusively praised the renovated stadium, including Charles Dryden: "That new playground on the west side is a poem of beauty and comfort and Mr. Murphy has reached far and wide for artistic effect . . . Among the rare creations are 1,200 regulation Spalding bats worked into the balustrades guarding the stairways. The upper boxes are railed off with iron piping ornamented with 460 gilded cast iron baseballs, facsimile reproductions of the playing article. At various places about the pavilion entrance cement Cubs may be seen climbing huge cement bats. This section of the zoo contains fourteen bears done in Sculptor Olsen's best zoological vein."[17]

Bill Phelon of *Sporting Life* gave his national audience a peek inside the Cubs' new digs. "Ornaments and statues, broad stairs with sweeping thresholds; an entire upper deck built atop of the pavilion; a calm confiscation of 50 per cent of the room formerly sacred to the bleacherites, and its annexation to the grand stand—all these things are in evidence, and completely alter the aspect of the park . . . As a piece of artistic skill and judgment, and as a palace of base ball, Cub Park is certainly a wonder."[18]

Murphy beautified the grounds with several smaller touches. He purchased $50 worth of long-stemmed roses and had them placed in the women's parlor. He added additional flower arrangements throughout the park to add a touch of elegance. Murphy also set out bowls filled with goodies for the fans. Some of the dishes contained candy for the youngsters, while the others held cigars for their parents.[19]

Murphy had devised a gimmick for the National League championship banner. It was tightly wrapped together at the base of the flagpole because it held hundreds of tiny pennants inside that would be sprung as gifts to the crowd at the moment the banner was unfurled. However, the enormous pennant refused to hatch when it reached its apex. The confused crowd murmured. Groundskeeper Charley Kuhn hastily lowered the flag and opened it up. The pennants spilled all over the ground anticlimactically. The blue banner was quickly reattached and run up the pole, where it flopped open to reveal its logo of a large baseball and a white cub with a bat. Frank Hutchinson described the low impact that the snafu had on the crowd in the next day's Chicago *Inter Ocean*: "The cheer would have been a peach had the flag opened on schedule time, but as the spring opening of Murphy's choice stock of pennants had been delayed the edge was taken off the spontaneous outburst and it became only a polite murmur." Fans quickly shook off any dismay at the blundered flag raising and cheered when the dapperly dressed Cap Anson strode out to the mound to throw out the ceremonial first pitch. Now the fans could really celebrate as game time neared. After all, Hutchinson said, the Cubs were playing the Reds, "who had been offered as the sacrifice by the schedule maker . . . Too easy!"[20] True to the reporter's contention, Chicago cruised to a 7–3 victory in an hour and forty minutes.

The fans amused themselves throughout the festive afternoon. They even shared their free bounty. With the Cubs ahead 5–0 in the sixth, Cincinnati's Hans Lobert hit a solo home run. When he took his position in left field in the bottom of the inning, impressed fans showered him with congratulatory cigars. Lobert returned to the bench with seventeen of them as well as a matchbox tossed in his direction by one particularly practical fan. His former teammate Orval Overall had to have chuckled at the sight of the fans' gifts of choice. Overall knew his old roommate didn't smoke.[21]

Murphy's palace earned rave reviews from everyone except the Cincinnati Reds. In the midst of getting the park ready for Opening Day, construction on the visitors' clubhouse fell behind schedule and was not completed by the time the season started. To compound the issue, groundskeeper Charley Kuhn had a flock of pet ducks that he kept at the ballpark. Over the winter, the fowl had set up shop in some new digs: the visitors' clubhouse. Kuhn removed the ducks before the season began, but he didn't clean up all the evidence that their presence had left behind. "The Reds managed to endure the comforts of home until they turned on the shower bath water which trickled thither and yon into forgotten angles and aroused unpleasant reminiscences of Mr. Kuhn's most interesting barnyard exhibits," Charles Dryden reported.[22] Garry Herrmann personally inspected the clubhouse and was repulsed by the filthy quarters. He told his team to dress at the hotel for the rest of the series and contacted Harry Pulliam to apprise the league president of the situation. For his part, Murphy acknowledged that work remained on the clubhouse, and he was trying to get it finished as quickly as possible. He didn't know anything about ducks. "I do not blame Mr. Herrmann for the alleged insanitary report of the dressing room set to President Pulliam. Garry was steered through a bunko inspection of the place by members of his own team, who were peeved and piqued by five straight defeats at the hands of my champions. I know what I'm talking about." With the homestand continuing, Murphy hired several men to fix the problem. He paid them double union wages to make the necessary repairs to ensure that the two showers, four sinks, and lockers were all in working order. He also had them paint the room.[23]

Pulliam responded to Herrmann's complaint by fining Murphy $25, the daily penalty for failing to "provide proper dressing room facilities for the opening game of the season."[24] Pulliam also instructed Murphy to reimburse the Reds the cost of hiring a carriage to take the team from its hotel to the park. However, the league president refrained from punishing Murphy further because the "Chicago club . . . ha(s) done everything reasonable to complete and provide comfortable dressing rooms for the visiting players, as provided for by the laws of the National League."[25]

The Cubs started the season well as they won thirteen of their first seventeen games, but a subsequent three-game losing streak dropped their record to 13-7 after twenty contests. The good news for Chicago was it sat atop the National League standings. The bad news was that three teams—the Pirates, Giants, and Phillies—were all within a game and a half of them. Chicago tightly clung to first place throughout May despite losing to the Pirates five times between May 6 and June 2. Although the Cubs' primary strength was their pitching staff, Murphy was growing increasingly concerned about Chicago's sluggish offense. Murphy thoughtfully reasoned that the Cubs could improve as the weather warmed up, but he also knew that Chicago was not going to simply run away and hide from New York and Pittsburgh as it had done the past two seasons. The team was barely hitting above .200, and it needed to increase run production if it was to have any hope of hanging on in the tight National League race.

Poor weather had wreaked havoc on the National League schedule into early May. Rain seemed to follow the Cubs everywhere. Weary of watching torrential downpours erode his team's playing surface, Pittsburgh owner Barney Dreyfuss deployed an innovation to protect the field. Dreyfuss hired the Pittsburgh Waterproof Company to design a tarpaulin that could be strewn across the field at Exposition Park to insulate it from adverse weather conditions. The Pittsburgh

Waterproof Company responded to the challenge by designing a giant tarp, measuring 120 by 120 feet, incorporating waterproof duck feathers. It took between fifteen and twenty minutes to deploy it. All told, Dreyfuss paid $2,000 for the tarp and its distributing system.[26] On May 7 rain washed out the game between the Cubs and Pirates, but Dreyfuss's new contraption protected the field. It was the fifth time the Pirates had been rained out at home since the nascent season had begun on April 15. Referred to as "the rain coat" by the players, it proved to be very effective at keeping the field dry even though the game had to be postponed.[27] Pirates player/manager Fred Clarke "is much pleased with his experiment, and while some alterations may be required from time to time, he is convinced that the cover will prove useful, not only in preventing postponements, but also in improving the playing field."[28] Murphy, however, wasn't overly impressed. No doubt the price tag influenced his opinion.

Back at home, Charlie and Louise Murphy liked living in Oak Park, and one of their great joys was their neighbors: three young girls who lived with their mother, Miriam Pannell. The Pannells rented the house at 240 Marion Street, next door to the Murphys.[29] The Pannell sisters: Gertrude, twelve; Lois, eleven; and little Helen, seven, in 1908, loved the performing arts and frequently appeared on stage in neighborhood productions. They assuredly kept Miriam plenty busy, which likely was a welcome distraction from the heartbreaking death of her husband. The new neighbors became friendly, and Murphy, who typically felt the same way about giving away free tickets to ballgames as his players did about the Giants, cheerfully made sure that Miriam and the girls received passes to every Cubs game for years.

Occasionally, Miriam rounded up her daughters and took them to the West Side Grounds. Murphy exuberantly greeted them and ushered the ladies to his private box, where they watched the game with him and Louise. Afterward, Murphy piled the Pannell family into his car and drove them to Rector's, a swanky seafood restaurant at the corner of Clark and Madison, where he treated them to dinner. "My sister Helen was his mascot," Lois Pannell fondly recalled. "She would have second breakfasts with him and he would read make-believe articles about her from the paper till her eyes were big as saucers. When he went away on trips he would send us postcards with pictures of little bears on them."[30]

The Pannells remained close to the Murphys' hearts even after Charlie and Louise moved across town, to Edgewater, several years later. The girls continued to visit them, and their trips traditionally ended with a jovial dinner where Gertrude, Lois, and Helen laughed at Charlie's silly jokes.

A decade later, in 1918, the Pannells once again had their world upended when Helen, now a teenager, was involved in a devastating car accident in which she suffered a fractured skull and a broken collarbone. The "vivacious and active young woman," who was "full of high spirits," missed so much school due to her injuries that she could not graduate from Oak Park High with the rest of her class. A year later, Helen fell ill with influenza during the worldwide pandemic. Thought to be on the verge of death, a determined Helen fought back fiercely and recovered, only to be stricken by pneumonia in the early weeks of 1920. On January 26 her condition rapidly deteriorated, and she was rushed to the hospital. Upon arriving, doctors immediately suspected that an abscess on Helen's lung threatened her life. They quickly huddled to develop a plan to remove it, but the surgeon never performed the operation. Just thirty minutes after being admitted to the infirmary, she died. Helen Pannell was eighteen.[31]

Miriam and her two daughters managed as best they could to cope with deep familial grief for a second time. Gertrude's marriage to Albion Holbrook injected some joy into the family the following year. The couple eventually had four children. Yet, sadly, Gertrude lost her husband in 1932, the same year she gave birth to their youngest child. Meanwhile, Lois became a stenographer and worked at city hall, where she became known for her keen writing skills. Lois also developed into a fine cook, and she shared her recipes with the readers of *Oak Leaves* and the *Chicago Tribune*. In her later years, memories of the fun times her family spent with the Murphys, including at the West Side Grounds, where she sat as a young girl in the owner's box and cheered on the

Cubs, moved Lois to write of Charlie, "The best way to live forever is to be nice to little children because little people never forget those who are kind to them."[32]

Thursday, May 21, was a special afternoon at the West Side Ball Park as the Cubs raised the purple and yellow World Series flag given to the organization by the National Commission in celebration of their 1907 title. Although oddly colored, the banner nonetheless represented the highest achievement in baseball and had been presented by the sport's governing body. Murphy hated how it looked, but the National Commission adhered to its color scheme. Harry Pulliam attended the game, and Murphy warmly welcomed his illustrious guest with a pregame tour of the renovated stadium. Murphy watched from the stands as the Boston Doves joined the Cubs in the outfield for the raising of the championship banner. A band played "The Star-Spangled Banner" as the flag was hoisted up the pole. This time, Murphy's stunt worked. As it unfurled, the large pennant successfully released a large school of small American flags that floated into the stands. Once the anthem ceased, several Cubs players retrieved what oddly appeared to be a smaller version of the biblical Ark of the Covenant from behind the fans sitting hundreds of feet from the field. Simultaneously, an enormous bouquet of roses was picked up by someone, although no one could tell who exactly because the flowers hid him from view. They all ambled toward home plate while the Doves' president, George Dovey, signaled to Murphy to join him on the field. Murphy excused himself from Pulliam and worked his way down the grandstand steps and onto the grass.

The Cubs carrying the case set it down between the teams, and the players gathered around it for a closer look. Curious Doves also hung around to get a close-up view of the proceedings. Dovey then stepped up and addressed Murphy, who removed his bowler hat to listen. "Here is a gift from the Chicago Cubs—twenty players and Treasurer Charlie Williams—for you, Charlie Murphy," Dovey announced. The present was a chest inscribed thusly, "Presented to Charles W. Murphy, our president, with best wishes of his Cubs, May 21, 1908." What lay inside the mahogany casket took Murphy's breath away. He gasped as the lid was lifted to reveal an engraved gold plate etched with the names of twenty players as well as Williams. Murphy's throat tightened as he was shown that below the plate lay a 107-piece set of pure silverware. Tears welled up in his eyes and, for perhaps the only time in his life, he struggled to speak. He expressed his appreciation and thanked the players for their generous gift, which was later estimated at close to $1,000. With the presentation over, the players dispersed to make their final preparations to play the game. Murphy collected the oversized flower display in his left hand and pinned it against his chest to keep from dropping the massive garland. As an overwhelmed Murphy made his way back to the grandstand, a smiling Dovey patted him on the back.

After the game, Frank Chance set aside the 11–3 thrashing the Doves put on the Cubs to explain why it was so important to the players to honor Murphy in front of the fans with such a lavish gift.

Declared Chance:

Every man on the team likes Mr. Murphy and would fight for him. As president of the club he has done us all so many acts of kindness that we feel more like brothers to him than mere employe(e)s. He is the most popular magnate in the country with the players—all of whom have heard of his generous treatment of the "Cubs" at all times. If he has a lower berth he gladly gives it up to the pitcher who worked that day. We regard him not only as the most shrewd owner in the country, but the most democratic in his bearing. Our hotel is good enough for him. Our troubles are his and, by the same token, he shares our joys. Men want to play for Mr. Murphy and all present members of the club are willing to be sentenced to work for life under him. They don't make 'em any better. His popularity with his players is one great reason for the success that the team has had winning flags.[33]

The championship feelings enveloping the Cubs were short-lived, because they took a sour turn during a four-game series against Pittsburgh that began on Memorial Day at the West Side Grounds. Chicago entered the series with a three-and-a-half-game cushion over their closest pursuers. The Cubs won the opener, but the Pirates stormed back and took the final three games of the series to draw closer to Chicago, but a more pressing problem was a violent brawl that erupted in the Cubs' clubhouse on June 2. The Cubs primary beat writers, including Charles Dryden, Sy Sanborn, and Frank Hutchinson, were careful not to divulge too many details about the fight. Following their 12–6 loss to the Pirates, the Cubs' postgame discussion about their defeat soured after Jimmy Sheckard directed a critical comment toward young infielder Heinie Zimmerman. Sheckard, a veteran player who always managed the club if Chance was indisposed, was certainly in a position to give his opinion about the second-year player. Zimmerman, however, took exception to Sheckard's remark and snapped back. Then all hell broke loose. Zimmerman's mouthy retort infuriated Sheckard, who angrily hurled an object at his teammate. Incensed by the escalation of the situation, Zimmerman grabbed a bottle of clear liquid and fired it at Sheckard's head. The vial smashed into Sheckard's forehead. The container burst open and released its contents—ammonia—into Sheckard's eyes. Sheckard screamed in searing pain as Chance threw himself at Zimmerman and rained down furious punches upon his head. Zimmerman fought back like a cornered wolverine, and Chance, unable to subdue him, yelled out for the others to help him. Several players rushed to Chance's aid, and they administered a whooping so severe it sent Zimmerman to the hospital. After a terrifying forty-eight hours, Sheckard's vision steadily improved, and the fear of permanent blindness evaporated.[34]

Infuriated by the brawl, which occurred on the heels of losing three in a row to Pittsburgh, Chance ripped into his team before it took the field against Boston. "What the P. L. said never may be known, but that it was something warm may be guessed from the fact his face was covered with perspiration, and it was not a warm day either," wrote Sy Sanborn.[35] Murphy was very angry with the situation, but he deflected the focus off the fight and onto the team's losing streak. He cursed the National Commission's flag for bringing his team nothing but bad fortune. "No more yellow pennant for me. I'll burn it or bury it," Murphy fumed. "It's a hoodoo color in baseball and we will hoist the red, white, and blue pennant which we had made for ourselves before we knew the commission provided a design of its own. We've had nothing but accidents and injuries and tough luck weather ever since the pennant was raised and it began on the day we raised it."[36] From afar, New York manager John McGraw reveled in the Cubs' increasing distress. Chicago had not been given much trouble winning the pennant during the previous two seasons, but they had not been strongly tested, he maintained. Would the Cubs persevere under increasing pressure? They have no chance to win if they can't, he said.[37] They were too busy fighting each other.

Entering August, the Cubs found themselves in second place in the standings, sandwiched between the first-place Pirates and third-place Giants. It seemed obvious that an exciting pennant race loomed on the horizon as only two games separated the three clubs but, with the suddenness of a Midwest storm, Chicago again hit the skids. The Cubs were thumped by the Boston Doves, 14-0, on August 1, which marked the beginning of a hideous fourteen-game stretch during which they went 4-10. By August 18 the slump had sunk the Cubs into third place and widened their deficit with Pittsburgh to 5.5 games. Stunningly, however, they didn't lose another ten games for the rest of the season.

Like many of his teammates, Johnny Evers read the newspapers. The feisty second baseman kept track of other teams and players around baseball. He soaked in all the news and notes, including the "Inquisitive Fans" column that appeared in the *Chicago Tribune*. Fans submitted their questions that stumped them about the sport, and the newspaper provided answers to their inquiries. Historian David Rapp identified one particular submission that affected the fortune of the Cubs' entire season.[38] On July 19 the *Tribune* responded to a question submitted by Joseph Rupp, who wanted to know whether a run counted or not in an interesting scenario. Rupp set up his question this way: There are two outs in the bottom of the ninth inning of a tied game. The home team has the winning run at third base. The batter singles and the runner scores. However, and this was the crux of Rupp's question, what if the batter stopped running before reaching first base because he saw the runner score, and the defense threw the ball to the first baseman standing on the bag? Does the run count because a force out was in order? "No. Run cannot score when third out is made before reaching first base," was the *Tribune*'s succinct reply.[39] Upon reading this bit of rule book minutiae, Evers filed it away for a time when it would be useful. He didn't have to wait long.

In early September the Cubs headed to Pittsburgh for a two-game showdown against the Pirates. Chicago found itself in third place, but just a game behind New York and half a game back of Pittsburgh. It would be a tight, taut pennant race. On September 4 the Pirates defeated the Cubs, 1-0, in ten innings, to extend their slim lead. However, the controversial circumstances in which they won became fodder for conversation throughout baseball. Murphy declared he would protest the game and have the result invalidated. While it did not appear likely that his complaint would amount to anything, Chicago's vehement protests changed its fate in a shocking way.

In the bottom of the tenth inning of the scoreless game, the Pirates' Fred Clarke led off with a single that eluded Cubs third baseman Harry Steinfeldt by a slim margin. Tommy Leach laid down a sacrifice bunt, which moved Clarke to second base with one out and the magnificent Honus Wagner striding to the plate. Mordecai Brown bore down. Wagner struck a hot shot, but Evers managed to deflect it, which held Leach at third base. With runners at the corners and one out, Brown hit Warren Gill with a curveball to load the bases. Brown then struck out Ed Abbaticchio to set up a confrontation with John "Chief" Wilson, who would go on to become a .300 hitter, but at this time was a young player who wasn't considered a particularly dangerous threat at the plate. So, of course, Wilson smacked Brown's first offering into center field for a base hit. A jubilant Clarke scored, and the Pirates began to celebrate their win. Cubs beat writer Sy Sanborn described for his readers what happened. "Gill, who was on first base when Wilson singled, ran only half way to second base and as soon as he saw the hit fall safely he returned and ran back to the Pirates' bench in a hurry to get his punctured slats manicured as soon as possible, never thinking it was necessary for him to touch second base in order to make the victory complete. He did not go within thirty feet of second at any time."[40]

Fully aware that Gill had stopped short of second base, the well-read Evers hollered at center fielder Jimmy Slagle to get the ball to him, which he did. Evers stepped on the bag and held the ball aloft for Hank O'Day to see it, but the umpire was already headed for the exit. Evers exploded. Gill was out, the run should not be counted, and the game ought to continue, but O'Day wouldn't hear of it. "Clarke scored before the out could have been made," O'Day told a protesting Frank Chance as he left the field. The game was over, and Pittsburgh was the winner. Evers, who was fully aware the rules stated otherwise, fumed. "Ol' Hank was mad at me anyway for an argument we'd had in St. Louis a few weeks before and you could tell that his whole attitude was he'd be damned if that little squirt Evers was going to get him in another jam," Johnny recalled years later.[41] Murphy filed a protest with the league, but the National Commission refused to overturn the result, and the Cubs were stuck with the loss. Chicago fell another game behind the Giants and Pirates, but the stage was now set for one of the most thrilling finishes to a pennant race in baseball history.

After the frustrating loss to the Pirates, Chicago responded by winning fourteen of its next nineteen games. That hot stretch nudged the Cubs ahead of Pittsburgh, but they still trailed the Giants by two games as the fierce rivals readied for an epic four-game clash in New York. Incredibly, the Cubs had played seven more games than the Giants, which theoretically gave New York more opportunities to extend their advantage. The internal strife had not broken the Cubs' spirit but instead galvanized their competitive natures. Both Sheckard and Zimmerman had healed and returned to active duty, and the team's offensive production had improved. However, the Cubs' stalwart left-hander Jack Pfiester, known as the "Giant Killer" for his effectiveness against New York, was ailing with a tendon issue in his pitching arm and, despite his attempt to loosen the knot, his availability for the series was in doubt. Mordecai Brown's sore arm was troubling him, but he declared himself fit enough to pitch. Meanwhile, the Giants continued to win behind the superb play of their stars: Christy Mathewson,

Mike Donlin, and Fred Tenney, setting them up with an opportunity to reclaim the pennant.

The series began in New York with a doubleheader on September 22. "At last the Cubs will meet their hated rivals on their own yard and we are but a couple of games behind," Dryden penned gleefully.[42] A tightly packed crowd of thirty-five thousand fans slowly shuffled into the Polo Grounds. The large throng momentarily bottlenecked in the front plaza, creating a scary scene, but police quickly intervened, and the only casualties were several smashed ladies' hats.[43] The Cubs sent them all home with their hats in their hands. Chicago won both ends of the doubleheader, 4–3 and 3–1, to climb within percentage points of first-place New York.

Back home, enthused Cubs fans called upon the *Chicago Tribune* to help them keep track of the third game of the series, and the newspaper gladly fulfilled their wish. The *Tribune* printed a notice above the fold on the front page that it would meet the demand of locals to stay abreast of the game. "Owing to the hundreds of requests by mail and telephone, The Tribune will install its automatic scoreboard in Orchestra Hall today and give a report of the Cubs and Giants game." The *Tribune* designed the event as a fundraiser for its hospital fund.

In spite of his troublesome elbow, Jack Pfiester would pitch for Chicago. The Giants, however, would not be at full strength. Fred Tenney, who was staying at the same hotel as the Cubs, woke up with a painful back, which compounded his ailing legs. He couldn't play, and it forced John McGraw to replace him with the highly regarded youngster Fred Merkle, who would be starting at first base for the first time all season.

Another large, if nervous, crowd filed into the Polo Grounds on that cloudy and consequential Wednesday. At 87-50-2, the Giants entered the game clinging desperately to first place, but their grip was slipping over the 90-53-3 Cubs. Christy Mathewson breezily dispatched the Cubs in the top of the first inning, which included Merkle's catch of a foul ball off the bat of Johnny Evers. Pfiester matched Mathewson's zero with one of his own, as he pitched around a lead-off walk in the bottom of the first. Chicago nearly scored the game's first run in the second inning, but an outstanding defensive play by Merkle denied them. Frank Chance smashed a single into left field for a base hit to lead off the inning. Harry Steinfeldt followed with a sacrifice bunt toward Merkle that the youngster handled cleanly. He recorded the out at first as Chance moved up to second base to give Chicago a man in scoring position with only one away. The Cubs had an opportunity to strike first, but Mathewson induced Solly Hofman to foul out to catcher Roger Bresnahan. That brought up Joe Tinker, who had made a name for himself throughout his career, in part because of his success against the ace Mathewson. Tinker climbed into the batter's box and coiled. Mathewson delivered the pitch. Tinker let the ball travel deep and unleashed a quick swing. With a loud crack, the ball jumped off Tinker's bat and shot down the first base line. Chance immediately sprinted away from second. The sinking liner looked destined for the outfield, but the vigorous Merkle, spry with fresh legs, dove headfirst to his left and extended his glove for the ball, snaring it inches from the ground.[44] Tinker couldn't believe his bad luck. Merkle's sparkling snag allowed Mathewson to breathe a sigh of relief as he turned toward the Giants' bench as the game remained scoreless.

Neither team could push across a run until Tinker again stepped into the box, in the top of the fifth. He smashed the ball to the opposite field again, but this time it got down for a hit. Right fielder Mike Donlin unsuccessfully tried to cut it off, and the ball scooted into the gap. By the time Donlin retrieved it, Tinker had torn around the bases and scored to put Chicago ahead, 1-0, as the crowd groaned. It was Tinker's fifth home run of the season. The Giants brought their fans back to life in the bottom of the sixth. Buck Herzog led off the inning with a sharp ground ball to third. Steinfeldt managed to corral it, but he rushed his throw and it sailed wide of Chance, allowing Herzog to hustle to second. Bresnahan sacrificed Herzog to third, which brought Donlin, who was in the midst of one of his truly great offensive seasons, to the plate. "Turkey" Mike singled to center to drive in Herzog and tie the score, 1-1.

The game remained deadlocked into the ninth inning. Mathewson retired the Cubs to give New York the chance to win the game in the bottom of the frame. He had pitched a tremendous ballgame with his mistake to Tinker the only blemish. The intensity of the game made nervous wrecks out of the twenty thousand fans in attendance, not to mention all the Cubs fans watching the *Tribune*'s ticker back in Chicago's Orchestra Hall. Jack Pfiester had matched Mathewson's effort, but he ran into trouble in the bottom of the ninth. Art Devlin laced a one-out single to center. Pfiester hunkered down against Moose McCormick. The Giants' left fielder made solid contact, but he hit the ball directly at Evers, who stabbed it and flipped it to Tinker, covering second to force out Devlin. However, they could not turn the double play, and McCormick reached first base safely with two outs. Up next was Fred Merkle, whose defensive gem in the second inning was the primary reason the game remained tied. The stadium erupted when Merkle, a right-handed hitter, ripped a Pfiester pitch into right field for a hit. McCormick tore around second and reached third, putting runners at the corners for Al Bridwell.

Bridwell, who had come to New York as part of the Fred Tenney trade, had enjoyed a nice offensive campaign for the Giants. The twenty-four-year-old finished third on the team with a .285 batting average in 1908. The left-handed hitter readied for Pfiester's delivery as the intense roaring of the fans enveloped Bridwell. Pfiester rocked and fired. Bridwell swung, and his bat firmly connected with the ball shooting it straight back, past Pfiester, and into center field. The fans screamed with delirium. Dozens of them jumped over the seat railing and spilled onto the field as McCormick touched home plate with the winning run. Seeing the swells of people invading the field, Merkle stopped running to second base, peeled out of the infield, and made for the Giants' clubhouse, located beyond center field, to avoid the mad rush.

Although the ensuing details have been debated for over a century, what isn't in dispute is that Merkle didn't touch second base, and it triggered the Cubs, who were in tune to the mistake after their recent experience with Warren Gill in Pittsburgh. The *Tribune* captured the machinations of what happened in its play-by-play:

Bridwell clouted the ball into center field and McCormick scored. As soon as Merkle saw the ball was going safe he did not run to second. In the meantime Hofman fielded the ball and threw to second to catch Merkle. (Giants pitcher Joe) McGinnity rushed out and intercepted the ball, and while the Chicago players were trying to take it away from him the crowd interfered. Evers and Tinker, however, recovered it, and the former touched second and completed the forceout of Merkle.[45]

Umpire Hank O'Day had worked the Gill game and was again on duty. Evers touched second base while holding a baseball and looked at O'Day as the crowd circled them all like buzzing hornets. After conferring with Bob Emslie, the second umpire working the ballgame, who had not seen the play, O'Day called Merkle out. The game could not continue, however, on account of the now hundreds, if not thousands, of fans on the field. The Giants declared they were victorious, and that McCormick had scored the winning run, but O'Day disagreed and declared the score remained 1–1. After the melee quieted down, Charles Dryden managed to find Frank Chance and asked him about the bizarre play. "Manager Chance said tonight he was glad the Chicago club filed that protest on the recent game in Pittsburg. He never expected to see the play come up again, but when it did the Cubs and the umpire were ready for it. Good thing O'Day has a retentive memory," Dryden reported.[46]

For his part, Dryden excoriated Merkle's lack of judgment. "In the ninth round Merkle did a bone-head base-running stunt identical with the recent exhibition which Mr. Gill, also a minor leaguer, gave at Pittsburg three weeks ago."[47] National League president Harry Pulliam upheld O'Day's decision, and the game was declared a tie. Lost in the aftermath was the fact that Merkle had saved a run in the second inning. Instead, by not running the bases according to the letter of the law, Merkle was called out in what became known as "Merkle's Boner."

The Giants won the series finale, 5–4, and reclaimed a one-game lead over the Cubs and Pirates with only a little more than a week remaining in the season. But Chicago caught fire, winning eight of its final nine games. New York won its last two games of the season to join the Cubs atop the standings, which forced a replay of the tied game with the National League pennant at stake.

The state of horse racing increased the already extraordinary interest in the Cubs-Giants game. New York officials had banned wagering at outdoor tracks, so gamblers sought different sporting events to engage in action. They targeted baseball. Suspecting that umpires Bill Klem and Jim Johnstone would work the game, individuals approached them with financial offers to influence the outcome of the game in the Giants' favor. Klem and Johnstone vehemently rebuffed the bribes on moral grounds, and they also explained that they hadn't even been given the assignment. When informed that they would be umpiring the game on October 8, the already stressed umpires asked Secretary John Heydler to reconsider, but they were the best arbiters available near New York. They each described how they had been approached—Klem under the stands after an earlier ballgame, Johnstone at a train stop—by shady characters asking them to cheat. Dr. Joseph Creamer, who had spent a large part of the 1908 season traveling with the Giants, counted out five $500-dollar bills for Klem if he guaranteed the game's result. Creamer implored Klem to see things a different way, as over $20,000 had been wagered on New York, but the umpire refused to budge. Klem and Johnstone wrote signed statements detailing the events and sent them to National League president Harry Pulliam, who locked them away. He did not tell anyone about the bribe attempt.[48]

In the days leading up to the replay game, Mordecai Brown received "black hand" letters that threatened to murder him if he dared pitch against the Giants and beat them. Brown took the letters to Charlie Murphy and Frank Chance and begged to get the start. "Let me pitch just to show those so-and sos they can't win with threats," he fumed.[49] However, Chance decided to go with Pfiester. A hostile crowd of gargantuan size circled the ballgame on October 8. Thousands of fans who had tickets couldn't get inside the Polo Grounds due to the sheer volume of people. The Giants got to a rocky Jack Pfiester in the first inning. The Cubs' southpaw drilled Fred Tenney with his very first pitch then walked Buck Herzog. Pfiester did get Roger Bresnahan on a

swinging strike three, but catcher Johnny Kling dropped the ball. However, in the midst of pouncing on it, he saw out of the corner of his eye
that Herzog had inexplicably wandered off the first base bag. Alertly,
Kling fired the ball to Chance, who tagged Herzog out. It was another
base-running blunder by the Giants. Following the double play, Mike
Donlin cracked a single down the right field line that scored Tenney
to give New York a 1-0 lead. Pfiester, who appeared to be wrestling
with the intensity of the moment, walked Cy Seymour, and Chance
decided that he had seen enough of the lefty. The Cubs' manager
summoned Brown, who had been warming up behind a large swath of
fans in right-center field. "Get the hell out of the way," Brown growled
as he shoved taunting fans. "Here's where you 'black hand' guys get
your chance. If I'm going to get killed I sure know that I'll die before
a capacity crowd."[50] Amid the boos and jeers, Brown struck out Art
Devlin to end the inning.

"Miner" Brown, so called because he spent his early years working
in the coal mines of Indiana, entered the Hall of Fame in 1949. Brown
won over two hundred games during his illustrious career. He threw at
least six shutouts in five consecutive seasons from 1906 through 1910.
He was truly one of the most magnificent pitchers of the Deadball
Era, and of his performance on October 8, 1908, Brown claimed, "I
was about as good that day as I ever was in my life."[51] When the Cubs
tallied four runs in the top of the third inning, highlighted by Chance's
two-run double, the game was all but over. Brown allowed a run in the
seventh inning but otherwise quieted the Giants' bats as Chicago beat
New York, 4-2, to win the pennant.

Brown retired Al Bridwell on a groundout to Tinker for the final
out of the game. As soon as Chance caught Tinker's throw, the Cubs
sprinted for their lives from an angry mob of New Yorkers pouring
onto the field with bad intentions, but they didn't reach the safety of
the clubhouse unscathed. Chance got walloped in the throat so hard
that the impact tore cartilage. Someone swung a knife blade at Jack
Pfiester that caught his shoulder. "We made it to the dressing room
and barricaded the door," Brown recalled. "Outside wild men were
yelling for our blood—really."[52] Rather than celebrate, the players

quickly changed clothes; then, after the raucous scene died down, six policemen escorted the Cubs back to their hotel in a patrol wagon. They collected their belongings and, again under the watchful eye of law enforcement, headed to the station, where they jumped on a train bound for Detroit and the 1908 World Series.

Back in Chicago fans, including Edythe Chance and Ruby Tinker, watching the recreation of the game at Orchestra Hall, erupted when the final out was posted. Charlie Murphy was euphoric with the Cubs' hard-fought pennant. Capturing their third consecutive National League flag, especially after such a trying season, full of internal strife and injuries, deeply satisfied him. "Manager Chance deserves a world of credit for his generalship, individual play, and incessant earnestness. Every member of the team is also deserving of unstinted praise. No gamer ball club has ever trod the diamond . . . I am glad our victory today was a decisive one, so that it cannot be charged to anything of a technical nature," Murphy gushed.[53]

The Cubs would once again take on the Detroit Tigers, who emerged victorious from a tightly contested American League race. Foremost in Murphy's mind was how to maximize the added reserved seats in the reconfigured ballpark for the World Series. Reporters from around the country typically sat in reserved seats, making them unavailable to the paying public. Inundated with requests, Murphy balked at giving away some of his choicest seats to the writers. He wasn't the only one who wanted to limit passes for baseball's marquee event. Earlier in the summer, the *Saturday Evening Post* requested passes from the National Commission to cover the World Series. Harry Pulliam acquiesced, but he warned Garry Herrmann that restrictions needed to be imposed because some of the stadiums had very little room to squeeze in all of the press.[54] Seats were meant to be sold to fans.

Murphy's stubborn refusal to work amicably with the newspapers irritated the reporters, who vehemently protested being ostracized. Several writers responded by banding together to establish the Baseball Writers Association of America, a new union for the scribes. Chicago's Hugh Fullerton and Sy Sanborn, who both knew Murphy well, were heavily involved in creating the organization, which sought to improve

working conditions as well as "assist the various club owners to eliminate from their press boxes the nonworking element which frequently
in the past has preempted much of the space assigned to working men
and made difficult the work of those whose sole purpose in life is to
satisfy the constantly increasing demand for baseball dope."[55]

Inexplicably, enthusiastic Cubs fans, determined to get reserved
seats for the World Series, found tickets nearly impossible to find from
official outlets and were horrified to discover that scalpers around town
had somehow acquired a vast number of them. The Cubs announced
that reserved seats for games in Chicago would be available for purchase at Spalding's on Friday, October 9, at 9:00 a.m. Droves of eager
fans lined up early around the sporting goods store with their money
in hand but, after waiting in line for hours, they were told that tickets
were unavailable because the printer had not delivered them yet.[56]
Undaunted, they showed up at the West Side Grounds on Saturday, the
day the series began, and waited in line for hours in hopes of securing
reserved seat tickets from the box office. However, after only a few
sales were made, the crowd was sent away empty-handed. A similar
scene occurred on Sunday morning.

Frustrated and disappointed fans who could not buy tickets for face
value were incensed to discover that, somehow, scalpers appeared on
the streets of Chicago throughout the weekend in possession of hundreds, if not thousands, of tickets available for purchase at exorbitant
prices. How were they able to procure so many tickets? The mystery
deepened when the Cubs returned 885 unused reserved seat coupons
to the commission as part of its receipt tabulations from Game Three.[57]
Confusion reigned over what had actually happened to the tickets,
and it initially forced Ban Johnson to awkwardly defend Murphy publicly. "Considering the shortness of the time which elapsed between
the deciding game in the National league race and the opening of the
world's series, one does not feel like criticizing any one," Johnson
told reporters.[58] The argument was made that this was not the first
ticket snafu in World Series history. The quick turnaround, political
heavyweights calling in favors, and issues with the printer all became
scapegoats for the debacle. However, fans heatedly pointed out, in

letters they wrote to the National Commission and local newspapers, that these lame excuses simply did not make sense. While Spalding's and the Cubs' office did not have tickets to sell, an ample supply of general-admission and reserved seats could be bought from scalpers at hotels and cigar stands throughout the city. The 1908 World Series played to this bitter backdrop in Chicago.

The series opened at Bennett Park in Detroit on Saturday, October 10, and just as they had done in 1907, the Tigers once again let the opportunity to take an early series lead slip through their paws. Ahead 6–5, Detroit pitcher Ed Summers retired Johnny Evers on a groundout to first to open the ninth inning, and then the wheels fell off. Chicago rapped six consecutive hits off Summers as it amassed five runs to flip its deficit into a 10–6 advantage. Mordecai Brown recorded the last three outs of the game to give the Cubs a 1–0 lead in the series. The teams hopped on trains to the Windy City for Games Two and Three.

Back in Chicago, Orval Overall locked horns with Bill Donovan in a tightly contested Game Two. Although it was played on a Sunday, only 17,760 fans showed up. It wasn't a minuscule number of fans, but the crowd paled in comparison to many previous iterations. Those that did attend witnessed a crackling pitchers' duel between Overall and Donovan. The game remained scoreless into the bottom of the eighth inning, when the Cubs broke the deadlock by scoring five times against the Tigers' right-hander, highlighted by Joe Tinker's two-run homer. The Tigers pushed across a run in the ninth on Ty Cobb's RBI single, but Overall polished off Detroit before it could mount a serious threat, as the Cubs won, 6–1.

The clubs were back at it again the following day for Game Three with Detroit needing a win to stay in the series. Meanwhile, disgust continued to build within the Cubs' fan base toward the ongoing issues with reserved ticket sales. Scalpers continued to wave around tickets that the fans refused to buy. Irritated fans encouraged each other to skip the game as a show of solidarity against Murphy, who they blamed for allowing scalpers to get their hands on tickets. While some of the scalpers had simply paid young people to stand at the front of the line for them at the box office, that did not satisfactorily explain how so many tickets had flooded the secondary market when fans had been turned away from the box office.

As the fans' frustration morphed into anger, Murphy remained silent. Whether he committed a series of snafus or committed disingenuous acts, the mounting strain of the situation deeply affected him. Prior to Game Three, Murphy collapsed in his office. The Cubs' team doctor rushed to his side, but he recovered well enough to complete the day's business. However, Murphy left the stadium and returned to his house rather than watch the game. The team issued a statement that claimed Murphy was suffering from pneumonia-type symptoms.[59]

Detroit added to everyone's misery by beating the Cubs and tightening the series to 2–1. Jack Pfiester blew a 3–1 lead as Detroit scored five times in the sixth inning on its way to an 8–3 win. Once again, the combination of the botched ticket sale and boycott by a group of fans impacted attendance, as only 14,543 fans, some from Detroit, sat in the stands. Following the game, the teams boarded trains for Detroit. Murphy stayed home.

The Cubs' pitching staff had led the team to an extraordinary number of wins over the past three seasons, and two of its stalwarts shut down the Tigers. Brown, the curveball maestro, fluttered and floated his pitches around the Tigers' bats in route to a complete-game 3–0 shutout in Game Four. Not to be outdone, Overall blazed his fastball past Detroit's hitters in his own complete game performance in Game Five. Overall retired the last twelve batters he faced as he blanked the Tigers, 2–0, to clinch Chicago's second consecutive World Series championship.

Not many baseball fans witnessed the Cubs' historic achievement. Shockingly small crowds in Detroit compounded the financial fallout for the players. Kept away by chilly weather, and the hopeless plight of their team, only six thousand fans attended Game Five at Bennett Park. The *Chicago Tribune* was all over the story, and it published a report that estimated an astounding fifteen thousand fewer spectators than anticipated attended the World Series games in Chicago due, in no small part, to the ticket scandal and that, all told, the players' share of receipts had taken a $25,000 hit. The financial loss infuriated Frank Chance, who felt betrayed, along with the rest of the team. They aimed no ill will toward their supporters who stayed away from the West Side Grounds, but they faulted Murphy personally for the catastrophe. The erupted fissure in their relationship stubbornly refused to heal.

Just over a week after the scandal broke, the *Chicago Tribune* reported that Garry Herrmann, chairman of the National Commission, "which at the request of hundreds of fans has undertaken to investigate the charges of ticket scalping at the recent world's series between the Cubs and Tigers, has sent letters to newspaper writers and others in Chicago asking for facts known by them to be true relative to the matter."[60] The organization vigorously defended itself. Murphy asked front office employee Charlie Thomas to write a letter of explanation that detailed what went wrong with the ticket sales. Murphy submitted Thomas's statement to Herrmann but not before leaking it to the *Tribune* for public consumption. Thomas blamed the printer for the debacle at Spalding's on the first day of the scheduled sale. Thomas was supposed to receive the tickets at 8:00 a.m., so he and his assistant could complete the reservations the Cubs already had accepted from their regular patrons before heading over to Spalding's, but they arrived more than ninety minutes late. Simultaneously, a gathering crowd filled their office wanting to buy reserved seat tickets. Thomas tried to prioritize selling tickets to fans that he recognized as frequent visitors to West Side Ball Park. Amid the chaos, the office phone began ringing off the hook. It was a representative from Spalding's wondering where the tickets were and when they would arrive at the store. "We informed them that it would be impossible for us to get over there with the tickets," Thomas said. "All we could do was to stay where we were, and do the best we could." Similar issues plagued the overwhelmed Thomas on Saturday and Sunday. As for the unused tickets the Cubs returned to the National Commission, Thomas explained that a hundred of them had been held in reserve for an emergency and that another large batch had been earmarked for a Detroit newspaper that wound up only using half of the seats it requested. As for the issue of scalpers getting their hands on a large number of tickets, Thomas acknowledged that it was probably true:

We had 6,234 reserved and box seats to dispose of for each game, and we endeavored to do so to the best of our ability. We could not follow every purchaser to see what he did with his tickets. The scalpers had tickets I am told; lots of tickets. I do not doubt it in the least. Every trick and influence obtainable was brought into play, undoubtedly, by scalpers to secure tickets," he declared. The bottom line, a defensive Thomas added with an air of disgust, was that the huge job was too much to handle with less than 24 hours of notice: "The whole thing, simmered down to one point, is this: Two men cannot be expected to take care of the demands of a whole city like Chicago satisfactorily and to every one's liking, especially when they have to do the work in an ordinary business office and with as short a time as we had in which to prepare for a series like the world's championship series.[61]

Letters from upset fans bombarded newspaper editors throughout town, and many of them were printed. It was a public relations disaster for Murphy. Fans' tempers flared, and their unheeded demand for a reasonable explanation kept them running hot. Murphy tried to calm the storm by apologizing in a letter to the *Chicago Tribune*. "We deplore the fact that all were not taken care of satisfactorily, because our great team has been handsomely patronized, and that support is heartily appreciated, both by the management and by the ball players," he said.[62]

After a drawn-out investigation, the National Commission added new oversight regulations on its selling practices, and it did so in writing. "To prevent a recurrence of this kind in the future, the commission will adopt rules and regulations governing the sale of these tickets by them for all coming world's series."[63] The commission made it a point to acknowledge that Chicagoans had been wronged by the Cubs and said it "will hereafter use its authority to prevent, as has already been stated herein, a recurrence of outrage and imposition on the Chicago baseball public such as it was subjected to during the last world's series."[64] The National Commission officially censured Murphy but did not discipline him, or the organization, further.

Two years later, Hugh Fullerton claimed that the National Commission had collected enough evidence to prove that someone in the Cubs front office colluded with scalpers, but it buried the information to avoid a larger scandal. "It had evidence regarding the disappearance of one big block of tickets from a ticket rack to which there were but two keys—and it had the evidence of Manager Chance that one scalper, caught with these tickets in his possession, stated that he procured them direct from a person connected with the club," Fullerton charged.[65]

In the meantime, the *Chicago Tribune* unleashed a fiery editorial, in the aftermath of the ticket scandal—titled "The American Game!"—in which it excoriated the increasingly problematic behavior of baseball's caretakers. "The diamond is clean. How long will it remain so if there is nothing but muck in the business management?" it pointedly asked. The editorial continued, "The exhibition which has been going on among the chief beneficiaries and high priests of professional baseball is the most discreditable page in the history of the game. If it doesn't stop and stop quick, if decency and fair play don't get a foothold in the management, and get it quick, the finish of professional baseball is in sight."[66]

The ticket scandal marred the high-water mark in Cubs' franchise history. It spoiled Murphy's relationships with the players and fans to a degree from which he never fully recovered. Murphy also alienated many of his fellow executives, particularly Harry Pulliam, who questioned the integrity of the Cubs organization.

7

THE WAR OF 1908–9

In late August, three weeks before the Cubs won the World Series, Joe Tinker and his wife, Ruby, celebrated moving into their new house in Oak Park by throwing a lavish party. Tinker, who later emerged as a notable vaudeville star in his own right, hired a number of exceptional musical talents to perform at the gathering of thirty guests, including Joe Bren, a ragtime composer, and his vocalist wife, who sang several numbers. Among the partygoers was Tinker's boss, and new neighbor, Charlie Murphy. Everyone enjoyed the festive evening.[1] How long ago the party must have felt to Murphy when he woke up on October 15. His Cubs were champions again, the first National League club to win back-to-back World Series titles, but the simmering anger the players and fans felt toward him overshadowed the triumph.

Atop Murphy's list of priorities following the just-concluded campaign was his annual meeting with Frank Chance to debrief the season and lay the groundwork for the organization's off-season plans, before the manager left Chicago for his winter home in Southern California. Inside Murphy's office, their conversation began amicably enough, but the chilly atmosphere became downright edgy when Chance asked Murphy to rework the financial terms of the four-year contract extension that he had signed on September 7. Chance had named the dollar amount of his deal, but the Cubs had resided in third place on the day Chance agreed to the contract, and the club's championship, combined with the loss of money from the ticket scandal, emboldened the field general to seek additional money.

Murphy balked. He told Chance that the increased revenue generated by the Cubs' title boosted the value of the manager's shares and dividends, which ought to suffice for increased earnings. Stoked to anger, Murphy burst into a condescending tirade in which he questioned several of Chance's proposed personnel moves, as well as a number of his managerial tactics, during the season. He piled on by needling Chance about losing the 1906 City Series to the White Sox, a random critique that remained a sore spot for Murphy. The hotly contested meeting reached a crescendo when Murphy took a personal shot at Chance by calling him a "fat-head" for inflating his own importance to the organization.[2] Murphy told Chance that he believed "the Peerless Leader was getting as much as he was worth," and then threatened to trade him.[3]

The intensity of Murphy's sudden reaction shocked Chance. More precisely, Murphy's searing criticisms cut him to the bone. Chance knew that he alone had determined the monetary value of his extension, but he hoped Murphy would see things his way and compromise. Chance never anticipated having his job performance questioned so severely, even though he accepted the reality that the players in the clubhouse bristled at his decision-making at times. After all, the Cubs roster was full of strong personalities, and Chance, a firebrand in his own right, understood that. Murphy had strong opinions as well, but he and Chance generally got along well. As a result, Chance tended to see the best in Murphy, in spite of his faults. However, Murphy's biting retort deeply offended him. "From that argument . . . he began telling me about the mistakes I had made managing the club," said Chance, in describing how the meeting with Murphy deteriorated. "One of his criticisms was so palpably unjust that I offered to let him write out his own statement of the case and submit it to the baseball writers of Chicago, and if any of them said he was right I would admit he was. He refused to do anything of the kind, and when he began to talk to trading me off to Cincinnati I concluded it would be better to make a change next year if he felt that way. My offer to give him $2,000 in cash if he would make the deal was on the level and still goes."[4] At that, Chance stormed out of Murphy's office "vowing he would not return until he was sent for."[5]

Murphy's flashpoint of anger fractured his relationship with Chance and threatened to deprive the franchise of its manager, not to mention break up the most famous infield in baseball. An infuriated Chance refused to go into the Cubs' office the following day, and he expressed his displeasure with Murphy to Sy Sanborn of the *Chicago Tribune* before he and his wife, Edythe, boarded their train for Los Angeles. "I would go to the Cincinnati team if they traded me . . . but I would not go to any other club in the league. I would stay in California rather than that. I'm going to buy an orange grove out there right away, anyway, and won't have to come back." While few of Murphy's associates avoided his barbs, Chance expressed his bewilderment at what he perceived to be an unwarranted outburst from Murphy. "I don't know but a trade would be the best way out of the difficulty, and told Murphy so. I'll say this for him. He never has shown a disposition to interfere with or critici(z)e my work before but has given me free rein for three years and has been mighty good to his players. I never knew a man to treat his players better. But, as I told him, he may think next year he knows enough baseball to begin to interfere. I could not stand the worry of that in addition to the other worries."[6] Several Cubs, including Mordecai Brown and Joe Tinker, met Chance and Edythe at the Northwestern Depot to say goodbye for the winter. Chance told them about Murphy's outburst, particularly the team president's threat to trade him to Cincinnati. "Well, boss, tell Murphy to throw me in with you for good measure," one of them cracked.[7]

Murphy shrugged off even the most personal of disputes, and he scoffed at the idea that his clash with Chance would have any lasting impact. Murphy's outburst was a momentary flash—a defensive reaction to a perceived business threat—and he did not mean anything personal by it. "In the management of a ball club there are always little disagreements. The same has been true of myself and Manager Chance, but nothing that would warrant calling out the militia or the police has happened. The story is amusing to me. Mr. Chance and myself are just as friendly as we always have been."[8] Murphy's assessment of the situation demonstrated his unwillingness to admit the intensity of Chance's displeasure with him, at least publicly. The two men had shared a good working relationship, but Murphy's criticisms had gone too far. Murphy worked closely with Chance and should have known he took things personally. As newspapers around the country picked up the story, stunned people around the game raised their eyebrows at Murphy's flippancy with Chance. Slack-jawed owners around the game would go to great lengths to keep a manager of Chance's ilk very content. Their views were mixed as to whether Murphy and Chance would be able to fix their relationship.

While members of the media close to Chance doubted the partnership could be mended, writers outside of Chicago thought of the trouble as a situational hiccup that would soon resolve itself. Jack Ryder of the *Cincinnati Enquirer* was among several reporters who revealed that a potential Chance trade to the Reds would include Hans Lobert and Dick Hoblitzell heading to the Cubs in exchange, but the sportswriter seriously doubted that the deal would be made. "The fans need not grow excited over the repeated reports from Chicago," Ryder warned.[9] For his part, the *Sporting Life*'s Bill Phelon could not see the deal coming to fruition either and suggested the warring Cubs leadership would eventually make peace. "Charles W. Murphy and Frank L. Chance are too good a pair of jolly gentlemen to quarrel. Both have real red blood in their make-up, both have positive ideas of their own, and neither is a quitter. It is only natural that two such men would have rows, and plenty of them, as to the management of a pennant club, and each should gladly let his share of the argument die down," Phelon observed.[10]

Chance received overwhelming support from his players. No fewer than five Cubs wrote letters to their manager over the winter declaring their intention to hold out as a group if Murphy refused to meet his demands. But, while he appreciated the loyalty of the players, Chance's disagreement with Murphy did not involve his teammates, and he did not want to be the reason anyone lost out on a salary during the upcoming season.[11]

Murphy nonchalantly ignored the increasing debris crashing around him from his fallout with Chance and turned his attention to the presidential election. On November 3, 1908, the American people elected William Howard Taft as the next president of the United States. An ebullient Murphy rushed to Cincinnati to celebrate the victory of Charles's younger half brother. However, the Queen City press only wanted to ask Murphy about Chance's status. "Frank has signed for four years and he is a man of honor. I am sure he will carry out his contract. Personally we are the best of friends, and I would want no other manager. We have argued now and then about matters of policy, but I have never interfered with his just prerogatives, and never shall," Murphy tried to assure everyone. However, Murphy's attention just now focused elsewhere. "President Murphy said his sole object in coming here was to shake hands with President-elect Taft," the *Chicago Tribune* reported.[12]

Jack Ryder caught up with Murphy in Cincinnati, but the talkative owner proved to be less loquacious than the beat writer had hoped. "President Murphy of the world's champions, who came to town to shake the massive mitt of Bill Taft, did not care to enter into a deep discussion of his little difficulty with Manager Frank Chance," Ryder conveyed.

That said, Murphy reiterated the situation from his perspective. "Chance has signed a four-year contract with the Chicago Club. He affixed his signature to this document on September 7, and the figures named in it were his own. Now you can draw your own conclusions. It does not seem at all probable to me that he will refuse to play ball under a recent contract, the terms of which were settled by himself."

Although Chance received much of the sympathy, Ryder empathized with Murphy's view on their spat, arguing that Chance had signed his contract when the Cubs did not have the upper hand in the National League race. Ryder argued that, after overtaking the Pirates and Giants to win the pennant and knocking off Detroit in the World Series, Chance "immediately jumped to the conclusion that his services were more valuable than he had rated them a month before and asked to have the document revised in his favor." Ryder supported Murphy's decision not to renegotiate the contract and excoriated other Cubs players for angling for raises. "So far Murphy appears to have all the better of the argument," Ryder told his readers. "It is well known that the continued success of the Cubs has made the members of the team money-crazy. No other club was ever so unanimously avaricious of the almighty dollar."[13] However, in the end, Ryder believed that the blowup would be smoothed over in due time.

Harry Pulliam carried a secret, and it weighed on his conscience like a heavy stone. He knew that he had to tell the owners about the attempt to bribe umpires Bill Klem and Jim Johnstone prior to the Cubs-Giants replay game but, in doing so, the National League president would risk the further wrath of John T. Brush and the New York Giants. Pulliam trembled at the thought of more psychological punishment. He loathed the frequently cold receptions he received around town for upholding Hank O'Day's ruling against Fred Merkle. Fans at the Polo Grounds hated the sight of Pulliam and let him know it. Pulliam shuddered to think that things could actually get worse.

Pulliam expressed his concern about gambling to the gathering of magnates at the winter meeting in December. The owners reelected Pulliam, but not unanimously as Brush refused to attend the meeting. Pulliam expressed his discouragement at the Giants' dislike of him and hinted that a specific issue was bothering him. The owners coerced the reluctant Pulliam to share what troubled him. He explained the bribe presented to Klem and Johnstone, to the astonishment of his audience. Pulliam told them that he had wanted to retain a lawyer to advise him, but he didn't have enough money to pay for it, so he locked the umpires' written testimonies away and stayed quiet. Pulliam's divulgence riveted Murphy, the primary beneficiary of their honest umpiring. "To my mind it is the most sensational and important thing that I ever heard of affecting the National League since I have been in it," Murphy told Pulliam. "I believe that is a God-send that you did not consult a lawyer. I think it is a fortunate thing that you did not consult the Board of Directors. I am free to confess that if you had consulted me, I would probably, in my Irish impetuosity, have flown off the handle, and there would have been a scandal. I have not the slightest doubt that all the claims in those statements are true. I have implicit confidence in both those umpires. I have implicit confidence in your honesty, and I am satisfied that this has disturbed your peace of mind night and day since it has happened . . . It rocks the very foundation of our sport."[14]

Murphy knew that Organized Baseball faced extinction without the public's trust, and he wanted to address the issue without any equivocation. "The perpetuity of our game is on the absolute faith and honesty of the sport," he said. The other owners agreed, and they spent the next several hours debating their options. Barney Dreyfuss wanted to go to the district attorney. Murphy thought the newspapermen ought to be apprised of the story without delay, to avoid any damaging leaks. "There has been a new era which has dawned in this country. This is the age of publicity. I am very strongly in favor of giving this thing out in its entirety, with the exception of suppressing the name of people whose names we could not use."[15]

The magnates sent Garry Herrmann and Charlie Ebbets to retrieve John T. Brush to include him in their discussions. Brush joined them the following day and expressed his dismay at Dr. Joseph Creamer's involvement in the developing scandal. Brush admitted that Creamer had traveled with the team throughout 1908 and openly confessed that the Giants had paid him for his services. However, Brush explained to the other owners how angry he had been at Secretary Fred Knowles for allowing Creamer access to the team, which had produced this unexpected expense. A furious Brush had written a check and then yelled at Knowles for his error in front of Creamer and John McGraw.

The magnates appointed a committee of Pulliam, Brush, and Herrmann to probe the matter and empowered it to retain counsel, if appropriate. Murphy knew that Pulliam was scheduled to travel to California, which generated the need for an additional committee member. The owners tapped Charlie Ebbets. Strangely, they appointed Brush as the committee's chairman in spite of his organization's close connection to the scandal. Pulliam wanted to show Brush a modicum of respect to avoid further animosity, and the owners wanted to demonstrate their belief in the innocence of the New York organization. In spite of their expressed intentions, the selection of Brush seemed unwise. The committee would examine the issue and report back at the spring meeting. In a move that was satisfactory to Murphy, the National League wrote a statement that explained that it was opening up an investigation into the bribery charges.

In the end, all the noise vanished without even a whimper. Baseball banned Creamer for life, but the doctor's backers did not face similar charges. Murphy's opinion over Klem's testimony oscillated as time went by. Murphy believed Klem, but he also thought that umpires had a tendency to exaggerate claims of poor player behavior in their game reports. Lawyer Delancey Nicoll informed the committee that Creamer had not committed a crime and, although stories swirled about the involvement of "Big" Tim Sullivan or possibly John McGraw, Christy Mathewson, and Roger Bresnahan, the punishment of the doctor closed the dubious episode.

National League president Harry Pulliam loathed the public shootout between Charlie Murphy and Frank Chance that splashed across the sports pages of America's newspapers. It was beyond bad for business. Murphy's inability to tamp his emotions angered Pulliam, and new rumors of Chance's possible retirement to the West Coast made Pulliam desperate to resolve the situation. Pulliam visited Chance in California to speak with him in person. Pulliam wound up sitting down with Chance twice, once before Christmas and again afterward, paying for both trips out of his own pocket.[16] During their conversations, Pulliam got the sense that, deep down, Chance wanted to return to Chicago, but Murphy would have to break the thickened ice between them. Chance admitted to Pulliam that he alone had set the financial terms of the extension, but he regretted signing it so hastily. That lament is what prompted Chance to ask for more money in his meeting with Murphy but, Chance added, he went into the conversation willing to live with the deal he had signed if Murphy denied the request. However, Murphy's acidic retort offended Chance's senses and hardened his resolve against Murphy. Pulliam empathized with Chance. Murphy's outburst annoyed the league president at a particularly sensitive time for him. Pulliam was suffering from serious bouts of depression and anxiety caused, in no small part, by the stress of living in New York during the aftermath of his unpopular ruling for Johnny Evers's Cubs and against Fred Merkle's local Giants in September. Following their meetings, Pulliam wrote Chance a letter in which he strongly expressed his desire to see the manager return to the Cubs in 1909. "I sincerely trust you will be back with us, because I want you and believe the National league can ill afford to lose you."[17] Pulliam then reached out to Murphy and encouraged him to visit Chance in Los Angeles to patch up their rift.[18] However, Murphy showed no indication that he planned on extending an olive branch.

Murphy's ambivalence infuriated Pulliam. On January 14 Pulliam expressed his outrage to fellow National Commission member Garry Herrmann. Pulliam alleged to Herrmann that he possessed evidence of underhanded behavior by Murphy relating to the final series between the Cubs and Giants during the just-completed season, and he was thinking of going public with it. "If Mr. Murphy wants any battle I will carry the war to Chicago, and I know something personally concerning the management of the business affairs of the Chicago club concerning the games played between the Chicago and New York clubs in the last series in the city of Chicago." Pulliam wrote, "that will not well in print" in pencil—perhaps omitting the word "look"—strongly hinting that he possessed damning information about the Cubs' conduct.[19] However, Pulliam never went public with the information, which remained a mystery. Herrmann acknowledged Pulliam's frustration but recommended that the league president not let Murphy, whom the Reds president had known for years, upset him so dramatically. "Keep on watching the flowers in Central park and murmur the spring song to yourself and think of 'your Kentucky' and the sausages at the Loughrey club and all your friends, and to hell with Murphy and Thomas."[20] Pulliam must have taken Herrmann's advice because his threat to expose Murphy fizzled upon arrival almost two months later.

The calendar turned to 1909 with no movement between Murphy and Chance, although a green shoot of hope sprouted in California. As planned, Chance purchased an orange grove on the eastern side of Los Angeles County, for $38,500, and he hinted to Chicagoans, in a reply to a telegram from the *Tribune,* that his return to the Cubs might still be possible.[21] "I wish I could let the Cub fans know if I was going to manage the team this year. It is up to President Murphy. Personally I hope to be with the Cubs. President Murphy knows the conditions under which I will manage the team. I will absolutely not manage under any other conditions. I am feeling great," read Chance's communiqué.[22] Rather than prepare for spring training, however, Chance relinquished his role as a bookmaker at the Santa Anita racetrack and turned his attention to the new ranch.

With the season approaching Murphy realized he had to take Chance's retirement threat seriously. Murphy penned a cordial note to Chance, who responded in kind. Their exchange of "friendly letters" opened communication but, by late January, their business impasse remained. "I want control of my team on and off the field, and Murphy opposes this. If he does not concede me this privilege, I will not return," Chance maintained.[23]

Murphy's standoff with Chance remained the feature conflict throughout the first month of the year, but anger bubbled throughout the rest of the Cubs roster against Murphy. Several players, particularly Johnny Kling and Mordecai Brown, remained frustrated at Murphy's unwillingness to follow through on a late-season declaration he had made to Chance that he would distribute a $10,000 bonus among the roster if the Cubs won the pennant. The players felt cheated because the ticket scandal during the World Series had cost them significant dollars, and now Murphy had yet to pay the bonus. Murphy had to move quickly to pacify their anger, or he risked a complete mutiny.

Murphy used the local press to get his side of the story out to the players, scattered throughout the country. He acknowledged having had a conversation about the money with Chance as they traveled together to the Polo Grounds for their replay game against the Giants. Murphy claimed that he came across a newspaper article in which New York owner John T. Brush suggested he would give Giants players the entire share of gate receipts that day. Murphy turned to Chance and said, "If he can reward them in that way, I see no reason why I cannot do the same thing." However, the National Commission strictly forbade the paying of additional bonus money. For his part, Chance warned Murphy not to break any rules.

Of course, the Cubs had won the game, and then the issue of the bonus hung in the air like smoke over the South Side stockyards. In the interview, Murphy explained that he had already written a check for $10,000 and turned it over to the National Commission, but complications with the rules had arisen that forbade him from distributing the money. The players wanted to be financially rewarded for winning a third straight pennant and second consecutive championship, but Murphy bristled at their aggressive posturing. "I am still anxious to see the money in the players' hands, and it will be placed there as soon as I can accomplish it without offending the commission," he said. "As for the portion of the 'grapevine dispatch' (all of which I believe was written in Chicago), which says Kling, Brown, and others will not have any dealings with me until I have fulfilled my promise, I will say, for one thing, I never made a promise to my ball players which I did not fulfill, and, for another, that the players named are under contract to play next season with the Cubs. There is no law compelling them to play ball. They will be with us if they want to. If not, that is their own affair."[24]

Despite the commission's rule against owners distributing reward payments, American League president Ban Johnson told Harvey Woodruff, the sports editor of the *Chicago Tribune*, that he would vote to make an exception in this case, not as a favor to Murphy, but to limit the damage of Chicago's World Series ticket issues. "While this rule against the giving of bonuses or rewards was adopted to be observed, there are mitigating circumstances in this case which in my opinion would justify granting the favor," Johnson said. "It is known that the Cubs and Tigers did not receive as their share of the world's series as much money as they would have received if there had been more time for perfecting arrangements for the sale of tickets, or if there had not been mismanagement or carelessness in conducting the sale in Chicago. These facts would seem to justify the commission in making an exception to the rule in favor of Mr. Murphy if he so desires."[25]

Woodruff reached out to Harry Pulliam to ask if he would give Murphy permission to distribute the bonus, as Johnson had decided to do.

Pulliam replied, "Ordinarily I believe in living up to our rules to the letter, but there are exceptions to all rules and, under the circumstances, and on the basis of the facts as stated by you in your telegram to me, I will join Mr. Johnson in granting Mr. Murphy permission to give the members of the Chicago Base Ball Club the sum of Ten Thousand Dollars."[26]

As Murphy and the commission hashed out the issues surrounding the bonus payment, Harvey Woodruff took it upon himself to broker peace between the Cubs' two most powerful cogs. On the surface, Woodruff, the sports editor at the *Tribune*, appeared to be an unlikely arbiter, but his long-standing relationships with both Murphy and Chance gave him unique insight into their temperaments. Woodruff had been part of the sports scene in Chicago for a decade, having first written articles for the *Chicago Times-Herald* as a college student. He dropped out of the University of Chicago in 1897 and soon became the sports editor at the *Times-Herald*. Afterward, he spent three years at the *Chicago Record* before landing a job as a sportswriter and copy reader for the *Chicago Tribune* in 1901. As a pair of youngsters only separated in age by one year, there is little doubt that Woodruff and Chance met during the latter's rookie season with the Cubs in 1898. Both shared a love of horse racing, and the two became friends during the ensuing years. If anyone could navigate the conflict between the two men, it would be Harvey Woodruff.[27]

Now, the bespectacled newspaperman found himself on a diplomatic mission to Los Angeles with the future of the two-time defending World Series Champion Cubs franchise hanging in the balance. Woodruff, who took it upon himself to operate as an intermediary "[on] behalf of the baseball fans of Chicago," arrived in Southern California on the morning of Saturday, February 6, and found Chance "madder than the proverbial wet hen." Just that morning, Chance had received a letter from Murphy that, according to Woodruff, contained a paragraph which he "didn't like a little bit." Now, Chance was busily making preparations to return to Chicago the following week but to sell his house and shares in the franchise instead of getting ready for the season. Woodruff, who knew Murphy as well, gave the owner the benefit of the doubt, expressing that the section of the letter that miffed Chance "possibly was thoughtless, and I do not believe intended to be insulting." Chance had just fired off his angry response to Murphy when Woodruff met up with him. "One hated to see that message go," Woodruff lamented. "Not because it was anything so terrible in itself, but because of the quick impulsive nature of Murphy, who sometimes says things and then is sorry afterward, and the temperament of Chance, with whom sarcasm leaves a scar."[28]

Incredibly, Woodruff managed to calm Chance down enough for the two of them to have a heart-to-heart conversation. Woodruff understood Chance. He knew the incredibly tough "Husk" Chance who boxed in the off-season, withstood being struck by bottles hurled from the stands, and even, according to Johnny Evers, lost the full volume of his voice for several months due to torn cartilage after a fan punched him in the Adam's apple after the 1908 replay game in New York.[29] Woodruff also knew Chance as the Peerless Leader. He understood how seriously Chance took managing the Cubs and how deeply he cared about developing his players. Woodruff appreciated how Chance acquired the struggling Orval Overall from Cincinnati in 1906 and nurtured the young right-hander through his difficulties, allowing him to build confidence and regain strength, which culminated in the rise of one of the best pitchers in the National League. Woodruff revealed just how well he knew the man by dubbing Chance "the most sensitive of men."[30] Woodruff alone could not assuage Chance's hurt feelings. Only Murphy could undo the damage he had caused, but Woodruff managed to elicit a confession from Chance that he wanted to stay in Chicago.

Seeing a sliver of an opening to present an outsider's perspective to the quarrel, Woodruff countered Chance's entrenched position with three points. First, Woodruff suggested to Chance that his salary was worth considering. Chance had just completed a three-year contract to play and manage the Cubs and, according to Chance, he "never asked or received any present or bonus outside the world's series money, the same as the other players" despite his multiple responsibilities. He would be throwing away the higher compensation included in the new extension. Second, Woodruff astutely noted that the value of Chance's shares in the club would lose value if he did not return, which would cost him financially. Finally, Woodruff told his friend that he "owed a duty" to Cubs fans who had so passionately supported the team and boosted the value of his original $10,000 investment five or six times in addition to three years' worth of dividends. Chance listened intently, and Woodruff could sense his friend's steely iciness beginning to thaw. He acknowledged Woodruff's points—his father-in-law could keep an eye on the orange grove—but Chance maintained he would not budge because of the principle of the matter. Nevertheless, Woodruff observed that his friend "was in a receptive mood."[31]

"Why not submit the whole affair to arbitration?" Woodruff asked Chance.

Chance replied that he was open to the idea but doubted that Murphy would consent. As the wheels inside Woodruff's mind churned about this latest development, he deftly interrogated Chance to ascertain the true depths of his anger toward Murphy. Woodruff wanted to glean specifics from Chance so he could formulate the best explanation of where things stood and communicate it to the Cubs president. Chance again expressed his anger at Murphy's poor treatment of him at the end-of-the-season meeting. However, he limited any further criticisms of Murphy to noting that the Cubs president "sometimes lacked tact" when communicating with players. Woodruff could feel a sense of hope welling within his heart when Chance expressed dismay at his conflict with Murphy. Reported Woodruff, "Chance said Murphy had treated him and the other players well, had kept his promises, and really it was unfortunate that troubles had arisen." Chance, who had a scheduled dinner to attend that evening, said goodbye to his longtime friend and headed out to Ocean Park.[32]

Charlie Murphy was at home that afternoon, in Oak Park, when the telephone rang. The call emanated from the *Chicago Tribune*, and the voice on the other end of the line informed Murphy that a message had just arrived for him from Los Angeles. A surprised Murphy listened as Woodruff's telegram of some 400 to 500 words was read to him.

The message relayed the sports editor's venture to Los Angeles and outlined Chance's position. Initially, Murphy scoffed, as he had done consistently throughout the off-season, but as the phone call wore on, he expressed a willingness to accept arbitration to settle the matter. Murphy's pragmatism outweighed his inclination to dig in further on his position, and he chose this moment to reveal a crack in his armament. Murphy gave the *Tribune* representative the go-ahead for Woodruff to broker peace, and he hung up.

Woodruff received word that Murphy had listened to his message and authorized him to mediate. Woodruff phoned Chance to tell him the news. As the two friends talked, Murphy sat in his house and contemplated the reality of the situation. Here he was, the owner of the two-time defending World Series champions—on the cusp of beginning a new season, in which the Cubs could become the first team to win four consecutive pennants—and he might lose his world-class manager over several unnecessary barbs. Furthermore, he liked Chance personally and wanted to continue working with him. Murphy picked up the phone and called the *Tribune*. He agreed to meet Chance halfway by acquiescing to several compromises. Murphy hoped it would be enough to convince the manager to return. Woodruff had just begun to work on a telegram to Murphy, detailing Chance's response, when he received the call from the *Tribune* with the proposal from the Cubs president. Woodruff immediately recognized that Murphy was meeting Chance in the middle and that a resolution was possible. Woodruff expounded Murphy's offer to Frank and then held his breath. "Chance thought over the matter for a moment and said that the conditions were perfectly satisfactory to him if only a little point could be arranged," Woodruff recalled. Daylight had long since given way to evening, but the mediator relayed Chance's single concern in a telegram to the *Tribune*. Although Chance's specific request cannot be ascertained, it seems reasonable to deduce that he wanted Murphy to pay the $10,000 bonus he had promised to the team. Although Murphy had probably made the commitment in jest, he understood that he did not have any option other than to relent and distribute the money.

Murphy climbed into his bed with the fate of his manager still unknown. Just before two in the morning, a ringing phone rustled Murphy from his slumber. Murphy listened as Chance's final request was relayed to him. He agreed to it, and arrangements were made for Murphy to be at the *Tribune* building at 4:00 p.m. to correspond with Chance directly. That afternoon, Chance again joined Woodruff in Los Angeles while Murphy arrived at the *Tribune* building. The two parties traded several messages, and when Murphy responded, "Yes, okay," the final line in the peace treaty between the two men was written. Chance and Murphy then "exchanged congratulatory telegrams which had at least the ring of apparent sincerity." Chance headed back to Ocean Park to make a different set of preparations. He needed to get ready for spring training, but first he needed to ask his father-in-law to keep an eye on his orange trees.[33]

Several weeks later, Murphy addressed the conflict over the bonus at the National League meetings. "I realize, however, that when you promise a ball player anything, if it is only a ten cent piece, you have got to give it. Whatever happens I am going to give the ball players a bonus. I cannot give them less than ten thousand dollars," Murphy told his fellow owners. Garry Herrmann told Murphy that the differences between the National Commission and the Cubs organization on the matter were ended, but he warned Murphy that any future missteps would result in a meeting with American League president Ban Johnson. He also told Murphy to keep future problems out of the press. "I will take your advice," said a remorseful Murphy. "It is good and I will heed it."[34]

Harvey Woodruff's adroit diplomacy allowed Cubs fans to exhale with relief as the truce they had longed to see came to fruition. "So that is the story of the war of 1908-09, which, while it may not rank in history with some of our other national wars, nevertheless was fraught with quite as much interest to 1,000,000 fans in Chicago," Woodruff concluded.[35]

A ten-day centennial celebration of Abraham Lincoln's birth had just kicked off in Chicago, and the peace agreement between Murphy and

Chance enhanced the mood. Murphy's wire burned up the following day. He cabled Chance to chalk up his offending telegram from Friday morning to a misinterpretation. Chance accepted Murphy's explanation, and the last burning ember of the conflict flickered out.[36]

Murphy's peace agreement with Chance meant that the Cubs had their manager back; however, Murphy's off-season troubles with the roster were far from finished. Over the winter, Johnny Evers wrote to Murphy from New York communicating his intention to sit out at least half of the 1909 season. The Cubs' dynamic second baseman suffered under the heavy weight of physical and emotional strain. His aching body did not feel up to the task of another arduous campaign, and his mother, Ellen, was seriously ill. Murphy seemed amenable to the arrangement.[37] As Murphy and Chance worked out their differences, the health of Johnny's mother continued to decline. Meanwhile, Evers got married. However, the *Tribune* reported that "Johnny Evers writes that his honeymoon was cut short by the illness of his mother. He has returned to Troy."[38]

On March 6 Ellen Evers died. Upon receiving the news, Murphy quickly purchased passage on the Twentieth Century train to New York so that he could attend the funeral.[39] Additionally, Murphy made arrangements to provide a wreath for the stage at St. Joseph's Church, the site of Ellen's funeral.[40]

Immediately following his truce with his boss in early February, Chance contacted Evers and encouraged his longtime teammate to rejoin the team as soon as possible. Despite Chance's attempts to change his mind, Evers did not want to return until June. Chance continued to communicate with Johnny, but he had to do it without applying too much pressure, or he risked alienating the mourning second baseman. It was a fine line to walk, but the two infielders, who played next to each other on the right side of the diamond, shared a special relationship despite the occasional conflict that had flared up over the years. The feisty Evers enjoyed needling his manager to watch him bristle. "Nobody on the club could talk to Chance like I could," Evers said. "He would have killed anybody else. He wouldn't hit me because I was too small. I knew that."[41]

Chance tolerated Evers's barbs in no small part because he understood and respected the fact that they both burned with a competitive fire to win. Chance's emotional quotient enabled him to connect with nearly all his players, particularly Evers. He knew when to apply pressure and when to take his foot off the accelerator. He also adeptly forced the issue at times and backed off when it would produce the result he wanted, as he had just demonstrated with Murphy. Chance understood that simply requesting Evers come back to play baseball would not be effective, so the Peerless Leader appealed to the Crab's competitive nature instead. Chance suggested that Evers would not be able to forgive himself if the Cubs fell so far behind the league lead during his absence that the team could not make up the deficit upon his return. Please reconsider your plans, Chance asked him.[42]

After laying his mother to rest, Johnny grappled with returning to the diamond. Evers's teammates shared Chance's suspicion that the little firecracker's competitive nature would compel him to return to the team. "Most of the Cub players expect to see Evers back with the club by the time the season opens or very shortly thereafter. No word from Evers himself has led them to this conclusion, but they have a 'hunch' that when the battle begins he will come out of his retirement," hinted a report in the *Troy Times*.[43] An anxious Murphy was taking no chances of losing his second baseman. According to the *Sporting Life*, Murphy and Chance "pressed (Evers) so hard that he decided to come back." Catcher Johnny Kling's absence also influenced Evers's decision, according to the report.[44] Word soon worked its way down from New York to Chicago that Evers would rejoin the team shortly.

Murphy reached resolutions in the Chance and Evers situations, but finding a settlement with Johnny Kling had dimmer prospects. In the midst of the World Series, several Kansas City businessmen met with Kling in Chicago to discuss adding the star backstop to their prospective ownership group. The owner of the American Association's Kansas City franchise, George Tabeau, wanted to sell the team, if he could get the right price. The local businessmen formed a group and approached Kling about taking on the dual role of player and manager for the team, if they acquired it. Kling agreed to join them, but he wanted $25,000 in club stock. Following the Cubs' victory over Detroit, Kling considered the very real possibility of leaving the Cubs. "'If I can get control of the Kansas City club I am willing to give up my fat job with the Chicago club and take charge of the team,'" Kling said.[45] He skipped a post-World Series exhibition game between the Cubs and Tigers in Indiana as he weighed his options.

Clark Griffith, the new manager of the Cincinnati Reds, paid Murphy a visit in Chicago in mid-December, hoping to pry away one of the Cubs' disgruntled stars in a trade. Griffith asked Murphy about the availability of Frank Chance or Johnny Kling and the Cubs president got a good laugh out of the request. Griffith "was told that President Murphy would not trade Chance or Kling for the whole Cincinnati club, including Manager Griffith and President Herrmann, and part of the Ohio river."[46] Murphy did not feel cornered by Griffith because he confidently believed he held leverage over both players, because they had signed multiyear contracts.

Kling sought permission from Murphy to take a leave of absence. Losing Kling for the year would be a substantial blow to the club. He was one of the best players in the National League, an excellent bat in the daily lineup and an even better defender behind the plate. Brown, Tinker, Evers, and Chance provided the Cubs with astonishing star power, and they overshadowed the importance of Kling—and Overall, too, for that matter—to the team. Kling became the first real test case for the newly defined roles of Murphy and Chance, and both men presented a united public front.

Chance returned to Chicago in February to prepare for the upcoming season. In interviews with the local press, he put to rest any lingering questions about his feud with Murphy (Chance denied Murphy had called him a "fat-head") but openly wondered about his catcher's situation. "As for Johnny Kling, I have heard of his retiring so many times that I try not to listen now when they are talking about it," Chance said.[47] The Cubs began spring training without their starting catcher. Chance gave him several weeks to report to no avail. Chance fired off a telegram to Kansas City, just after St. Patrick's Day, telling Kling to

report to the club. Kling's reply slammed the door shut on his return
for the 1909 campaign.

> Don't expect me this season, as I find it impossible to trust my
> business here in other hands. No question of salary, but my man-
> ager here is not capable of handling my affairs in the proper way.
> Things are breaking too well for me to leave, as my prospects here
> are the brightest.
>
> Best wishes to you and the boys. John G. Kling.[48]

It was becoming clear that Kling had remained away from Chicago
for reasons other than possibly joining the Kansas City ownership group.
Kling, an excellent pool player, had recently opened a billiards parlor
in Kansas City, and he viewed his business prospects as bright. His loss
was a blow to his teammates, but they weren't surprised he quit. They
believed that Kling remained angry at Murphy for a scuttled business
deal that appeared to involve Reds president Garry Herrmann. Kling
wanted to open a billiard hall in Cincinnati, but he believed that Murphy stymied his pursuit for property by accusing Herrmann of tampering. The potential deal collapsed, and Kling blamed Murphy. Kling's
telegram may have surprised Murphy and the fans, but his teammates
were well aware that he had a "grievance" against Murphy, regardless
of whether it was "real or imagined."[49] Murphy's actual involvement
in the billiard situation remained unclear.

Kling did not mention the bungled business deal as a reason for
quitting, suggesting that he would have been happy to return to the
Cubs. "'Chance is a good fellow and Murphy is a good fellow . . . But
business is business, and I've simply got to pass up the game for one
year. I haven't a kick coming and it isn't a question of salary. If I played
ball I would be perfectly willing to return to Chicago at the same money
I received last season. But I've got a proposition here that will make
me $150,000 in ten years. I have been figuring for a long time and
have come to the conclusion I must remain here this summer,'" he
said.[50] Kling had leased a "large building" and transformed several
floors into a billiard hall. The remainder he sublet at a profit. The

lease still had nine years to go before it expired. The total investment was $75,000, and Kling wanted business to remain robust during the summer months, which had not typically happened while he was off playing baseball.

Speaking from Shreveport, where the Cubs were playing an exhibition game, the always candid Chance still felt good about his club in spite of Kling's absence. "The loss of Kling unquestionably will be a blow to the Cubs, but it will not put us out of the running. Kling's loss may weaken us. I am willing to admit it does, but I do not for one moment believe his loss will be a vital one. We will win the pennant of the National league just the same," he said.[51]

The Cubs already had Pat Moran—who Chance said was the best catcher in baseball outside of Kling—on the roster, but he swung a deal with St. Paul of the American Association, on March 27, for backstop Tom Needham as insurance.[52] The trade cost Chicago pitcher Fred Liese and $1,000. Kling, who was in the midst of a multiyear deal, would have to repay the organization the thousand dollars if he wanted to rejoin the team, a not insignificant sum considering he had made $4,500 in 1908.

While Murphy tried to be diplomatic, Chance struggled to hide his displeasure with Kling. Chance had handled his agricultural business prior to leaving California, and perhaps his irritation stemmed from Kling's inability to balance his billiards hall with his responsibility to the team. Chance began shopping Kling around to evaluate the type of trade package the catcher could glean. Murphy did not interfere. Chance contacted Clark Griffith in Cincinnati, but the two managers could not find common ground for a trade. Nevertheless, Chance made no secret of his desire to deal Kling the second he received a decent offer.

Back in Kansas City, the press informed Kling of the trade speculation surrounding him, on April 7, and he vociferously defended his actions.

"Murphy might as well make up his mind that he isn't going to have my services this season," said Kling last night. "How many times have I got to say that I will not leave Kansas City this summer? Evidently a ball player's word doesn't count for much. At any rate, I have already ordered uniforms for the Missouri Athletic Club City league team and I am not throwing away any money. Then, yesterday, I posted a forfeit of $150 to play the winner of the Weston match, the games to be played here in May. I guess I am going to toss off that $150?

"I will admit that I have been drawing a good salary for playing with the Cubs. I am not asking for an increase, but I know that by staying here and taking care of my business I can make more money here than I can by playing ball."[53]

Kling may have felt that the fans would eventually turn against him but, for now, they wanted him back. Ring Lardner reported that Kling received "fully 100 letters" from Cubs fans and that the catcher "invariably looks sad" as he reviews his mail. "'What will we do without you?' one 'lady bug' asked him. 'Who will nail the flying runners at second base? Who will drive in the runs that win for the Cubs? John, please return. Save the day for your friends.'"[54]

Kling brushed aside any emotional pull returning to the Cubs may have held for him. After all, he had signed up to compete in a city bowling tournament held at Royal Alleys that night.[55]

The Cubs entered the 1909 season undermanned to take on a powerful Giants outfit that had acquired Red Murray, Bugs Raymond, and Admiral Schlei from the St. Louis Cardinals in exchange for Roger Bresnahan. However, Murphy remained optimistic about his team's chances to capture a fourth consecutive pennant. He knew Evers would return during the season, the sooner the better. As for Kling, "Both Chance and myself expect him to come back, but we will win again if he does not," Murphy said.[56]

1. Charlie Murphy's life changed forever after he moved to Cincinnati, where he began his journalism career with the *Cincinnati Enquirer* in 1892. Murphy spent thirteen years working for Queen City newspapers. *Cincinnati Commercial Tribune*, January 26, 1905. Courtesy of the Cincinnati Public Library.

"BUM" AT THE BENCH SHOW.

2. Saved from the life of a stray as a young pup by a police officer, Bum, a shepherd/collie mix, frequently tagged alongside Charlie Murphy for a decade as the latter ran around town covering stories all over Cincinnati. *Cincinnati Commercial Tribune*, June 17, 1901. Courtesy of the Cincinnati Public Library.

3. (*opposite top*) Charles P. Taft hired Charlie Murphy to write for his newspaper, the *Cincinnati Times-Star*, in 1902 and agreed to finance the purchase of the Chicago Cubs three years later. Courtesy of the Library of Congress, Prints & Photographs Division, photography by Harris & Ewing, LC-DIG-hec-01542

4. (*opposite bottom*) Despite his relative youth, twenty-eight-year-old Frank Chance quickly established himself as the leader of the Cubs following the tragic illness of manager Frank Selee in 1905. Courtesy of the Chicago History Museum.

5. (*above*) Following the 1905 season, Charlie Murphy's blockbuster trade for outfielder Jimmy Sheckard shocked the baseball world and earned him Chance's respect. Courtesy of the Library of Congress, Prints & Photographs Division, LC-USZ62-28946.

6. Walking off the field with Boston owner George Dovey, Charlie Murphy carries a large bouquet after a pregame ceremony, on May 21, 1908, during which he received a 107-piece silverware set from the Cubs players and treasurer Charlie Williams for his role in winning back-to-back World Series championships. Courtesy of the Chicago History Museum.

7. President William Howard Taft, a passionate baseball fan, waves to the enthusiastic crowd as he enters the West Side Grounds on September 16, 1909. Taft's visit to the stadium proved to be one of Murphy's great triumphs as owner of the Cubs. Courtesy of the Chicago History Museum.

8. By 1911 Charlie Murphy had established himself as one of the National League's most influential figures. However, despite his success, tumult surrounded him as he pushed the envelope and consequences awaited him just on the other side of the horizon. Courtesy of the Library of Congress, Prints and Photographs Division, LC-DIG-ggbain-02685.

9. Charlie Williams, Johnny Evers, Frank Chance, and Joe Tinker essentially grew up together as members of the Cubs organization during the first decade of the twentieth century. However, it ended during the 1912 off-season. Williams joined the front office of the Chicago Federal League organization, Evers replaced Chance, who took over the New York Yankees, and the Cincinnati Reds hired Joe Tinker as manager. This picture captured them together in Chicago for the final time before the four men went their separate ways. Courtesy of the Chicago History Museum.

10. Charlie Murphy always felt more comfortable talking baseball and competing at card games with players and managers than he did circulating among the owners, who criticized him for not building alliances in the boardroom. Courtesy of the Chicago History Museum.

11. Following the Horace Fogel scandal, many of the National League owners wanted to oust Murphy, but it took the firing of Johnny Evers, during the fierce battle with the Federal League, to help them succeed, in the spring of 1914. Taken in December of 1913, this picture proved to be Murphy's last Winter Meeting group photo. Courtesy of the Library of Congress, Prints and Photographs Division, LC-DIG-ggbain-13107.

12. Murphy's love of show business inspired him to build a theater in his hometown of Wilmington, Ohio. He spared no expense, and the auditorium astonished locals as the entranceway ushered them into the house when it opened on July 24, 1918. Courtesy of the Clinton County Historical Society.

13. Murphy ordered the equivalent of seventy train cars of sand and gravel, nineteen cars of bricks, four cars of lumber, and half a car of carpets and light fixtures. Murphy passionately pursued perfection for the theater and wound up spending a quarter of a million dollars on it. Courtesy of the Clinton County Historical Society.

14. In a rare surviving photograph taken during his later years, Murphy had cast away his mustache, but he never lost his love for baseball. Courtesy of the Chicago History Museum.

A PAIR OF PRESIDENTS

While the wounds incurred during the scrap between an obstinate Charlie Murphy and a proud Frank Chance slowly mended, as the season drew near, the fallout between the Cubs owner and National League president Harry Pulliam only deepened. They remained at odds over the World Series ticket scandal, and Pulliam continued to publicly criticize Murphy. Pulliam had long ago grown fed up with the National League owners' disregard for the rules when it suited their organizations, either blatantly or through subterfuge, and their blaming him for enforcing regulations. He viewed the ticket scandal as yet another example of blatant indiscretion that undermined the authority of the National League presidency. "I am sick and tired of controversy and being put in the attitude of a notoriety seeker for simply asking that the rules be lived up to and a fair measure of equity be dealt to the players," Pulliam complained to Garry Herrmann in the spring of 1908.[1]

On the cusp of February's National League meeting in Chicago, percolating tensions exploded, and the rift between Murphy and Pulliam widened into an irreparable gulf. Pulliam had inserted himself into the argument between Murphy and Chance during the off-season. He contacted Chance and let him know that the National League wanted the Peerless Leader to remain with their organization. Pulliam's audacity irked Murphy, who thought the president was involving himself in a team situation that was none of the league's business. In early February someone leaked four letters, written during the clash between Murphy and Chance, to the Chicago *Inter Ocean*. The newspaper published them, on February 9, in what appeared to be an orchestrated attempt, on the part of the leaker, to pin the blame for the conflict between Murphy and Chance squarely on the former. Harry Pulliam either wrote or received all the letters, giving the impression that he was leaking the communications to paint Murphy in a bad light. However, Pulliam bristled at seeing the letters in the press, although he refused to back down from Murphy. He wrote a letter to the *Chicago Tribune* denying he was the source of the leak. "I never before was accused of being a foul fighter, even by my enemies, and I need no assistance in handling Mr. Murphy. Mr. Murphy's specialty since coming into baseball has been insulting people and then apologizing. As far as I am concerned that must end, and I well know that the public is not interested in the trouble between Murphy and myself."[2]

Although he tried to exude confidence in public, Pulliam felt tremendous personal stress over his open conflict with Murphy and long-running feud with John T. Brush and the Giants over the Merkle ruling. Rumors that Pulliam was drinking more frequently started to quietly circulate among the increasingly alarmed owners. Pulliam felt as though he were the parent of squabbling children, who responded to his authority by thoroughly ignoring him. Pulliam had a lot on his mind on the eve of the winter meeting in February, and he sounded perilously close to snapping. "I'm sick of all this winter baseball. I am anxious for the real season to open, when I can pick up a newspaper and learn the result of a good ball game instead of the latest brand of mud hurled broadcast by the 'magnates,'" Pulliam admitted in a show of vulnerability.[3]

In his mind, Pulliam's participation in brokering the truce between Chance and Murphy had been a success, which had kept one of the National League's biggest stars in place. Even though he had been a minor player, Pulliam felt underappreciated for his part in resolving their differences. Although he would have liked to be recognized for his role, he settled for retaining the Peerless Leader in Chicago. He also remained mad at Murphy, who he believed had stirred up an unnecessary controversy. "I'm glad Chance is back and that he has patched up his differences with President Murphy. He's a great manager and the Cubs might have their troubles with a less experienced leader, although a ball team of their class ought to win with almost any kind of management," Pulliam said.[4]

Pulliam gave the keynote address at a banquet attended by members of the Baseball Writers' Association of America at the Auditorium Annex in Chicago on February 16, and some attendees thought that the president might use his speech to reveal what he knew about Murphy's alleged dealings in the Cubs-Giants series, which he had hinted at for a number of weeks. Instead, Pulliam shockingly unleashed a verbal assault on the National League owners, which quickly got back to them. Murphy, along with several other team presidents, did not hear Pulliam's inebriated diatribe as they had ventured over to the Academy earlier, where they had all watched Joe Tinker perform on stage in the appropriately titled play "A Home Run."[5]

The following day, the magnates convened to discuss the business at hand, and it quickly emerged that they were all thinking about what to do about Harry Pulliam, who had ripped them the previous night. Outspoken and unfiltered around his peers, Murphy unloaded on Pulliam:

I am absolutely unwilling to jeopardize my business interests any further through kindness of heart or generous impulse. I believe that it is our duty as men having large interests at stake, not to jeopardize them any further, and I for one am unwilling that Mr. Pulliam shall exercise any further official function with this League while he is in the condition that he is in.

Therefore, I think we should devise ways and means to protect our interests, and also to protect the man. We have to do something immediately. Whether it would be proper to vote him a vacation or how to handle it, so that the public won't know just what has happened, or whether we owe it to the public to let them know—but I think the man should be put in some sanitarium.

I have no feeling of unkindness towards Harry. I like him personally, as we all do, but I find that it has got beyond the time of tolerance and forbearance.[6]

Boston Doves president George Dovey followed up on Murphy's comments by confessing that he had struggled with alcoholism before he had gotten sober in the mid-1890s. Dovey saw his former self in the current face of Harry Pulliam. "I can state from my own personal experiences that when I had reached his condition of drink there was no relative of mine could do anything with me," Dovey admitted to the group. Once initiated, suspicions about Pulliam's behavior tumbled out like baseballs from an upended ball bag. Dovey said Pulliam had told him about flippantly spending large amounts of money on the West Coast. Thomas Logan, a Reds shareholder, recounted a conversation in which he overheard Pulliam complain that he would quit his job as National League president if he didn't have to financially care for his sister. Pulliam also expressed dismay at his salary which, he argued, paled in comparison to Ban Johnson's $15,000. The owners agreed something had to be done, but they weren't exactly sure what to do. It was a difficult issue. They bandied about the idea of calling Pulliam's relatives to conduct an intervention. Murphy suggested contacting a local physician he knew who could assess Pulliam, but he did not want to be held personally responsible if the plan went haywire. "You know what my relations with Mr. Pulliam are at this time," he said.

"What is the difference?" Herrmann retorted.[7]

Despite having won back-to-back World Series championships, Charlie Murphy and the Chicago Cubs prepared for the 1909 season with an unusual number of questions to resolve with their on-field personnel. However, the organization's brand had never been stronger. With three consecutive National League pennants under their belt, Murphy and Chance had overseen the establishment of Organized Baseball's first twentieth century dynasty. The Cubs' star players earned accolades for their performances from writers and fans across the country, and Murphy reaped a financial windfall as the team's value increased significantly with each successful campaign. To cap it off, Murphy and the Cubs deepened their relationship with Chicago and, in turn, came to represent the city around the country.

On April 12, with the season opener against St. Louis only two days away, a frustrated Frank Chance voiced his displeasure at his inability to pencil either Johnny Evers or Johnny Kling into Chicago's Opening Day lineup. "Let them all quit. If we have nine men left by Wednesday afternoon we will be out on the west side to play Bresnahan's club. I guess we can scrape together enough to make it a legal game."[8] One player Chance knew would be in uniform was Orval Overall, and the skipper selected him to start the season opener against the Cardinals.

Chance had decided to split the catching duties between the capable duo of Pat Moran and Jimmy Archer, but it had become more apparent throughout spring training that the team would feel the loss of Kling. Heinie Zimmerman, who had pleasantly surprised his manager with excellent play during the exhibition season, would replace Evers at second base until the latter's return. While Chance admitted that not having two key players would impact the club in the short term, he remained confident. Chance thought the Giants, Phillies, and "the Pittsburg Club" would be the contending teams jostling with the Cubs for the pennant.[9]

As teams continued with their preparation for the season, a cultural debate over playing games on Sunday intensified throughout the Midwest. At stake for contemporaries was no less than the idea of baseball as a democratic sport, a thoroughly laughable concept considering the exclusion of African Americans, but one they debated nevertheless. In 1909 teams in Missouri, Indiana, and Minnesota listened intently to heated debates over various legislative proposals addressing the legality of playing games on Sundays.[10] Known as "blue laws," these established regulations sought the eradication of nonreligious leisure activities on the Sabbath. According to historian Steven Riess, "Working-class Chicagoans vigorously opposed the state's blue laws and other morals regulations, and city officials, who exercised considerable home rule, did not enforce the detested restrictions."[11] The Cubs had eighteen Sunday home games scheduled for the 1909 season, but conservative politicians, buoyed by supportive religious leaders, pushed to outlaw the practice once and for all.

Beginning in 1878, the National League banned Sunday games; however, each organization was allowed to determine its own policy following the merger of the American Association and the National League in 1891. Charlie Murphy's predecessor, Jim Hart, initiated the practice of Sunday baseball in Chicago for the 1893 season. Fearing reprisals from the middle class, the organization, under Al Spalding, had shunned playing on the Sabbath, but the possibility of a new team moving into the Windy City and taking market share on Sundays spurred Hart into action. Hart leveraged the Sunday opening of the Columbian Exposition of the 1893 World's Fair to argue that baseball games ought to be played on that day of the week as well. Chicago played its first Sunday game on May 14, 1893, in front of 13,500 fans.[12] As far as club officials were concerned, there was no going back.

Murphy had been involved with the issue of playing Sunday games since his short stint in the New York Giants' front office. During an exhibition game on April 9, 1905, three police officers in "citizens' clothes" arrested the Giants' Offa Neal, along with two members of the opposing Emeralds, for "violating the Sunday law." The three ballplayers were scheduled to appear the following day, and Murphy "gave security for their appearance."[13] Playing games on Sundays was good for business. It gave blue collar workers with the day off an opportunity to attend. However, Murphy hesitated to publicly argue for Sunday baseball because it would elicit suspicion of his business practices. However, he found subtle ways to encourage supportive public commentary.

Reverend Thornton Anthony Mills found himself with complimentary season tickets to see the two-time defending World Series champions after he informed his congregation that he found nothing inherently wrong with baseball games on Sunday. Reverend Mills ripped a proposal to ban the practice, calling it "class legislation." The working class had no way of ever visiting the ballpark while they were on the clock. Eliminating Sunday games would take away the one opportunity many of them had of enjoying a leisurely day at the yard. Murphy learned of Mills's sermon and promptly sent the preacher the passes along with a letter in which he wrote in part:

I want to say to you that your sermon on base ball coincides exactly with the views expressed by the late Bishop Potter, of New York, who held that Sunday base ball was a good thing from a moral standpoint. I am reluctant to discuss this phase of the base ball business because selfish motives would be attributed to anything I might say. But I could not refrain from dropping you a few lines after reading what you had to say in your sermon at the Church of the Christian Union in Rockford.[14]

While the debate over the accessibility of ballgames to all economic classes raged, another conversation about attendance occurred in Chicago at the National League annual meeting in mid-February. Charles Comiskey's White Sox had been implementing a promotion called "Ladies' Day" for several years before Murphy enacted it in 1908.[15] The owners discussed issues surrounding female attendance at their ball parks, specifically the free admission women received on Ladies' Days. Generally, Ladies' Day promotions admitted women into the ballpark without charge for designated games throughout the season if they were accompanied by male escorts. The owners believed the presence of women elevated the prestige of the baseball game to a "clean" leisure activity appropriate for all members of society. According to historians Harold Seymour and Dorothy Seymour Mills, the practice of Ladies' Day emerged as the role of women in society changed during the post-bellum period. "No longer did the genteel prudery of an earlier day confine them to the home," they argue. Following the Civil War, American women began to engage in outdoor games including archery, tennis, and cycling. They also attended baseball games. The Knickerbockers, an amateur team in New York, held the first Ladies' Day in 1867. Following baseball's professionalization, owners continued the promotion to great success, beginning with the Athletics and Orioles; both franchises dubbed each Thursday home game as Ladies' Day in 1883.[16]

Even so, just over twenty-five years later, several owners, including Murphy, believed that Ladies' Day had served its purpose and ought to be eliminated. Murphy enthusiastically supported women attending games, but winning had increased the Cubs' popularity, and Murphy, out for additional dollars, believed he could sell the seats that women currently occupied for free. Murphy encouraged the entire league to get rid of the promotion. "John T. Brush told me 'You are a fool; it don't get you a dollar.' I said 'I am watching it this year, and I will find out;' and the same bunch come day after day, and they never pay a dollar. I think we ought to abolish ladies' day. We are business men. We can say that the League is against it," Murphy argued to the other National League owners, including Dodgers owner Charlie Ebbets, who heartily agreed with him.

Murphy reiterated his nuanced stance so his position would be completely understood. "I would suggest that Mr. Heydler say that the League has not abolished ladies' day, and he does not want to discourage the ladies from coming, but it abolishes their coming in free," he clarified.[17]

Women were encouraged to attend ballgames by an authority no less influential than Edythe Chance, the Peerless Leader's wife, who embodied the modernizing relationship between women and baseball. She implored housewives to expand their worldview by forgoing their stereotypical activities and visiting the ballpark instead. "'If more women would forsake bridge whist and pink tea, sofa cushions and kimonos, and turn out to watch the cleanest sport in the world, there would be more robustness and fair-mindedness among our sex,' Mrs. Chance said. 'If women would only come out and expand their lungs to the fresh air by "rooting" for the "home team" there would be less work for the doctors.'"[18] Edythe's provocative comments appeared in newspapers throughout the country, including the *New York Times* and *Sporting Life*. While it is true that Edythe Chance and Charlie Murphy stood to financially profit from increased paid female attendance, as franchise shareholders, the relationship between women and baseball continued to evolve during the Progressive Era. Owners and sports-writers established the narrative that baseball was a "clean" sport, which encouraged more women to attend games. Simultaneously, as more women went to the ballpark, baseball earned a more reputable place in society. The Cubs were emerging as an important representa-tive of Chicago to the nation, and their quest for a fourth consecutive pennant beckoned all locals to participate. Murphy made it clear to the other owners that he wanted women in the stands at Cubs games; he just believed the team's popularity made the Ladies' Day promotion obsolete. The owners unanimously passed a resolution that signaled their intent to take the matter up with baseball's "proper authorities."[19]

Without Evers and Kling, the Cubs still managed to win eight of their first thirteen games. Following an eight-game road trip, Chicago returned home to face the sputtering Pirates, who arrived in the Windy City a game under .500. However, the series at the West Side Grounds altered the trajectory of Pittsburgh's season. Its pitching staff allowed only four runs in thirty-eight innings, capped off by a brilliant complete-game, eleven-inning shutout performance by Babe Adams. The Pirates swept the Cubs on their way to a 20-6 May record as they entrenched themselves as the frontrunners in the National League.

One bit of good news for the Cubs arrived in the person of Evers, who pulled into Chicago with Murphy, aboard a train, for the series. Evers had agreed to a two-year contract and began to work himself back into playing shape.[20] He walked in his season debut, a pinch-hitting appearance in the third game of the Pittsburgh series. Complicating matters, Chance received word from the National Commission that Evers was ineligible to play because he had failed to properly report to the club in the spring.[21] Although the matter was quickly resolved, the Cubs promptly lost Chance to a shoulder injury that forced him out of action for weeks. Everywhere the Cubs stepped during the 1909 season seemed to be on ground that gave way.

Despite its challenges, the 1909 season included a remarkable bright spot: the developing connection between the Cubs franchise and the president of the United States, William Howard Taft. Murphy had known Will Taft for a number of years, having lived in Cincinnati and having gone into business to buy the Cubs with the commander-and-chief's older half brother, Charles. The Tafts were Cincinnati's most influential family, and Murphy had become intimately familiar with their role in the social, political, and sporting dynamics of the

Queen City during his time as a reporter. Murphy had encouraged Will to come out to watch the Cubs before he was elected president. Prior to the 1907 season, Murphy sent complimentary passes to Taft—then secretary of war—and his wife, Nellie, and invited them to visit whenever they wanted. Murphy sent passes numbered 152 and 153 and included a note that looked ahead optimistically. "The sentiment of the middle west is being crystalized for you as president, and as we already regard you as next president, I will be pleased to have you occupy the president's box at the Chicago park at some future time, when it will be convenient."[22] Taft warmly received the season passes as well as Murphy's assessment of the political climate. "Thank you for your kind expressions. If the sentiment you refer to grows as fast as the prestige of the Chicago club under your management it will certainly be formidable."[23]

Murphy had also mailed Secretary Taft a season pass before the 1908 season got underway. That time, Taft did not have 151 names called prior to his own. Murphy, always the marketer, looked ahead to the Republican Convention that would be held in June. Murphy delightedly told Taft, who had been campaigning for the nomination, "We have this day sent pass No. 1 to President Roosevelt, and although the phrase may be hackneyed and stereotyped by this time, we are taking extreme pleasure in sending pass No. 2 'to the next President.'" Murphy offered Taft his own interpretation of the current political environment as it related to the presidential primary. "Please pardon me for taking up any of your time, as I realize how busy you are just now, but I want you to know that Taft sentiment in Chicago and throughout Illinois is growing every instant, and by the time of the convention in June I do not think that there will be any doubt of your nomination on the first ballot."[24] In March Murphy lunched with Charlie and Annie Taft along with their daughter, Louise. They playfully held a mock National Republican Convention and nominated Secretary Taft for the presidency on the first ballot.

Murphy believed that the baseball establishment would support Will Taft's quest for the presidency. Murphy told Charles Taft that he would "take the stump" for his younger half brother in baseball circles, but it might not be necessary. "Taft sentiment is being crystalized rapidly in the baseball profession," Murphy informed him.[25] Garry Herrmann, National Commission member and president of the Reds, was an important cog in the wheels of Organized Baseball and Republican politics in Ohio. Charles Taft had been working hard behind the scenes for months to solidify support for his younger brother's candidacy. In the process, he learned that Hamilton County members of the State Central Committee in Ohio threatened to not endorse Will for the presidency unless the organization simultaneously announced its support for Senator Ben Foraker's reelection bid. Alarmed, Charles contacted Herrmann and informed him that this idea would lead to Will's defeat. Senator Foraker did not support Teddy Roosevelt's railroad regulatory reform program, which led to a falling out between them. Charles Taft chastised Herrmann and told him that linking support of Will to the anti-progressive Republican senator from his home state of Ohio would "seriously injure his standing in the other states especially in the middle and far west."[26] In another letter, Charles pointedly told Herrmann, "Do not delude yourself in this matter."[27]

In spite of any obstacles, real or perceived, Will Taft comfortably captured the Republican nomination on the first ballot at the Chicago Coliseum in June. He was Roosevelt's hand-selected heir apparent, and the president's support virtually assured his nomination. An ecstatic Murphy sent a congratulatory telegram to Taft. "Everybody in the world who knows you is overjoyed at your nomination. Your election is positively certain," he gushed.[28] The Cubs learned of Taft's nomination upon arriving in New York for a series against the Giants. Frank Chance expressed the sentiment of the ball club in a telegram he sent from the road: "You have made a home run with the bases full, hearty congratulations from all the Cubs and myself."[29]

In October of 1908 the Cubs beat Detroit in the World Series. Less than three weeks later, on November 3, Taft captured 329 electoral votes to defeat William Jennings Bryan for the presidency. The Cubs and Taft jubilantly shared in each other's victories. Chance sent another congratulatory message to Taft, and the president quickly wrote back.

My dear Mr. Chance:

I beg to acknowledge the receipt of your telegram of the 4th instant and to thank the manager and the members of the Cubs for their good wishes, which I assure you I very much appreciate.

Very sincerely yours,
William H. Taft[30]

Now, several months after the inauguration, Murphy's dream of having President Taft attend a Cubs game came to fruition not just once but several times in 1909. The Cubs stopped in Pittsburgh to play on May 29 in coordination with President Taft's visit. Taft was in town to attend to the fifth annual meeting of the Western Associated Yale Club, an alumni association of his beloved college, along with several other presidential duties.[31] Taft already had a full slate, but he enjoyed baseball tremendously, and Murphy "hoped and expected" that the president would drop in on the game at Exposition Park.[32] Murphy's hopes were realized when Taft's staff left his afternoon open after the president lunched at the Commercial Club. Pittsburgh became the place to be. Charles Taft arrived in town to spend the day watching his team with his presidential sibling. Murphy made sure to be there.

Pirates owner Barney Dreyfuss prepared a private box for the president and his party, but Taft politely declined the offer. "'I want to get right down among the rooters—the baseball bugs,' said the President. 'The boxes are all right, but I want to mingle with those in the stand.'"[33]

A huge crowd turned out to see the president, and they were not disappointed. The Taft brothers, Will with his thick mustache and Charles with his flocculent beard, starkly stood out to the adoring fans. They sat in the same row in the grandstand, along the first base line, with secretary of state Philander Knox and Arthur Hadley, the president of Yale, between them. All four hatted gentlemen smiled throughout the afternoon. Murphy spent part of the game conversing with Dreyfuss near the presidential party.[34] Sitting in the stands earned President Taft admiration from the fans. He only increased his credibility with them when he stood up "about the fourth inning" to participate in "the general stretch, whereupon the crowd, which was watching his every move, indulged in a roar of approval."[35]

After the Pirates took a 2-0 lead in the bottom of the second inning, President Taft teased Charles about the current state of affairs for his older brother's ball club. The *Pittsburgh Post-Gazette* reported that it appeared that President Taft and Secretary Knox had made "a few wagers" with Charles and President Hadley before the game. "Want to withdraw and call it off?" they teasingly asked Charles, who indignantly replied, "I am no quitter. We have this game cinched." A three-run rally by the Cubs in the top of the sixth inning made Charles happy, as it put them in the lead, but Will's Pirates tied the game in the bottom of the seventh on Honus Wagner's RBI infield hit. The Cubs broke the game open by scoring five times in the eleventh inning, and Mordecai Brown finished off his complete game effort as Chicago won, 8-3.

After the final out, President Taft explained to the local press how a day at the ballpark was good for his soul. "'It was a great game and I am glad I was fortunate enough to be present,' said President Taft as he was leaving the grandstand. 'Yes, I am passionately fond of baseball, and this recreation this afternoon has relieved me of any fatigue I may have felt from the busy day I have put in. It looks to me as if the Chicago and Pittsburgh clubs are evenly matched. I certainly enjoyed the contest, and I must say that your Pittsburgh baseball fa(n)s know how to root; they also know how to show their appreciation of good plays by members of the visiting team. An afternoon at the baseball game is a good thing for any man, particularly if he has been tied up in an office burdened with business cares.'" The baseball fans of Pittsburgh loudly cheered the president as he made his way out of Exposition Park.[36]

Taft's visit thrilled Murphy. Several years later, Murphy wrote an article for *Baseball Magazine* in which he explained how the presence of the president of the United States at the ballpark validated the merits of baseball. Despite the prestige of his position, Taft's preference for sitting in the stands rather than a private box demonstrated that "it was not Taft, the President, but Taft, the fan, who wished to see this game . . . Here he showed his democratic spirit by munching peanuts and drinking lemonade just like any other fan out for an afternoon of pleasure and relaxation," wrote Murphy. "While the writer is not officially authorized to speak for the President on baseball or on any other subject, he feels safe in asserting that Mr. Taft will always love baseball so long as the game is kept clean and square," Murphy added.[37]

Murphy aptly paid tribute to both the president's personal enjoyment of baseball and his own warm feelings for the Taft brothers. However, the article also exemplifies the important role Taft played in creating overwhelmingly positive public relations for the sport, especially early in his administration, and the opportunistic Murphy wrote the piece to further intertwine his business and the White House. In fairness, by the time *Baseball Magazine* published Murphy's article, in 1912, President Taft did not enjoy much popularity to speak of as he headed toward defeat in his reelection bid.

The 1909 season developed into one of the most historically important campaigns in the annals of the Pittsburgh Pirates franchise for reasons beyond hosting the president. Led by the incomparable Honus Wagner, they reeled off thirty-nine victories in forty-seven games in May and June to build a seven-and-a-half-game cushion in the pennant chase. Pittsburgh capped off its incredible run with an 8–1 win over the Cubs on June 29 in their final game at Exposition Park. The following day, the two teams opened Forbes Field, a spectacular new million-dollar "plant" long dreamed of by Barney Dreyfuss. The *Pittsburgh Post-Gazette* proudly declared on its front page that "future historians when writing of the greatness of Pittsburgh doubtless will refer to the opening of Forbes field as an epoch—no an event."[38] The overwhelming response by the fans demonstrated that the business of baseball was booming in the "Iron City." An enormous crowd of 30,338, dressed in suits and gowns, stuffed themselves into every nook and cranny of the new facility to watch the game. The attendance set a new official record for baseball as neither New York nor Chicago publicized "actual figures."[39] Frank Chance collected the first hit in the stadium's history, an RBI single in the top of the first inning, and Ed Reulbach pitched the Cubs to a 3–2 win on a warm, sunshine-filled afternoon.

The victory was particularly satisfying for Murphy because Dreyfuss had recently ripped him in the newspapers for the former's vote against Pittsburgh on a protested game played between the Reds and Pirates in April. Dreyfuss called Murphy a "rat," and he suggested that the Cubs owner had lied to him about how he would vote on the Pirates protest. Dreyfuss believed Murphy changed his mind to support the Reds because they could not threaten the Cubs in the standings like the Pirates. Interestingly, Dreyfuss did not take any issue with Charles Ebbets of hapless Brooklyn, who also voted against Pittsburgh. The Pirates were emerging as a legitimate threat to the National League order, and Dreyfuss was politicking hard to gain traction for his club behind the scenes, but the episode again emphasized the dysfunctionality of the National League.

On July 29, just before 9:30 p.m., inside his room on the third floor of the New York Athletic Club, despondent National League president Harry Pulliam lifted a revolver to his right temple and pulled the trigger. The bullet tore through his face, destroying his right eyeball and severing his optic nerve, but it left him alive. He dropped to the floor in utter agony. "I think he struggled on the floor for two hours and that he was so overcome with the intense pain that he tried to get to the telephone to send for me. He probably got the receiver off the hook and then lost his strength entirely," Dr. T. Hamilton Burch said later.[40]

A phone operator noticed that Pulliam's wire was open and attempted to contact him but received no response. Thomas Brady, an employee of the club, was dispatched to Pulliam's room to check out the strange situation. When the young man arrived, he heard the mangled Pulliam moaning in pain. He unlocked the door and rushed into the room nearly tripping over Pulliam, who lay prostrate on the floor. Brady's eyes adjusted to take in the ghastly sight of a limp Pulliam, in his underclothes, bleeding profusely from his shattered head. Brady immediately called for help. Dr. J. J. Higgins of the club quickly arrived to tend to Pulliam, as did Dr. George Shrady, a New York coroner. Pulliam's gruesome injuries prevented him from being transported to a hospital, so he was gently lifted onto a sofa in his room. "He was in a pitiable

condition," Shrady bemoaned. "He was semi-conscious but irratio-
nal."[41] Medical personnel gingerly moved Pulliam to his bed where,
per law, he was placed under arrest for attempting suicide.[42]

Shrady stayed with Pulliam throughout the calamitous night, but
the doctors could not do anything to save him. The forty-year-old
Pulliam died at 7:35 the following morning. "I have no doubt that Mr.
Pulliam shot himself with intent to take his life," Dr. Shrady said. "I
have the pistol and the bullets it contained and also the bullet which
plowed through the front part of his head, destroying one eye and
knocking out the other so that it rolled on the floor. It may be said that
ill health probably caused Mr. Pulliam to kill himself. He had been in
a sanatorium. Mr. Pulliam was decidedly irresponsive when I asked
him last night why he shot himself. He continually tried to rub his
eyes, and even tried to push his thumb in the right eye socket. When
I questioned him all he said was 'What shot?' and would not answer
me. He continually asked that I rub his head."[43]

Murphy was noticeably quiet about Pulliam's suicide in the days
following his death. Murphy gave out news regarding possible player
transactions to the local press, but he conveyed relatively little about
Pulliam other than giving a short response to a question about who
would take over the presidency of the National League. "I had too high
a regard for Harry Pulliam to be discussing his successor so soon after
his death," he said.[44]

For the first time in their brief histories, the National and American
Leagues both postponed their games on the day of Pulliam's funeral.
Murphy traveled to Louisville, where he joined the other National
League owners as honorary pallbearers. Only Giants owner John T.
Brush, who still nurtured his grudge against Pulliam, was absent. Prior
to moving into the National League office, Pulliam had worked for
Barney Dreyfuss, beginning in the front office of the Louisville Colo-
nels and then in Pittsburgh following the organization's rebirth as the
Pirates. Manager Fred Clarke and Secretary William Locke traveled
with Dreyfuss to the service. Honus Wagner desperately wanted to
join them, but a serious injury compelled his doctors to forbid him
from traveling. A devastated Wagner wept.

Approximately 1,200 people attended the service at the Cave Hill Cemetery chapel, including a deeply saddened Jim Hart, who had worked with Pulliam in Louisville: "I consider Mr. Pulliam one of the finest men I have ever had the pleasure of meeting. He was honest to a fault and took every one's troubles to heart as if they were his own."[45]

While saddened by Pulliam's suicide, many of the people who moved in his circle were not surprised. Nevertheless, speculation over the reason Pulliam shot himself appeared in many of the stories about his death. Francis Richter described Pulliam's struggles in his piece for the *Sporting Life*: "Mr. Pulliam was of extremely nervous temperament, and worried excessively over National League troubles. Personal criticism, however slight or well intended, was to him almost unbearable. He also was obsessed with the idea that the success of the National League rested entirely upon his shoulders, and complained frequently that the burden was too heavy for any man to bear. Occasional controversies with various club owners bore hard upon him and matters were not mended by the arbitrary stand he took upon many matters."[46]

Although Murphy encouraged his peers to wait on naming a successor out of respect for Pulliam, the owners promoted National League secretary John Heydler to serve as president.

While Charlie Murphy had experienced President Taft watching the Cubs in person, it was Barney Dreyfuss, not Murphy, who had served as host. Now, it was Murphy's turn. Congress's passage of a controversial piece of legislation proved to be fortuitous for Murphy's desire to throw a patriotic party for President Taft at the West Side Grounds. One of the integral components of Taft's first year in office involved the Payne-Aldrich Tariff Act, which he "eagerly" signed into law on August 5, 1909.[47] During a brief respite with his wife, Nellie, in Massachusetts, Taft relaxed in preparation to embark on a nationwide tour to sell the American people on the merits of the compromise piece of legislation. The trek would take the president from one side of the country to the other, over the course of nearly two months, beginning with a visit to Chicago. The *Chicago Tribune* tabulated the president's railroad journey would crisscross America to the tune of 12,759 miles and declared it the "GREATEST PILGRIMAGE EVER UNDERTAKEN BY THE HEAD OF A NATION."[48] Following a speech to the Boston Chamber of Commerce on September 14, one day before his fifty-second birthday, Taft boarded the *Mayflower*, his private train car, and headed west.

Upon being selected as Taft's initial tour stop, the city of Chicago buzzed for two weeks with preparations to welcome the president on September 16. "Never in the history of the city's career as host to distinguished men of this and other lands has more care been exercised in preparation for a season of entertainment," reported the *Chicago Tribune*.[49]

Murphy learned of Taft's possible trip to Chicago at least a month prior to his visit, and the weather conspired with him to reconfigure the Cubs' schedule to coordinate a day when the president could visit the West Side Grounds. A game between the Giants and Cubs on June 9 had to be postponed because of a wet field, and a make-up contest was scheduled as part of a doubleheader on August 14.[50] However, neither game could be played that day because another storm had unleashed its fury on the city. A particularly vicious crack of lightning—most likely a Tigers fan—took out its frustration on the Cubs' symbol of victory. Sy Sanborn reported, "The storm which destroyed so much other property hereabouts robbed the Cubs of the flagstaff which has been graced by so many pennants during its existence. Lightning struck the tall mast and shattered its top for a distance of perhaps twenty-five feet, which was carried away by the wind." The strike ripped the championship pennant from its high perch atop the post, and it flapped away in the wind. The flag was located nearby, but the event loomed ominously. "The emblem of Cub-prowess was found on top of the roof of an adjoining house, and the superstitiously inclined will know why if it comes to pass that the Cubs fail to win their fourth straight," warned Sanborn.[51] Murphy immediately began his search for the perfect lumber to replace the obliterated wooden flagpole.

The summer storms provided Murphy with an opportunity to come up with a perfect solution for hosting Taft. The original postponed game would now be moved again, but this time it was to accommodate the president. An "(a)nnouncement was made yesterday that the

postponed game with the Giants, which was to have been played off
on Sept. 17 here, has been advanced in the schedule to the open date,
Sept. 16, when President Taft will be welcomed to our fair city, so as to
give the nation's executive opportunity to accept an invitation to see
the world's champions," an article in the *Chicago Tribune* explained.[52]

Murphy flew into a frenzied organizing mode. Workers adorned
the ballpark with bunting and flags. Important dignitaries throughout
local politics and the National League received invitations to attend
the game. Murphy was inundated with seat requests, but administer-
ing to the needs of the Hamilton Club, President Taft's official city
hosts, as well as the Commercial Club, emerged as his top priorities.
Murphy worked with the baseball committee of the Hamilton Club to
provide access to tickets for three thousand of its members and their
guests. They would each be given an American flag and a Hamilton
Club pennant upon arriving at the stadium. The plan called for all of
them to stand and wave their flags while simultaneously bursting into
a loud rendition of "Hail to the Chief" as Taft entered the stadium.
Murphy ensured that five bands—sixty-two pieces in total—would be
on hand to provide the music. President Taft would be seated along
the first-base line, about halfway up the grandstand. The attendance
of the clubs and excitement over Taft's presence at the park left tickets
to the ballgame in short supply.

By the date of the president's visit, the Cubs' hope of capturing a
fourth consecutive pennant hung by a thread. Despite an impressive
91-42 record, Chicago trailed Pittsburgh by five and a half games with
twenty-one contests to play. The good news for Chicago was it was
back home for a seventeen-game home stand that would see it through
the first weekend of October. The bad news arrived in the form of the
team's old rival, the New York Giants, who rolled into town in a disappointing third place looking to spoil any remaining hope the Cubs
had of moving up in the standings. Christy Mathewson would pitch
the series opener.

In the midst of preparations for Taft's visit, Manager Chance considered the unique circumstance as he mulled over his starting pitcher for
the afternoon. Initially, Jack Pfiester, the left-handed "Giant Killer," was

scheduled to pitch, but an injured middle finger put his start in jeopardy. The backup plan called for Ed Reulbach to start if Pfiester couldn't go. In the end, however, with the president in attendance and Mathewson taking the hill for the Giants, Chance took an entirely different tack and gave the ball to Mordecai Brown on two days of rest. Meanwhile, Murphy attended to the business of ensuring that everything at the ballpark went off without a hitch. Arranging unprecedented security precautions fell to Murphy and the Secret Service. He wouldn't know until after the game whether his efforts would pay off.

President Taft's train pulled into town at 11:12 a.m., three minutes early, on September 16. The "auspicious weather" assured large crowds at each outdoor stop on Taft's itinerary.[53] As planned, Chicago's school children lined the streets of the eight-mile route taken by Taft's motorcade, which wound through downtown from the station on Fifty-Fifth to the Congress Hotel. The students jubilantly sang songs and waved flags. The president warmly doffed his hat and waved his handkerchief in return with his trademark smile, grinning from ear to ear.

Later that morning, Taft wrote a warm telegram to his wife, Nellie, providing her with a description of the overwhelming reception by Chicagoans. "Have just finished a parade through the street of Chicago welcomed by 150,000 school children stretched along for nine miles on both sides of the Boulevard. It was the greatest sight I have ever witnessed and the continuous welcome calling for enthusiastic response from me at every turn made my right arm and neck tired with the effort. Certainly it surpassed any welcome that I have ever had. I go (to) a baseball game this afternoon after a luncheon at the commercial club . . . I send love."[54]

The blocks surrounding the West Side Grounds teemed with people trying to catch a glimpse of the president, and when Taft's motorcade pulled up to the stadium on Lincoln Street, reverberating shouts went up from the crowd. "The cheering was started by the 'knothole' audience which lined the sidewalks twelve deep and sat on the roofs and in the windows of houses adjacent to the park," reported the *Chicago Tribune*.[55] Moments later, the crowd inside the ballpark erupted with cheers and flag waves as Taft entered the stadium through a turnstile.

On cue, the assembled bands switched from playing rag time to "Hail to the Chief."[56] Secret Service agent P. G. Drautzberg flanked the president and scanned the crowd for any warning signs of danger, but he only saw cheering Chicagoans thrilled to welcome President Taft, whose prioritization of attending the game had clearly won the adoration of the city's baseball fans. The president waved to the crowd as Hamilton Club president George Dixon and other members escorted the remainder of the president's party into the ballpark, including Governor Charles Deneen, General Frederick Dent Grant, secretary of war Jacob Dickinson, Captain Archie Butt, and the new Chicago chief of police, Le Roy Steward.

Murphy had arranged for Taft, once inside the ballpark, to be escorted to the field, where he greeted the players from both teams. The players arranged themselves, and the president shook the hands of the Cubs before meeting the Giants. "Now, see that you put up a good game," he good-naturedly implored them.[57] Following the player introductions, Taft was escorted to his seat, located three rows behind the boxes aligned with the first-base bag. Someone handed him a glass of lemonade, and Taft guzzled it down. As first pitch approached, newspaper photographers in the aisle next to Taft annoyed the president by continuing to snap away with their cameras. "Now you fellows hurry up and get through," Taft instructed them. "I want to see the game."[58]

Excitement pulsed through the stands as Brown and the Cubs took the field. Many of the fans in the stands expressed hope to one another that "brother's team," a reference to Charles Taft's stake in the Cubs, would find a way to win and put pressure on the front-running Pirates. However, a defensive miscue, with two outs in the top of the first inning, allowed a Giants rally to build. Art Devlin singled in two Giant runs and quickly dented the crowd's enthusiasm. Chicago got a run back in the bottom of the second when Jimmy Archer singled in Joe Tinker to cut the deficit in half, but Mathewson tightened the screws on the Cubs' offense and they got no closer.

Local dignitaries made their way over to shake Taft's hand throughout the game, including Cap Anson, who was one of the first to greet the president. After several innings, with the game proceeding smoothly,

Murphy ventured out to visit with the president. He brought a slice of Ohio, Taft's home state, with him in the forms of Garry Herrmann and Cincinnati mayor John Galvin. They all shook hands and chatted.

Taft enjoyed himself immensely. He scarfed down popcorn (declined peanuts) and engaged in friendly banter with those around him. At one point he wondered aloud, "How many people are here?"

"Forty thousand," replied congressman William Wilson.

The suspicious president wasn't buying it. "I'm asking with a judicial mind, not a Chicago mind," he quipped.[59]

Murphy estimated there were between twenty-eight thousand and twenty-nine thousand in attendance. It wasn't a record crowd, but it was close.[60]

Taft even stood up in the seventh inning and stretched his legs, according to Richard Tobin of the *Inter Ocean*, "just like 'real fans' do."[61]

Mordecai Brown pitched well, but it was not enough as the Giants won the game, 2–1. The *Tribune*'s "Sy" Sanborn came away impressed with Taft's dedication as a fan after closely observing him throughout the game. In his game recap that appeared the following day, Sanborn concluded, "A leading constituent might be confiding an important party secret to the presidential left ear while another citizen, whose name appears often in headlines, might be offering congratulations on the outcome of the battle for revision downward to the right auricle, but while both ears were absorbing messages from friends both presidential eyes were steadily watching Christy Mathewson and the Giants revise downward the standing of the Cubs. That is the test of the true ball fan and William Howard Taft qualified as president of the United Fans' association of the U.S.A."[62]

Only in the aftermath of Taft's visit did the magnitude of Murphy's achievement come to light. Due to the unique nature of the rescheduled game, the organization did not have tickets for reserved and box seats for the date of September 16. As a result, Murphy had an easier time making seating arrangements for the president's party and the large number of Hamilton Club members. However, it also made security a bit trickier as anyone who acquired a ticket printed for June 9 could use it to get into the ballpark. The Chicago police department, Secret

Service, and Murphy coordinated and implemented exhaustive security measures to keep the president, along with all the fans who attended the game, safe. Law enforcement agents, along with members of the building department, cased the ballpark the day before the game. Three "watchmen" stayed at the stadium overnight from Wednesday into Thursday to keep an eye out for any suspicious activity. Law enforcement officials arrived at the ballpark early in the morning and stationed themselves beneath the section in which Taft sat, while fifty Secret Service agents patrolled the stadium during the game. A grateful Chief Steward personally thanked the Cubs for their assistance in facilitating such a smooth event.[63] All in all, the day proved to be a personal and professional triumph for Murphy. "The way in which the event was handled reflected great credit on every one connected with it, from President Murphy, who conceived and planned it, down," Sanborn declared.[64]

Despite the success of Taft's visit, the Cubs' loss to New York dropped Chicago to six and a half games behind the league-leading Pirates. Pittsburgh had simply outdistanced itself by a safe margin during the first half of the season. Murphy believed that several factors prevented the Cubs from winning a record fourth consecutive pennant. "Injuries to Manager Chance, with the late condition of our pitchers, put the Cubs in a rut that endured long enough during the spring to force the champions behind Pittsburgh," Murphy said. "The Pirates seem to have the best chance of the pennant because they have played sensational winning base ball and are entitled to the honors. Chicago will strive for the honor again next year with new faces on the club."

A dejected Chance lamented the organization's missed opportunity. "Defeat after such a bitter race is a hard blow to the Cub team as well as to myself. I had hoped to set the new record in base ball by winning four pennants in the National League, but the case now seems hopeless," admitted the Peerless Leader. The Pirates followed through on their great promise. Pittsburgh succeeded the Cubs as World Series champions by beating the Detroit Tigers (again!) in seven games.[65]

Following the season, Johnny Evers approached Murphy and asked for a personal favor. Evers's younger brother, twenty-three-year-old

Thomas, needed work, and the Census Bureau had emerged as a possibility as the department geared up to conduct the census the following year. Murphy gladly obliged and contacted Charles Taft on the young man's behalf. "This young man is a brother of John J. Evers, the second-baseman of the Chicago National League Club, and I have told you very often how highly I think of 'Johnny,' not only as a ball player, but as a man," Murphy wrote.[66] Whether Thomas got the job working for the government remains unclear, but Murphy was happy to engage Taft as a personal favor for Evers.

Despite all of the excitement surrounding the Cubs organization and President Taft, the season ended too early for everyone. With the magnificent streak of consecutive pennants swept away, an earlier-than-usual off-season greeted the team. The Pirates proved to be the class of the National League in 1909, and there wasn't much else one could say about it. Cubs right fielder Frank Schulte, who led the club with sixty runs batted in during the season, also dabbled in poetry in cahoots with Ring Lardner of the *Tribune* during the season, and they summed up the Cubs' broken pennant streak thusly:

> I've heard some reasons, nice and fine,
> Why we lost out in nineteen nine.
> Some say the pitchers lost their grip;
> Some say the infield had the pip;
> Some say the outfield couldn't hit.
> Some say the catchers didn't fit:
> Now, here's my reason, nice and fine.
> Why we lost out in nineteen nine:
> The Pirates won more games than we
> And didn't lose as many—see?[67]

THE FINAL PENNANT

Many American youngsters who grew up during the Progressive Era embraced Teddy Roosevelt as a heroic figure, but many lads who lived in the Chicago region admired a second great man, the lionhearted Frank Chance. One such fledgling, the son of Charlie Murphy's physician, lived in Oak Park. Born on July 21, 1899, Ernest Hemingway grew up alongside the Cubs. Young Hemingway participated in a variety of sports, but he claimed that baseball was his favorite. "I played it and loved it more than any other game," he wrote in a letter to his friend A. E. Hotchner. "Was a mediocre fielder, worthless second baseman, pretty good emory ball, knuckle ball and nothing ball pitcher," recalled Hemingway, the self-assessing scout. "Learned to throw knuckle ball from Eddie Cicotte (probably mis-spelled[*sic*]). Could always hit."[1] Hemingway also read Ring Lardner, the baseball writer who covered the Cubs on a daily basis for the *Chicago Tribune* beginning in 1910. Hemingway's initial successful writings were impressions of Lardner's style.[2]

Hemingway digested pitching lessons from Cicotte, the Chicago White Sox right-hander, who later entangled himself in the Black Sox scandal, and writing pointers from Lardner, but he comprehended as a teenager that following Chance's example taught him something about the finer points of becoming a man. During high school, Hemingway played football all four years as a reserve lineman. His lack of size limited him to the 135-pound team through his junior year before he joined the varsity squad as a senior.[3] Football inflicted physical pain on Hemingway, but Chance's stoicism poignantly modeled physical toughness and endurance to the impressionable youth: "I used to have piles bad in football season (they'd stick them in and tell you to hold them up all night and you would be awake all night thinking you were holding them up and they would be out already) I would say Dear Lord I know this isn't as bad as what Frank Chance has to go through every day but please give me courage to bear it like he does."[4] Biographer Michael Reynolds contends that, "Hemingway's generation came of age with a new definition for manhood: a man must excel in competitive sports." According to Reynolds, Hemingway complied: "It was never a game with Hemingway: fishing, hunting, tennis, boxing became tests of manhood." Nor were they games to Chance, who was a renowned boxer in the off-season. Johnny Evers once told sportswriter Grantland Rice, "A ball game with Frank Chance was war, not a pink tea."[5] Although not a soldier, Chance's self-reliant toughness rivaled the vision of the strenuous life fashioned by Teddy Roosevelt and expressed by many of the characters Hemingway would later write into existence.

Chance's strength of will, however, could not overcome the multiple blows to the head he suffered at the plate. Pitches that struck the side of Chance's skull undoubtedly damaged his hearing, and the repeated trauma inflicted substantial pain. "Frank Chance couldn't duck if they threw at his head," wrote Hemingway with the exasperation and worry of an admirer. "After he had his first concussion when I think it was Marquard hit him he would freeze and nobody ever threw anything to him that wasn't high and inside. Finally he got such awful headaches that it was tough for me, a punk kid, to see him."[6]

By the 1910 season, the finish line of Chance's playing career was nearing with rapid velocity. Chance had appeared in only ninety-three games in 1909, the lowest total of his career since 1902, when he was a young part-time player. A shoulder injury forced Chance out of action for six weeks, from mid-May through the end of June. The physical toll of playing baseball painfully tormented Chance's body, but his sharp mind and unquestionable toughness continued to bend the Cubs' clubhouse to his will. Although the Cubs knocked off the White Sox in the City Series after the 1909 season, it didn't mean much. The disappointment of losing out on the pennant to Pittsburgh, who had gone on to win the World Series, deeply stung Chance. He restlessly stewed throughout the off-season. The second-place finish reinforced his hunger to win, and he would accept nothing less than the same commitment from his team in 1910.

A disappointed Charlie Murphy drew little satisfaction from the 1909 season, even though the Cubs won 104 games, but he took some solace in the ticket scandal that erupted during the 1909 World Series. The National Commission, which had taken over the sale of World Series tickets from clubs, as part of the process restructure in the aftermath of the 1908 outcry, didn't fare any better than Murphy and his outfit had the year before. The commission arranged for undercover agents and local police to monitor the stadium box offices and local establishments near Forbes Field and Bennett Park, where scalpers were known to operate, but it could not have botched the sale more if it tried, particularly in Detroit. Sure, police officers nabbed some scalpers out front of Bennett Park but, in their overzealousness to crack down, they actually kicked Tigers fans out of line. "It was because members of the commission and the Pinkertons they brought over from Chicago did not know a thing of the prominent patrons of the Detroit club. They refused to sell them tickets, while the scalpers were getting all they wanted for the same reason. Congressman Edwin Denby, George and John Nestor, who buy dozens of tickets a day in the regular season, were among those who were kicked out of line," criticized one report.[7] Clearly, selling World Series tickets to fans was harder than it sounded. At least the Cubs' front office had recognized its most valuable customers.

The Cubs "barnstormed" for several weeks after their City Series against the White Sox ended, a common practice of playing postseason games to make a little more money after the close of the season. Among the exhibition contests, Chicago played a particularly intriguing series against the Leland Giants, an independent team of Black ballplayers managed by Rube Foster, a savvy businessman and an outstanding pitcher. The series began on October 18. The Cubs played without either

Evers, who had returned to New York following the birth of his son, or the recuperating Chance, but they otherwise fielded a strong squad.

Murphy attended the series opener at Gunther Park, located on the north side of the city. Chance was also there to watch. The Cubs beat the Giants, 4–1, behind the pitching of Mordecai Brown, in front of over two thousand fans. However, the incredible toughness of Giants center fielder Joe Green left the most lasting impression on everyone at the game. After Green reached third base in the eighth inning, he took a large lead off the bag, and Cubs catcher Pat Moran thought he could pick him off. As Moran released his throw to Harry Steinfeldt, who was covering third base, Green hurried back to the bag and slid. The awkward impact broke Green's leg. Moran's throw wildly missed Steinfeldt and sailed into left field. Green immediately got up and hopped on one leg as fast as he could toward home plate. However, the Cubs executed a relay play and tagged Green out just before he could score. Overwhelmed with pain, Green collapsed and had to be carried from the field.[8]

Three days later, the Cubs met in Murphy's office to divvy up the money they had earned for beating the White Sox in the City Series. It amounted to over $700 a man, including treasurer Charlie Williams, to whom the players had voted a full share. Additional revenue from other exhibition games was also distributed.[9] Later that afternoon, Murphy and the Cubs returned to the field as they resumed their series against the Leland Giants. Murphy sat in the stands alongside longtime baseball scout Ted Sullivan, who had discovered Orval Overall in a previous life. The Giants jumped out to a 5–0 lead in the third inning against Ed Reulbach. The Cubs scored single runs in the fourth and eighth innings but still trailed by three runs entering the ninth against the dazzling Rube Foster. Chicago's offense was kept at bay, in part, by the Giants' defense, which twice successfully pulled off the hidden ball trick to nab Cubs base runners. However, Chicago finally got to Foster in the ninth inning. The Cubs put together a four-run outburst, capped off by Frank Schulte's sprint for home from third base, while the two teams debated with the umpire about the slow tactics of Foster. Timeout had not officially been called, so Schulte sprinted for home.

Foster fired the ball to the plate, but Schulte slid under the tag to give the Cubs a 6–5 lead they did not relinquish.[10]

Mordecai Brown returned to the mound and outdueled Giants' left-hander Pat Dougherty, 1–0, in the final game of the series. Miserable weather made for difficult playing conditions, and the game was called after only seven innings. Although the Cubs had swept the series, the talented Giants had proven that they could compete with one of the National League's top clubs. Several months later, the magnates embedded a new clause into the players' contracts for the 1910 season that barred them from playing exhibition games without the written consent of the owner. Harvey Woodruff, the sporting stalwart of the *Chicago Tribune*, who had helped Murphy and Chance reconcile, reported that the close series between the Cubs and Leland Giants, as well as a lackluster performance by the Detroit Tigers in Cuba, alarmed all the owners because it harmed the teams' reputations.[11]

Charlie Murphy missed the final game of the Cubs' series against Leland because he was delivering an address to the Young Men's Christian Association at the Oak Park Club that evening. It was one of his final engagements as a member of the Oak Park community, as he planned to soon move to Edgewater, a neighborhood on the western shore of Lake Michigan, where waves lapped the backyards of the homes on Sheridan Road. Murphy primarily spoke to the attendees about the global growth of baseball. He cited the recent printing of baseball's rules in at least seven foreign languages, by a Chicago publisher, as evidence of the sport's increasing audience. Of course, Murphy also told them tales about the Cubs. He believed that the team's intelligence was one of its keys to success and that no player epitomized its savvy more than Johnny Evers.[12]

With the players dispersed for the winter, Murphy turned his full attention to the business operations of his franchise. Failing to win the pennant had cost the organization a significant sum of money, but he didn't blame the team for finishing in second place. The Cubs had become the first team to win over a hundred games and not advance to the World Series. They had actually performed admirably in the face of Johnny Kling's desertion and injuries throughout the roster. With the

West Side Grounds renovated and a strong roster still intact, Murphy pondered new ways of expanding the business. He floated the idea of extending the regular season from 154 games to 168 games to his peers. Murphy wasn't the only one who favored the concept. Brooklyn's Charles Ebbets and John Taylor of the Boston Red Sox voiced their support for a longer season. Despite their support, the suggestion to lengthen the schedule failed to gain widespread traction in the American League and was scrapped.

While baseball owners and reporters droned on about the schedule expansion idea, the wily Murphy initiated his real master plan. Over the past four and a half years, Murphy had risen from an indebted vice president of the Cubs to running the franchise himself as the majority shareholder with two World Series titles to his credit. The same ambition that convinced Charles Taft to loan him the funds necessary to buy the team now fueled Murphy to an even grander design. Murphy was not satisfied with simply being a successful baseball magnate; he wanted to be a business titan. He had conquered the baseball world, and now he turned his eyes toward creating a new entertainment model that amalgamated sports with the performing arts. Why should he doubt his capabilities? His ambition, energy, and work ethic had produced successful results harkening back to his teenage years in Wilmington as a clerk at Dan Fogel's drug store. Murphy's tactics had ruffled plenty of feathers along the way, but he didn't really have many sworn enemies with whom he couldn't smooth things over, with the exception of American League president Ban Johnson. But animosity in baseball circles ran deep toward the abrasive Johnson, so did it really matter? Steeped in confidence, Murphy forged ahead with his dream to build an empire.

The first step of Murphy's quest dovetailed with John T. Brush's newfound purpose of dethroning Ban Johnson as the leader of Organized Baseball: get rid of Harry Pulliam's protégé, John Heydler. Brush had been ill for a number of years and sensed that he finally had an opportunity to regain the control he had lost in the merger war of 1902–3 between the American and National Leagues. Brush wanted to oust Heydler and replace him with someone more influential over the National Commission. Murphy eagerly supported Brush's attempt to replace Heydler because he needed someone friendlier to his own interests. Ban Johnson would never support Murphy's grandiose plan in any way, so Murphy wanted someone in charge of the National League who would protect him. Replacing Heydler would curb Johnson's power. Murphy not only wanted a stronger ally personally, but he also wanted the National League to become more effective at counteracting Johnson. Murphy believed that Johnson was too old-fashioned and unwilling to disrupt some of the traditions of baseball to improve its business model.

Murphy had a problem with Heydler beyond his business scheme. Heydler had cracked down on rowdy behavior by National League players throughout his months in charge, and an angry Murphy thought the president had unfairly targeted the Cubs. Bill Phelon, who had known Murphy for a number of years as the Chicago correspondent for *Sporting Life*, thought Heydler had done a good job, and he questioned Murphy's displeasure with the league president. "Charlie Murphy, master of the Cubs, is a grand little fellow, even if many folks don't like him. Any dislike to Charlie Murphy is, as a rule, among people who don't really know him . . . But—even though I may go sharply counter to the ideas of Mr. Murphy—what earthly reason is there for not standing by John Heydler?" inquired Phelon.[13] Despite Phelon's criticism, Murphy wasn't alone in his displeasure with Heydler. In addition to Brush, Ebbets also wanted to thwart the president's reelection bid.

Murphy had an ideal candidate in mind to replace John Heydler: Jim Hart, his predecessor in Chicago, who had received some notable support for the position in the past. Murphy approached Hart about the possibility of becoming the next leader of the National League in late October. Flattered, Hart provided Murphy with a list of requirements that he wanted met before he even considered the possibility. Hart demanded that he be able to retain his business interests and continue living in Chicago. He also wanted to name the league's secretary and treasurer himself. Hart believed his list of asks so egregious—not to mention that the owners would have to agree to rewrite the National League constitution to see them through—that Murphy would naturally balk, and Hart could elegantly escape having to turn him down. To Hart's surprise, Murphy said he would get to work on meeting Hart's demands straightaway. Rumors began to circulate in the press that Murphy was aiming to make Hart the new man in charge. Uncomfortable with the publicity and uninterested in the job, Hart wrote a letter in late November to the press that explained he did not want to be considered for the role.

Thwarted by Hart, Murphy traveled to New York to strategize with Brush and Ebbets about what to do next. The three owners wanted a new president, even if they had not yet reached consensus on either the ideal replacement or the procedure. Murphy tried to keep his trip from becoming public, but his presence was detected. Murphy claimed that he was visiting Brush because of the latter's illness, but nobody believed him. Ebbets batted away any notion that he was involved in any sort of mischief. "It is true that I have talked about Heydler with Murphy, but I am not pledged to vote against him," Ebbets dubiously proclaimed to inquiring reporters. Ebbets later couched his frustration with Heydler in a disingenuous declaration that he was not part of Murphy's voting block: "I have nothing against Heydler either personally or officially. While he may have made mistakes, so would any man in his position. I have nothing to say about the protested game he decided against us, nor do I wish to criticize anything he has done while in office. If there is any so-called conspiracy to unseat him I am not a party to it and know nothing of it."[14]

Although impossible to prove, it is highly likely that Murphy and Brush found a few minutes alone to discuss a vital, and extremely controversial, next step in Murphy's grand plan: the purchase of the Philadelphia Phillies. Murphy had heard that the Phillies, and their ballpark, could be bought for the right price, but the loathing for syndicate baseball complicated matters. Murphy was well aware of the hostility held by many who worked in the baseball industry toward syndication, but their distaste for the practice didn't faze him. Nor did it bother Brush, who had been simultaneously involved with the Reds and Giants earlier in his career. Murphy's pursuit of the Phillies dovetailed nicely with the Heydler conundrum, because he could then

install a figurehead in Philadelphia and direct his vote against the
league president. Brush knew just the right person for the job: Horace
Fogel, who Brush had hired way back in 1887 to manage his team in
Indianapolis. Fogel had taken the helm for the New York Giants in
1902 but was fired during the season. He spent a few months as a
scout for the Giants before he joined the *Sporting News* as a columnist. The following year Fogel was part of a group that tried to buy the
Phillies, but it lost out to another collection of bidders that included
Barney Dreyfuss, which fueled animosity between them. Now, six
years later, Brush figured correctly that Fogel, who wanted to work
with the club, would willingly sign on as a front man for Murphy, if
given the opportunity.

With Jim Hart no longer an option, Brush and Murphy needed a
new presidential candidate, and the anti-Heydler faction coalesced
around the controversial John Montgomery Ward, a veteran of sixteen
seasons in the National League. The versatile former ballplayer was an
outstanding pitcher and outfielder who had also managed. Ward had
attended law school in the off-season and graduated from Columbia
in 1885, after which he fought for players' rights. Ward drew the ire of
the establishment by railing against the reserve clause in players' contracts that bound them to one franchise in perpetuity, and he played
an instrumental role in organizing professional baseball's labor force.
In 1890 Ward left the National League to play in the newly constituted
Players League, an organization he created, which had folded after
one year. He spent four more seasons playing in the National League
before retiring after the 1894 season.

Although Ward emerged as a candidate for the Brush-Murphy faction of National League owners, he was anathema to American League
president Ban Johnson. Although Johnson raged in the background at
Ward's potential candidacy, he astutely wrote a stern, yet calm, letter to
Garry Herrmann, largely for the purpose of being released publicly to
give the anti-Ward faction political cover. "The unbounded prosperity
the game has enjoyed under its present government should serve as a
safety valve to any prejudiced act that might tend to destroy a healthful,
sound, and sportsmanlike condition in baseball." In other words, John-

son was warning Brush and Murphy that they risked sparking another war between the leagues if they somehow managed to elect Ward.[15]

Meanwhile, Murphy furtively worked toward acquiring the Phillies. He talked the deal over with Charles and Annie Taft, and they jumped on board as investors. Taft supplied a large chunk of the capital needed to acquire the club without his name being publicly connected to the transaction. The Tafts also joined Murphy in pursuing the ballpark purchase, although that would not take place until the end of the year. The Tafts and Murphy wanted to remain silent partners to avoid accusations of running a syndicate operation in which they boosted the roster of the Cubs at the expense of the Phillies. It was a bold and underhanded idea. If word got out, the National Commission would terminate the transaction, expose the scheme, and ruin their reputations.

In late November Murphy traveled to Philadelphia to meet with Horace Fogel. Murphy worked to arrange the deal over the next forty-eight hours and, on November 26, 1909, the Philadelphia Phillies were purchased and Fogel was announced as the new president of the franchise. Four prominent local men were selected as officers of the club and formed the local group of "buyers" that accompanied Fogel. The *Philadelphia Inquirer* reported the purchase price as $350,000, and Fogel told the newspaper that he had acquired 987 of the 1,000 issued shares. All told, it gave the appearance that the local consortium had spearheaded the buy when, in fact, Taft and Murphy were behind it. Fogel steadfastly denied that the Cubs' owners had supplied his investment group with capital, but the lie didn't fool anyone. Eventually, Fogel admitted that Murphy had offered to help him make the deal happen but said little else. Fogel confessed that he had entered negotiations to acquire wayward Cubs star Johnny Kling, which raised even more questions.[16] The Baker Bowl, the home of the Phillies, was not included in the sale, but its status would be resolved in the coming months.

As the winter meeting approached, Cubs treasurer Charlie Williams emerged as a candidate to become the next secretary of the National League if the magnates reelected John Heydler. Williams refused to inject himself into the process, but he acknowledged that he would take the job if it was offered to him. Heydler thought highly of Williams, as did many around baseball, and he had asked the Cubs treasurer to work on behalf of the league during the 1909 World Series, but Williams had to decline because he had duties to perform for his team. If the Chicago organization was guilty of massive ticket fraud in 1908, it didn't curb Heydler's interest in promoting Williams or hurt the youngster's reputation around the sport. Williams traveled to New York the following week and attended the meeting in case he was tabbed for the post.[17]

However, it increasingly appeared that Charlie Williams would be taking his brief sojourn to New York for fine dining and a show rather than a new appointment with the National League. Barney Dreyfuss announced that the Pirates would support Heydler's reelection, and he scoffed at the idea that he would lose. "I do not think there is the slightest possibility of there being a change," Dreyfuss said.[18]

However, the well-connected Garry Herrmann hedged his commitment. "I always have been for Mr. Heydler, but if I find out there is no chance for his election I will not vote for him. I will vote for the next best man rather than cause a row, but that man will not be John M. Ward."[19]

As the owners settled into their opposing sides of the issue, Charles Ebbets announced that he would support Ward and join Murphy, Brush, and Fogel in the anti-Heydler camp. It posited the four owners against Herrmann, Dreyfuss, and John Dovey, who had recently assumed the presidency of the Boston Doves, following the death of his brother, George. The final decision rested on the shoulders of Stanley Robison, the owner of the St. Louis Cardinals, who had yet to publicly state for whom he intended to cast his ballot.

Outraged at the prospect of serving on the National Commission alongside Ward, Ban Johnson continued to rant that war would descend upon the leagues if he was elected. Johnson blamed Murphy, not Brush, for Ward's candidacy and went so far as to suggest that the Cubs owner had demanded that all National Commission rulings favor the National League. "Do you think we are going to allow a man of Murphy's caliber the balance of power in a thing as big as baseball?" Johnson thundered. Johnson accused Murphy of favoring Ward because he was an associate of Henry Taft, the younger brother of Charles Taft. "I wrote a letter to Garry Herrmann telling him my objections to Ward, and I sent a copy of the letter to every one of my clubowners, and every one of them (e) ndorsed it," Johnson added.[20] This tense dynamic between the executives hung thick in the air as the winter meeting opened in New York, at the Waldorf Astoria Hotel, on December 14, 1909.

Stricken with illness, Brush remained at home for the initial sessions, but his absence did not blunt his impact on the proceedings. Well aware that Brush had his voting bloc aligned and united, Herrmann knew that Heydler didn't have five votes in the room to be reelected, so Robert Brown, a Louisville journalist known throughout baseball, emerged as an alternate candidate. The first official ballot revealed how Stanley Robison of St. Louis would vote, and the result was a 4-4 tie. Robison had cast his lot with the Herrmann-Dreyfuss faction in support of Heydler. The deadlock continued, as Brush refused to relent. After several days of unceasing discussion, the meeting drew to a close, and Brush faced the very real possibility that Heydler would continue as league president simply because a replacement had not been named. It was clear that none of the group that included Herrmann, Dreyfuss, Robison, and Dovey would break away to push Ward over the top. Brush's only move was to offer up a moderate alternative candidate that the magnates could support. Feeling compelled, Brush willed himself out of bed and went to the hotel for a face-to-face confrontation.

Brush spoke ardently in favor of Ward, but ultimately, his words did not sway any votes, and it remained clear that Ward did not have a path to election. The Heydler faction generously offered Brush the opportunity to submit a different candidate. Initially, he refused and futilely argued Ward's case. Eventually, however, Brush realized that it was a meaningless exercise, and he retreated into his bunker to come up with another name. Brush caught everyone off guard when he submitted the name of Thomas J. Lynch, a former National League umpire. Amenable to everyone, Lynch sailed through the confirmation process and was unanimously elected president of the National League, 8–0. The astute Lynch wanted Heydler retained in the league office as secretary, the role he had so admirably performed before Harry Pulliam's death. Heydler had been a young umpire when Lynch was operating as one of the finest arbiters in baseball. Brush assented, and Heydler was handed a shiny new three-year contract to resume his role as National League secretary, which he readily accepted. Left empty-handed, Charlie Williams rejoined Murphy in Chicago. Brush had been defeated, which meant that Johnson remained the towering figure in the sport.

Following the tumultuous few weeks, Murphy returned to Chicago for a brief spell before he headed southeast to Wilmington, where he spent Christmas with his mother, Bridget. On his way to visit his family, Murphy stopped in Cincinnati, where he sat down with Reds manager Clark Griffith to talk trades. Griffith was one of many managers interested in prying the ostracized Johnny Kling away from the Cubs. McGraw and the Giants had also expressed interest, but Murphy would never trade Kling to New York. The Reds were also interested in Rip Hagerman, a young right-handed pitcher who had made thirteen appearances for the Cubs during the 1909 season. The Reds had a thirty-two-year-old pitcher, Bob Spade, who intrigued Murphy. Griffith met up with Murphy, and the two men sat down for several hours but could not strike an accord. At one point during the talks, Murphy dangled Mordecai Brown, who immediately piqued Griffith's interest. Murphy claimed he was joking, but Griffith didn't find any humor in it. Murphy was irritated that Griffith's demands for the Reds' players were so preposterously high. Thinking nothing of his jest, Murphy left Cincinnati for Wilmington to celebrate Christmas before Griffith could give him an answer on Brown, leaving the Reds skipper angry. "He may have a better scheme up his sleeve, but you can count me out of it," Griffith fumed. "I am done with trying to deal with a man who is so afraid that he couldn't tell to whom his own soul belonged."[21] Upon hearing the rumor, Mordecai Brown indifferently shrugged.

On New Year's Eve, an announcement was made that the Tafts had officially acquired the Baker Bowl from Colonel John I. Rogers and A. J. Reach and, in turn, leased it to the Phillies organization for ninety-nine years. The Tafts paid $215,000 for the title to the ballpark and, apparently at the behest of Rogers and Reach, made a $35,000 contribution to the Pennsylvania Institution for the Instruction of the Blind.[22] Interestingly, Rogers admitted that, although they sold the stadium for $250,000, it would be worth twice as much in a decade. Meanwhile, Horace Fogel tried in vain to deflect insinuations that the transaction meant the Tafts owned the team itself. "Mr. Taft does not own one dollar's worth of stock in the Phillies. He took over the park as an investment and also to strengthen the position of the National league in Philadelphia," Fogel claimed.[23]

However, Fogel had hosted his sportswriter friends for a celebratory dinner at the ornate Hotel Majestic on Broad Street to toast his group's acquisition of the Phillies. During the party Fogel confessed to his cohorts that his good friend Charlie Murphy had pulled the strings behind the Phillies' sale, but Fogel maintained that Murphy had not bought into the club itself. "Mr. Murphy does not own a share of stock in the club. The stock is owned solely by Philadelphians. There is no Western syndicate concerned in the transaction," Fogel stressed.[24] No one in baseball believed him.

Murphy also refuted suggestions that he owned any stock, and even though the Tafts' acquisition of the Baker Bowl raised questions, he argued that there was nothing to it. Murphy released a statement in which he claimed that Bill Shettsline of the Phillies had approached him to speak with Taft about buying the ballpark the previous year. He refuted the reports that suggested something nefarious was afoot.

"Neither Mr. Taft nor myself owns stock in the Philadelphia club. Invidious persons have circulated mendacious reports to the contrary, to hurt the National league. I did not think it policy to make any comment on these stories until after the completion of the deal for the Philadelphia park, which had to be closed before Jan. 1, 1910. Neither Mr. Taft nor myself favors syndicate baseball . . . My activity at Philadelphia was entirely in behalf of the National league, and I have no apology to make to those who are envious of

the successful culmination of the two big deals at Philadelphia,"
said the implacable Murphy.[25]

Although insistent that they had not bought the team, the pair of
Charlies made little effort to conceal their involvement in the Phillies'
business arrangements even though the concept of syndicate baseball
was deeply frowned upon. Taft and Murphy were in Philadelphia at
the time of the club's sale, and they both talked to the press, although
they gave largely evasive answers. Nonetheless, reporters learned a
few pertinent bits of information. Murphy confirmed that he was the
Cubs' majority owner by way of possessing 53 percent of the franchise's
stock, while Taft retained a 25 percent interest in the franchise. Taft
also acknowledged the purchase of the Phillies' ballpark. "I am interested in the success of the Philadelphia Club to the extent of hoping
that the owners make enough money to pay the price of the lease,"
Taft told reporters.[26]

Fueled by his unrelenting confidence in his promotional capabilities,
Murphy believed that with an upgraded roster, enhanced by a splash
of circus magic, the Phillies could evolve from an irrelevant National
League franchise into a new kind of amusement powerhouse. Murphy
initiated his plan to merge the ballgames with theater and circus acts.
Bill Phelon believed that Murphy was uniquely positioned to fulfill
his vision of becoming an entertainment mogul on a national scale.
"The Philadelphia deal, engineered, despite all talk and gossip, by Mr.
Murphy's capital, is but an item in a scheme of gigantic proportions...
Mr. Murphy, backed by unlimited capital, wishes to become not only
a base ball magnate, but an amusement promoter of the Klaw and
Erlanger magnitude. The idea is one of huge possibilities," admitted
the admiring Phelon.[27] Marc Klaw and Abraham Erlanger operated a
theatrical management company out of New York City that booked
acts in the best theaters across the country. To demonstrate his commitment, Murphy acquired a 50 percent interest in the Baker Bowl
from the Tafts.

Adding a stake in the stadium to his growing portfolio allowed Murphy to combine sports and entertainment. Murphy planned to hold

doubleheaders of a different kind at the Baker Bowl. Baseball games would be held in the afternoon, which would be followed by theater performances in a hippodrome on the grounds.[28] It wasn't an original idea; the Philadelphia Athletics of the American League had already tried something similar, but Murphy believed his marketing skills, and Annie Taft's connections in the theater world, would make the project a smashing success. Murphy's strategic maneuvers were like a bolt of lightning from a clear sky in the mind of Bill Phelon, who had originally questioned Murphy's unwillingness to support another term for Heydler. Now Phelon grasped the full scope of Murphy's vision: "First thing of all, the magnates do not understand the ambitions and the business capacities of Charles W. Murphy. They still figure the little president as a busy hustler and a troublemaker, a sort of sawed-off firebrand in base ball, and in base ball only. They see in the deal for the Philadelphia Club only an evidence of Murphy's insatiate desire to possess power in base ball circles and to make himself the main figure of a diamond syndicate. All well and good—but how far short of the actual facts!"[29]

A rumor circulated that a deal between the Cubs and Phillies was on the table that would send Jimmy Sheckard to Philadelphia in return for Sherry Magee, an exciting young outfielder. The Phillies wanted to install Sheckard as their new player/manager, but Chance told Murphy no, and the proposal evaporated.[30] The mirage of the Phillies as an independent operation remained intact but the mere presence of the rumor suggested otherwise. Chance may not have liked this particular trade proposal, but it didn't change the fact that the Cubs had tried to fleece Philadelphia.

At the end of the 1909 season, the Cubs returned to their various caves throughout the country, but hardly any of them hibernated during the winter. Orval Overall returned to California, where his gold mine investments monopolized much of his time. A few hundred miles south, Frank Chance worked his ranch in Glendora, where the skipper grew oranges, fished, and took care of his animals, including a young cow named Teddy. On his land in Bellevue, Kentucky, Harry Steinfeldt engaged in his favorite hobby, horticulture. Steinfeldt kneaded the dirt and planted rows of roses, but he was particularly affectionate toward his Japanese violets. For the second off-season in a row, Joe Tinker starred in a vaudeville show. He appeared in "A Great Catch," alongside Sadie Sherman, which opened at Chicago's Haymarket Theater on January 10, 1910. All the Charlies in the Cubs front office attended the show: Murphy, Williams, and Thomas. Mordecai Brown showed up to support his teammate. Garry Herrmann could be spotted in the crowd as well. Hank O'Day, the umpire who called Fred Merkle out and who lived in Chicago, was also there. The crowd enjoyed the musical (Tinker sang a song titled, "Slide! Slide! Slide!") and showered the actors with praise after it concluded.

Herrmann remained in Chicago for several days after the show, and Murphy reached out to him to schedule a meeting, presumably out of a hope to reignite trade talks over pitcher Bob Spade. The two magnates spoke and agreed on a meeting time, but Murphy didn't show up, which left Herrmann frustrated. That happened two more times. "I tried to see Murphy three times in Chicago last week, but every time I went to the appointed place he was missing," Herrmann told reporters the following Monday: "He called me by telephone and asked me to come around to see him. I went, but couldn't find him. Again, he called me up and again I went. The third time I went and he was still away. Then I made up my mind that we could get along just as well as if he never existed."[31] Rather than communicate with Herrmann to alleviate his anger, Murphy kept the reason behind his absences a mystery.

Back in Ohio, Murphy's sister, Katie, the youngest sibling of the family, who suffered from dementia praecox, a term not used in modern medicine but frequently referred to as a forbearer of schizophrenia, had died. She had passed away on January 4, 1910, at the Athens State Hospital, where she had been institutionalized for nearly thirteen years. A grief-stricken Murphy attended the opening night of "A Great Catch" to take his mind off her death. He mingled with friends, supported Tinker, and enjoyed the show for several hours of respite before he returned to the family tragedy the following morning.

Murphy never spoke about his family's struggles publicly, and he feigned a response to pacify Herrmann's criticism without mentioning Katie's death. Murphy claimed that he had overslept, and therefore missed the first meeting, while Herrmann had to return early to Cincinnati, which forced the cancellation of another. Meanwhile, Bridget Murphy and the boys had Katie's body brought back to Wilmington, where they laid her to rest in Sugar Grove Cemetery next to her father. Conflicting records make it difficult to determine her exact age, but she was no older than thirty-five.[32]

The success of Tinker's show expanded its run to include several Midwestern cities outside of Chicago. Tinker was originally scheduled to appear in Kansas City, the home of Johnny Kling, in January, but a schedule change postponed the performance until March. Tinker wanted to talk with Kling about rejoining the Cubs. Tinker called on Murphy to discuss the Kling situation. Kling remained angry with Murphy, because he felt like the latter had been responsible for trying to thwart his billiards business. Murphy denied it, and many of Kling's teammates had come to believe that Garry Herrmann had actually been the one behind it. Murphy knew that Tinker maintained a close friendship with Kling, and he happily paid for the shortstop's train fare to visit the Cubs' former catcher. Kling remained ineligible to return to the National League, because the National Commission had labeled him a contract jumper, but the first step in getting him back involved talking him into wanting to be a Cub again. Tinker adamantly pressed Kling over lunch. Tinker argued that Kling's business would explode in value if he reestablished himself as one of the premier players in baseball, but he had to first smooth things over with Murphy. The following day, January 19, at 2:00 p.m., Kling called Murphy, and they talked out their issues over the phone. Murphy, who could put aside his own frustration and smooth things over with just about anyone, expressed his excitement at having Kling back in a Cubs uniform, and Kling agreed to apply for reinstatement. Tinker returned to Chicago, but he wisely remained silent about the development so as not to alienate the members of the commission.

In Chicago, Murphy received two exciting pieces of news regarding President Taft. Murphy opened a letter informing him that Taft would again be attending a Cubs game during the upcoming season. Taft's team had scheduled a trip to Pittsburgh on May 2 and blocked off the afternoon for Chicago's visit to Forbes Field, and Murphy, who eagerly circled the date on his calendar, was encouraged to attend. Additionally, Taft would be in the Windy City on St. Patrick's Day to speak to the Irish Fellowship Club of Chicago.

Looking ahead to Taft's visit, the Irish Fellowship Club acquired four large strips of sod bursting with shamrocks from the grounds surrounding Rostellan Castle in County Cork, Ireland. The prized grass traversed the Atlantic, a journey taken by so many of Ireland's immigrants, and arrived in America aboard the *St. Louis* of White Star Lines for President Taft to stand upon when he delivered his remarks in Chicago.[33] The sod was transported to the La Salle Hotel and put on display for the public to see in the days leading up to St. Patrick's Day. Despite its best efforts to plan, the response to the sod overwhelmed the hotel. Chicago's Irishmen and women stood in excruciatingly long lines to catch a glimpse of the thin slice of Erin's land. The club allowed as many people as possible to see it. Overcome with emotion, the tears of the weeping Irish relentlessly washed the grass anew. Before he left to join the Cubs in New Orleans, Murphy offered the club $100 for the sod.[34] He wanted to install it near home plate at the West Side Ball Park, where it could become a public shrine of sorts. The club politely declined Murphy's overture. On March 17 Taft delivered his remarks to the club with his feet firmly planted on Irish ground. "This is the greatest St. Patrick's day celebration ever held on American soil," exclaimed Irish Fellowship Club president M. J. Faherty.[35] No one in the audience disagreed.

On Friday night, February 26, 1910, a train pulled out of Chicago and headed toward West Baden, Indiana, for the commencement of spring training. Only half of the team was aboard, but the missing players had alternate plans to meet the group in either West Baden or New Orleans, where the team was scheduled to begin its exhibition season. Embittered by losing out to the Pirates, the Cubs prepared for the season with renewed vigor and saltiness tinged with anger. "We're not afraid of Pittsburg, New York, Cincinnati, or any of the rest of them now, but if we get off two or three games in the lead the fight will be a joke," Frank Chance insisted.[36] The Cubs core was getting a bit older, but one could hardly accuse them of aging. Although Chance, Steinfeldt, and Brown were entering their midthirties, several players, including Reulbach, Schulte, and Hofman, remained in their prime. Pitcher King Cole, a twenty-four-year-old right-hander whose fastball hummed like an engine, established himself as a newcomer of promise in the rotation.

One of the more entertaining debates during spring training involved Solly Hofman and Ed Reulbach, who playfully argued over which new father had the most intelligent baby. They were both incredibly devoted to them: Hofman to his daughter, Mary Jane, and Ed to his son, Edward, which made it all the more disconcerting when young Edward suddenly became very ill. A doctor diagnosed the baby with diphtheria, and Reulbach rushed to St. Louis to be with his wife and son. Murphy and Chance couldn't replace either Reulbach the teammate or Reulbach the pitcher, but they wanted to fortify the rotation so that the team could start the season well while it waited for Ed's return. Reulbach, who pitched at Notre Dame before turning professional, did not get nearly the amount of ink some of his teammates did, but the organization knew how valuable he was to its success. He had led the National League in win percentage for three seasons in a row from 1906 through 1908.

Reulbach's concerned teammates breathed a deep sigh of relief after they received word that his son's condition was improving, but they only had a short reprieve before they learned that Ed himself had contracted diphtheria. As the team began its exhibition schedule, Reulbach took a turn for the worse. He received an anti-toxin treatment from doctors to combat his bacterial infection. After several tenuous days, Reulbach responded to the treatment and slowly regained his strength. The pleased doctors told him that he was recovering, but his body could not handle baseball for quite a few weeks.

Reulbach's illness galvanized the Cubs to make a move. Murphy failed to pry Bob Spade away from Cincinnati, and he needed to find another pitcher before the season started in less than a week. Murphy traveled with the team to Indianapolis, where the Cubs continued their exhibition schedule. Murphy's purpose, however, did not center on the team's performance but on conferring with Chance on finding a replacement for Reulbach. They believed that the margin for error in the National League would be razor thin, and a poor start could sink their season. The pitching staff needed to be at full strength.

Chance wanted to acquire Harry McIntire, a veteran right-hander, who had performed reasonably well for a terrible Brooklyn team. McIntire had a career record of 46-98, but that belied his notable pitching ability. Brooklyn stunk, and it would be bad again in 1910, so Charlie Ebbets did not have any reason to keep him. Chance and Murphy believed that the five-year veteran could effectively assume Reulbach's role until the latter returned, but the price would be substantial. Murphy was undeterred and agreed to trade a valuable trio of young prospects to Brooklyn for McIntire. The Cubs players were ecstatic. "The illness of Reulbach left us in a bad way, but I firmly believe that McIntyre will be a winner for us and that we will not miss big Ed half as much now that we have a right-hander we can depend on," said Chance.[37]

With the pitching staff shored up, the last outstanding question pertaining to the Cubs' roster was the eligibility of Johnny Kling, who had decided to apply with the National Commission for reinstatement that spring. With the regular season quickly approaching, Chance lost his patience with the National Commission's untimely decision-making process. On March 25 the commission—made up of Ban Johnson, Thomas Lynch, and Garry Herrmann—met in Cincinnati. Kling's reinstatement request was among their top orders of business. They agreed to allow Kling to return to the Cubs, but they could not come up with a satisfactory penalty to appease each of them. With trains leaving to take them back to Chicago and New York, respectively, Johnson and Lynch turned to Herrmann on their way out the door and told him to orchestrate a compromise to resolve the matter. The issue would be revisited in a week's time. Chance blew a gasket. "Johnson doesn't want Kling to get in condition by the time the season opens. Otherwise the national commission would announce to the world what it has done without any further red tape," he fumed.[38] Murphy wanted Kling back, and he readily manipulated the facts of the case to get his star catcher back into the fold. Murphy told the commission that he had granted Kling a leave of absence only a few days after their conversation on March 4, 1909. "This statement on the part of Mr. Murphy is misleading to say the least," argued the commission.[39] In its ruling, the commission revealed that Kling's leave paperwork wasn't filed until seven weeks later, which suggested that Murphy had originally been very much against the idea. Nevertheless, on March 28, Kling was given permission to play for Chicago again but with several stipulations. He had to pay a $700 fine for playing semi-pro baseball in Kansas City, he had to play for the $4,500 salary that was commensurate with the last year of his original three-year contract, and the Cubs couldn't trade him during the 1910 season. Kling bristled at having to accept a below-market salary and mulled over his options in Kansas City while the spring exhibition season rolled on.

Joe Tinker wasn't worried about his friend's return. He knew it was just a matter of time before all the details were ironed out and Kling donned a Cub uniform again. "I took some trouble in the Kling case, but I feel that I am well repaid now that he is sure to play with us for I believe we have the pennant as good as won with him on the club. I like the honor of being on a championship ball team, and I also like the money that we will make if we win this year, so I won't figure I did that work for nothing if the Cubs came back into their own," Tinker said.[40]

Chicago opened the season on April 14, in the Queen City, against the Reds. Orval Overall got the starting nod against his former team but lost the game, 1–0. Cincinnati promptly beat the Cubs again, 5–3, the following afternoon. Chicago rebounded to win seven of its next nine games as it arrived in Pittsburgh, on May 2, to begin a three-game set against the Pirates in front of President Taft. Murphy traveled with the team so that he could catch up with the president. Charles Taft had hoped to meet up with him there, but something came up, and he could not attend. A large throng of fans enthusiastically welcomed the chief executive to his first game at Forbes Field. Taft sat in his customary seat along the first-base line with his party, which included secretary of state Philander Knox and Count Johann Heinrich von Bernstorff, the German ambassador to the United States. Before the game, Frank Chance, Johnny Evers, Honus Wagner, and Fred Clarke approached President Taft and asked him to autograph baseballs for them, and he happily complied. Several years later, Murphy told Taft, Chance "still treasures the ball which you tossed out to him at Pittsburgh, upon which you wrote your autograph."[41] Murphy waded through the crowd to shake hands with the president, and the two spoke as the band got into position to play "The Star-Spangled Banner." Following the playing of the national anthem, Taft threw out the first pitch, and the Pirates proceeded to beat the Cubs, 5–2.[42]

Chicago lost six of its next ten games, and the disappointing stretch was capped off when Cliff Curtis, who finished the season with a 6-24 record, pitched his Boston Doves to a 4–1 win at the West Side Ball Park, which dropped the Cubs into fifth place in the National League, with a record of 11-11.

Chicago's start was Chance's worst nightmare, but he and Murphy made several personnel changes that shook up the moribund Cubs. They sold catcher Pat Moran to the Phillies to make way for the return of Johnny Kling, who finally returned to the lineup on May 9. Chicago then dealt outfielder Doc Miller to the Boston Doves in exchange for Lew Richie, a talented young pitcher who had flown under the radar, with several losing franchises, early in his career. Chance started Richie against the Doves on May 15, and the hurler responded with a complete-game shutout, a 4–0 win that ignited an eleven-game winning streak. Richie dazzled while King Cole emerged as a stalwart in the rotation. The two young hurlers infused new life into Chicago, which roared up the standings from fifth place into first on May 25. Another hot stretch in June, during which the Cubs won 11 of 12 games, established a 4.5 game cushion between Chicago and the second-place Pirates.

Horses remained ubiquitous on the streets of Chicago, but automobiles increasingly appeared on the thoroughfares of the Windy City.

Car companies heavily advertised in Chicago's newspapers, as owning a motorized vehicle became more accessible to the public, albeit primarily the wealthy. Orval Overall's father, Daniel, had purchased the first car in his town of Lemon Cove, California, and the Cubs pitcher was so taken with it that he bought one of his own. Johnny Evers and Frank Chance bought cars too.

On May 20 a wet playing surface caused the cancellation of the scheduled game between the Dodgers and the Cubs. Evers and Chance had driven their new automobiles to the ballpark and excitedly offered to take several people home after the game was postponed. Solly Hofman and Jimmy Sheckard hopped into Chance's car and left the stadium. Evers, who had only owned his car for two weeks, filled it with gas, and his brother, Joe, Johnny's young mechanic, and George Macdonald, a writer for the *Chicago Journal*, climbed into the open carriage and headed north on Lincoln Street.

Evers slowed his touring car to a crawl as it neared the intersection of Lincoln and Van Buren Streets. A streetcar moved along the tracks of Van Buren approaching the intersection. Both Evers and the trolley driver stopped their vehicles. Then each of them, anticipating that the other was going to stay still, accelerated. The streetcar barreled into Evers's car, which gave way and folded into a contorted heap. As suddenly as the crunching of metal had begun, it vanished into silence. Shaken but okay, Evers checked on Joe and his mechanic, who were shocked and dinged up but otherwise in one piece. Evers spun around to check on Macdonald, who had been sitting behind him, but he wasn't there. They yelled out for Macdonald and frantically scanned for him. They pried themselves out of their seats and discovered him lodged underneath the car. Racing with adrenaline, they managed to wriggle the car off of Macdonald, which unveiled the ghastly sight of his mangled body. George, a thirty-one-year-old husband and father of a toddler, was rushed to the hospital, where doctors performed surgery. They removed pieces of his broken skull, reconnected severed arteries atop his brain, and prayed he hadn't lost too much blood. But it was too late. George Macdonald remained unconscious throughout the night, and he died the following morning.[43]

Several days later, Macdonald was laid to rest by his wife and child along with friends and family. A destroyed Evers, who had tightly clutched Macdonald's father and profusely apologized to him for the accident, managed to attend the funeral although it was incredibly difficult for him. Acutely aware that Evers was wracked with guilt, Charlie Murphy gathered together the Cubs front office, and they all attended the funeral to honor the dead and offer support to the living. Overall was there, too, as was Chance. Chicago White Sox owner Charles Comiskey also paid his respects.

Overwhelmed with grief and anxiety following Macdonald's death, Evers was interviewed as part of an investigation to determine the cause of the accident. Ultimately, both parties were cleared of wrongdoing. They had simply miscommunicated, but that was little consolation to Evers. "I never regretted anything so much as this. Macdonald was a prince of a fellow and one of my friends. I am mighty sorry for his father and his wife," said a choked-up Evers. The devastating crash stunned the unflappable Chance. "I lay awake most of the night thinking of the accident. It preyed on my mind as nothing has done for a long time. Today I am looking for some one to buy my machine. I don't want to take any risk myself and I don't want the chance of hurting some one else," he confessed.[44]

In spite of a slew of injuries, neither Pittsburgh nor New York mustered a serious challenge to Chicago during the dog days of August, and the Cubs cruised to their fourth National League pennant in five years, a stunning fifteen games clear of the Giants.

Chicago clinched the pennant on October 2 by beating Cincinnati, 8–4. A jubilant Chance paid for his players to eat and drink whatever they wanted during a postgame party. Chance had good reason to be happy. Despite a slew of injuries and other challenges, the Cubs won 104 games in 1910, which propelled their five-year total of victories to over five hundred, a remarkable achievement for Chicago's core group of players. King Cole and Lew Richie finished the year with a combined record of 31-8. Solly Hofman, the defensive genius, swung a magical bat all season. "Circus" Solly finished third in the National

League with a .325 batting average and drove in eighty-six runs, both career-high marks. His season was worth 5.3 wins above replacement, which trailed only Sherry Magee of the Phillies in the National League. Johnny Kling failed to regain his old offensive form but still managed to hit .269 in ninety-one games.

Murphy toasted the team's success and marveled at the sustainability of its winning formula. "For the Cubs to have won the National league pennant four times and a world's pennant twice, with the possibility of a third, in the five years since I have been connected with the club is a source of great personal gratification to me, but the credit, of course, belongs to Manager Chance and his men," an elated Murphy said.[45] Chance uncharacteristically gloated over the productivity the new players had brought to the ball club. His anger at losing the pennant in 1909 boiled over in his interview with the press after the game. "I was a true prophet last spring if never before. If you will take the pains to look it up you will find that I said that we would win the pennant this season because we strengthened our club while the other contenders stood still," an indignant Chance crowed.[46]

In spite of the joy of the moment, the Cubs had a pressing issue heading into the World Series against Connie Mack's Philadelphia Athletics. Johnny Evers could not face the A's because of a gruesome foot injury he had suffered in Cincinnati. He broke his right ankle and shredded ligaments when his foot got caught underneath him as he slid into home plate. Evers's ankle dislocation sickened home plate umpire Hank O'Day, whose stomach remained so queasy that he could neither eat dinner nor smoke a cigar that night. "I knew things must be pretty bad when Hank can't smoke," Evers quipped. He spent several days in a Cincinnati hospital before returning to Chicago, where his leg was set and put in a cast. Evers remained confident that his teammates could finish the job without him. "I think the Cubs will beat the Athletics in decisive fashion, as the pitchers are in good shape and the players feel sure they can annex another world's championship," he said. Alas, they did not.[47]

Orval Overall, who had missed a significant number of games during the summer due to the deep pangs of a sore arm, struggled in Game

One, lasting only three innings in a 4–1 loss to the A's in front of nearly 27,000 fans in Philadelphia. The Cubs offense did not fare any better as it managed only three hits. Game Two began in promising fashion. Chicago loaded the bases with two walks and a single with one out in the first inning, and Heinie Zimmerman gave the Cubs a 1–0 lead with a sacrifice fly to center field. The A's took the lead by scoring twice in the bottom of the third against Mordecai Brown. The game remained close before Philadelphia's bats broke out in a six-run seventh inning, highlighted by Danny Murphy's two-run double, as the A's beat Brown and the Cubs, 9–3.

The stunned Cubs tried to regroup in Game Three as the series shifted west to Chicago, but a remarkable pitching performance by Philadelphia's Jack Coombs shattered their hopes. Coombs had tossed a complete game for the A's in Game Two, and he returned to the mound on just one day of rest to pitch Game Three. Chance countered with Ed Reulbach for the pivotal matchup. However, the pitchers struggled early. Each team tallied a run in the first inning and scored twice in the second frame, but only Coombs settled into a rhythm. Chance replaced Reulbach with Harry McIntire, who had performed well following his acquisition from Brooklyn, in the third inning. Lead-off hitter Bris Lord smacked a ball to left field off of McIntire, and only a sparkling running grab by Jimmy Sheckard prevented it from being an extra base hit. However, Eddie Collins reached on an infield single. Then Frank "Home Run" Baker launched a screaming line drive into right field that skipped in front of Frank Schulte, struck him in the leg, and bounded away into the grass beyond. Collins scored easily and Baker scampered into third base as Philadelphia took a 3–2 lead. The fans groaned as McIntire, who could not control his spitter, hit the next batter, Harry Davis, with a pitch to bring up Danny Murphy, who had already burned Chicago in Game Two. He did it again. Murphy crushed a three-run homer to right field, and the A's held an 8–3 advantage.

Frank Chance was furious with the home run call. He claimed that the ball had actually landed in front of the screen that served as an outfield fence, and that the hit should be ruled a ground rule double. Chance asked umpire Hank O'Day to change the homer to a two-base hit, but O'Day, who was working behind home plate, told him to talk to right field umpire Tommy Connolly. Chance discussed the decision with Connolly but went berserk after the umpire refused to change his call. Chance informed Connolly that the latter belonged in the Ananias Club, a euphemism used by the press whenever Teddy Roosevelt referred to someone as a liar. "I'll pay your initiation fee," Chance was overheard telling Connolly. The Cubs manager was thrown out of the game.[48]

With his five-run cushion now firmly established, Coombs settled in and pitched the rest of the way for Philadelphia as it took a commanding 3–0 series lead with a 12–5 win.

Philadelphia's offensive outburst astonished Cubs fans, who were accustomed to their pitchers' dominance. To many of them, the struggles of Chicago's pitchers could be explained away by an assortment of injuries and accruing age, but the Phillies' hitters had a secret. They had been stealing signs in the American League, and they deployed the subterfuge during the series. Their scheme was extraordinarily simple but extremely effective. As each Philadelphia hitter coiled to hit, the on-deck batter, who had stationed himself at an angle where he could read the catcher's signs from behind, would give a verbal signal to indicate which pitch was coming. Johnny Kling and the rest of his teammates did not catch on to the scheme quickly enough, and the Phillies built an insurmountable series lead.[49]

Chicago gallantly fought off the A's in Game Five by scoring in the ninth inning to force extra innings. Sheckard won the game for the Cubs in the tenth, when his single to center scored Jimmy Archer from third base to give Chicago a 4–3 win. The team's relief and renewed vigor proved to be short-lived, however. Buoyed by yet another strong pitching display by Coombs, a five-run outburst by the A's in Game Five gave them a large lead, and they easily defeated the Cubs, 7–2, to win their first World Series championship in front of 27,374 fans at the West Side Grounds. Coombs won three games in six days to cap off his astounding campaign, during which he had led both leagues with thirty-one wins and thirteen shutouts in the regular season.

Murphy was disappointed but gracious in defeat. Chance also had kind words for Connie Mack's club, but not being at full strength gnawed at some of the players. Injuries and heavy workloads had left their pitchers vulnerable, and the A's had capitalized. "You know and I know that Mordecai Brown, or Overall, or Reulbach, or any of the rest of our pitchers can win when he is in his stride. In this series none of them was right, and there you have the whole thing in a nutshell," elucidated a disappointed Solly Hofman.[50] Overall was so disgusted with his performance, and the criticism it engendered, that he threatened to never pitch again.

Whispers around baseball not only gossiped that Philadelphia had stolen Chicago's signs but insisted that Charles "Chief" Bender, the outstanding Athletics pitcher, had extensively scouted the Cubs in person during the regular season. Bender identified ways in which the Cubs' pitchers were tipping, or giving away, their pitches, and he passed that information along to his teammates during the World Series. *Sporting Life* published a story under a headline that read "The Athletics' Signal Tipping Pitching System and Inside Ball Made Cubs Look Foolish in the World's Series."[51] It was an incredibly embarrassing outcome for the Cubs considering their reputation as a team that exceled at the intellectual side of playing baseball.

With their loss to Philadelphia, the end of the Cubs' winning era was at hand. None of the players on the 1910 National League championship team ever appeared in another World Series for Chicago. The next pennant-winning Cubs season occurred in 1918. By then, World War I had been fought, Jimmy Sheckard had been dead for five years, and the Cubs featured, of all players, Fred Merkle.

10

"MURPHY ALONE IS MY ENEMY"

Ban Johnson just wouldn't let it die. Whenever the American League president pontificated on the growth of baseball, which was often, Johnson praised the success of his philosophical approach to running the sport as its primary catalyst. He demanded a clean sport, void of cheating and complaining on the field, and his long-term contract infused his position with authority, unlike his various counterparts in the National League, who were forced to operate on a one-year pact, a difficult political task. In an open letter to the press prior to the 1911 season, Johnson blustered. "Skill and sportsmanship in the players, fairness and firmness in the umpires, well-kept fields, of such dimensions that a fast runner may complete the circuit of the bases on a fair hit to their limits in any direction, skirted with mammoth fireproof stands and crowded to their capacity with real enthusiasts from all walks of life, are, from my viewpoint, essential elements in twentieth century base ball, whether a position in a league race or the championship of the world hinges on the result."

Johnson also made it clear that he would continue to seek the eradication of detrimental behavior by owners, managers, and players that threatened baseball's reputation. One of his primary targets remained the nefarious activity of ticket scalping. Two and a half years after the scandal that rocked the 1908 World Series, Johnson continued to use the episode to attack Charlie Murphy and promote the National Commission as an agent of moral enforcement that worked on the behalf of baseball fans. "It is our desire to give the public the best possible accommodations and eliminate from the series ticket scalping and kindred evils. Nothing will do more to estrange patrons from the game than the treatment accorded them in this city in the last World's Series between Detroit and Chicago. It is a prudent and sensible club owner who does not have the dollar always in mind in the operation of his base ball property," pontificated Johnson.[1]

Murphy, accustomed to the long stream of criticism directed at him from the American League office, dismissed Johnson's badgering, but the Cubs' treasurer, Charlie Williams, quietly fumed. Johnson's blathering letter to the press simply glossed over the fact that the Cubs had just hosted the A's in the World Series without major incident, and it ignored the results of Williams's own discovery that had inadvertently helped him solve, at least to some degree, the mystery of how scalpers had acquired postseason tickets.

The answer arrived in the mail. Williams had partnered with Johnny Evers in a shoe store that opened in Chicago around the same time that the Cubs played in the 1910 World Series. To market its grand opening, Williams mailed advertisements about the store to fans who had purchased World Series tickets through Chicago's front office. Williams already had their addresses on file, so he slipped letters to the patrons in the mail and hoped they would procure some curious customers who wanted to meet a ballplayer and purchase new footwear at the store's celebration. Much to his surprise, fifty of Williams's letters returned to him unopened with notes that indicated no one with the name inscribed on the envelope resided or worked at the listed address. The replies immediately raised his hackles. Where had all these recent ticket buyers gone? It dawned on Williams that clerks at these offices had written falsified letters on their companies' letterheads to request World Series tickets that they then plucked from the mailrooms and turned over to scalpers. Williams may have been disappointed that his advertisements came back to him still sealed, for the sake of his shoe store, but at least he now had some sort of explanation—and a modicum of inner peace—for at least one aspect of the bewildering ticket anomalies that had eluded him.[2]

During the weeks following the season, an agitated Murphy brooded over the performance of the umpires during the recently concluded

World Series. Traditionally, the vast majority of the magnates fumed over calls that went against their teams, and Murphy was at the forefront of the movement. Tommy Connolly, an American League umpire, drew Murphy's ire during the series for ejecting Frank Chance in Game Three after the Cubs' skipper profanely argued a home run ruling. Connolly's action incensed Murphy, but the umpire staunchly defended himself. "Chance came to me next day and held out his hand and apologized and said he was sorry the thing happened. The decision was right, proper and just, and Chance's apology the next day is proof."[3]

Connolly's explanation did little to pacify Murphy, who mulled over ways he could force changes to the umpiring system and, in doing so, embarrass the American League arbiters and, by proxy, Ban Johnson. He wanted the umpires to be held accountable for their actions and, somewhat oddly, one of his primary metrics of success for them was a physical exam. On the surface, Murphy's idea appeared petty, but it received a warm response from Sporting Life. Murphy "is going to father a resolution . . . to compel umpires to undergo a course of Spring training just like ball players, for eyes, wind and muscle, after a long Winter of idleness or rust. Not a bad idea, all things considered . . . Evidently the magnates are coming to the point where the umpire is to be taken just as seriously as the ball player—which is as it should be," the magazine argued.[4] With an eye toward gaining leverage over Johnson by publicly embarrassing Connolly, the National League owners agreed to implement Murphy's proposal.

The key tenant of Murphy's training proposal that caught journalists' attention was an eye test designed to ensure that the umpires possessed excellent vision without the aid of glasses. "Ball players and the more excitable base ball 'fans' generally are ready to agree that every umpire is as blind as a bat at noonday, and it should prove gratifying, as well as satisfying, to this class, as well as to the general public, when it is known that every umpire's eyes have been tested by an oculist and found to be all right," read a passage in the Philadelphia Record, which Sporting Life saw fit to reprint.[5]

National League president Thomas Lynch ordered all nine of the National League umpires to undergo eye exams. All of them passed with flying colors. Hank O'Day had perfect vision, although Bill Klem and Bob Emslie could only see better than average. Regardless, it was enough for Lynch to declare his crews fit for the season and claim superiority over the American League. "All oculists reading these reports must agree that the seeing power of the National League umpires is normal in every instance, and that several of them are blessed with vision considerably better than the average man possesses," Lynch boasted. "I doubt if the vision of nine other men selected at random would begin to approach this record."[6]

Before engaging with the tasks of the winter months, Murphy ventured to French Lick, Indiana, where he enjoyed some downtime to unwind from the long season. Upon returning to Chicago, Murphy's characteristically busy off-season commenced. Undeterred by Johnny Evers's tragic accident, Murphy joined the ranks of motorized vehicle owners in mid-November, when he purchased a touring car. Most likely, he enjoyed regaling his family with tales from the road during his days in Wilmington to celebrate Thanksgiving. Upon his return to the Windy City, Murphy hosted delegates from throughout the minor leagues at their convention.

Despite all of his comings and goings, Murphy's thoughts never wandered far from his ball club. Questions about the team's future viability as World Series contenders plagued not only Murphy but the entire organization. The youthful Philadelphia Athletics had dispatched the veteran Cubs with an ease that, in part, exposed the increasing age of Chicago's roster. The Cubs, who played with a competitive rage matched by few teams, had given their maximum effort in hundreds of games for five consecutive seasons, and fatigue, along with injuries, had saturated their bodies. Philadelphia had hit them like a locomotive and punctured a hole in the cocky cocoon that encapsulated the Cubs. Joe Tinker could only shake his head in admiration for the Athletics. "We have every batter classified, what he hits—usually—and where and how he hits—usually. We know all about every pitcher another team can know. We know what he has got and how he uses it. We know every weakness of everybody we go up against. In short, we reduced base ball to a card index system, as I said, and here comes along a young, ignorant, enthusiastic team, simply bubbling over with vitality and pepper, and tears up our card index system and before we can formulate either an attack or defense they take three games and have the series right in their mitts," Tinker marveled. Simply being a winning team wasn't acceptable to either Murphy or the players, and Tinker knew that changes needed to be made for the Cubs to keep pace as World Series contenders. "We are young in years, but old in base ball, and every year takes a little more of the fund of nervous energy a man must have constantly on tap to keep his pepper up," the shortstop admitted.[7]

Losing the World Series bothered Murphy, and the stories about the sign-stealing scandal published throughout the off-season embarrassed him. It all reflected poorly on the franchise, and he would not stand pat. Not winning championships affected his reputation, the value of the business, and his leverage within the game, and it was simply unacceptable. In a way, his own successes had pushed his expectations beyond a realistic level. The Cubs' roster needed upgrades, particularly to its pitching staff, before the 1911 season, but Murphy still believed the team's core pieces could win, so he was going to make changes at the roster's edges. He had no reservations about churning out players who did not perform. Chance knew Murphy wasn't going to tolerate losing the World Series. Earning the players' respect had once motivated Murphy, but now winning the next championship drove him. "He doesn't care whether the players like him or not," Chance said of his boss. "He pays salaries for ball players and allows me to decide whether the money is earned or not. Sentiment cuts no figure with him, and whatever I may suggest to benefit the team you can rest assured that Murphy will O.K. it."[8] Chance was equally committed to winning and, it was no secret, the 1911 Chicago Cubs would look different on Opening Day.

On Wednesday, December 7, 1910, an extraordinarily cold Chicago day, an estimated eighteen thousand to twenty thousand garment workers, many of them women, bundled in head scarves and long coats, took to the streets amidst the freezing temperature and whipping wind as part of an ongoing strike against their employer, Hart, Schaffner & Marx. The strikers marched through the west side of the city, from Walsh's Hall on Milwaukee Avenue to the West Side Grounds. Upon reaching the ballpark, the large pool of protestors reshuffled into smaller groups, based on either their shop membership or nationality, to listen to a series of speeches by union leaders.

Charlie Murphy welcomed the strikers to the stadium and, along with treasurer Charlie Williams, secretary Charlie Thomas, and former outfielder Jimmy Slagle, helped prepare more than seventy thousand sandwiches and coffee for the workers. Following the speeches, which were delivered in six languages, Edward Nockels, secretary of the Chicago Federation of Labor, informed the protestors that Murphy had food and drink for them. The strikers' loud cheers for Murphy pierced the cold air, likely the only time they praised a wealthy business owner that day. Murphy, Williams, Thomas, and Slagle ushered women into rooms beneath the stands for the food. The appreciative workers, many of whom were going without a full complement of food without their pay, gladly partook of the meal. The *Inter Ocean* relayed the story of a father whose family needed sustenance. "One man, grasping five sandwiches in his bony hand, stepped up to Williams and asked for a sixth. 'I have six children at home and I want one for each of them,' he said when told that he had been supplied already. He got the sixth sandwich."[9]

The local press reported on the demonstration without quoting the loquacious Murphy, an appropriate strategy by him in light of the meaningful event. Throughout his life, Murphy encouraged the women around him. Perhaps the garment workers' cause moved him to action. He had also cared for people and causes in his personal life in a way that he never engaged at work. A cynical view would interpret the meal as a recruiting event for ingratiating the Cubs to the community. Considering the antibusiness nature of the strike, Murphy would have been taking an unnecessary risk by inserting himself in their movement if something went awry. In the end, the event went smoothly, and Murphy earned kind words for his support. In total, forty-five thousand strikers participated in the movement over the course of twenty-two weeks before it came to an end, with an agreement, in early February of 1911.[10]

Although Murphy had paid his players reasonably well over the years, cracks in that reputation started to show, as Cubs players began to age, following the 1910 season. Murphy targeted Orval Overall, who he wanted to take a substantial pay cut following an injury-marred campaign, but the big right-hander had no intention of taking less money. The two men didn't like each other very much. Murphy was miffed that Overall's arm injury had persisted throughout the previous season. Murphy complained that Chance was protecting Overall because of their personal friendship, which only frustrated the manager and alienated Orval.

After the loss to the Athletics, Overall and his wife, Ethel, spent the off-season with Mordecai and Sarah Brown in California, where the teammates worked on their mining operation. In February Brown returned to Chicago to prepare for spring training. However, without a contract for 1911, Overall remained on the West Coast. Overall's injury had contributed to his poor performance in the World Series, which exacerbated matters; it hurt Overall's pride and dinged Murphy's pocketbook. The wound of Murphy's contract offer panged Overall, and he refused to sign it.

Murphy demonstrated his faith in some of the team's core players by agreeing to multiyear contracts with Joe Tinker and Johnny Evers, but he concluded that it was time to part ways with third baseman Harry Steinfeldt, who had been a stalwart at the position for the past five seasons. Heinie Zimmerman, who had hit .284 in a part-time role in 1910, made the decision easier. At twenty-four, Zimmerman was a full decade younger than Steinfeldt and, along with pitcher King Cole, who had already been rewarded with a $1,000 bonus from Murphy as well as a substantial three-year contract, represented the infusion of youth that the roster needed. Tinker had voiced his desire to play third base, but inserting Zimmerman instead, and leaving the veteran shortstop in his spot, strengthened the club. The Cubs released Steinfeldt, who briefly caught on for nineteen games with Boston before his career came to an end. Solly Hofman, fresh off an outstanding

1910 campaign, wanted a salary increase and threatened retirement to create leverage, but he and Murphy settled on a number both could live with, and the popular player, known for his outstanding defense, returned to the fold.

The 1911 season got off to a painful beginning for Frank Chance and the Chicago Cubs and eventually thwarted the team's strong start. On April 24 George Suggs of the Reds uncorked a wild pitch that struck Chance in the back of the head as he tried to spin out of the ball's path. The frightful blow stunned him and scared observers, but it didn't keep him out of action for long. Days later, Chance severely sprained his ankle sliding into home plate while scoring from second base on a Frank Schulte base hit. He missed a little over a week but returned to the lineup on May 6. Johnny Evers, too, struggled physically and mentally in the aftermath of the severe leg injury that had ended his 1910 season, along with the collapse of his shoe business, and spent significant time away from the team.[11] In spite of their injuries, the Cubs played solid baseball throughout the campaign's opening months and found themselves atop the National League race on June 21, when they hit a rough patch. Chicago dropped six of its next nine games and slipped out of first place.

Murphy recognized that Chance remained hobbled, and he made a trade for reinforcements in hopes that Chicago could remain in con-tention. Johnny Kling, who had been regarded as the best catcher in the National League before sitting out the 1909 campaign, had not regained his old form, and after he got off to a sluggish start at the plate during the 1911 season, Murphy and Chance shipped him to the Boston Rustlers, in June, as part of an eight-player deal. The Cubs received outfielder Wilbur Good and a veteran backstop, Peaches Graham, as well as two additional players. Trading Kling was the price of doing business, and the emergence of catcher Jimmy Archer made him expendable.[12]

Chicago arrived in Cincinnati for a late-June series that would be played in suboptimal weather conditions. A scorching hot spell tortured large swaths of the United States, leading to scores of deaths, destroyed

crops, and an angry, overheated polar bear, Lena, who clawed her trainer's head on Coney Island.[13] The heat compelled the *Chicago Tribune*
to initiate a fundraiser to provide ice for poor families with babies, who
were in danger of contracting illnesses from drinking spoiled milk.

During warm-ups prior to the series opener, Jack Ryder of the *Cincinnati Enquirer*, who had watched Chance play against the Reds countless
times, immediately recognized that the Cubs manager was struggling
with the oppressive humidity. Chance batted clean up and played his
customary first base but went 0-for-4, although the Cubs won the
game, 3–2. In his game story for the *Enquirer*, Ryder noted that, "Frank
Chance, in no shape to play in the heat of the afternoon, still gamely
took his place in the lineup to strengthen the team and try to get the
Cubs off their losing streak."[14]

Ryder's concern for Chance went beyond either the heat or the
skipper's early-season ankle injury. Everyone knew that Chance had
frequently been hit in the head by pitches throughout his career. One
report stated he had sustained an astonishing thirty-six cranial bean-
ings, and they were the leading cause of the excruciating headaches
he suffered from with increasing frequency.[15] The following day, prior
to the second game of the series, Chance suddenly collapsed, during
his pregame routine, on the field. Ryder described the scene thusly
for his readers: "Chance ran forward to field the ball, when suddenly
everything went black for him. He stumbled to his knees, while the
ball bounded over his shoulder and went on to the outfield. Chance
remained on his knees for a minute or two, with his hands clasped to
his head, before any one noticed his predicament. Then Zimmerman,
Tinker and some of the other players rushed over to their beloved leader
and assisted him to rise to his feet." They helped Chance back into the
clubhouse, where he received medical treatment, and he went back
to the team hotel to rest. His condition improved slightly, but something was clearly wrong. "I do not know what I shall do until I see my
physician in Chicago to-morrow," Chance told Ryder that evening.
"They tell me here that I may have to lay off for a few weeks and go
to the country for a rest. Of course, this is the last thing that I want to
do, but if necessary I shall have to stand for it."[16]

Chance intermittently managed the team over the next few weeks, but his physical condition restricted him from playing. Another severe headache attacked him in Brooklyn, and a week later Murphy announced that Chance would pilot the Cubs from the bench while young Vic Saier would be taking over first base for the remainder of the season. Chance made just one more plate appearance and, overall, he played in just thirty-one games. Without Chance, Evers, Kling, or Overall for large stretches, the Cubs miraculously didn't collapse but, in the end, they never threatened New York and finished the season in second place, a distant 7.5 games behind the Giants.

One of the few pieces of good news for Murphy during the 1911 season involved a significant business deal that established baseball's largest sponsored sign inside the West Side Grounds and offset the lost dollars of failing to reach the World Series. Over 130 feet tall by 168 feet wide, the scoreboard loomed large over left field. Murphy inked a three-year deal with the *Chicago Tribune* to advertise the newspaper on the board, which displayed American League scores for fans in attendance. The *Tribune* boasted that it just might be the largest painted sign in the world.[17]

Six months later, on Saturday, April 13, 1912, a rain shower punctured the sweltering humidity oppressing Cincinnati, which had cancelled the early-season afternoon contest between the Cubs and Reds. With no game to play, Charlie Murphy received word from Frank Chance that the manager wanted to speak with him privately. The Cubs had lost the first two games of the season to the Reds, and perhaps Chance needed to discuss an issue pertaining to the club. Chance did, and the player he desired to talk about was himself. With yet another blinding headache, Frank knew that he could not play that afternoon, but it was more than that. The headaches that had plagued him throughout 1911 were continuing with a vengeance. His condition had improved over the winter, but an attack in Nashville sobered Chance up in regard to his new physical reality. The intense Cincinnati heat brought on another headache, and it buckled the unassailable Chance dismissively. Upon hearing Chance describe his deteriorating condition, Murphy counseled him to stop playing. He suggested that Chance again manage from the bench, an idea to which the Peerless Leader agreed. "I cannot guard against danger of another collapse in any way except by keeping out of the heat and sun," Chance reluctantly admitted. "I have learned that fact to my great regret."[18]

While the end of Chance's playing career made headlines in Chicago, it was quickly swept aside by news coming out of the North Atlantic Ocean on April 15. The colossal ship RMS *Titanic*, sailing its maiden voyage from England to New York, had struck an iceberg and was helplessly sinking in deep, cold waters. Chicago, along with the rest of the world, read in horror about the deaths of more than 1,500 of the ship's 2,240 passengers and crew. Among the drowned was Major Archie Butt, an aide and friend of William Howard Taft, who had met Murphy at several Cubs games he had attended with the president.

Frank Chance continued to power his way through the summer even though he lost most of his hearing in his right ear. Still, he piloted the ball club as well as he could in the final year of his four-year extension, but by mid-August he was coming to terms with the fact that this could be his final season in baseball as an active player or manager. Fortunately, Dr. Wilfred Fralick in New York suggested to Chance that a blood clot was the most likely culprit behind the headaches, and he recommended surgery.

On August 15, 1912, the Cubs won their sixth game in a row, a 5–1 thrashing of the Giants in front of a raucous crowd of thirty thousand at the West Side Grounds, to pull within five games of first-place New York. Afterward, Murphy and Chance talked about the victory together. Winning the game had given both men a particular shot of adrenaline that only beating the hated Giants in front of tens of thousands of home fans could deliver. Buoyed by the win, Murphy asked, "What do you think about managing the team next season?" Resigned to his fate, Chance reluctantly confessed that he didn't think it would be possible. Murphy tried to think positively by reminding him of his upcoming surgery. "You wait until after the operation before deciding to quit, and maybe your health will be all right."[19]

The hope created by Chicago's winning surge soon faded as the team struggled in September, while the Giants continued their winning ways unabated on their way to winning the National League crown for the second consecutive year. Murphy's optimistic attitude soured, and his frustration boiled over after Chance suspended slugger Frank Schulte without pay for the rest of the season, for drinking, on September 8. It pained Chance to send Schulte home, but discipline was of the utmost importance to the Peerless Leader.

Schulte's suspension immediately raised Murphy's suspicion that deviant behavior throughout the roster hindered the Cubs' play on the field. Murphy was already annoyed that the Cubs were falling out of the pennant race, and he was looking for something to blame. The thought that imbibing by the players could be a root cause of the team's shortcomings infuriated him. There was no question that Schulte was in the midst of a down year following his 1911 MVP season. Murphy claimed that he had received information that members of the Cincinnati Reds had made it a "habit" of taking Cubs players drinking the night before games.[20] Deeply disappointed by the choices of Schulte, the team's best player, Murphy's emotions again got the better of him. He proceeded to recklessly, and unfairly, project Schulte's behavior onto the rest of the roster and, in doing so, undercut the authority of Chance, who tried to do the right thing for the clubhouse's culture even though it made winning games more difficult. It was a dangerous game for Murphy to play, but he committed himself to eliminating all drinking by every player during the season.

Chance's operation was scheduled for September 17. Just before going into surgery, Chance decided to lift Schulte's suspension. After conferring, Murphy and Chance reinstated the outfielder. Chance then turned his attention back to his hospital admittance. With his wife, Edythe, by his side, Chance underwent the operation, performed by Dr. Fralick and assisted by the Cubs trainer, Bert "Doc" Semmens. Fralick removed a blood clot "from the nerve center at the upper extremity" of Chance's spine. Following the seventy-minute surgery, Fralick announced to the concerned baseball world that it had been a success.[21] Chance would spend a few days recuperating in the hospital, but everything had gone well.

As Chance recovered, Murphy continued to stew over Schulte's behavior. Murphy knew that other franchises—specifically the Pittsburgh Pirates—had bandied about the idea of implementing a clause in players' contracts that forbade them from drinking or smoking during the season to ensure maximum performance. Murphy concluded that he would adopt the proposal and insert the stipulation into the players' contracts for 1913. However, he decided to immediately make his grievance public. When Murphy next met with journalists, with the season still ongoing, he tore into the players he suspected of lacking sobriety. "Booze, cigarettes and late hours beat us out of the pennant this year, but it won't beat us out of it again. I have spotted the men who are not taking care of themselves, and they will obey the commandments, or get off my team. I cannot afford to lose any more pennants," Murphy warned.[22]

Murphy's accusations alienated the players, and by calling it "my team" Murphy ignored Chance's investments—physical and financial—in the club. Murphy's move to ban alcohol consumption by all the players insinuated that Chance could no longer competently do his job and implied that stricter measures were needed to compensate for the manager's deficiencies. Chance learned of Murphy's comments while still in the hospital. Murphy declared that he had identified misbehaving players while the manager had either missed the signs or willingly looked the other way. Murphy's comments, especially after Chance had painfully gutted out the season, were too much for him to bear. Lying in his recovery bed, a wounded Chance blasted Murphy. "I feel these charges keenly. Reading them in the papers has set me back. I could hardly sleep last night. I cannot figure out what Murphy is trying to do. Apparently he is sore because I lost the pennant and wants to rasp somebody, but he is not going to rasp me." Chance expressed regret at having to single out Schulte for suspension, but he insisted that it was the right decision to maintain order. "There probably were other men who were out, but I happened to catch Schulte, and he was the goat," Chance admitted. The players did enjoy a beer after a game at times, but they never drank prior to taking the field, Chance said. The skipper expressed dismay at Murphy's unwillingness to wait until after the season to discuss the new policy, but he again theorized that Charlie was upset at losing out on the pennant. Murphy and Chance had never missed out on the World Series in consecutive seasons before, and that failure deeply ate at both men with one major difference. "I think just as much of my team when it is losing as when it is winning. Murphy only thinks of the team when it is winning."[23] No team, Chance argued, would win four pennants and two championships if they played hungover. Even though he didn't philosophically disagree with the prohibition clause, Chance made it plain he would not sign a contract that contained it. While convalescing, Chance wearily summed up his frustration: "I've been too long in the business to be insulted like this."[24]

After taking a step back and calming down, Murphy realized that watching Frank Schulte's name get drawn through the mud bothered him. He felt guilty. "It would have been much better if Schulte could have been penalized without publicity. Now that this matter has been talked about so much, however, I desire to say that in my judgment Schulte has been more sinned against than sinning," Murphy said.[25] But it was too little too late. The players were furious with Murphy, and he couldn't walk it back.

Feeling trapped, on Saturday, September 28, with Chance's return to Chicago imminent, Murphy released a statement in which he implied that the Cubs' manager had resigned his post. Murphy explained that he had known since his conversation with Chance on August 15 that his managerial career was over. Murphy had asked Chance, whose contract expired at the end of the season, about continuing at the helm in 1913, and Chance had confessed that he would rather not. "Realizing that Frank had not been in the best health for a few years, I was not surprised at this reply, and I have not counted on him to manage the Cubs in 1913 since that day, especially as I have seen it stated in the public prints from time to time that he contemplated retirement," Murphy said. He went on to suggest that Chance couldn't physically do the job anymore: "Managing a major baseball club is a hard job for a well man, and now that Mr. Chance has declined to manage the team again I hardly know whom I shall select. It doubtless will be some one from the team, as our greatest success has been attained under a playing manager."[26]

Murphy's preposterous comments held enough kernels of accuracy to ring true to his own ears, but it had no chance of convincing the public. While Chance had indeed contemplated retirement because of his poor health, he had never announced his intention to retire. In reality, Murphy had used Chance's words against him. Chance heard about Murphy's statement just as he was boarding the Twentieth Century Limited in New York. With his pain reduced, a shocked and angered Chance put his full vigor on display for the sports writers. He admitted that he had told Murphy on August 15 that he did not want to continue managing, but Murphy had said he still wanted him in charge, and they would discuss the issue after the season. "Since my operation I feel much better," a renewed Chance declared. "The doctors tell me I will be as good as ever next year. Consequently it is up to Murphy whether I manage the team next year. However, he must give me either a contract as manager or my absolute release."[27]

A contingent of fans and media greeted Chance as he disembarked from the train, in a plaid coat, the following morning in Chicago. Chance acknowledged their cheers and had his photo taken alongside Cubs treasurer Charlie Williams. Murphy was nowhere to be seen. Announcing that his operation had profoundly reduced his pain, Chance reiterated his position to, among others, Sam Weller of the *Tribune*: "I have not resigned; I never will resign, and what's more, I'm ready to sign a contract to manage the Cubs next year."[28]

The local press hounded Murphy for his side of the story, but the owner morphed into a baseball version of Herman Melville's Bartleby the Scrivener. He deflected questions from the Chicago reporters for the next several weeks by repeating the same clipped retort: "I have nothing to say."[29]

Tension between the two men ratcheted higher after the season. In early October, Chance sold his 10 percent interest in the Cubs to

Harry Ackerland, a Pittsburgh native and president of Fleishmann Distilling, as well as a friend of Murphy antagonist and Pirates owner Barney Dreyfuss. Chance enticed Ackerland to buy the stock, in part, by promising that he would return to manage the Cubs in 1913, as long as Murphy offered him a fair contract.[30] Put at ease, Ackerland agreed to pay Chance $40,000 for his hundred shares, an excellent return on his initial investment.[31] Murphy now had a new minority owner with whom he had to contend.

In the aftermath of Ackerland coming aboard, Murphy made a bold personnel move. On October 12 Murphy demoted the Cubs' star pitcher, Mordecai Brown, who had missed a large chunk of the season with a knee injury, to Louisville of the American Association. However, Chance believed that Murphy had dumped Brown out of spite rather than performance. Although Murphy did not disclose anything about Brown's status publicly, Chance was convinced that Murphy had unfairly punished Brown by forcing him to stay in the minor leagues. Murphy released another statement, on October 20, in which he praised Brown but said it was time to move on from the injured pitcher. "It is not pleasant to let Mordecai Brown go, but it can't be helped. This lion hearted fellow, who has done so much for the west side club, practically drew a full season's salary for nothing in 1912 and even then he is not repaid for what he has done, but we can't keep him forever," Murphy said.[32] However, Chance chafed at Murphy's comments because he believed the owner had intentionally left out an important element of Brown's demotion. According to Chance, "My first real trouble with (Murphy) came when he sent Mordecai Brown to Louisville with the provision that Louisville was not to give Brown a chance to go to any other major league team. This meant that Brown would have to play forever in the minors or quit baseball. And this after Brown had practically by his individual efforts won four pennants for the Cubs."[33]

According to William Grayson, who served as president of the Louisville franchise in 1912, he and Murphy had developed a scheme of illegal "farming." Grayson produced several letters from Murphy that he claimed proved that, in 1911, Murphy had released young players to Louisville, who did not make the Cubs roster, to trim the roster down to its limit. In exchange, Louisville covered the draft price of players to the National Commission for their rights. Murphy then sent a personal check to Grayson to cover the cost. Grayson improved his squad for free, while Murphy repeatedly benefited by having a fungible transaction lever that he could pull whenever he needed to stash a player in a minor league. In this instance, the move Murphy wanted to make involved Brown, an incredible contributor who had won 186 games for Chicago, including his immortal performance at the Polo Grounds in the replay game of 1908. Murphy, though, had no time for reminiscing about the past. The club needed to improve now. Unwisely, Murphy preferred to demote Brown rather than give him a fresh start with another organization in either the National or American League.[34] A local businessman and Cubs supporter, Charles Weeghman, took particular note of Brown's demotion.

With Brown now watching his former teammates from the stands, the Cubs blew a 3–0 series lead against the White Sox and lost their crosstown postseason showdown in seven games. The White Sox thumped the Cubs, 16–0, in the finale, sparking rumors that the Cubs threw the game to spite Murphy, a charge Chance vehemently denied. If Murphy had any remaining doubts about replacing the manager, losing four straight games to the Sox made the decision for him. Murphy went to work behind the scenes to facilitate a change. Joe Tinker, Johnny Evers, and Charlie "Red" Dooin of the Philadelphia Athletics emerged as the top candidates, but first Murphy needed to orchestrate Chance's permanent exit.

As soon as rumors of Chance's possible dismissal leaked into the public sphere, Cubs fans throughout the city flooded Murphy's office, in the Corn Exchange Building, with angry letters—some of quite substantial length—voicing their deep displeasure at the owner's decision to not reconcile with the manager. The forty-two-year-old Murphy donned his spectacles to read the endless stream of pointed correspondence triggered by his lack of loyalty to Chance. Murphy absorbed, and even understood, their complaint, but he pointed to the fact that the Cubs had played consecutive seasons without winning a pennant, in addition to being embarrassed in the postseason City Series against the White

Sox, and he considered it an organizational failure that he wouldn't allow to continue. On the heels of Chance's dismissal, journalist F. C. Lane of *Baseball Magazine* visited Murphy at team headquarters. Although he had not been speaking to local reporters, Murphy allowed Lane into his inner office for a forthright conversation. Surrounded by mail, Murphy picked a random envelope out of the pile, opened it, and read aloud the letter's contents to Lane. The fan blasted Murphy for four pages, but Charlie shrugged it off. "I get a lot of these. This one sounds as though the writer was perfectly sincere. But what are you going to do? You can't please everybody. I don't expect people are going to like me. What difference does it make if they don't? The team is the whole story. The owner doesn't count," Murphy told Lane. Murphy had become immune to being mocked for his unorthodox ways. "I have had so many knocks in the press and elsewhere of late that I don't mind them anymore," he said dismissively.[35]

Murphy prioritized winning as the most important marketing tactic of his hardline business approach, and Frank Chance's popularity among the Cubs' faithful was an abstract feeling that neither pitched well nor produced base runners. Murphy didn't believe sentimentality ever won baseball games, and the Cubs had lost too many of late for his liking. His methods often troubled him after the fact, but he had the ability to compartmentalize his guilt and move forward, a defense mechanism he had long possessed. Murphy understood that not re-signing Chance was a hard conclusion for many fans to understand, but he felt like seeking admiration from them would only distract him from figuring out a way to dethrone the Giants in 1913. He believed they would love the Cubs regardless of who played or managed as long as they won. Nevertheless, as he reflected on the organization's accomplishments over the past seven seasons, Murphy believed that the iteration of Chance's Cubs had done something special and deserved high praise. "Whether I have done it or whether Chance has done it or whether we only took and built up the material that others left us, the fact remains that the club has given Chicago winning baseball and Chicago ought to remember it."[36]

Murphy's attempt at sentiment did not play well with either the Chicago public or Chance, so he altered his public relations approach. Murphy argued that he wanted to infuse the team with youth and speed to offset its aging core, which could no longer compete for championships, but his comments only succeeded in further inflaming the situation. An exasperated Chance couldn't believe what he was hearing. In an epic rant to his friend Harvey Woodruff, Chance laid bare all his accumulated frustrations with Murphy. "Speed, speed! Of course we need more speed. That's what I have been telling Murphy for three years," Chance exclaimed. "What Murphy needs is scouts and nerve enough to spend some money for players. He has his brother for a scout. I told him he ought to get two or three experienced base ball men, somebody who would know a player if he saw one. And then he talks about speed," he fumed.

Instead of boldly talking with the local press about his decision, Murphy hid behind yet another statement explaining the organization's divorce from Chance:

On Aug. 15, 1912, Frank Chance was asked about managing the Cubs in 1913 and he replied: "I would rather not." That, of course, eliminated him. A manager is desired who wants the job, some one who will enthuse over it, and not have to be forced to accept it. No one can succeed to a superlative degree without enthusiasm. He must like his task, and not take the job merely for the renumeration involved. When the season is over he must be champing on the bit like a young colt with anxiety for the next campaign to begin. He must be full of optimism for the future, and such a feeling should be infectious.

Murphy wanted to turn over the Cubs roster and start fresh with a squad of young, fleet players.

In the history of every club a time arrives when reorganization is necessary ... No one cares who owns the ball club or who manages it so long as it wins games, but the fans who contribute to the support of the game are entitled to fast, aggressive baseball. Of course a waning star has many friends, but the memory of the public is fleeting and a man who wears a uniform must make good all the time—every minute he is in action.

He took a not-so-subtle shot at Chance by declaring that he wanted the Cubs' next manager to live in Chicago during the off-season so he could handle the day-to-day operations of the club.[37]

Predictably, Chance bristled at Murphy's statement: "Murphy never hired me. Jim Hart did that. Murphy found me here and kept me because I made good. I don't owe him anything."[38]

In addition to alienating Chance and many Cubs fans, Murphy's attitude ran off the team's primary external candidate for the managerial role the following day. Philadelphia's Red Dooin removed himself from consideration for the Cubs job after observing the growing discord in Chicago. "Even if the position were offered to me I would not step into that mess."[39]

With Dooin's departure from consideration, Murphy's choice came down to Joe Tinker or Johnny Evers.

In the meantime, Chicago mourned the impending loss of their beloved Peerless Leader, who had sacrificed so much to help turn the Cubs into a winning franchise. He had arrived in the Windy City as a raw twenty-one-year-old catcher in 1898 and was leaving as a two-time World Series champion. He had taken over as manager for the beloved Frank Selee under difficult circumstances and guided the Cubs to 768 wins in his nearly eight seasons at the helm. It had been a remarkable run for Chance, who had left an indelible mark on the Chicago Cubs. Harvey Woodruff penned a column in which he captured the essence of what Chance meant to the city and to the game of baseball. "Personally, Chance is one of the most likeable fellows in the baseball profession. His friends are legion. He has no enemies. His players swear by him and it is their sense of loyalty to his many fine qualities which has been a great factor in the success of the Cub machine. The retirement of Chance will be a distinct loss, not only to the Chicago Cubs and the Chicago public, but to the game of baseball."[40]

As Murphy deliberated behind closed doors about offering the job to Tinker or Evers, Chance headed back to California shrouded in uncertainty. His recovery had gone better than expected, but he knew everything could spiral when the heat returned. He was also an unaffiliated baseball man for the first time since he was a kid. Before boarding his train home,

Chance expressed his gratitude for his time with the Cubs. He said, in part, "I have given Chicago the best I had. Chicago has given me the best it had. I always will remember Chicago, my friends here, and the Cub fans. I hope they will remember me."⁴¹ Although Chance tried to spin events positively, it was a bitter end for him. "The game of baseball has been good to me. I have been successful and have made enough to keep me for the rest of my life in comfort. However, I am not satisfied with the way I am leaving it. I am sorry that it seems as if I have been driven out of the game . . . I feel that the fellows who played under me are my friends and that Murphy alone is my enemy, so I guess there is nothing to regret."⁴²

On October 24, 1912, Charlie Murphy selected Johnny Evers over Joe Tinker as the Cubs' new manager. Murphy and Evers agreed to a pair of five-year contracts. The first pact tied Evers to the franchise as a player, while the second deal added his new managerial duties. Still irritated by Chance's renegotiation after the 1908 season, Murphy wanted to ensure that Evers could not demand his managerial salary be reworked. Anxious to avoid another contentious standoff, Murphy included a bonus structure in Evers's contract that paid him additional compensation based on the Cubs' finish in the standings. For his part, Evers quickly agreed to the terms. He never wanted to play anywhere other than Chicago, and he happily signed the contracts without reading them.

Over four hundred Cubs supporters throughout the city celebrated Evers's hiring at a banquet thrown for the new manager at the posh Sherman House. Evers autographed everyone's menu as a souvenir of the festive evening, which lasted into the wee hours of the morning. Murphy lavishly praised Evers, telling the audience that the new manager might find himself elevated to a front office role sooner rather than later. "I am planning a trip around the world and if I go I will make Evers head of the club as well as manager. He is fitted for the position, for he has the brains to grasp anything."⁴³

Unlike Murphy, who made no mention of the recently departed manager, Evers lauded Frank Chance for his tremendous work in Chicago, which drew a thunderous ovation from the gallery. Evers promised he would do all he could to return the Cubs to the World

Series, where he hoped they could once again play the White Sox. The banquet generated a groundswell of excitement for Evers, who proved himself a motivational speaker capable of rallying public support. He knew the clubhouse would require the same attention.

The biggest piece of Cubs news other than Evers's hiring centered on Tinker's imminent departure from the franchise. Murphy gave the longtime shortstop permission to look for a managerial position elsewhere, and Garry Herrmann, who had been keeping an eye on the developments in Chicago, made no secret of his interest in securing Tinker to lead the Cincinnati Reds. Tinker mulled over his options, but he made it clear that he could not return to the Cubs under the franchise's new leadership structure.

"I see that Tinker says he could not play baseball under me. At the same time he said we were good friends. Now, it doesn't make any difference whether we are friends or not," noted Johnny Evers, Tinker's longtime double-play partner, frequent nemesis, and new boss. Evers called Tinker the league's best shortstop, but it was clear that the duo would not remain teammates. "If he can get the job of manager in Cincinnati, I wouldn't want to stand in his way," Evers said.[44]

Murphy admitted that a Tinker trade must be approved by both him and Evers, and the Cubs' new skipper proved tough to please. After weeks of wrangling, during which a pensive Tinker kept himself distracted by performing vaudeville, Murphy and Herrmann hammered out a complicated deal, acceptable to all parties, in mid-December that sent Tinker to Cincinnati as part of an eight-player trade. As part of the transaction, the Reds paid Detroit $7500 for young infielder Red Corriden, who they then sent to the Cubs in the deal. Murphy expressed warm feelings for Tinker and wished him well. "I am pleased that Joe Tinker has a chance to manage the Cincinnati team. The trade did not shape up as rapidly as I expected it would, but all the time I was anxious to see Tinker given the opportunity to advance which he desired so much. I think the trade finally made will benefit both teams," Murphy said.[45] Evers, however, squashed any notion of sentimentality and simply stated that, without the Peerless Leader's supervision, he couldn't fathom playing alongside Tinker anymore. "Tinker and I could not have played on the same team without Chance on the bench, and that was all there was to it."[46]

Not only did Garry Herrmann manage to wrangle Tinker away from Murphy, but he also ensured that Frank Chance remained a manager at baseball's highest level. Herrmann arranged for the Reds to claim Chance and, on November 9, Murphy released Chance to the Reds on waivers for $1,500.[47] Herrmann then made it possible for Chance to be rehomed in the American League.

New York Highlanders owner Frank Farrell had let it be known through back-door channels that he wanted to hire Chance, who was interested in taking a year off to recuperate. Regardless, it was a stunning physical turnaround for the first baseman. Dr. Fralick's operation miraculously had improved Chance's health to such a degree that his baseball career could continue. "He has a rugged constitution and a remarkable will power," Fralick said. "His ailment was never serious and I have treated many similar cases successfully. In justice to Chance I make this statement, absolutely sure of my ground."[48] Bringing Chance to New York would give the American League a star manager, opposite John McGraw of the Giants, in the game's largest market.

In this way, the core of the Cubs' 500-win club disintegrated. Suddenly, Tinker and Chance had their own franchises to lead, while Mordecai Brown remained trapped in the minors. Charlie Murphy now exercised more control over the Cubs than at any point during his tenure. By parting ways with three of Chicago's iconic figures, Murphy put the target for the team's success squarely on himself. Watching Chance, Tinker, and Brown leave the Cubs grieved the fans, and anything short of a National League pennant in 1913 would roil the increasingly dissatisfied public against Murphy.

On January 7, 1913, Chance arrived in Chicago from California to meet with Farrell. A party of friends warmly greeted Chance as he stepped off the train. Joe Tinker and Johnny Evers were there to say hello, as was Charlie Williams, who had grown close to Chance over the years. Less than forty-eight hours later, after Farrell offered to make him the highest paid manager in the history of baseball, and the sudden onset of freezing weather insidiously swept through his orange crop, Chance was convinced to sign on to manage New York. Farrell knew Herrmann deserved all the credit for making Chance's arrival possible. "I want to thank you for the assistance you gave me, without you I could not have secured the man," Farrell told Herrmann. "I want to say that at any time or place I can be of any service to you I am at your command."[49]

Murphy tried to blunt the headlines of Chance's agreement with the newly christened "Yankees" by agreeing to terms with Roger Bresnahan, a good catcher who had spent the past four seasons in St. Louis. When reporters pressed Murphy about Chance coming to terms with New York, the Cubs' owner emphasized his own team's new acquisition. "We feel so good here over the acquisition of Roger Bresnahan to the Cubs for the next three years that we have been able to think of little else," Murphy contended. "Still, we can pause in our elation long enough to congratulate Farrell on securing Chance."[50] It was a foolhardy attempt to deflect attention away from the headlines created by Chance. It didn't work. Chance's situation continued to receive higher billing in the local newspapers.

Chance's reception at the train station proved to be the final time he was with Tinker and Evers before the three men went their separate ways. The broken Cubs' double-play combination of Tinker to Evers to Chance, which had matured during countless hours spent together across eleven seasons, now belonged to three different franchises. The Reds and Yankees were elated to welcome Tinker and Chance into their folds. As for Evers, in spite of his favorable first impression, the Cubs' future remained shrouded in murkiness, like the thick smoke that so often enveloped Chicago itself, but one thing could not have been clearer: the dynasty had ended.

11

"ALL IS FAIR IN LOVE AND WAR"

During the winter of 1912, Charlie Murphy found himself embroiled in his most scrutinized controversy yet, and it had nothing to do with the departed Frank Chance. The uproar involved Murphy's nefarious scheme involving the Philadelphia Phillies and, in the end, it irreparably damaged his reputation around the game. It all started when Murphy stirred the pot in mid-August, as the second-place Cubs desperately tried to close the gap with the front-running Giants. The St. Louis Cardinals were visiting New York for a three-game series when Giants skipper John McGraw asked St. Louis manager Roger Bresnahan, his former catcher, to join him during an off-season worldwide tour of exhibition games to promote baseball. Bresnahan declined McGraw's overture. Perhaps sensing that McGraw exuded a bit too much chumminess with his protégé, a seemingly unprovoked Murphy sharply questioned Bresnahan's personal integrity in running his team, during an interview, suggesting the Cardinals put forth less than their best effort to beat New York. "I want to see the Cardinals play the game against the Giants and play it right up to the hilt. I can hardly believe that Bresnahan would allow himself to be drawn into a financial scheme whose success might depend entirely on his own team losing and a rival team winning . . . Not even a suspicion can be permitted right now," Murphy asserted.[1] Murphy had reveled in provoking the New York Giants for years, and perhaps he sought an ounce of payback against Bresnahan for the "poker raid" setup back in 1905, but his wild accusation that the Cardinals were tanking games, late in the season, against the league-leading Giants made zero sense in light of St. Louis's series victory. Perhaps Murphy remained frustrated at the Cardinals' lackluster performance against New York in 1911, but publicly assassinating Bresnahan's character marked a notable escalation in Murphy's behavior.

Murphy wanted to further disrupt the Giants so, oddly enough, after making a successful push for umpire eye exams, he developed the narrative that they were benefiting from favorable umpiring. Nearly all the National League owners felt like the victims of poor calls at one time or another, but they primarily kept those complaints behind closed doors. Murphy knew that he couldn't risk alienating National League president Thomas Lynch, a former umpire whom he had respected during his younger years as a baseball reporter in Cincinnati, with direct accusations of crooked calls favoring New York, so the Cubs president concocted a course of action that kept his name from being publicly associated with the scheme. In September Murphy contacted Phillies president Horace Fogel and leaned on him to push the pro–New York umpire conspiracy. Fogel completely owed his presidency to the Cubs ownership, and he could hardly turn down Murphy's request to publicly bludgeon Lynch and his umpires.

After the Giants swept a doubleheader from the Phillies on September 6, 1912, Fogel expressed his dismay at the umpiring in the series. Within earshot of reporters Sid Mercer and Grantland Rice, as well as fans, Fogel loudly complained that the Chicago club was correct, the Giants received favorable calls, and umpire Al Orth's poor decisions proved it by robbing Philadelphia of victories that day. Mercer wrote up Fogel's outburst in his game story for the *New York Globe*. Fogel's accusation created a nightmare scenario for National League officials, who now had to fend off claims of fixed games, and things only got worse.[2]

On September 29 the *Chicago Evening Post* published a sensational article, written by Fogel, that accused National League umpires of favoring the New York Giants. Fogel, who was genuinely frustrated with decisions against his team, pointedly criticized Lynch who, the Phillies president asserted, was only "a figurehead president with a greater power behind him."[3] Fogel argued that the real "power" in the National League played ball at the Polo Grounds, and he claimed that the umpires feared angering John T. Brush and John McGraw so as not to jeopardize their chance to work the World Series, a plum assignment that also paid well.[4] According to Fogel, the Giants had won up to twenty-one games—three against each opponent—during the season due to the assistance of favorable calls.

Condemnation accosted Fogel from all sides as the baseball world reacted in anger to the hit piece. Nobody realized that Murphy had read and approved of Fogel's article prior to its publication. John McGraw, in spite of his own reputation, or perhaps due to it, blasted Fogel's insinuations. "It has always been Fogel's way to blame umpires for the Phillies' defeats, and his latest squeal is only one of many that he has made since he got control of the Philadelphia Club."[5] Essentially lying on his deathbed, a feeble John T. Brush, Murphy's longtime mentor, who had just two months to live, summoned Giants secretary Joseph O'Brien and asked him to contact Lynch to organize an investigation into Fogel's charges.

Suppressing his emotions, a livid Lynch provided a composed, yet pointed, statement to the press in which he declared his commitment to thoroughly vetting Fogel's accusations. Lynch said, in part, "As far as President Fogel's attack on the President of the National League is concerned I care nothing. My 25 years' record in base ball speaks for itself. The cowardly attack on the honesty of the umpires and the game itself is a different matter, however, and cannot be overlooked. I shall take these charges of President Fogel before the Board of Directors of the National League, which has sole jurisdiction."[6]

Fogel's public suggestion of fixed ballgames sent the entire National League into an intense frenzy, and it filed seven formal charges against him in October. Charles Taft, Fogel's primary financial backer, demanded that Fogel sell the club by October 26, but the Phillies president dug in his heels and refused to part with the team, despite receiving an offer of $750,000. Fogel's defiance raised the mild-mannered Taft's ire, and he wanted the Phillies sold immediately.

"Mr. Taft does not dictate the policies of the Philadelphia Club, nor has he any voice in the matter," Fogel countered.[7] Taft did not yet realize that Fogel had written his controversial article at the urging of Murphy, who inconspicuously went about his business as the mayhem unfolded.

On November 26 the figureheads of the National League filed into the Gold Room inside the Waldorf Astoria Hotel to hear the Fogel case. Under the examination of league lawyer John Toole of the Boston Braves, Fogel denied that he believed the umpires fixed games, although he expressed his anger over rulings against his Phillies. He maintained that other owners and players shared his sentiment. Fogel admitted that he had penned the article that appeared in the *Evening Post*, but he argued that he wrote it to advance his position that umpires assigned to work the World Series ought to be selected by the president of the alternate league to eliminate any bias, in their regular season work, aimed at getting the postseason assignment.

Fogel took significant heat early in the trial, but the dynamic changed during the testimony of W. S. Forman, the sports editor of the *Evening Post*, who exposed Murphy's involvement with Fogel's article. Forman testified that he had received the article directly from Murphy, allegedly on Fogel's behalf, which had raised the editor's suspicion.

Trapped by Forman's testimony, Murphy tried to wriggle off the hook, but his argument failed to persuade anyone. Murphy confessed that he had seen Fogel's story, but he claimed that he couldn't remember exactly when the article started to condemn the umpires. Murphy testified that he had read only the first three pages of the copy before setting it aside. He then backtracked and stated that he had actually read only its first page. Murphy later admitted, "I did acquiesce and did authorize Forman, as he says, to tell Fogel to write the story; but I did not intend to attack the umpiring, and I want to say I am sorry that attack was made."[8]

In the end, the National League owners sympathized with Fogel, Murphy's pawn, but they nonetheless convicted him of five charges, and they banned the Philadelphia president from ever again representing a baseball franchise on their councils.[9] Murphy, too, submitted a guilty verdict and the entire controversy was officially blamed on Fogel, but the owners were irate at Murphy, who had essentially publicly called their sport fixed. Murphy avoided punishment and, in the aftermath of the event, blamed the *Evening Post* for exaggerating his role. "The *Evening Post* is hounding me because I fired Frank Chance. It is a play for circulation. There is nothing else to it. This man Forman is crazy, and his paper is a liar," Murphy insisted.[10]

Murphy's criticism of the *Evening Post* incensed Forman. "It came to me from Murphy's office, and if Murphy had not approved that story it never would have been published," he said. "The man who is morally responsible for that article and the charges it contained is Murphy himself, and I have Fogel's own word for it that he wrote it simply 'to help Murphy fight his battles' in the National League."[11]

Anger in the press boiled against Murphy for egregiously sautéing one of their own: Fogel, a former journalist. Newspapermen used Murphy for his unyielding content, which filled their columns, but Forman demonstrated that Murphy had turned the tables and was using them in his public relations game, and they resented it. Jack Ryder held nothing back in his assessment of the proceedings: "The testimony to-day showed that Murphy was the instigator of the obnoxious article, and that probably it would never have been written but for him. Now that Fogel is up against it Murphy deserts the poor tool who did his bidding and hides behind an alibi. It was a sorry spectacle." Ryder also recognized the severe consequences for any baseball official who politically aligned with Murphy in the future: "Murphy will doubtless go free, but he will never again be a power in the league or have the slightest influence in its councils."[12]

Murphy didn't save Fogel from the owners' wrath, and Charles Taft, who wanted the bad publicity gone, agreed to part with the Phillies to squash the turmoil. Taft rid himself of the franchise on January 15, 1913, in a deal with an investment group led by former Pittsburgh Pirates secretary William Locke for an amount believed to be, at minimum, north of $300,000. Fogel was bounced from Organized Baseball, but the triumvirate of Charlie and Annie Taft and Murphy emerged from the scandal with the Baker Bowl retained in their possession and, as part of the sale terms, Locke agreed to a lengthy lease of the ballpark guaranteeing the savvy investors a reliable revenue stream for years to come.[13]

The new-look Cubs entered the 1913 season with Johnny Evers at the helm, but without Frank Chance, Joe Tinker, or Mordecai Brown, a new crop of ballplayers needed to lead the way for Chicago to achieve notable success. Demonstrating that money can serve as an effective apology, Murphy stunningly mended fences with Roger Bresnahan to counter the bad publicity generated by the Chance firing and Fogel controversy. Murphy expected that the veteran Bresnahan would catch a considerable number of games for Chicago during the upcoming campaign.

Following the roster turnover, Murphy's preseason preparations included selecting a new spring training site. For the first time, the Cubs would prepare for the season in Florida. Murphy struck a deal with Tampa Bay businessmen to sponsor the team's hotel and food expenses in exchange for the profits produced by a series of exhibition games featuring the Cubs. With the exception of Murphy botching the number of needed rooms at the hotel—he should have let Charlie Williams handle those reservations—which left several of the team's party temporarily without quarters, the plan went smoothly. The Cubs played a notable three-game series against a team from Havana that drew a large number of invested locals with ties to Cuba. During the latter stages of camp, the team worked its way north to play exhibition games in several cities to generate additional revenue and lay the final groundwork for the season.

The Cubs roster underwent several additional changes during the spring. Veteran pitcher Orval Overall, unable to come to terms on a contract with Murphy during the off-season, abruptly announced his retirement, leaving a huge hole in the team's starting rotation. Fortunately, Murphy, fully attuned to the dearth of reliable starting pitching on the team, revisited talks with the right-hander and got Overall under contract with a boost in salary. However, Murphy sold the contract of veteran outfielder Jimmy Sheckard to the St. Louis Cardinals to open up an outfield spot for the Cubs' youth movement. Changes weren't limited to the team's playing roster. Murphy unexpectedly had to hire a new trainer upon the Cubs' return to Chicago. During the trip home, Bert "Doc" Semmens had taken exception to a biting remark from the mouthy Evers and punched the new manager in the face. Murphy dismissed Semmens, but the trainer quickly caught on with Cincinnati, where Joe Tinker hired him to work with his stable of Reds. "I am sorry I had to hit Evers, but it was one of these sudden quarrels—a flash, a wallop, and all over—but it put me into a new position that I think I'll like much better," Semmens said.[14] Without the firm leadership of Chance keeping everyone in line, Semmens was happy to leave Chicago.

The Cubs wrapped up their spring exhibition schedule by defeating the Minneapolis Millers, 12–0, at the West Side Grounds in early April. In the hours that followed, alarming word reached Murphy that two of the Millers' players had been potentially stricken by smallpox and exposed the Cubs' players to the virus. The St. Louis Cardinals had arrived in town to open the regular season, but the startled Cubs' focus was strictly on finding evidence of possible exposure. Murphy called in Dr. W. K. Murray to examine each player for any indication of the threatening illness. Following the appointments, a relieved Murray relayed that he had not observed any signs of smallpox. He expressed confidence that the vast majority of the players had already been vaccinated and required no further treatment outside of close observation. Rain in the city further hampered any hankerings of opening the season on time, and the first two games against the Cardinals were postponed.

Chicago's season got underway on Saturday, April 12, 1913, during a frigid afternoon that only four thousand brave souls dared to battle. The Cubs did not give their supporters many opportunities to get warm by cheering, as St. Louis won the game, 5–3. The highlight of the day occurred during the pregame ceremony. Mayor Carter Harrison gifted new skipper Johnny Evers 180 pieces of silver and a large floral bouquet in the shape of a baseball diamond to celebrate the latter's ascension to the managerial seat. Surrounded by bunting, streamers, and a brass band, Harrison threw out the ceremonial first pitch to umpire Brick Owens. It was all downhill from there.

Despite losing their opener, the Cubs' productive offense carried them to twelve wins in their first seventeen games. With a record of 12-4-1, Chicago sat atop the National League standings by two games

over the New York Giants, and Murphy felt good about his reconfigured
club. However, his optimism faded as Chicago's favorable start hit the
skids in May. The Cubs' potent bats cooled off, and the questions surrounding the quality of the pitching staff were definitively answered:
it wasn't very good. By the time the team began an East Coast road
trip on May fifth, Cubs pitchers had allowed a hundred runs, the most
in baseball. Chicago lost twelve out of its next fifteen games, as they
tumbled out of first place and landed with a thud in a fourth-place tie
with St. Louis. By early May Murphy knew his team was in trouble. He
mulled over his team's struggles with Garry Herrmann, who wanted
to wait a little bit longer before declaring his new-look Reds under
Tinker a complete disaster. "I doubt the method of loading up with
high priced players, who are slipping; but, of course, that is none of
my business," Murphy told his Cincinnati counterpart. "I could use
the same sort of advice in regard to our club, and if some of our high
priced pitchers do not show more, I will have t(o) supplant them with
young and ambitious men."[15] Several days later Murphy left Chicago
to meet the team in Philadelphia, so that he could discuss the Cubs'
deteriorating play with Evers.

As the Cubs stumbled through their East Coast swing, the city of
Chicago buzzed with excitement over the highly anticipated return of
one of its most beloved adopted sons: Frank Chance. On May 17 the
Chicago White Sox held Frank Chance Day at Comiskey Park as the
Windy City welcomed home the manager of the New York Yankees.
Hundreds of cars lined up in the city streets for a lengthy morning
parade featuring Chance, who joyfully waved to his adoring fans. Illinois governor Edward Dunne and Mayor Harrison, no doubt interested
in having their pictures taken with the popular Chance, participated
in the festivities.

The boisterous crowd, an elaborate embroidery of Cubs fans, Sox
fans, women, men, young, and old, clamored with joy when it was
announced that Chance, who typically played in a reserve role for New
York, would start at first base. The pregame festivities reached their
climax just prior to the first pitch, when Chance made his way to home
plate, where he met Governor Dunne, Mayor Harrison, and White Sox

manager Jimmy Callahan for a ceremony where he received an elaborate horseshoe of red carnations and roses eight feet in height. Photographers from every paper throughout the city vigorously snapped photos
of the four men as the fans' raucous cheers enveloped Chance. His
atypical smile shone through his natural stoicism in devoted warmth.
"It was a wonderful testimonial to the warm spot Chicago has in its
heart for the young Lochinvar who came out of the farthest west more
than a dozen years ago, stole a bride from among its fairest daughters,
and gave the city in return a proud place in the annals of baseball," Sy
Sanborn wrote of the Windy City's reception for its beloved knight.[16]

Charles Comiskey may have benefited from the boosted attendance
generated by Chance's return, but he also deeply respected the man,
and he gladly shone the spotlight on his adversary. "It's a grand day.
It surely shows that Chicago still loves her once popular favorite and
I hope that it will continue to feel the same toward him, even if he has
a trailing club. It will not give me any pain if we lose today's game."[17]
The White Sox owner needn't have worried much. New York was not
very good despite Chance's presence, and the Yankees struggled all
season. Chance grounded out in his only at bat, and, despite taking a
2–0 lead, the Yankees lost, 6–3.

When the White Sox had announced Frank Chance Day in March,
the *Chicago Tribune* had published a cartoon by Sidney Smith that
depicted Charlie Murphy standing on two stacks of newspapers so he
could peer through a knothole in the stadium fence to catch a glimpse
of the proceedings. A large bead of sweat clings to his face as the crowd
serenades Chance with affection. Usually, Murphy organized parades
and elaborate pregame entertainment, but there was no sign of him
anywhere at Comiskey Park for Chance's visit. Upon his return to
Chicago from his East Coast meeting with Evers, he holed up in his
house, away from the press and public. Anticipating questions about
the Cubs' dismal performance and Chance's return, Murphy clammed
up and avoided making any public comments except to suggest that a
potential personnel change to the pitching staff was close at hand. It
was an ineffective attempt at distraction. Chance still retained hard
feelings toward his former boss, and Murphy knew that the public sided

against him for moving on from the skipper, so he wisely remained out of sight.

The Cubs rallied hard in the waning weeks of the season, winning 21 of their final 30 games, but it was not nearly enough to keep pace with the Giants, who won an astounding 45 out of 58 games in June and July and coasted to the National League pennant. Chicago finished the season in third place with 88 wins, 13.5 games behind New York. Their solid final month did not offset the harsh reality that the Cubs had won fewer than 90 games for the first time in a decade.

There were several bright spots for the club. Third baseman Heinie Zimmerman batted a team-high .313 and led Chicago with ninety-five runs batted in. Young first baseman Vic Saier provided the Cubs with hope for the future. He hit .289, smacked fourteen homers, and drove in ninety-two runs. The twenty-two-year-old Saier also led the National League with twenty-one triples. The pitching staff rebounded a bit late in the year, but it still allowed over four runs per game. Everything added up to a decent season but one that fell far short of the high expectations shared by Murphy and the fans.

Fittingly, the Cubs lost their postseason City Series to the White Sox, which only further perturbed Murphy. He fumed at several of Evers's in-game managerial decisions, including not using faster pinch runners in late-inning situations. Murphy's ire crested when he learned that Evers had been seen socializing in public with White Sox manager Jimmy Callahan. Evers vigorously maintained that Callahan had simply extended a warm, friendly invitation to him and his wife, Helen, but Murphy wouldn't hear of it. Although he wanted to retain Evers as the Cubs' second baseman, an agitated Murphy wanted to find a new manager.

Ownership's support for Evers deteriorated throughout the season. Murphy and Charles Taft felt the first-year manager's explosive temper got him ejected from games too frequently, which cost the Cubs not only his managerial acumen but his bat in the lineup, and they weren't paying Evers to neither play nor manage. In particular, the stoic Taft recoiled at the uncouth nature of Evers's demonstrative behavior. It was one thing for Evers to play for the team, but to lead them as its manager required self-control, Taft believed. But putting the entire blame on Evers wasn't entirely fair. He had openly displayed his feistiness ever since joining the Cubs as a twenty-year-old in 1902, and ownership knew his temperament before hiring him.

Following the loss to the White Sox, Evers went to Murphy's office to collect the bonus money owed to him for the Cubs' third-place finish in the National League standings. Murphy quietly wrote Evers a check for $1,000. Ominously, there was not a lot of talk exchanged between the two loquacious men. "You are going away, are you?" Murphy asked simply.

"Yes," replied Evers, who was leaving Chicago for Excelsior Springs in several days for some downtime.

"Well, all right," was all Murphy said as he nodded and handed Evers the check.[18] Evers left and spent the next few days gathering up his things for his trip. As Evers packed, his mind churned through the changes he wanted to make for the 1914 season. Murphy had already made his decision: Evers would be fired as manager, but first he needed to line up a replacement.

As the 1913 season unfolded, a potential threat to Organized Baseball emerged in the form of the Federal League, a new minor league that soon set its sights on competing at the highest level. Hugh Fullerton, baseball's ace journalist, reported, "They are neither seeking war with the powers of Organized Baseball nor avoiding it. The new league has no intention of trying to secure players from major league clubs."[19] However, the Federal League reconsidered its strategy, in June, after Federal League president John Powers publicly accused the Chicago Cubs and St. Louis Cardinals of tampering with two signed players attached to the Chicago Federal League team: Tom McGuire and Leo Kavanagh.[20] The organization decided its teams could pursue players from the American and National Leagues in the off-season, under the condition that they had not already signed their contracts for 1914.

Hampered by low revenue, the Federal League limped through the 1913 season, but its survival demonstrated a staying power that caught the attention of additional investors, around the country, who yearned to get into the booming business of baseball. The sprouting league also caught the attention of American League president Ban Johnson, who expressed his concern that, although the American and National Leagues could nonchalantly brush it aside, the American Association faced a legitimate threat to its livelihood. In no way did Charlie Murphy want the Federal League to flourish in Chicago, and he actively undermined the efforts of the franchise, run by Charlie Weeghman, a local restaurateur and former Cubs fan. Murphy had successfully fought off the American Association in previous years, but now he needed help to crush the nascent aspirations of the Federal League in the Windy City.

Signing quality players paved the surest way to legitimacy for the Federal League, and Joe Tinker emerged as a primary target. Following a disappointing seventh-place finish in his first season at the helm, the Reds manager had a falling out with his boss, Garry Herrmann, who wanted to have a member of the front office follow Tinker throughout the season to help the team run more efficiently. Tinker, who demanded all the responsibility for the Reds' performance or nothing, balked. Desiring to replace Tinker, Herrmann traveled to the winter meeting determined to find a trading partner for the shortstop. The owners arrived in New York, but Charlie Murphy didn't join them. He missed the gathering because he and Louise had sailed across the Atlantic Ocean, aboard the *Lusitania*, to begin a two-month tour of Europe that was scheduled to last through the new year. It wasn't too soon to crack *Titanic* jokes for Ring Lardner, who teased his readers about Murphy's shipmates in his *Tribune* column.

ABOARD THE LUSITANIA.

Fair Tourist—I'm just sure we're going to run into an iceberg.

Escort—No; C.W. Murphy's aboard.

F.T.—What of it?

Escort—If we run into anything, it'll be a gold mine.[21]

Just prior to the winter meeting, Joe Tinker stopped in at the Corn Exchange Building and informed a Cubs front office employee that he wanted to reclaim his old spot at the West Side Grounds. A cable was immediately sent across the pond to Murphy. With the desire to replace Evers top of mind, the news yanked Murphy's attention away from his vacation and back to baseball. He wanted Tinker in a Cubs uniform again, this time quite possibly as the team's new manager.

Murphy sped back to America aboard the *Olympic* with a palatable solution to the Evers situation within reach. He disembarked in New York on December 10 and immediately looked for the nearest reporter to ask about Tinker's status. "I thought he was manager of the Reds. What is all this talk about his being on the market?" Murphy asked the scribe, who apprised him that Tinker wanted a reunion in Chicago. Murphy straightened up and, with his usual panache, declared himself a contender for the ballplayer's services. "I want him and will pay the price for him. I will pay real money," Murphy proclaimed. "I can't say what I will offer until I see Herrmann. I did not know until now that Tinker was to quit the management of the Reds," he added disingenuously. When told by the reporter that Brooklyn's Charlie Ebbets had offered Herrmann $25,000 for Tinker, Murphy, ever the showman, removed one of his gloves and displayed a dollar bill tucked in the fold of his hand. "I will give more real money for Tinker than any other man."[22]

Murphy correctly surmised that his theatrics guaranteed that the news wires would pick up the story of his desire for a reunion with Tinker and convolute the trade talks between Cincinnati and Brooklyn. Alerted to this new development, Herrmann engaged Murphy to gauge his sincerity. Murphy offered to swap Roger Bresnahan and Red Corriden for Tinker. The underwhelmed Herrmann declined the proposal but agreed to give Murphy an exclusive forty-eight-hour window to marshal a better offer.[23]

Murphy left New York for Chicago, where he hoped to sit down with Tinker, discuss the situation, and put together an acceptable package for the Reds. As Murphy's train rolled toward Chicago, Herrmann had drinks with Ebbets and other baseball officials and writers where, in front of the group, they finalized a deal for Tinker. The agreed-upon trade sent Tinker to Brooklyn in exchange for $25,000 on two conditions. First, Tinker would receive $10,000 of the money as a one-time bonus payment and, second, Ebbets needed to pay the player $7,500 per season on a multiyear pact. "Tinker will make Brooklyn a first division team, if not a pennant factor," Ebbets proudly told reporters. There was just one problem: Tinker had no interest in playing for Brooklyn.[24]

A crewman awakened Murphy aboard his train and handed him a telegram: Tinker had been sold to Brooklyn. The news surprised Murphy, but there was nothing he could do about it. "I am sorry to lose Tinker, for I thought we were pretty sure of getting him, but I wish him all the luck in the world," Murphy said. "He will strengthen any team, and ought to make Brooklyn a factor. Of course, the deal is not closed until Tinker consents, but I have no reason to believe he will not."

For his part, Tinker made it clear, at least publicly, that he would let the process play out. "While I would much prefer to play in Chicago I owe it to my family to do the best I can with the baseball that is left in me," he said, with an eye toward the $10,000 bonus.[25]

Just as the Tinker deal looked done, all hell broke loose. The Cincinnati Reds Board of Directors balked at only profiting $15,000 off the sale of the franchise's huge star—members wanted at least players in return—and it overruled Herrmann's decision to move Tinker. Reds fans also strongly disapproved of the swap, which further pressured Herrmann to alter the structure of the deal if he hoped to salvage it. To top things off, Ban Johnson told Herrmann that he loathed the agreement, because it created a new precedent in which a player received part of the money changing hands between organizations.[26] Slightly panicked, Herrmann wrote Ebbets a letter without the knowledge of the Reds board members and asked him to redo the trade as a "favor absolutely on the 'square'."[27] Ebbets declined to revisit the transaction's terms and grew frustrated with Herrmann for seeking to break their agreement. The disputing factions gave the opportunistic Murphy an opening, and he contacted Herrmann, on December 15, with the hope of rekindling talks. Murphy also made sure to publicly tell his fan base that he was going all in on getting Tinker back in a Cubs uniform. "I want Tinker for our club, and if I find I am in position to bid for him I will do my utmost to get him," Murphy promised.

Tinker did nothing to dissuade his former boss's persistence. "I am going to do all I can to swing the deal to Chicago. If President Murphy wants to bid for my services I am going to demand that the Cincinnati club give him the chance," Tinker said.[28]

Murphy's and Tinker's machinations incensed Cincinnati and Brooklyn, but their shared frustration did not bridge their differences. Ebbets wanted to meet face-to-face with Tinker to smooth things over and, hopefully, agree to terms on a contract. Simultaneously, Ebbets shot Murphy a curt telegram in which he warned the Cubs owner, "Please keep your hands off."[29]

Ebbets traveled to Cincinnati and met with Herrmann, on December 20, to hash out their disagreement. Although the angry board pressed Herrmann on all sides, there wasn't anything that could be done. He had already signed off on the trade. The Reds dealt Tinker to Brooklyn in exchange for $25,000, with $10,000 going to the player, and contacted President John Tener's office to record the transaction. Tinker's rights now belonged to Brooklyn.[30]

Although Brooklyn held his rights, contract negotiations between Tinker and the team fell apart. Ebbets's desired meeting with Tinker never occurred, and the aggravated Brooklyn owner decided not to meet the player's asking price of $7,500 a season over three years. Brooklyn's new manager, Wilbert Robinson, called Tinker to explain Ebbets's position. "Ebbets has stated that he will not pay more than he had made up his mind to pay. If you will not accept his offer, then Ebbets will take the chance of losing the $15,000 he paid Cincinnati," the Dodgers' skipper told Tinker.

"Well, you have lost $15,000," an angry Tinker spat into the phone.[31]

In the midst of the turmoil, Johnny Evers read a newspaper article that suggested Murphy wanted to replace him with his old double-play partner. Prompted by his wife, Evers sought out Murphy at the Cubs office, inside the Corn Exchange Building, to pin him down about the rumor. Murphy evaded Evers for several days, but on December 27 he couldn't avoid his manager any longer. Murphy allowed Evers into his personal office and informed him that he wanted a new manager:

> John, I have got a very painful duty to perform. While I think the world of you we have decided to make a change. We have had a meeting of the Board of Directors, and I have got to report back to them on January 7th when we have another. Now, in this change, we are going to get a much older man, and a man that is not play-ing. We do not think you can play and manage at the same time.[32]

Murphy pointed out that, in addition to having been ejected from games, Evers had not properly deployed the young, able base runners that the organization had acquired at the beginning of the season in several situations during the City Series loss to the White Sox.

An upset Evers tried to remain calm. "Well, you are the boss, Mr. Murphy, if you have decided that way, well and good."

Murphy, who, at this stage of his life, tended to equivocate when faced with interpersonal confrontation, made an awkward attempt to soften the blow. "What have you got to say for yourself?"

Evers, who never shied away from an opportunity to express his feelings, exploded. "I have no chance in the world to say anything because you have already given me worse treatment than the lowest criminal would get in court."

Murphy recoiled in the face of Evers's frustration. "Well, I have not decided this thing yet. I have practically decided, but I want to hear your end of it," Murphy stammered.[33] In reality, Murphy wanted to keep Evers as the team's second baseman, but he preferred to hire either Tinker or an alternative candidate, umpire Hank O'Day, who had done some scouting work for the Cubs in addition to managing the Reds in 1912, to pilot the team, but neither one was under con-tract. Evers intensely defended himself, and Murphy wavered in the face of his persistence. Murphy backtracked on his position to extinguish the confrontational argument. "Well, we have this meet-ing on January 7th, and I will take it up, and probably everything might be all right."[34]

Unbeknownst to Murphy, the attuned Federal League had been plotting to snatch Tinker away from the National League. Charlie Weeghman had quietly reached out to Tinker and made him a lucrative offer, with the added bonus of returning to Chicago with his Federal League outfit. Murphy was caught flat-footed when, hours after his conversation with Evers, Weeghman stunned the baseball world by pulling off an unthinkable heist: he inked Tinker to an exorbitant three-year, $36,000 deal. Serious ramifications of the transaction reverberated throughout Organized Baseball. The failed negotiation between Ebbets and Tinker meant the National League had lost one of its most well-known stars. Ebbets desperately wanted to file a lawsuit against Tinker for breaking his contract, but the precarious nature of the reserve clause convinced him to lay down his sword.[35] In the aftermath of the fiasco, Ebbets weakly tried to save face by accusing Murphy of discouraging Tinker from signing with Brooklyn even though everyone in baseball knew the shortstop's price.[36] Murphy's reputation made him an easy target, but Ebbets and Herrmann, who had not followed through on his promise to give Murphy forty-eight hours to acquire Tinker, were the ones responsible for losing Joe Tinker to the tuft-hunting Federal League.

Weeghman's deep-pocket signing of Tinker frustrated Murphy's reunion plan with the shortstop, and now his fractured relationship with Evers was saturated with distrust. Tinker's jump to the Federal League created another problem for Murphy. The Cubs had several key players who remained unsigned for the 1914 season. With Tinker taking over as manager of the Chicago Federal League outfit, Murphy feared the former Cubs shortstop would gleefully poach his players. Murphy penned a letter on New Year's Eve that warned each unsigned Cub that his franchise retained their rights. "Any attempt to violate or disregard this contract will be legally resisted, and this communication may be regarded by any unthinking players as a timely and kindly warning of the intention of the Chicago Club management to protect its interests."[37]

Murphy still wanted to replace Evers, but now he desperately needed the second baseman's help to keep the roster together. A week after

Murphy told Evers a change was in the works, Murphy invited him over to his house. Murphy wanted to send Evers on a recruiting mission, but he knew that required smoothing things over. Murphy began the conversation by conveying his appreciation to Evers for the job he had done managing the club in 1913 and expressed optimism that their partnership could continue to work moving forward. "I think you done fine, and if it is all right, we will go ahead," Evers recalled Murphy telling him.[38] Evers's managerial contract stipulated that the front office was responsible for signing players, but he magnanimously agreed to help Murphy anyway.

Murphy and Evers traveled to Cincinnati, where they spent several uneventful days together prior to the Cubs' board meeting on the seventh. When nothing concrete regarding his job status emerged from Murphy's sit-down with the directors, primarily Charles Taft, Harry Ackerland, and Charles Schmalstig, Evers departed town and crisscrossed the country for ten days signing up Cubs players, with one notable exception. Confusion between Evers and Jimmie Johnson resulted in a missed meeting in Tennessee and caused Murphy to send Hank O'Day to Chattanooga to sign the player instead. It was not the first time O'Day had taken on work for the Cubs. Murphy employed the umpire to scout young ballplayers in the off-season and make personal recommendations as to whether they ought to be signed by the organization. Although Evers didn't realize it at the time, O'Day's involvement in the Johnson signing indicated that Murphy was now considering the National League umpire as a strong candidate to take over as manager.

As Evers traversed the United States, Murphy voiced his displeasure with the lack of aggressiveness on the part of Organized Baseball to get its unsigned players under contract. He believed that losing Tinker was only the beginning of the National League's troubles if the necessary moves weren't made to squash the growing threat of the Federal League. "If I owned the Brooklyn club I would take immediate steps to enjoin Tinker from tampering with ball players. After that if he persisted in sending out telegrams to players under contract I would have him arrested," lashed out Murphy.[39]

Murphy tried to build a consensus by stoking the protectionist passions of Garry Herrmann but with unsatisfying results. The politically savvy Herrmann had no intention of following the rough-and-tumble Murphy into a proverbial alley for a street fight, even against the under-capitalized Federal League. The Fogel controversy remained fresh in everyone's mind and greatly hindered Murphy's efforts to establish political alliances. Murphy did not make this connection, and he remained perplexed at Herrmann's seemingly apathetic response. Murphy didn't fully appreciate the degree to which the other owners no longer trusted him. Dissatisfied by the lack of an urgent response from the National Commission, an increasingly agitated Murphy indicated to Herrmann that he would take matters into his own hands. "All is fair in love and war, and this certainly is a war condition, and we should try and do something to wipe out this movement as soon as possible, something as you say, which will have a crushing effect upon the insurgents."[40]

Locally, Murphy continued his efforts to thwart Weeghman. Murphy had developed many business connections throughout Chicago over the past eight years, and he tapped them for their knowledge of Weeghman's financial circumstances. Murphy learned that Weeghman, who owned a local restaurant chain, had invested a large amount of capital in the Federal League venture and was deeply frustrated at his penny-pinching peers, who were not following through on their pledge to sign major league–quality ballplayers to compete with Organized Baseball. Murphy also gleaned that, in the weeks following his jump to the Federals, Joe Tinker had become increasingly wary of the Federal League's precarious financial situation and could be coerced back to the National League with the right offer.

Murphy's intel proved correct. Weeghman was spending an extraordinary amount of money to compete with Organized Baseball, and Murphy attempted to portray him as financially overleveraged in the hope of discouraging players from signing with the Federal League, as well as rallying the other owners to his cause. "I have been informed that Weeghman, the authentic backer of the Chicago club has failed twice in business, and I know that he was refused certain loans the day before yesterday at the banks here," Murphy told Herrmann on January 10.[41] Murphy reiterated his contention to Herrmann several weeks later. "I have no fear here about the Federal League," he maintained, "because I know that Weeghman and Walker cannot make money on account of the tremendous expense they are assuming."[42] Weeghman may not have turned a profit in baseball right away, but his successful restaurants ensured he possessed free cash flow. Murphy remained on edge, and his injection of optimism into his communications with Herrmann was merely a change in strategy to provoke the National League to act. Privately, Murphy remained anxious.

Fed up with waiting, Murphy developed a strategy of his own. Without consulting the National Commission, or any of the National League owners, Murphy crafted a plan that called for Charlie Ebbets and the Brooklyn franchise to meet Tinker's demands on a three-year contract worth $7,500 per season, in addition to giving the shortstop the $10,000 bonus that had been bandied about in the earlier negotiation. Ebbets would have to uncomfortably stretch his budget to make the $32,500 package work, but the moribund franchise could rebrand itself under the expert eye of Tinker, making the plan palatable, Murphy believed. Murphy surmised that the loss of the star shortstop would scuttle the Chicago Federal League operation, and he intended to make sure it stayed buried by offering a cash settlement of $27,500 to Weeghman and his business partner, William Walker, for their abandonment of the club. Murphy figured that the payment could be split equally by either the National and American Leagues or each individual franchise. It seemed like the perfect proposition to Murphy, and Tinker confirmed his suspicion. The cornerstone franchise of the Federal League could be squashed in the blink of an eye for the slim price of $60,000. "This would, no doubt, kill this Federal League movement for 1914, and, J.T., says forever," Murphy informed Herrmann.[43]

Murphy nearly pulled it off. Ebbets traveled to Chicago and held productive talks with Murphy, Tinker, and James McGill, the owner of the American Association's Indianapolis franchise. According to historian Dan Levitt, "McGill . . . was included because the settlement would also allow the Federal League's Indianapolis backers to buy into his club."[44] The dizzying array of nuances to the plan was seemingly coming together when Federal League president Jim Gilmore heard about their ongoing conversation and kicked his organization into action to recruit Weeghman to remain in the fold.

With Weeghman's commitment to the Federal League teetering on a knife's edge, he met with American Association president Thomas Chivington, on January 22, 1914, to discuss another proposal. Weeghman wanted to own a baseball team in Chicago, and Chivington delivered that opportunity to him. Chivington offered Weeghman the American Association franchise in St. Paul, which he was free to move to Chicago.[45] Without consulting either Comiskey or Murphy, Ban Johnson gave the American League's consent to allowing a new American Association franchise into Chicago, because it meant pulling Weeghman, the pecuniary linchpin, out of the Federal League, which would assuredly collapse into rubble without its primary pillar. "It is my judgment that even if we are unable to accomplish anything at this time, we should grant the American Association the privilege of placing the franchise in this city. It will cover the territory on the North Side, and serve as a barrier to an entry into Chicago of any interests that are hostile to organized baseball," Johnson explained to Garry Herrmann.[46]

In the meantime, Johnson hoped that political pressure applied to Chicago officials by Organized Baseball would complicate matters for either the American Association or the Federal League's chances of permanently placing a team on Weeghman's north-side property.[47]

The possibility of Weeghman moving an American Association franchise to Chicago infuriated Murphy, who raged at the idea of his territory being invaded. Murphy worried that his franchise could be devalued by anywhere from one-third to one-half as a result of the added competition. Murphy simmered at the thought of another league prospering at his expense, and he fervently argued his case to Herrmann. "The Federal League can't last and the American Association can last, and would cut down our attendance, and make constant conflicting dates in Chicago and divide up the newspaper space, and hurt not only the Chicago Club but the entire National League, and

I prefer if necessary to go to law about it," an increasingly desperate Murphy implored.[48] Despite his loud protestations, Murphy's complaints fell on deaf ears.

The day after the meeting between Chivington and Weeghman, the National League held a vote on allowing the American Association to relocate a club to Chicago. Seven owners supported the plan, while Murphy cast the lone National League vote against the arrangement.[49] Cracks emerged in the wall of support for the idea after several owners learned of Murphy's desire to oversee Chicago, as they wished to exercise autonomous control over their own territories in future disputes. Charlie Ebbets immediately regretted his vote and voiced his concern over the idea in a letter he sent to all the National League presidents. "I believe this legislation is a mistake," he said. "I am firmly of the opinion that even though five, six or seven clubs might vote for the entry of a minor league organization into any club's territory it should not be effective however without the consent of the local club."[50] The owners rescinded their support, and the proposal failed. Weeghman could not settle an American Association team on the north side.

As Murphy grappled over the Feds, Johnny Evers successfully jaunted throughout the country enticing the Cubs players to put pen to paper on 1914 contracts. He even convinced young star Vic Saier to sign a multiyear extension, in spite of a nice offer from the Federal League. Evers, however, remained bothered by his conversations with Murphy, and he returned to Chicago determined to have another meeting to hash out their differences. Evers had signed a pair of five-year contracts when he accepted the Cubs' managerial job. The first pact tied him to the organization as a player, while the second deal made him the skipper. Evers had signed the contracts without reading the fine print, which left him unaware of a clause they contained that allowed Murphy to dismiss him with ten days' notice. That provision took Murphy off the hook for paying Evers for the remainder of the deal. A movement afoot in the American League questioned the wisdom of retaining that clause in the player's contract, but it remained embedded in the National League.[51]

When Evers returned to town he heard a rumor that the highly esteemed Charlie Williams, who had started his career with the Chicago franchise as a young scoreboard operator, during the playing days of Cap Anson, before rising through the ranks to become the Cubs' treasurer and traveling secretary, would be joining Charlie Weeghman's operation as the new secretary and treasurer of the Chicago Federal League club. Evers informed Murphy that Williams wanted to jump to the Federal League. "I expected so," Murphy replied.

Evers wanted to discuss his contract further before he left for his off-season home in Troy, so the men arranged a meeting at Murphy's home for Saturday, January 31, to talk things over but, on the morning of their scheduled conversation, Murphy telephoned Evers's wife, Helen, and told her he had taken ill and couldn't see anybody.[52] Murphy suffered from lumbago and rheumatism, and they possibly flared up at this moment of high stress. For his part, Evers believed Murphy avoided him on purpose, which is the more likely scenario. Infuriated by the snub, Evers penned an angry letter to Murphy.

My dear Mr. Murphy: -

I sincerely hope you have recovered by the time you receive this and will read same over carefully. I was indeed disappointed at not being able to have the talk with you that I expected yesterday afternoon, for if you remember, you told me when I went on my last long trip, signing up many of your players, that you would think things over and we could continue our talk, and now I am denied that. Now I am sure you know very clearly what my position is after our last talk, and what I think I am entitled to, as we went through pretty nearly everything, and I have shown you, on this last trip, and many times before, that I was square and loyal to you and the Chicago Ball Club, and I will confess your actions of some four or five weeks ago have made a thorough impression on me, and it is by just such an action that you have made me look out for myself.

NOW HERE IS MY POSITION: I WILL NOT PLAY ANYMORE
UNDER ANY SUCH CONTRACT AS GIVES YOU THE RIGHT TO DO
AS YOU INTENDED A SHORT TIME AGO, AND IF NECESSARY, I
WILL NOT PLAY AT ALL[53]

In spite of his frustration, Evers softened his tone at the letter's close.

Foot-note: Mr Murphy, I know you will understand thoroughly
my feelings in this matter, and that it is purely one of business,
as you so often have said to me, and that all the sentiment I ever
possessed has been taken clean out of me. JOHN.[54]

Rather than being moved to reconcile their discord, Murphy believed
that the letter was his ticket to removing Evers without any backlash.
Murphy contacted his attorney, Edwin Cassels, and asked if Evers's
refusal to play under his current contract could be legally construed
as a resignation. Cassels affirmed that it could. A relieved Murphy
stashed the letter away for safekeeping, in case he would need evidence against Evers, who had just quit his managerial post as far as
Murphy was concerned.

Lost amidst the Evers skirmish, Charlie Williams's decision to bolt
from the Cubs for the Federal League dealt another blow to Murphy, one the Cubs president failed to fully appreciate. Both Williams
and Weeghman were very well-connected, and it is likely they had
crossed paths previously, but Joe Tinker almost assuredly had played
an important role in convincing his longtime friend to leave the Cubs
and join him on the north side. The beloved Williams, who had always
been given a playoff share by the players, took a salaried position to
work for Weeghman, indicating that he was ready to move on from the
tumult brewing ever more intensely within the Cubs organization. Williams's last act with the Cubs was a notable one. In October he nabbed
four scalpers, during the City Series against the White Sox, selling
marked-up tickets on Thirty-Fifth Street, and had them arrested.[55]
Williams still bristled over the insinuations aimed at the Cubs' front
office over the 1908 World Series ticket scandal.

Losing Williams was a costly mistake by Murphy. Williams had grown up across the street from the West Side Grounds and worked his way up the organizational ranks since running the scoreboard during his teenage years.[56] Although he publicly thanked Williams for his years of service, Sam Weller of the *Tribune* reported that Murphy was already working on lining up a replacement within an hour.[57] Saying goodbye to another popular mainstay of the organization created another wave of resentment toward Murphy within the fan base. Watching a beloved player suit up for another organization stung, but their diminishing skillsets made it somewhat more palatable. However, Charlie Williams aged like fine wine. He knew as much about traveling throughout the eastern United States as anyone, and he was a walking, breathing personification of the team's history as a conduit to the Cubs' past. On February 1 George Nye, a longtime Cubs fan, organized a dinner at the Bismarck Hotel for eighteen of his friends. Nye announced that they were starting a club to drop their loyalty to the Cubs in favor of Charlie Williams and the Chicago Federals when the season opened in the spring. Nye told the amenable group that he wanted to quickly expand the nascent organization by recruiting Williams's friends on the West Side. They all readily agreed.[58]

Hiring Williams was another coup for Weeghman, who continued to make inroads on the north side of town. He hired architect Zachary Taylor Davis to design a stadium on a lot he owned at the intersection of Clark Street and Addison Street. Although thwarted in his effort to acquire an American Association club, Weeghman plowed ahead with his grand design for his nascent Federal League franchise.

Murphy had won the battle against the proposed American Association invasion but, in the end, his shortsightedness lost him the war, as Weeghman now had no other choice than to continue on his current path in the Federal League. As the situation crystallized, the other National League owners' frustration with Murphy intensified as the Federal League slowly but steadily grew in strength, and Ban Johnson resumed contemplating his strategical choices against losing ground to it. Behind the scenes, Weeghman remained cynical of the Federal League's viability, and his skepticism opened the door for one last attempt by Organized Baseball officials to lure him away. Behind Murphy's back, they offered Weeghman the chance to buy the Cubs. Although the exact machinations of the overture remained unclear, a movement within the National League to bounce Murphy from its ranks was clearly underway and gaining momentum. Otto Stifel, the primary owner of the St. Louis Federal League franchise, who had rescued Mordecai Brown from the minor leagues to manage his club, admitted that prior to an important conversation with investors, Weeghman had been pitched the deal of a lifetime. "Just before we went into that meeting Weeghman had been offered the franchise of the Chicago Cubs for $400,000. It was a bargain figure," Stifel claimed.[59] However, Phil Ball, minority owner of the St. Louis franchise, delivered a passionate address that exhorted his colleagues to ante up to take on Organized Baseball, which compelled Weeghman to stay the course and assured Murphy's competitor would remain open for business. The Chicago Federal League team would play baseball in 1914.

"THE MALICIOUS MISTAKE
OF MR. MURPHY"

On February 9, 1914, Charlie Murphy left Chicago for New York to attend the National League winter meeting with an important mission to accomplish: hire Hank O'Day as the Cubs' new manager. Johnny Evers remained an employee of the club—Murphy still hadn't fired him—which complicated matters significantly. Murphy needed to give Evers official notice of being let go to start the ten-day release clause in his managerial contract but, oddly, he hadn't done it yet. Additionally, Murphy had to clear an administrative hurdle of his own making to employ a league umpire as a manager. After Garry Herrmann had tapped O'Day to pilot the Cincinnati Reds prior to the 1912 season, Murphy had shepherded a motion through the National League Board of Directors that required any team hiring an umpire to pay the league the cost of finding a replacement arbiter. Now, claiming that he was operating on war footing against the Federal League, Murphy wanted to sign O'Day without paying anything, but he knew his peers would sternly oppose him. Upon arriving at the Waldorf Astoria Hotel, Murphy sought out Giants president Harry Hempstead and strongly hinted to him that Evers was creating tension within the organization and asked for help eliminating the required fee to hire an umpire. Hempstead, who had taken over the franchise following the death of his father-in-law, John T. Brush, suggested that Murphy could hire O'Day by simply paying the minuscule figure of $10, because the rule did not require a specific dollar amount.[1] "I thank you," Murphy replied.[2]

Meanwhile, Johnny Evers arrived in New York City, at the behest of the new National League president, John Tener, to provide league officials with testimony of his complaints against the Cubs president in their contract dispute. Tener, a former ballplayer turned politician, was just starting his tenure as president, and he would not take over the role full-time until his term as the governor of Pennsylvania expired in twelve months. Unlike his predecessors, Tener had demanded, and received, a multiyear contract and, with it, the leverage to more effectively corral the National League owners, who had spent a lot of time railroading past presidents operating on one-year deals. From the outset Tener firmly warned the magnates that only by working together could they improve their business. Tener sought to further strengthen his organization by improving executives' relationships with the players, and giving Evers a platform to express his dissatisfaction with Murphy was part of that process.

The meeting started on February 10 in the hotel's Sun Parlor. During the gathering's opening session, the owners were discussing the status of umpire contracts for the upcoming season when Murphy interjected his desire to hire O'Day. Murphy's request snapped Pirates owner Barney Dreyfuss to attention. Dreyfuss reminded the group that Murphy had recently led the passing of a resolution against the hiring of umpires without penalty. "You are right, Mr. Dreyfuss, we passed a resolution, but we could not foresee then a Federal League war," Murphy responded. "This is a war measure, and I know it means increased gate receipts, and I am right in the stronghold of this Federal League, and I think there should be some exception made, and that I should be allowed to engage this man O'Day."[3]

Dreyfuss remained unconvinced. "When Cincinnati took Umpire O'Day away, you did not think that way, and as I remember it, you were in favor of a resolution that if that was done again, that the club securing the umpire should pay for him," he responded. Dreyfuss viewed O'Day as a valuable asset to the National League, and he maintained that Murphy shouldn't be able to get him for nothing.

"I do not think that is the way to look at it when a war is on," Murphy rebutted. "This man is a native of my town, and was born within a stone's throw of my ball park." Murphy did not think that the National League was doing enough to help him fend off the Federal League, and the least they could do was save him some money.

Murphy's argument annoyed Dreyfuss, who didn't equate hiring O'Day with a war measure. Murphy was far more vulnerable for firing Johnny Evers than for hiring O'Day. In the end, the owners sided with Dreyfuss: Murphy needed to financially compensate the league but, ultimately, with several of them under the impression from Murphy that Evers had actually resigned from his post, they allowed the hiring to proceed. Murphy agreed to pay a modest $500 and, in turn, the owners freed O'Day from his contract, but they added a stipulation to the transaction that he would immediately return to the National League as an umpire when his tenure in Chicago ended.[4]

During the break that followed the session, Boston Braves owner Jim Gaffney ran into Johnny Evers downstairs inside the hotel. Gaffney informed Evers that Hank O'Day had just been released from his contract so that Murphy could hire him to manage the Cubs. Gaffney's news stunned Evers, especially the day before his hearing and with spring training just a few weeks away. Far from having quit, Evers simply wanted to rid his managerial pact of its ten-day clause and stay on as the Cubs' skipper. Cognizant of his swirling emotions, Evers composed himself and discussed the situation with President Tener that afternoon as the two men readied for the following day's meeting. During their conference, Tener listened as Evers complained that Murphy had not treated him fairly. Evers emphasized to Tener that he had not resigned and that any insinuation to the contrary was false. The new president encouraged Evers to make his case to the National League Board of Directors.

Johnny Evers entered the Sun Parlor at 4:15 p.m. the following afternoon and sat down in front of the National League's power players. Evers brought magnetism of his own as one of Organized Baseball's brightest stars and most audacious personalities for over a decade. He had fought their teams ferociously on the field but, in the end, they all belonged to the same league. John Tener opened the meeting by setting the standard that, under his leadership, "every player and every club owner shall have his day in court, and that fairness and justice shall be meted out to him, I asked Mr Evers if he would care to bring his case before the meeting of the Board today, and he said he would, and he is here for that purpose."[5]

Evers proceeded to outline how his fallout with Murphy had developed over the past several months. He described how Murphy considered firing him, in part, because he could not sell advertising after the Cubs' underwhelming season. Evers then shared how Murphy backtracked on his threat and asked him to travel around the country to sign up Cubs players before the Federal League could get to them, which Evers successfully did. After Evers returned to Chicago, he sought out Murphy to discuss his contract situation. He expressed his willingness to sign a new, single pact as player and manager for a length of time of Murphy's choosing, so long as it eliminated the possibility that he could be turned back into just a player with ten days' notice. "Can it be fixed so I can be assured of my position to go out there with confidence in talking to these players, and everything like that? Suppose I should go out and call some player, and two weeks later be playing alongside of him as a player myself, my life would be like a dog," Evers explained.[6] Evers's grievance failed to move Murphy, who claimed that he could not alter the managerial document. The owners listened intently as Evers expressed his frustration that Murphy did not resolve this issue prior to his recruiting trip, even though Evers was contractually exempt from signing players for the organization, then avoided him upon his return to Chicago when they were set to discuss the contract question further. Evers admitted that he expressed his anger over the matter in a heated letter he wrote to Murphy on February 1, but Evers revealed that he had no idea the Cubs were hiring O'Day as manager until he ran into Gaffney the previous day.[7]

Murphy began his defense by submitting both the player and managerial contracts, as well as the letter Evers had written him on February 1 expressing his displeasure at their cancelled meeting. The documents were read aloud so that each executive could be familiarized with their content. "I might say," Murphy pointed out after the stenographer entered the documents into the record, "that this section of the letter in which he says 'I will not play anymore under any such contract as gives you the right to do as you intended a short time ago, and if necessary, I will not play at all,' is what I claim to be a resignation."[8]

In a vacuum, Murphy made a compelling argument. "I would not sign anybody to manage the club that I could not let go, when I felt it was to the interest of the club to do so," he told the gathering. Evers wanted to change the contract that he had signed, and Murphy simply wasn't going for it. "Well, I thought then that the contract should stand, and I had had a very bitter experience with Mr Chance, and that is why it was embodied in the contract, that there should be no prize asked for, or any bonus demanded or any additional compensation not specified in the agreement," Murphy said. He went on to praise Evers for his handling of the team's pitching staff during the 1913 season but pointed out that he and Charles Taft thought the tempestuous manager got ejected too frequently.

Evers asserted that he had never sought to renegotiate the fiscal terms of the agreement as Chance had done, and he refuted any comparisons to his former manager.

I did not want to tie Mr Murphy down. As I remember, he said at one time during this argument, "I am going to be the big guy in Chicago, and nobody will be over me," and I told him they did not have a chance to get over him, and he went on and said, "If you are trying to hold up this Club, talking about the Federal League people, if you are, it is a holdup." I said, "Mr Murphy it is nothing in the line of a holdup. It is a question of being secure, whether it is one year, two years, three years, or five years. It is not the money consideration at all." Now if Mr Murphy will go back far enough to show that Chance held him up, he would know that my end of it has been entirely different all the way through, in all my dealings with him.[9]

Evers's mention of the Federal League immediately made all the board members sit up straight. Their guts cringed further as Evers recalled being out recently with friends at the Planters Hotel when Ned Hanlon, along with Charlie Weeghman and William Walker, Federal Leaguers all, came over to his table to say hello. After a brief conversation, Evers accepted Weeghman's offer of a ride home in his car, as they lived about five blocks apart. On the way to the house, the sly Weeghman teased Evers about his contractual status. "It has got to be a joke around here that Murphy is laughing up his sleeve that he has got you to a contract that he can toss you out in ten minutes," Weeghman needled.[10] An irked Evers reported the conversation to Murphy, but it still didn't move the Cubs owner to rework the deal. Evers also dropped several more bombshell revelations. Evers revealed that O'Day had suggested to him, nearly two weeks ago in Chicago, that he would be replacing him as the Cubs manager. Additionally, in response to a question from Dreyfuss, Evers stated that he still had not received ten days' notice that he was being fired by the Cubs, which meant he was technically still the team's manager. The owners, struggling to comprehend what exactly the Cubs president was doing, peppered Murphy with questions about Evers's firing. "I have only had two days," Murphy responded defensively, in reference to his time at the New York meeting. "When I get to my office, I want Mr Cassells to draw it up, my attorney."[11]

The issue swirling around Evers's contract, however, quickly faded into the background, because Charlie Weeghman's entrance into the conversation turned up the temperature in the room. The lurking Federal League terrified the owners, even though Murphy and Evers continued their testimony without emphasizing it. Murphy didn't pick up on their intensifying apprehension. He went on to deny several of Evers's charges, but no one was even listening to the contract squabble anymore. The magnates realized a really serious problem lay in front of them, and they were wondering if Murphy understood its magnitude. Weeghman had already nabbed Tinker, and now he was zeroing in on signing Evers, a potentially disastrous public relations blow to the National League that they simply could not allow to happen.

In the waning moments of the testimonies, John Tener interrupted the proceedings to announce he had a train to catch back to Philadelphia. He looked at Evers and assured him that the National League would treat him fairly. Charlie Ebbets, the chairman of this meeting, echoed Tener's sentiment and expressed optimism that the matter would be quickly handled. John Toole was not a member of the board but, as minority owner of the Boston Braves, he had quietly sat in the room and intently absorbed all that Evers had said about his deteriorating relationship with Murphy. As Ebbets concluded the meeting of the Board of Directors and reopened it to all National League members, Toole, the respected lawyer who had tried Horace Fogel on behalf of the National League in 1912, raised his voice:

> I desire to make a suggestion before Mr Evers leaves the room. I move you that the National League at this time guarantee to Mr Evers the performance of this contract, by a resolution to be passed by the League, pending the time when the disposition of it may be arranged, in whatever way may be figured out later, but that the carrying out of the contract which Mr Murphy made with Mr Evers, as manager of the Chicago Club, be guaranteed to Mr Evers by the National League. If this matter is allowed to go two or three weeks, every day increases the difficulty of reaching an amicable and agreeable understanding in the matter, and the parties are here now.[12]

Toole recognized that the prowling Federal League could have Evers signed, sealed, and delivered in hours if they allowed him to walk out of the room.

The owners passed Toole's resolution unanimously. The National League officially guaranteed both of Evers's contracts. Toole expressed his satisfaction that the relationship between Evers and the National League would continue even if his connection to the Cubs would have to be severed. Despite being pleased with his salary guarantee, the reality of the situation stung Evers deeply. The little ball of fire that the owners knew as one of their toughest opponents painfully dropped his emotional guard before them:

"I can assure you that, at any time, in fact, the principal part of this thing to me is the ambition which Mr Murphy has knocked out of my carcass, to remain with one club until I finish," Evers said bitterly. "I cannot do it now, and I feel as though I am hurt so much, that possibly I will not be the same sort of ballplayer some place else that I would be with Chicago. In that way, it is going to jeopardize my playing. As I told Mr Murphy, when he first started in this argument, it was not the financial consideration I was arguing over, but simply the principle of sticking with one club. I wanted to stay there, but he has made it impossible for me to do so. If I go some place else, I do not know how long I will last. That is the only thing. I have been loyal to the National League, and I hope to continue that way, and I think I am. In fact, I know so. I am not of that character that would do anything that would leave anything behind me that was distasteful to anybody connected with the National League or with base ball."[13]

Despite his claim, the owners knew Evers might use the situation to leverage a better deal from his next team, but they only cared about keeping him in the National League. They could work out the details later. Done with his testimony, Evers exited the room, his career in Chicago finished. The enraged owners then pivoted to Murphy with fire in their eyes.

Murphy listened as Ebbets's voice pierced the suffocating quiet and defended Brooklyn's failed negotiations with Joe Tinker, and he also spoke for his peers when he insisted that the National League could not afford to lose Evers too. "It would be a great blow to each and every club, and to the National League, to take any chance of Mr Evers going down to the Knickerbocker Hotel, and there being signed up by the Federal League tonight," Ebbets bellowed.

Philadelphia Phillies owner William Baker agreed that the Federal League would stop at nothing to sign Evers if word of the breach with Chicago reached them. "They will never let him rest between times," Baker said.[14] The owners resolved that Murphy must find a trading partner for Evers before the winter meeting ended. There was no other choice.

"You have placed us in this position," Ebbets pointedly told Murphy. "We have guaranteed him the $40,000. It is going to cost the League possibly more than it cost you in giving him up, but it may cost the League a great deal more, untold thousands, if Mr Evers is permitted, at this juncture, to get away from us."[15]

A troubled Harry Hempstead expressed his dismay to Murphy at being asked to help Chicago hire O'Day based on what he had just learned. "I did not think Evers would have anything to do with the Chicago Club, but I did not dream it was merely on a letter of that kind, which is merely a plaintive letter, trying to have you re-arrange something, so he will know whether he is up in the air, or down in the street, or is secure in his position, and I am terribly sorry, to say that I would permit O'Day to go until I know just what the difficulties were between you and Evers," the upset Hempstead told him.[16]

Murphy recoiled under the weight of Hempstead's disappointment and committed to doing all he could to ensure Evers remained in the National League. "I realize it is almost as unfortunate as the Tinker matter, probably a little more so, coming at this juncture, and I have great reluctance to do what I have done, but the construction of that letter which I have stated is not my construction," Murphy said.[17]

The owners hoped that facilitating an Evers trade within their ranks would close the matter. When Murphy indicated that he preferred not to entertain monetary considerations in exchange for Evers, Ebbets exploded.

You have got us in a position here, Mr Murphy, and you have to take, in a measure, what we want. It is seven clubs you have got here into a hole, damn it! We do not want Evers so much as to get out of the position we are in, and to say where he shall go. You took O'Day from us, as Mr Hempstead says, and you have got a manager. You did that with your eyes open . . . Now, let us be fair, and do not start to say what YOU want until we get some solution, some way out of it.

"There is no occasion for any excitement about it," Murphy replied, trying to lower the temperature in the room. "Keep calm."[18]

Gaffney and Ebbets expressed their interest in acquiring Evers during the roll call, but before Murphy could leave the room to negotiate with them, Barney Dreyfuss expressed his anger that he, too, had supported letting O'Day out of his umpiring contract based on the flimsy evidence of Evers's letter. It didn't read like a resignation to him. "I do not know whether it was his intention, or not, but I was deceived as to the status of Mr Evers' case."

"Not purposely, I can assure you of that," Murphy replied.

"I was not deceived by the fact you wanted to let him out, because I heard that four or five months ago, directly or indirectly, but I was deceived as to his resigning as manager," Dreyfuss explained to Murphy.

"I cannot see that Mr Evers did any wrong," Dreyfuss said to the group before turning back to Murphy. "I never had any use for the man personally, but that is neither here nor there, and I think we should do him justice. I think that your action, in regard to Mr Evers, in showing him up in the way you have in the newspapers is reprehensible to a very high degree, and puts not only your self but the whole National League in a ridiculous position."

Murphy tried to deflect Dreyfuss's critique. "Talk about the Tinker case. Don't concentrate on me," he managed.[19] But Murphy could no longer divert anyone's anger with self-deprecating humor or a sheepish apology. The genuinely heightened stakes against the Federal League had created a wall of stern resistance that he could not scale. Murphy had gone too far, and he knew it.

Murphy tried to shield himself from the onslaught of criticism by hiding behind his lawyer's assertion that Evers's letter was a resignation. Charlie Ebbets perked up when Murphy again mentioned Edwin Cassels.

"Did not you say that this," Ebbets began haltingly before his frustration level steeled his resolve to reveal a private conversation between Murphy and himself several weeks prior. "Did not the lawyer say that this was what you were looking for, the opportunity to get rid of Evers, or something like that?"

"Yes," Murphy confessed. "Yes, he said that."[20]

Murphy's admission elicited exasperation from the executives. They sat in stupefied silence as Ebbets, whose guilt washed away faster than his team's annual postseason hopes, burst on their behalf and berated Murphy. "You prejudiced my opinion, when you told me that in confidence, and I told you that you were a . . . fool, but you said you had gone through with it, and made up your mind, and you told me what the lawyer said, and I shut up. Now, I told you that you should not have done it, in Chicago, and I am sorry about this—I never did it in my life before, to tie a man down to a personal interview like that, I never did it in my life, but you have got us all in a tight place," a flustered Ebbets blustered.

"Don't keep repeating that," muttered the chastised Murphy. "I know we are in a jam [sic]. Let us get out of the jam, and not keep reiterating that."[21]

The only real solution, as everyone in the room saw it, involved the Cubs trading Johnny Evers to another National League team on the spot. Drawing out the process would alienate Evers and push him into the waiting arms of the Federal League. Murphy, scorned and shunned, wanted to make everyone happy with him again, and he readily acquiesced to the idea of dealing Evers. Boston and Brooklyn had already been identified, during the roll call, as the only two teams interested in trading for Evers, and Cubs minority shareholder Harry Ackerland advised Murphy that the trade be consummated before the session adjourned. Murphy agreed, and he left the room with Jim Gaffney to discuss parameters of a trade between Chicago and the Boston Braves. After several minutes of discussion, Murphy agreed to swap Evers to Boston in exchange for second baseman Bill Sweeney, pitcher Hub Perdue, and cash. They returned to the boardroom and Ebbets joined Murphy outside to talk about Evers, but the deal with Boston was already done. Murphy spurned Ebbets and headed downstairs to give out the details of Chicago's trade with Boston to the Associated Press.

The news of Evers's departure stunned everyone in Chicago. Newspapermen rushed to the Cubs headquarters to learn more about the story. Newly elevated secretary Charlie Thomas handed the reporters a press release that Murphy had written before his departure to New York that announced the hiring of Hank O'Day as the new manager of the Cubs, a move no one had seen coming. Murphy quoted himself as saying, "While we are sorry Evers will not be with us we feel mighty good over securing O'Day, the former battery partner of Connie Mack. I have known O'Day for many years and I do not know any man who knows more practical baseball."[22]

The story made the front page of the *Tribune*, so splashy was the development. Murphy followed up the press release by providing interviews defending his decision. "Evers could not control his temper on the ball field, neither could he control the players and I firmly believe that, if O'Day had been in charge of my team instead of Evers, the pennant would have been won," Murphy argued.[23] The fans would forget about Evers once O'Day returned the Cubs to glory, he believed. However, accurate or not, Murphy only made his situation more precarious by disparaging the popular Evers and referring to the Cubs as his own, in the press, in an attempt to limit the damage from the day's events. It only made it easier for fans, players, and National League executives to side against him.

Jim Gilmore, Joe Tinker, and Charlie Weeghman immediately pressed Evers to sign with the Federal League and offered him a three-year contract for $45,000 with a $10,000 upfront payment. Evers's lawyer told him that he was a free agent and could sign with anybody for any amount, and Evers strongly considered the offer. Panicked, John Toole and Garry Herrmann managed to get an audience with Evers. They were told by Evers's lawyer that he wanted a $35,000 bonus to stay in the National League and no assets for his services sent to the Cubs. After tightrope walking through the rigorous negotiation for the next twenty-four hours, they hashed out a deal with Evers. The National League agreed to pay him a $25,000 bonus paid in two installments. The National League paid the initial $15,000 while Boston absorbed the $10,000 cost of the second installment. Meanwhile, the Braves agreed to accept his Cubs contract as it was currently constituted, per Evers's request. After several heart-palpitating moments, Evers agreed to extend his stay in the National League.

As long as he no longer played for Murphy, Evers was content to move to another club, and he claimed that sentiment now ran throughout the Cubs' roster. "Take it from me that if Mr Weeghman had tried to sign the Cubs every one of them would have deserted Murphy. I know what I am talking about," Evers said. "I stuck to Murphy through thick and thin. I never showed any disrespect for him. I was loyal and painstaking. But after the deal Chance got I might have known I would get the same."[24] Evers's emotional response may be understandable, but it certainly wasn't true. Tinker, for instance, would have signed with the Cubs, if allowed.

Reinvigorated by his anger, Johnny Evers had one of his finest seasons as a professional ballplayer in 1914 for the Boston Braves. He earned his large paycheck and then some. Evers won the National League's Most Valuable Player award as he hit .279 with twenty doubles and forty runs batted in. The Boston franchise won its first pennant in sixteen years and followed it up by making quick work of the Philadelphia Athletics in the World Series. Evers hit .409 as the Braves swept the A's in four games. It was the third championship of Evers's career.

It was clear that the knives were now out in full force for Charlie Murphy, and that his days as a National League owner were numbered. As the National League's winter meeting wound down to a close, Charlie Ebbets, who benefited the most by faulting Murphy for the Federal League problem, again took off the gloves and had another go at the Cubs president for his outsider way of doing business:

> Now, if he would only do as every one of the other fifteen clubs do, and mix around socially and agreeably, and think, "We are Charley, and we are Jim, and we are Jack together," and we all have a common purpose,—if he would do that, I think much of his trouble would be wiped away, and would be simplified, but he has the eternal suspicion that the National League, an honor-

able body of men, who can handle my money at any time, to any extent, he has a suspicion that some one of them are going to do him an injury. Now, if he would by mix around, I think he would find so quickly that while they make mistakes, yet they are doing that which is best for the interests of all, and of the Chicago Club, too. That is all I care to say.

Silence overtook the room after Ebbets finished, and all eyes locked onto Murphy. They wanted to know how he would respond to Ebbets's criticism, an opinion that, frankly, most of them shared. Murphy could perhaps win them over again with a moment of sincere self-awareness, a trait he possessed but frequently ignored in favor of his competitive business nature, but instead he winced in the face of Ebbets's verbal lashing. "I move we adjourn," the defeated Murphy mustered.

Unsurprised and unmoved by that meek response, Ebbets tacked on his own ending to Murphy's sentence: "And accept the invitation of Mr Hempstead to go to luncheon with the New York Club. All in favor say Aye, contrary No. It is unanimously carried, and I would suggest we go down by special stairway to get the dinner."[25]

Following a gathering of American League owners that same weekend, American League president Ban Johnson telephoned his National League counterpart, John Tener, to inform him that the situation with Murphy had become untenable. Johnson issued a public warning to National League owners: "The American league has become tired of the blunders of this man, and for the good of baseball I think a change in the ownership of the Cubs is necessary. Just how this problem can be solved I am not at liberty to discuss at this time, but the American league is determined to purge baseball of persons within the ranks who are enemies of the sport," he bellowed.

Murphy scoffed at Johnson's latest threat. "These fellows have been trying to throw me out of baseball for a long time, but they only make me laugh. I shall pay no attention to them until they try to injure my property rights. Then we will see how far they will go," Murphy warned.[26]

Upon returning to Chicago, Murphy declared to reporters his intention to shut Johnson up for good by suing him for slander and conspiracy to kick him out of baseball. "Now, listen and get these exact words," Murphy seethed. "I'm going after that big——, Ban Johnson, tomorrow morning for conspiracy and slander. Be sure to get those words—big——. There's a suit of clothes in it for every fellow who gets them in his paper." Murphy went inside his office for a few minutes before he returned to vent some more. "What has Johnson done to fight the Federal league? He's been helping them out, if anything," Murphy fumed. "While he sat back and did nothing I've had to fight the 'outlaws' single handed in Chicago. Mr. Comiskey being away and unable to take a hand in the war. I've had to protect Comiskey as well as myself."[27] Comiskey was on a global baseball exhibition tour and was in Rome, far away from Chicago.

Murphy aimed to take Johnson down, and he was willing to spend the money to do it, even if it cost him six figures. Murphy painted Johnson as an egomaniac and a failed opportunist. "Johnson takes advantage of every new man who joins our league. He tried to get an interest in the Cubs in 1905 when I bought the team. He asked August Her(r)mann to supply $25,000. The letter for money was written to John E. Bruce and I have a copy of it," Murphy claimed.[28]

Johnson ignored Murphy and moved ahead with his plan. He had already coerced the American League owners into granting him the power to remove team officials who undercut the interests of Organized Baseball in its fight against the Federal League. Johnson demanded that the National Leaguers follow suit. Johnson even made veiled threats about linking up with the Federalists in a joint venture to create a new league to avoid a continuation of a business relationship with Murphy. "I can say now that we will go to any extreme to eliminate Murphy from organized baseball," Johnson raged.[29] Johnson called *Chicago Tribune* scribe Sy Sanborn a "good guesser" for his speculation that American League clubs could break the National Agreement and pursue a partnership with several Federal League clubs. "That theory is not at all impossible," Johnson told him.[30]

A rampant rumor raced around Chicago that the National League might force Charlie Murphy to sell the Chicago Cubs. The day Murphy returned from the winter meeting, a group of local businessmen wrote him a letter asking for his price, but Murphy ignored them and focused on making final preparations for the spring exhibitions.

Hugh Fullerton heard the increased chatter involving his longtime friend Murphy. Fullerton gave his readers detailed insight into Murphy's tension within National League circles. "His extraordinary success during the first five years he owned the Cubs aroused much envy, and his actions aroused bitter enmity. He has quarreled with almost every man in baseball—and made a fortune doing it.

"Just now he is out with almost everyone in baseball—and laughing at them, declaring they cannot drive him out of the game.

"Hate him or like him, he is always interesting—and that is something," Fullerton wrote.[31]

The National League magnates heeded Ban Johnson's instructions and resolved to empower John Tener to operate unilaterally. Tener set out to resolve the angst around Charlie Murphy once and for all. He scheduled a meeting for all the National League owners, in Cincinnati, on February 21. Tener mulled over his choices, but he really only had two options. He could force Murphy to either conform or sell his stake in the Cubs.

Seemingly alone without an ally in the game, Murphy went into the office the morning of the twentieth, but he didn't feel well. He knew the owners were angry at him, and that any support he retained was quickly slipping away like sand through an hourglass. Murphy might be able to hang on if the problem only featured the National League owners, but Ban Johnson's involvement made escaping this predicament very difficult. Murphy did not want to give up the Cubs, but he would never surrender his independence. They all adhered to Johnson. Murphy began to feel sick. His muscles ached. Stress saturated his body. Murphy's train left for Cincinnati that evening, but at noon he informed Charlie Thomas that he was leaving the office. Instead of heading to the station, Murphy drove home, where he changed clothes and slipped into bed. He wasn't going to be their punching bag.

Meanwhile, the serious-minded Taft climbed onto his train bound for Cincinnati and encountered a host of baseball officials on board, including Charlie Ebbets and Jim Gaffney. A reporter caught Taft's attention and asked for his views on the Charlie Murphy situation. Taft listened with pursed lips as the journalist listed Murphy's short-comings. The quiet and dignified Taft then turned to the writer and said politely, yet firmly, "I intend to back Murphy to the limit and will resist any effort to oust him from the National League."[32] The train jerked forward and pulled out of the station.

As the trains carrying the magnates converged on Cincinnati, word reached Garry Herrmann that not only was Charlie Murphy not aboard one but he was ill in bed at home. Herrmann had seen Murphy pull this move before, but he saw that nothing could be done about it. "I don't know just what we can do or what we shall do," he confessed.[33] Tener arrived, and he made the decision to thin out the meeting's participants.

On February 21 Tener discussed Charlie Murphy with Taft, Harry Ackerland, and John Toole. The talk lasted four hours. Taft felt a strong sense of loyalty to Murphy and remained apathetic to the idea of removing him. However, Tener, Ackerland, and Toole expressed their worry over the potential ramifications for the Chicago market in the ongoing battle with the Federal League. Ultimately, for the good of the National League, Taft acquiesced and agreed to buy out Murphy, who received an evening telephone call at home with an offer for 529 of his shares that he couldn't refuse. Taft asked Murphy to retain one share so that he could remain a voting member of the board until it was reorganized.[34] Murphy agreed. "I sold out at 7 o'clock over the long distance telephone," Murphy told reporters that night. "Mr. Taft offered me more money for my 53 per cent of Cubs stock than I ever thought was in the world. I accepted without quibbling. I am through with baseball and its controversies and squabbles. I'm the happiest man in the world tonight."[35]

Charles and Annie Taft had been in business with Charlie Murphy for nearly a decade. Investing in baseball had increased the wealth of all parties. However, the increasingly tumultuous circumstances involving Murphy and Organized Baseball could no longer be ignored.

Taft bought out Murphy for the substantial sum of $500,000 broken down into two parts. First, on March 18, Taft declared a 100 percent dividend on all Chicago Ball Club shares, and Murphy received a check in the mail for $50,000. Second, Murphy agreed to give Taft five years to pay the remaining balance of $450,000 owed to him so long as he could keep the 530 shares as collateral. Taft consented.[36] Additionally, Murphy retained his stake in the West Side Grounds.

Several weeks later, the National League informed Taft that the Boston Braves would not be trading either Bill Sweeney or Hub Perdue to Chicago as compensation for Johnny Evers, per Evers's own request. The Cubs would also have to pay their allotted portion of Evers's $25,000 bonus, $10,000 of which the National League had agreed to pay.

"What was the twenty-five thousand dollars put up for?" Taft asked.

"In order to save the malicious mistake of Mr. Murphy," John Toole replied.

"And in order to carry out the delivery to Boston," John Tener added.[37]

Taft, who expressed his support of the National League and dedicated himself to its "phalanx" posture against the Federal League, accepted the terms. In response, the National League paid Boston $4,000 for the rights to Sweeney, which it then transferred to the Cubs. Sweeney agreed to go to Chicago and went west for the 1914 season. Technically, the National League met Evers's demand of not compensating the Cubs, but it found a workaround that provided a second baseman for Chicago.

While Charlie Murphy made a substantial profit on the sale of the Cubs, his reputation lay in tatters. Despite their once amicable relationships with Murphy, not to mention their tremendous personal and team success during his ownership tenure, Johnny Evers and Frank Chance could hardly contain their glee at his demise, a sad ending to their years together. "I am happy if I helped in getting Charley Murphy out of baseball," said Evers. "It is rather hard for me to leave Chicago now after playing here for so long, but it isn't so bad when I think of the good the whole mess has accomplished."[38] Chance shared his former teammates' disdain for their former boss. "'Murphy,' he said, 'is a menace to organized baseball. He has played politics in the National league and has given the Federal league an opportunity to get a foothold. I do not think the Federals have a chance to succeed. There is no more call or use for a third major league than there is for a wagon with a fifth wheel. But had it not been for Murphy there would have been no Federal league. It would not even have been talked of.'"[39]

Understandably, Chance remained bitter, but it clouded his judgment. The Federal League featured Joe Tinker in 1914, not Johnny Evers, and that resulted from the botched transaction between Brooklyn and Cincinnati. Murphy would have acquired Tinker to manage the Cubs had he not been traded to Brooklyn. Charlie Ebbets sought to assuage any frustration toward himself during the winter meeting for a reason; he had failed to get Tinker under contract. Garry Herrmann also largely escaped blame even though he had misled Murphy about an exclusive forty-eight-hour window to deal for Tinker. Murphy would have found a way to make that trade to reunite with his neighbor and rekindle the fan base. Where might that have left Evers? It's likely that Tinker's reacquisition, especially if he had become the new manager, would have alienated Evers, and it's possible he would have wound up jumping to the Federal League. Although Evers and Chance disliked Murphy at the end of their tenures in Chicago, not all players shared their opinion, but conflict with those two huge stars had created insurmountable problems. Murphy's increasing unwillingness to create alliances with owners had compounded the problem and left him politically vulnerable, which made him the casualty of the Federal League conflict.

Murphy tried to take the disappointing close to his time with the Cubs in stride. He wanted to relax after scratching and clawing for years on end. "This has been a strenuous winter season, between the Federal league and the bickerings of owners of 'organized' clubs. I will try and forget it all and right now am at peace with all the world. I have made my pile and I have quit work for all time. I wish Mr. Taft the best of success," Murphy said.[40]

In Murphy's eight full years as club president, the Cubs earned four pennants, won two World Series championships, and never finished below third place.

Although Murphy had helped transform the Chicago Cubs into one of the crown-jewel franchises of professional baseball, his days as a prominent figure in Chicago had ended. Now it was time for something new. The forty-six-year-old Murphy looked outside the Windy City to refurbish his reputation, and his beloved Wilmington called him home.

13

SHOW BUSINESS

The day after he agreed to sell his majority stake in the Cubs, the *Cincinnati Enquirer* surmised that the now unencumbered Charlie Murphy "will probably devote his attention to the show business."[1] For his part, Murphy was ready to take a break. Sitting in a large chair inside his warm home as a blizzard raged outside, Murphy told Sam Weller of the *Chicago Tribune* he wanted to take a step back before deciding upon his next move. "I'm going to take a long rest, a real rest, such as a man can have only when he hasn't a care in the world. I'm nearly worn out over worry and fuss in baseball. I haven't made any plans whatever. But I don't expect to retire from business life yet," he said. "After I've had this long rest I suppose I'll get into some business activity, but it will not be anything as confining as running a baseball club."[2]

Newspapers across the country plastered stories about Murphy's expulsion from baseball throughout their pages. The news was so big it made a paper in Canada as well as a German language publication in America.[3] Murphy's foes, particularly American League president Ban Johnson, had succeeded not only in ousting him from the sport but in publicly admonishing him as well, but a sanguine Murphy took it all in stride. "Perhaps I did have enemies, and perhaps I deserved to have them," Murphy reflected thoughtfully. "There are a few men in organized ball today that I personally don't care for. But I'm through with all of them now, and I'm able to say, 'I've got mine,' and go along without hating anybody."[4]

Murphy was ready to exit stage left. "Somebody else is going to worry about building a new grand stand for the Cubs. Somebody else is going to fuss over managers and players and a thousand little details of running a ball club. Somebody else is going to be jeered by a mad public. From now on I'm going to be a fan, a regular howling crazy fan, because I will always love the game. I'm going out there and yell 'rotten' at the umpire and I'm going to roast the visiting players and eat pop corn, and just have a grand old time." Murphy smiled. The baseball business had been very good to him. Financially, in addition to the $450,000 of stock he controlled, Murphy retained a significant stake in two stadiums: West Side Grounds and the Baker Bowl, which supplied him with consistent rental income from the Cubs and Phillies.[5]

While baseball officials congratulated themselves over Murphy's removal, not everyone understood their excitement. Popular writer Damon Runyon, while admitting he had observed Murphy's career in Chicago from afar, nevertheless, expressed his dubiety over the necessity of booting the Cubs president from his post. "We never heard that Charles Webb Murphy acquired his money by graft, or by robbing widows or orphans. We never heard that Charles Webb Murphy ever committed any indictable crimes whatsoever, although his taste in weskits merits the consideration of any grand jury. We have heard him accused of numerous heinous baseball offenses, but we cannot recall now what they all were, and whatever they were, they probably have no bearing upon the future well-being of the nation," Runyon concluded wryly.[6]

Murphy officially separated from the Cubs front office on March 18 at a special meeting of the Board of Directors. Murphy resigned and helped elect Secretary Charlie Thomas to the team's presidential post. Charles Taft would represent the Cubs at National League meetings as the principal owner, while Harry Ackerland and Charles Schmalstig, Taft's personal secretary, retained the bulk of the minority shares. Thomas took over the organization immediately.[7]

As the insouciant Murphy relaxed in his home upon the shore of Lake Michigan, the conflict between Organized Baseball and the Federal League continued to rage. Arguments over player signings, fiscal matters, and the continued uncertainty surrounding the level of Charlie

Weeghman's commitment to the Feds soured any real momentum toward a peace agreement between the two consortiums. The Federal League failed to pilfer a substantive number of quality players from Organized Baseball and, predictably, floundered at the ticket office in a number of markets, considerably limiting their leverage in talks. Financial cracks in the ground beneath the Federal League continued to widen, and Weeghman, once again, looked for a way out. On October 14, 1914, Weeghman met with Garry Herrmann and expressed his interest in purchasing the Chicago Cubs as one facet of a more complex settlement between the leagues. As part of the potential peace treaty, several other Federal League owners would buy into Organized Baseball franchises, while the remaining organizations would be absorbed into the minor leagues. Weeghman followed his productive meeting with Herrmann by contacting Charles Taft to gauge the latter's interest in selling the Cubs. They met at a hotel in New York. Taft candidly consented to Weeghman's buying the team, and the two men spent the next several weeks negotiating a framework for the deal.[8]

Murphy had kept to himself throughout the season, but word of Weeghman's impending pact with Taft roused him out of his baseball hibernation. Weeghman's brand new ballpark, just over six miles north of the West Side Grounds, threatened Murphy's rental agreement for his own stadium. The Cubs would move up the road and take Murphy's revenue stream with them. Murphy, who continued to retain his majority stake in the Cubs as collateral, remained quiet in the public eye but roared to life behind the scenes. Rather than make waves in the press himself, Murphy supplied *Chicago Tribune* writer Sy Sanborn with an anonymous source that dispassionately explained that the former Cubs president had neither received complete payment for his shares nor wanted to terminate the stadium lease agreement. Additionally, the source told Sanborn, Murphy wanted the team to remain on the West Side. Murphy fielded telephone calls from other reporters, but he declined to answer any of their questions directly other than to acknowledge that he retained a lengthy lease agreement with the team. Sanborn accurately concluded that Taft had not yet paid Murphy, which left the former Cubs president in complete control of the situation. "The transaction was one in which Murphy accepted obligations backed by stock in the club in exchange for said stock. C.W. Murphy, therefore, remains a considerable factor to be reckoned with in local baseball affairs," Sanborn concluded.[9] Stunned baseball officials scrambled to address the new revelation. A possible solution emerged in the form of a new stock issuance following a merger between the Cubs and the Chicago Federal League team, but Murphy wasn't interested in it. Despite having been expunged from Organized Baseball, the underestimated Murphy possessed more control over its business than ever.

Charles Taft reached out to Murphy, and the latter agreed to visit his longtime friend, in Cincinnati, on November 16. Murphy broke his ongoing silence with reporters, but his tone struck a different chord. He explained himself earnestly but without the bursts of emotion that he had famously shown during the last few years of his ownership tenure. "During the past season I have had some peace of mind and have enjoyed being out of the limelight," Murphy divulged. However, he sternly frowned upon the Cubs being sold or moved. "Charley Weeghman is a fine fellow personally and would no doubt be welcomed into the ranks of organized baseball, but his park is too small for National league games and it has not got the required transportation facilities. I am in favor of keeping the Cubs on the west side."[10]

Now free from the intensity of pressure from other league owners, who most assuredly wanted to end the Federal League once and for all, Murphy pressed Taft to dismiss Weeghman as a suitable buyer. Over the course of the next several days, in Cincinnati, Murphy's cajoling won over Taft. Murphy emphasized the location of the team on Chicago's West Side as the primary reason for keeping the team away from Weeghman. The population of the Windy City skewed to the west, and their loyal fans continued to buy tickets in prodigious numbers. Murphy and Taft could also keep their paying tenant. Taft agreed and sent a letter to Weeghman that called for an immediate end to their negotiation.

With his stake in the team and stadium intact, Murphy returned to Chicago and publicly downplayed Weeghman's level of involvement with Taft: "Charley Weeghman has no option on the Cubs, either verbal or written, and never has had . . . Weeghman has for a long time, no doubt, wanted to be a big league magnate, but that ambition cannot very well be achieved. The Cubs will remain on the west side, where they belong and where they have been loyally supported."[11]

Weeghman bristled at Murphy's insertion into the proceedings, but there was nothing he could do about it outside of declaring that, yes, indeed, he had held an option on buying the Cubs. "I do not care to answer Mr. Murphy's statement further because he is a neighbor of mine and I have a fine bulldog at home which I prize very highly, and I'm afraid Murphy might poison my dog."[12] Weeghman, who knew that Murphy had outmaneuvered him, tried to assure anyone who would listen that he may have been knocked down but not out. "It looks like war, doesn't it?"[13] The collapse of the talks between Taft and Weeghman stunned Ban Johnson and John Tener, who both believed they were close to a settlement with the Federal League. Now, they were back to square one.

Murphy's shocking victory marked his revenge against Weeghman, a former Cubs fan, who had cited Mordecai Brown's demotion to the minor leagues at the hands of Murphy as his initial motivation for buying a baseball team in Chicago.[14] Despite Weeghman's efforts, Murphy had successfully boxed him out, at least temporarily, and simultaneously prevented peace between Organized Baseball and the Federal League. Cubs fans, whose love for their team's former president had devolved into scorn following Frank Chance's firing, could not have been more thrilled with the unexpected development. Murphy had materialized, seemingly out of nowhere, just in time to rescue their team from relocation. The fans dusted off their old adoration for the man who had helped deliver them four pennants and two titles. Frank McDonald spoke for many Cubs supporters who lived in the neighborhood surrounding the West Side Grounds. "As a patron of the national game for a long period of years, and as a resident of Chicago's great west side, I think your attention should be called to the fact that in the opinion of the rank and file of west side fandom Mr. Charles W. Murphy, former president of the Cubs, has performed the most signal service in their behalf that ever was performed for them when he interposed his successful protest against the carrying out of the plan to take the famous National league club away from our section of the city. From what I hear from the well wishers of the Cubs and the game in general the feeling toward Mr. Murphy is one of sincere gratitude."[15]

Satisfied that the Cubs were staying put, a content Murphy boarded a train for a two-week trip to Wilmington. He looked forward to relaxing, catching up with old friends, and spending Thanksgiving with his family.

In due time, the *Cincinnati Enquirer* proved prescient. The day after Charlie Murphy's time in the National League inner circle closed, the *Enquirer* suspected he would wind up in show business and, indeed, his love of live performances, affection for his hometown, and desire to refurbish his tarnished brand coalesced into a vision of building a state-of-the-art theater.

Murphy already possessed significant, and titillating, playhouse experience. In 1909 he joined a venture, led by Harry Askin, manager of the Grand Opera House, to operate productions at the La Salle Theater, located on Madison Street in the heart of Chicago's downtown loop. Murphy had loved the theater since his youthful days performing in Wilmington. As an adult, he frequently attended shows throughout Chicago, and he was naturally drawn to help run a stage of his own. It didn't hurt that he knew the theater building's owner well: Annie Taft. However, no sooner had Askin and Murphy prepped their offer to Taft than trouble over the lease created a condition in which they quickly realized that they had caught a tiger by its tail.

Mort Singer operated the La Salle Theater Company and paid an annual lease of $8,500 to Taft for the use of the auditorium. Singer's lease was set to expire on April 30, 1909, so Askin and Murphy readied to move in on May 1. Singer, however, hotly contested the transition. He claimed that he had agreed to a five-year extension of the lease through communication with Charles Schmasltig, Taft's representative, and had already made financial commitments well beyond the lease's expiration date as a result. The problem? He didn't have a signed contract to prove it. Nevertheless, Singer's attorney, Lessing Rosenthal, filed suit in Superior Court and received a temporary injunction. Rosenthal ridiculously tried to portray Murphy as a menacing presence looming over the entire situation. "There is a danger that Charles W. Murphy and others in this conspiracy will attempt to take over the premises by stealth. They may attempt to take possession of the theater Saturday afternoon during the performance unless restrained," Rosenthal claimed.[16] Although the chance to get into the theater business thrilled Murphy, he stopped well short of donning a mask and weapons to take one over with his friends. Singer stayed and his play, "The Golden Girl," continued its lengthy run.

Rosenthal's silly argument about Murphy belied the complex situation surrounding the lease, which kept the question of the theater's status tied up in the court system. In late May Murphy and Askin, who were both thoroughly unamused by Rosenthal's insinuation of potential violence, filed a response in court in which they vehemently denied all of Rosenthal's charges, including conspiracy. Over the ensuing weeks and months, they received several legal victories against Singer, who continuously appealed while maintaining possession of the theater. In June of 1910, over one year after filing his initial lawsuit, Singer lost again, this time in appellate court. It was the final straw. Ironically, with Singer out of town, court "custodians" carried out a secret raid on the theater to oust its current tenant, a vaudeville show, and take possession of the theater before handing it over to Askin and Murphy. The officials forced carpenters to dismantle sets, told orchestra members to fetch their instruments, and razed the dressing rooms. Among the items left behind, they found a loaded gun and a pair of pink tights.[17]

Five years later, Charlie Murphy wanted to erect an auditorium all his own. Murphy had plenty of time on his hands without a ball club to run, and he was getting fidgety. Building a theater in his hometown of Wilmington seemed like the perfect remedy. He wanted to bring the world-class productions seen at the La Salle Theater to Main Street in Wilmington, and he also yearned to orchestrate another large project. He loved to conduct, and this project would put a baton back into his hand. On top of that, Murphy wanted to create a new legacy for himself, apart from baseball. He desired to become a figure who had gone off to the big city, made good, and then returned home to share his bounty. He was self-aware enough to realize that baseball history would not treat him particularly kindly, and that he would not be able to alter that national narrative, so he turned his attention homeward. Murphy genuinely loved the people of Wilmington, and he wanted to give them a gift that they could all be proud of. Ultimately, at the end of his life, Murphy wanted to be buried at home, in Wilmington, but the idea of people having to scout around Sugar Grove Cemetery to find his grave repulsed him. He endeavored to make his memorial site obvious: a sparkling world-class theater that hovered over Main Street.

Murphy noodled over his theater plans for a number of months. In 1915, he took his annual Thanksgiving trip to Wilmington to visit his family, but this time he wanted to scout out potential building sites. Murphy spent time catching up with family and friends. Charlie attended a football game where he conversed with his old classmate, Henry Farquhar, who eagerly told him about the ongoing development of Wilmington's manufacturing sector, including a plant that produced more auger bits than any other in the world. Murphy was impressed by Wilmington's commitment to its economic development. The townspeople had passed a $350,000 bond measure to raze a full block of buildings and build a new courthouse on South Street, just one block east of Murphy's childhood home, beginning in January. Wilmington residents could take trains to Cincinnati and Columbus, and the city's Commercial Club was relentlessly recruiting railroad executives to build a new line to Dayton.[18] Everything Murphy saw and heard about his hometown's maturation process emboldened his theater plan. He wanted to create a central hub for entertainment and commerce, a building that included a large house for performances as well as retail space for local businesses. He concluded that the best place for it would be in the heart of Main Street, where he conceptualized it as the future cultural and social centerpiece of Wilmington.

Two particular parcels of land caught Murphy's attention immediately. The adjacent properties sat in a centralized location, on the south side of Main Street between Mulberry and South Streets, directly across the street from the Cub Theater, a movie playhouse operated by his brother Frank and just one block east of the family home where his mother, Bridget, continued to live. The lots had separate owners: Dr. Eldorado Briggs and William Schofield. Murphy contacted them both and explained his plan. Briggs quickly accepted Murphy's offer for his lot, known by locals as the "Ziegler property," named after the family who had previously owned it for decades; however, Frank Schofield, William's son, was not ready to sell their parcel on such short notice. William Schofield, an Englishman who had successfully run the Wilmington Woolen Mill for years, owned several pieces of real estate in town but, now in his nineties, the elderly gentleman did not conduct business as rapidly as he once did.[19] Murphy and Frank Schofield held three amicable conversations about the sale of the property, but they could not agree on financial terms. The Schofield family wanted some time to think things over, and Murphy agreed to write them from Chicago at a later date.[20]

With one lot in his possession, Murphy initiated a public relations campaign to support his new project. Before returning to Chicago, Murphy announced his acquisition of the Ziegler property and outlined his grandiose vision for entertaining locals in the revamped downtown. "To my way of thinking, Wilmington is the best town of its size in the state, and, in addition to helping my brother Frank, I want to do something for my birthplace . . . We want to erect on Main street the handsomest and best equipped opera house in Southern Ohio, so that Wilmington can enjoy first-class theatrical attractions, lectures, operas, conventions and the best pictures to be had," he declared.[21]

Following his return to Chicago, Murphy continued having conversations with the Schofields, but those suddenly halted when tragedy struck their family. Both William and his wife, Anna, were stricken with influenza in early January. Their children focused solely on helping them recuperate, but their parents' condition rapidly deteriorated. On January 18 news of Anna Schofield's death saddened the community. Less than three weeks later, on the morning of February 8, William passed away. They both died in the family home.[22] Reeling,

Frank Schofield, who had continued living with his parents after his brother and sisters moved out of town, concentrated on planning two funeral services. He gave very little thought to negotiations over the Main Street property, which the Schofield children had just inherited.

As spring emerged from a receding winter, Charlie recruited both of his brothers, Frank and Jim, to help him. Frank, incredibly experienced at running a theater, would run the day-to-day operations and communicate with the press, while Jim would oversee construction and serve as the primary contact for businesses interested in renting space in the new building. Charlie Murphy had several important decisions to make. He first had to rethink the theater's design, because its footprint now had to fit on just the one lot. That quandary posed a challenge for whomever Murphy selected as the architect for the job, an important task he and Frank were working to complete. Additionally, the theater needed a name. The sooner it had one, the faster Murphy could create promotional signage to post around the construction site.

By March, the Murphy brothers had selected Dittoe, Fahnestock, and Ferber, an architectural firm out of Cincinnati, which had also been chosen to design the new Wilmington courthouse, to draw up plans for the project. The firm selected Charles Ferber, a veteran architect with ample experience, which eschewed his age—he was only twenty-seven—to be the lead designer. Ferber's initial rendering included 52 feet of frontage space for the theater along Main Street, including its main entrance. The depth of the facility would stretch back 175 feet, a reasonable space to construct a large stage and two floors of seating for upward of 1,200 patrons, an optimistic stretch goal. The theater would be three stories in height with the top floor reserved for high-end apartments, a highly welcome development due to Wilmington's housing shortage, caused by its booming economy. The firm initially submitted its proposal to Frank, who liked the design and forwarded it on to Charlie for final approval. As conversations over the plan culminated, Jim and Frank worked with the Wilmington Gaslight & Coke Company and the Breeze Plumbing plant, the building's two primary tenants, to efficiently and effectively move them out.[23]

The Wilmington community buzzed with excitement over the construction boom underway in 1916. In addition to the theater, construction crews busily erected apartment buildings and single-family homes to infuse supply into the housing market. Simultaneously, construction on the new St. Columbkille Catholic Church, a $30,000 project going up on Mulberry Street just north of Main, got underway. All of these projects flanked the expansive new courthouse, which was being built on Shadagee Square. Each brick laid served as a physical reminder of Wilmington's economic health, which supplied locals with jobs, encouraged population growth, and boosted the financial outlook of the town. "When it comes to activity this summer you can put it down in your little old dope book that the capital of Clinton is going to be some live old 'burg,' as those inclined to the use of slang would say," the *Wilmington Daily News* excitedly reported. "Some business for a 5,500 town, eh?"[24]

Plans for the theater moved along swiftly throughout the summer. Charles Ferber finalized the theater's measurements and solicited bids from contractors. Murphy approved the final design, but an issue with the property line on the lot's western edge stopped the process in its tracks. The Walker Memorial Building, located next door, actually encroached over the property line onto Murphy's lot. Murphy contacted the city, which owned the building, to figure out what to do. They rapidly reached an amicable solution. The city offered Murphy use of the building's eastern wall as the western wall for the theater. Joists could be inserted directly into the wall to reinforce it, which would cohesively unite the two buildings. In exchange, the city asked Murphy to sign a quit claim deed that prevented him from making future claims on the Memorial Building property. Additionally, through the deed, the city asked Murphy not to add weight to the wall that could impair its integrity. Murphy agreed. In the meantime, Murphy hired a construction company that tore down the Ziegler property building in late August, and excavators moved in to haul away the huge pile of bricks baking in the sun as the locals looked on with excitement.[25]

As progress on the theater site continued throughout the summer, Murphy doggedly explored ways to buy the Schofield property. His inability to fulfill his initial vision incessantly gnawed away at him. He didn't want to settle for a smaller facility, but the Schofield lot remained elusive. Murphy distracted himself, in part, by focusing on the interior design of the theater. He obsessed over every detail. In November Murphy selected the seats and signed a contract with the Heywood Brothers and Wakefield Company, a popular furniture manufacturer based on the East Coast, to provide them. An ebullient Murphy penned a letter to the *Wilmington Daily News* with the exciting news. "They are mahogany with green velvet upholstering and gilded standards and no picture-house outside of Cleveland or Cincinnati has anything like them. The seats have springs and will be soft to sit in and they are comfortable, because they will be twenty inches wide. They are really good enough for the Metropolitan Opera-House in New York. Wait till you see them!"[26] Murphy frequently sent letters to the *Daily News* from Chicago to apprise locals of the latest happenings concerning the theater.

The following spring a sudden development with the Schofield property halted the theater's construction. On the morning of April 4, 1917, Frank Murphy made a startling statement to the local press. He announced that Charlie had completed a deal to buy the Schofield lot and that the theater design would undergo a major reconfiguration. Said Frank, "There have been a number of obstacles encountered in building the theater, but my brother has set his head to give his home town and county a big improvement and the difficulties he has met have only made him the more determined to go ahead. He will be here within a few days and will be glad to tell you anything you want to know to tell the public."[27]

In the year since William Schofield's death, Frank Schofield had sold his interest in the family property to Murphy; however, Schofield's three siblings remained unamenable to selling, so Murphy, tired of fruitless negotiations, hired a local lawyer named G. P. Thorpe to file a suit in partition with the court that requested that either Murphy's interests in the lot be "set off" or that a sale of the lot be forced with the proceeds evenly distributed among the three remaining heirs who maintained interests. The suit was a game changer. John Schofield,

Miriam Outcalt, and Elizabeth O'Neill relented and agreed to sell their holdings to Murphy. On April 3 the parties agreed to a deal with Murphy for a reported total of $8,900.[28] Murphy delivered the money to them before the sun set. The transaction immediately shut down construction, but Murphy didn't care. He was thrilled. The theater could now be expanded an additional 16 feet in width with an increased number of business spaces. "I expect to make it the finest combined business block and theater in Southern Ohio," Murphy said.[29] The *Wilmington Daily News* responded positively to the sale of the Schofield property. "This assures the improvement of West Main street in a complete way, and words are weak to express what it will mean to Wilmington," it reported.[30]

The theater's design needed to be redone immediately, and Charles Ferber embraced the change in plan. Born in Cincinnati on June 22, 1891, Ferber had already displayed a prodigious talent for architecture during his young career. As a teenager, he trained at the Ohio Mechanics Institute, an institution founded in 1828 where students learned skills relevant to the industrializing economy. He joined a local architectural firm, in 1909, for four years then moved to Chicago for additional experience. Ferber relocated to San Francisco in 1913 and spent two years working for the Reid brothers: James and Merritt, two incredibly influential architects on the West Coast who designed several Bay Area landmarks, including the Fairmont Hotel. The Reid brothers were also responsible for the Hotel del Coronado just west of San Diego, the largest hotel in the world upon its completion in 1888. Murphy told the people of Wilmington that Ferber had worked on the Panama-Pacific International Exposition, otherwise known as the world's fair, held in San Francisco in 1915, while at Reid & Reid.[31] Ferber returned to Ohio in 1915, where he spent the next three and a half decades designing buildings for a number of different firms.[32]

Ferber took special pride in designing the theater in Wilmington, and he assured Murphy that it would be "prettier than anything in Cincinnati."[33] Murphy clearly expressed his expectations to Ferber, who worked diligently to please his challenging client. Murphy took it for granted that the theater would be more magnificent than anything in the Queen City. "When the theater is completed Wilmington need not take a back seat for any town or city in the country when it comes to having a comfortable and cozy place of amusement," Murphy trumpeted.[34] In addition to being a gift to Wilmington, Murphy viewed the theater as a mausoleum of sorts for himself, a heavenly place where his spirit could live on. The theater's beauty needed to stand out on its own accord. "We want innocent and harmless amusement of such character as to chase away the blues from those who patronize the place," Murphy said. "It must radiate joy and sunshine and good cheer. There is enough trouble in the battle of life without going to the theater to find more. We want no gloom, nor mystery—only those things that we understand and which amuse us." Subconsciously, Murphy was building a place in Wilmington where the fearful little boy inside of him could peacefully rest without feeling the threatening presence of his father or the embarrassment of poverty. "We want to uplift the people and one way is to amuse them properly and drive away melancholy and depression."[35] He was talking to himself as much as anyone in Wilmington.

Such was the challenge facing Ferber as he revisited his blueprints. Ferber designed the interior of the theater to generate a deep sense of the Italian Renaissance through the use of curved lines. Ferber divided the stage from the house with a proscenium arch forty feet in height to frame the action of the performance. The Italians first utilized the technique during the sixteenth century, and it eventually became a common feature of theater design. Although some architects used straight lines to create proscenium arches, Ferber designed a true arch that not only framed the stage but encapsulated the entire house.

After a delay of nearly two weeks following Murphy's announcement, work on the expanded theater site resumed. Workers pulled out the embedded steel pillars to make way for the new floor plan. Meanwhile, Ferber traveled to Chicago to meet with Murphy, who had recently been inspired by a new business building he had seen in the Windy City, perhaps at the behest of his friend Joseph Downey. The Murphys lived a few houses down from the Downeys on Sheridan Road, and the couples had become friends. Murphy frequently consulted with

Downey, a prominent contractor responsible for Chicago's Illinois Central Railroad Station, about the theater.[36] The building Murphy saw showcased a "novel feature," second-story business rooms with display windows. Murphy wanted to repurpose the theater to feature something similar, so Ferber eliminated the previously drawn second-story offices and created a series of eleven "modern and convenient" business rooms to replace them.[37] Inspiration struck Murphy again that summer when he happened upon another new edifice in Chicago, with a large basement "constructed in such a way as to make a splendid show room," according to the *Wilmington Daily News*. Murphy immediately wired Ferber and his brother, Jim, that the basement of the theater had to match what he just saw. Ferber huddled with the contractor to discuss what it would take to make the alteration. They sent Murphy a message with a list of expenses that totaled in the "many thousands of dollars." Murphy was undeterred. "Make the change," he told them. The theater could no longer open on time, but Murphy didn't care. It needed to be perfect. The construction workers, some of them assuredly shaking their heads in disbelief, knocked down the standing walls and hauled the disposed chunks of concrete away.[38]

Since the beginning of its construction, Murphy had referred to his pet project as the "Clinton Theater." In a marketing sense, the name appealed to a wider berth of potential patrons from throughout Clinton County. Additionally, the name lent credence to Wilmington being the governmental seat of the region. Signs reading "Clinton Theater" hung around the site providing Jim's contact information to businesses interested in renting space. Murphy loved spending time with his childhood friends whenever he returned to Wilmington, especially Charles Fisher. On one particular visit, in the fall of 1917, Fisher brought up the name of the theater to his friend. "Clinton is alright," Fisher admitted, "but what about calling it the Murphy Theater?"[39] It was an emotional moment for Murphy. The advice validated a new narrative around the Murphy family name and expressed deep appreciation for his generosity to the community. Murphy agreed with Fisher and renamed it the Murphy Theater. An encounter with another Wilmingtonian settled any remaining doubts Murphy may have felt. "When I was there last a prominent member of the Clinton County Bar walked in to see what we were doing. Turning to me he said: 'Well, Charley, it is probably better to have your monument here on Main street than over in Sugar Grove Cemetery.' The more I have thought to what he said, the more convinced I am that he was right," Murphy contended.[40] The theater developed as a monument to the Murphy family as much as a gift to the community. "My mother sat in her front window and saw the walls go up a layer of brick at a time and she will now, I hope, soon see a big sign go up on the rear and two sides of the auditorium walls reading Murphy Theater. When the theater is completed Wilmington need not take a back seat for any town or city in the country when it comes to having a comfortable and cozy place of amusement"[41] His family and hometown would be associated with the best of the best.

It took a little over two and a half years to complete the theater, and Murphy spared no expense. The final cost: $250,000, the equivalent of nearly $4.7 million in today's dollars. In total, the *Wilmington Daily News* reported that Murphy had ordered 175 train cars worth of materials that "would make a train one and one quarter mile long."[42] The theater required seventy train cars of sand and gravel, nineteen cars of bricks, four cars of lumber, and half a car of carpets and light fixtures, just to name a few of their contents.

Charlie and Frank used the theater's opening as a fundraiser for the Clinton County Red Cross. They set ticket prices at ten cents and fifteen cents for seats and auctioned off the private boxes to the highest bidders. The demand for tickets was extraordinary, so Murphy decided to hold three shows. The schedule called for speeches, musical acts, and a pair of films—"Say, Young Fellow," starring Douglas Fairbanks, and "Good Night Nurse," featuring "Fatty" Arbuckle—during the first two performances. The late show only included the movies, but it gave more people the opportunity to experience the theater's inaugural day.

The Murphy Theater stunned patrons when it opened on July 24, 1918. People began gathering out front of the theater early in the afternoon hoping to secure a ticket to the first performance. The swelling crowd soon overwhelmed the box office, and it quickly became clear that not everyone would be able to fit inside the auditorium. People had ventured from all over Ohio to attend the grand opening. Residents of Sabina, Lynchburg, Cleveland, and—of course—Wilmington represented a few of the communities. In the midst of his preparations, Murphy eyed the crowd and noticed several elderly folks standing in line as well as a few mothers cradling infants in their arms. Quietly, he slipped outside, collected those individuals, and snuck them through the basement door. An ebullient Louise Murphy found Charles Ferber in the crowd and thanked him for his work. "You must now tell your friends at home that the reason Cincinnati does not grow faster is that it is too close to Wilmington," she teased him.

Overwhelming crowds suffocated Main Street all day trying to acquire tickets. Murphy encouraged patrons to donate money to the fundraiser, and many of them responded by overpaying for their tickets. In total, the box office sold three thousand tickets, which raised over $600. The auction for the boxes raised another $599. Those fortunate enough to get inside gawked at what they saw, beginning with the foyer. Ornately carved wood, colorful paintings, luscious flower arrangements, and a sparkling black and white checkered floor warmly greeted visitors with open arms. Large windows at the back of the lobby invited natural light into the auditorium and gave the theatergoers a view of the house. Two large doorways on either side of the windows yawned wide and ushered the visitors down carpeted aisles without sound as the flooring, including the stairways in the balcony level, hid a thick layer of cork that muted their footsteps. Murphy had ordered a large chandelier from Paris, and it proudly sparkled overhead.

The small town basked in the glow of big-city lights. "In a blaze of glory, with an enthusiasm that rarely manifests itself even among the patriotic and rigidly sensible people of Wilmington and Clinton County, and with an eagerness marking the acts of the men, women, and children, the new Murphy Theater, the gift of Charles W. Murphy, of Chicago, to his home town and to the people of the present and of future generations, was formally opened and dedicated to pleasure and patriotism Wednesday," beamed the *Wilmington Daily News*.[43]

It was a different sort of Opening Day, but the energy still flowed through the former Cubs president as "the happy, jovial, genial Mr.

Murphy was ablaze all day." Murphy's friend Charles Fisher served as the master of ceremonies for the first two performances. The Wilmington Oratorio Society sang its rendition of "The Star-Spangled Banner," and the Wilmington Band provided additional musical numbers. Judge Clevenger gave a few remarks to the crowd in which he thanked his longtime friend Charlie Murphy for his generosity. Several other speakers and musical acts entertained the crowd, and Fisher asked Murphy to say a few words to those in attendance.

Murphy could hardly contain his excitement as he proudly looked out over the sold-out audiences full of children. "I am being told that this thing is a white elephant from a financial standpoint. I know that, of course, I knew it the day I started to erect it. But let me say to you that money is not the only income and return on an investment. I sat here this afternoon and saw the happy-faced children in the mezzanine boxes—there by the thoughtfulness and the generosity of Mr. Denver—and I want to say that I was repaid many times over for having built the theater, just in watching them and thinking that I had brought pleasure to the little boys and girls out at the Children's Home," Murphy jubilantly proclaimed.[44] He thanked everyone for their support and admitted it overwhelmed him. "I would like to grab everybody in Wilmington, Clinton County, and Southern Ohio, in fact, and give each one a hug like a polar bear and implant a kiss on each cheek like they do in France when a soldier is decorated for bravery," he exclaimed. "My wife feels the same way. I have run out of adjectives in attempting to fittingly describe the great opening."

Following the shows, Murphy attempted to get a table at Heller's Restaurant, but it was so full of patrons that no seats were available. Relayed Murphy, "The proprietor threw (u)p both hands when he saw me and acted like a passenger in a stage-coach being held up, when he said: 'If you build any more theaters I wish you would do so in Chicago.'"

"'Nonsense,' I replied. 'I've come in to get my commission on your sales for the day.'"

Joking aside, Murphy marveled at the amount of money raised for the Red Cross. "Just think of the bandages, pajamas and other things that the money taken in yesterday will buy for our gallant soldiers in France. We must all back up those boys in the trenches until they march triumphantly into Berlin, grab hold of the Kaiser, take away his cheese knife sword and tin helmet and send him where he belongs—I can't mention the place here," he said.[45]

Editor W. J. Galvin wrote a column that appeared in the *Daily News* the following day in which he called Murphy a "go-getter" and praised Wilmington's iconoclastic native son for ignoring his skeptics. Wrote Galvin,

His ideas didn't suit the architects and the others associated in the work of paving the way for the finest theater in Ohio—but when the show-down came Wednesday evening, it was Charley Murphy's theater they dedicated and it was built just the way Charley Murphy wanted it built.

That's the way Murphy ran the Chicago Cubs—the greatest baseball team fandom has ever seen. Every other magnate in the country will take you over in the corner and tell you confidentially that Murphy couldn't run a ball team and that he was a joke as a magnate, but now Murphy has the bank-roll and other guys are keeping the door-mats of the Bank Presidents warm trying to raise money enough to meet their pay-rolls.

And Murphy incidentally won about all the National League pennants in sight and gathered in a few World's Series on the side—then he quit while the quitting was good.[46]

Galvin's commentary intended to do more than praise Murphy for his generosity. It aimed to reshape Murphy's reputation. Galvin defiantly argued that Murphy deserved credit for ignoring the conventional route. "Cut-and-dried methods don't cut any ice with Charley Murphy," he declared. Murphy built a beautiful theater, and then, when better ideas came along, he bankrolled the remodeling. Murphy's dismissive attitude toward the running costs earned Galvin's admiration and respect. Traditional methods and processes were overrated. "The idea is to deliver the goods—and Charley Murphy has delivered 'em," Galvin proclaimed.[47]

Murphy basked in the glow of the theater's opening the following day. He marveled at the sheer number of people that came out for the event. "That opening handed me the greatest surprise and delight of my life. Where did the people all come from?" he asked. "I have seen many large crowds—some of them at the world's series netting me thousands of dollars—but none gave me the real pleasure that I got Wednesday," he said. Murphy's family experienced similarly intense feelings. The Continental Club of Wilmington had presented Murphy with a silver cup to show its appreciation. "My mother and my wife and I had a good cry last night over it," Murphy said. Bridget Murphy was so overcome with emotion that she cradled the cup in her arms and did not fall asleep until past four o'clock in the morning.

Murphy's most enduring memory would be the smiles on the faces of all the children. "It was worth all I invested in the Murphy Theater to hear the 'kids' scream with delight at 'Fatty' Arbuckle and his screen companions. I witnessed that three times and it made me extremely happy," he said.[48]

The Murphy Theater cultivated curiosity well beyond the purview of Clinton County. *Western Architect*, a monthly journal with a sweeping subscription base across the country, featured five photos of the theater in its November 1919 issue.[49] The pictures focused on the auditorium's luxurious design and the ornate artwork produced by the painstaking work of the plasterers, carvers, and painters, which could be seen on the outside of the seating boxes, affixed to the walls, and embedded in the ceilings. In the end, Charlie Murphy not only oversaw the building of a breathtaking theater, but he also paved an avenue for Wilmingtonians to proudly see a small piece of themselves on the national stage.

NARRATIVES

The year 1918 proved to be a monumental one for Charles Webb Murphy. He celebrated his fiftieth birthday in January and hailed the opening of his Wilmington theater in June. Life after being a National League president continued to be bountiful for him. During the ensuing years, Murphy took up his pen again and wrote articles for a host of publications. He also traveled aplenty with his wife, Louise, and watched his nephews grow up. Amidst it all, Murphy remained connected to baseball. Many of his journalistic endeavors incorporated his thoughts on the game he loved. He took over complete ownership of the Baker Bowl and shocked the baseball world again, this time by reestablishing his relationship with the Chicago Cubs. Murphy continued to attend ballgames and cheer as loudly as ever.

Murphy's baseball career became the subject of narratives in the mass media in the years that followed his exit from the National League. In 1916 *Baseball Magazine* ran an editorial written by F. C. Lane, whom Murphy had known for years, that called Murphy "genial, witty, an associate of rare talent and charm," but the passive-aggressive compliment rang hollow in light of the piece's true intent. "A sinister shadow has long rested on baseball in Chicago. The empire city of the west has been welcomed in the personality of Charles Comiskey, princeliest of magnates. But the National League club with all its glorious traditions has not been thus endeared to the public, and the reason is,—Charles Murphy." The editorial excoriated Murphy for reemerging from the shadows to thwart the sale of the Cubs to Charlie Weeghman. "Shakespeare says the evil that men do lives after them. Certainly the influence of Charles Murphy that had become evil to the National Game lived after him and was quite as irksome and unwelcome as his original presence," Lane said.[1]

For years Murphy's loquacious, insightful, and sometimes controversial quotes had captured the imaginations of baseball writers and their readers and helped the business of baseball flourish. Now, without any fear of losing this largess or of losing his vote, his detractors pushed the narrative that he was to blame for all that ailed the National League. Murphy's reputation had been permanently sullied. Murphy understood better than anyone what they were doing. Lane's hit piece would have sent a younger Murphy into a furious frenzy. Instead, with a little distance between himself and the boardroom battlefield, Murphy displayed a newfound depth of emotional patience, but he nonetheless defended the way he had run the Cubs and suggested that no one had a substantively good reason for taking issue with his business practices. Murphy authored a thoughtful response directed at Lane that appeared in the following issue. "I have just read your editorial comment concerning me in the February number of Baseball Magazine. Of course, it is not pleasant, but I am used to taking my medicine. I am like the little boy and the castor oil. As the bottle was held above his head, he said: 'Mother, you can make me take that, but you can't make me say I like it.'"[2]

Although Murphy had profited handsomely from his Cubs investment, he challenged the crux of Lane's narrative as intellectually elitist. "It seems to be a crime to succeed in the eyes of those who fall. It also seems to be a crime in baseball for a man to run his own business. That is what I did. I paid my players the top price and got their maximum efforts. When they were no longer able to deliver major league ball of the championship brand, which the public had a right to demand, I let them go. Was that fair to the public? I think it was." If Murphy was guilty of anything in terms of baseball operations, it was being ahead of his time.

Murphy continued to reengage the public as a writer, and he opined on his own legacy as well as popular topics around baseball. Murphy explained the machinations of his ownership tenure, from his perspective, in a series of articles for the *Chicago Evening American*. Those stories appeared under the auspices of providing readers with an "inside look" at baseball, but the autobiographical pieces also served as vehicles for Murphy to present his own narrative without interference from any editorial desk. In spite of F. C. Lane's criticism, Murphy also wrote for *Baseball Magazine*.

Murphy remained as opinionated as ever, but his softer tone revealed that his most combative days were behind him. His articles disclose a man who wanted to be better understood. He wanted to reconnect with the fans with whom he felt a genuine kinship because he shared their deep love for baseball. He had never belonged to the elevated class of baseball owners and writers, who were not members of American society's upper crust but were nevertheless gatekeepers of the sport.

In one of his articles for the *Chicago Evening American*, Murphy discussed the difficulty of starting out as an owner with the press corps in both New York and Chicago against him. Murphy believed that John T. Brush's decision to hire him had angered many New York writers, who thought that they were more qualified to have been selected as the Giants' press agent. In Chicago, the popularity of Charles Comiskey, the venerable owner of the White Sox, who went out of his way to cultivate a positive relationship with the press, impacted the acceptance of Murphy in Windy City baseball circles. Murphy had known Comiskey for decades, going back to their days in Cincinnati. It was no surprise to Murphy, whose brash style ensured that he would always play second fiddle to Comiskey, that he never received the praise of the affable White Sox owner, whom Murphy liked very much. "Comiskey has made himself popular and is the possessor of much personal magnetism," Murphy said admiringly. Lane's editorial comments comparing Murphy and Comiskey in *Baseball Magazine* publicized what Murphy had already known privately.

Murphy genuinely liked Comiskey, but he felt like a portion of the Chicago baseball community didn't want to give him a chance from the start. Sitting back in retirement, Murphy admitted that the criticism sometimes bothered him: "The other major league club was operated by Comiskey, a native son, whose father was famous as an alderman, and the question was frequently asked, 'Who is this guy who has the gall to come out here and try to successfully operate a baseball club in competition to the Old Roman?'"[3] Even though he preferred to be loved, Murphy prioritized running his business over any personal feelings, and that meant he alienated people. "I was as popular with the fans as a bag of rattlesnakes would be if turned loose in the bleachers at a double-header," he joked.[4]

While he ran the Cubs, Murphy did not care if the writers disliked him personally as long as they provided free publicity. It was a mutually beneficial relationship. Murphy intentionally provoked writers, with a wink and a nod, for a while—he and John T. Brush engaged in a battle to see who could lock out the most reporters that covered each other's team one year, to keep the flames of the Giants-Cubs rivalry properly stoked—but he admitted that his temper had gotten out of control at times and had interfered with his true intention of maintaining personal and professional relevance for himself and the Cubs. Murphy's deepening self-awareness allowed, perhaps even compelled, him to acknowledge that he had rarely let any slight, real or perceived, slip by unchallenged. "Then my temperament was too much like that of Evers and Tinker for me to stand abuse without getting back," he confessed.[5] These days, however, portended a kinder, gentler Murphy, who had taken to retirement from baseball like Tinker to a Mathewson fastball, which is to say adroitly.

In his later years, Murphy reflected on his relationships in baseball. He always felt closer to the players than he did to his fellow executives. "As indicated, I had my troubles with pass fiends and the baseball powers, but I must honestly say that I did not find it so much trouble to handle the famous Cubs because most of the players were intelligent fellows who knew when they were treated properly. I traveled with the men a great deal, played cards with them on the trains and at the hotels on rainy days and enjoyed their society. I never did like some club owners—go to the swellest hotel in town and send the boys to a cheaper place," Murphy said.[6]

However, Murphy's stories left out the frayed endings to many of those friendships. Murphy tried to keep the Cubs winning, and he never gave in to the sentiment of re-signing aging players to significant contracts to appease anyone, no matter how well they had once performed in a Cubs uniform. The strategy left him vulnerable to plenty of second guessing when the crop of Chicago's young players failed to maintain the organization's high standard.

Murphy's columns for *Baseball Magazine* addressed a variety of topics, including how his occasionally contentious relationships with reporters affected his connection with Cubs fans over the years, even though he believed that their high attendance marks demonstrated he couldn't have been that unpopular. "Some of the reporters ... dearly loved to pan me," Murphy wrote. "I was a shining mark for a long time for what a prominent movie star would doubtless characterize as German propaganda—meaning inspired yarns knocking me for an ulterior purpose." Although the events surrounding the Federal League had bothered him at the time, Murphy never took reporters' criticism about that topic too personally. The negative press he received played into his business flywheel strategy, a strategical concept that would not be written about extensively for another century.[7] "Of course, there is much pure fiction printed about men in baseball now and then and baseball men are often put in a false light with the fans by ill-advised stories. In the off-season, though, the columns must be filled and I have always felt it is all 'water on the wheel,'" Murphy explained.[8] He had enthusiastically covered the off-season winter meeting as a young reporter, and he expected nothing less from the current crop of scribes.

Murphy also pointed out that his aggressiveness, or indifference to tact, distracted his associates from understanding the transformational aims of his methods. He refused to accept being a member of the status quo. "Another thing I have noticed is that the fellows who never get knocked are the ones who go along the line of least resistance and do nothing. If you do nothing and say nothing and carry water on both shoulders everybody will be with you—and you will be a plain mutt."[9]

Murphy pushed the conventional norms of baseball to win and improve his business model. Gambling, however out-of-the-box, proved to be one area that he refused to indulge in any way, and he used the national platform provided by *Baseball Magazine* to encourage the

sport's leadership to eliminate it at all costs. "There must be no tem-
porizing about the gambling evil. It has existed for forty years, but of
late at most of the parks it has become a genuine nuisance. A crowd of
boisterous 'tin-horn' gamblers congregate in a box and by their antics
disgust those who go to baseball for the love of the sport," he said.[10]

Peace between Organized Baseball and the Federal League arrived in early
1916. As part of the settlement, Charlie Weeghman acquired the Chicago
Cubs from Charles Taft on January 5, 1916, and merged them with his Federal League franchise, the Chicago Whales. Weeghman and his partners
bought 90 percent of the Cubs for $500,000. They purchased the 530
shares controlled by Murphy, Annie Taft's 250 shares, Charles Schmalstig's
100 shares, and Mary Walsh's (John's widow) 20. Harry Ackerland retained
his 10 percent stake. Taft paid the shareholders accordingly, including
Murphy's $450,000, as well as an additional 5 percent interest payment
from the date of sale.[11] Murphy satisfied the press's demand for his opinion on the deal. "If the Cubs are sold to Mr. Weeghman as is reported
from Cincinnati, I wish him all the success in the world. Personally he is
one of the best men in the game. The same is true of Joe Tinker," added
Murphy of the organization's manager.[12] He felt no personal animosity
toward Weeghman and acknowledged that the new owner might very
well lead the franchise more effectively than he had. "Mr. Weeghman will
make a better president of the Cubs than I did. He has a better poise than
I possessed; he will not hit the ceiling when made the victim of malicious
attacks; he brings to the game a better temperament."[13]

Murphy played nice in the press, but the Cubs' impending move
to the north side complicated his position. Murphy, along with Annie
Taft, retained the West Side Ball Park and its lease with the team.
The *Chicago Tribune* reported that Weeghman agreed to assume the
lease debt obligations for two years, which was well short of the nearly
hundred years remaining on it. Murphy knew it was neither the time
nor the place to raise a ruckus about the lease, so he let it go for the
time being.[14]

As for the actual move of the National League ball club to the north
side of the city, Harvey Woodruff, the newspaperman who rescued

Frank Chance's relationship with Murphy in 1909, believed that only time would tell, but the organization's new stadium, or "plant," Weeghman Park, would play an outsized role in deciding the team's financial success. "Whether the transfer of the Cubs to the North Side after their tenure on the old West Side lot, is a wise business move, can only be determined by attendance results. The Federal League plant is modern, with hardly enough seating capacity for a club striving for a pennant . . . The North Side or Federal League grounds are easy of access. The question is whether the old fans, who resent to a certain extent, the transfer, will follow their team to the new location," Woodruff said.[15]

Weeghman combined the Cubs and the Whales, his Federal League franchise, into a new corporation, valued at a million dollars, which forced a reevaluation of Charlie Murphy's impressive business savvy. New Cubs beat reporter James Crusinberry of the *Tribune* acknowledged that Murphy had understood the future growth of baseball before his contemporaries. "It was just ten years ago last October that Charles W. Murphy and Charles P. Taft purchased the west side club from James Hart. The price was $105,000. At the time the general opinion was that Murphy and Taft had paid as much as the club was worth, and many thought they had given too much," Crusinberry wrote.[16] For his part, Murphy always believed that he had underpaid for the Cubs. Sitting in the stands with Jim Hart in 1905, Murphy had recognized the true value of the organization, especially when he considered its roster of talented young players, whom they were watching on the field. Time proved Murphy correct.

On May 19, 1918, a rainy late spring Chicago day, Charlie Murphy went to church. Former Chicago White Stocking turned evangelist Billy Sunday was preaching the final sermon of his latest revival campaign, a ten-week series at a local tabernacle. Murphy wasn't alone. Over thirteen thousand people crammed into the humid church to hear Sunday, who began his presentation by introducing the crowd to his former manager, Cap Anson. Sunday was thrilled to see Murphy. "You got in, old top, in the last half of the ninth inning," Sunday exclaimed. "Yes, I ought to have come oftener," Murphy admitted.[17]

After the Cubs officially relocated, and with Charlie Weeghman's money safely tucked away in his bank account, Charlie Murphy decided the time had arrived to do something about his ballpark lease. He filed a lawsuit against the Chicago Cubs arguing that the organization had broken its long-term lease by moving out. Murphy estimated that he was losing around $12,000 a month without the Cubs, and he wanted to be compensated for it. He fired off several additional lawsuits against the newly constituted Chicago National League Ball Club and, after that failed, the National League, but Murphy's attorney, Edmund Cummings, struggled to gain traction in court. As he waited for the lawsuits to play out, Murphy allowed army training corps programs from local high schools to conduct drills inside the eroding stadium, which otherwise sat vacant.[18]

Alfred Austrian, who represented the Cubs, succeeded in having Murphy's initial claim against several of the team's shareholders, including Charlie Weeghman and William Wrigley Jr., dismissed, and he continued to fend off an undeterred Murphy, who vigorously pursued more litigation. Austrian assured his clients that Murphy couldn't beat him. "I have been contesting Mr. Murphy's right to get all the money in Chicago for a good many years," Austrian told the National League owners in 1920. "Perhaps some day he will get some of it, but he hasn't yet."[19] Austrian's assessment proved correct. He repeatedly defeated Cummings in court.

Although the Cubs had irritatingly migrated to the north side of town, they always remained close to Charlie Murphy's heart and, astonishingly, he rejoined the organization's shareholder fraternity in 1919. Who exactly had the audacity to sell stock to Murphy remained unclear, but to say that the news stunned the baseball world would be an understatement. "Just say that I think baseball is coming back big and I want to be in on it," Murphy told Harvey Woodruff. Murphy kept everyone guessing the identity of the seller and the number of shares transferred by refusing to divulge any additional details, but the story was indeed true. The Cubs' front office confirmed that Murphy had indeed been given a stock certificate, but it, too, did not provide any insight.[20]

Yes, Murphy wanted to make sound financial decisions and remain close to baseball, but his failed litigation against the Chicago Cubs encouraged him to get as close as he possibly could to the organization so as to influence its decision-making. He couldn't beat them in court, so he rejoined them. "I hope and think the Cub management will eventually see the wisdom of returning to the west side location and building a modern, up to date plant capable of accommodating the crowds which would attend games of a championship team," he said.[21] Weeghman, however, had no intention of abandoning his northside location, and he never did. However, his struggling restaurant business soon took a heavy financial toll on Weeghman and forced him to sell the ball club to minority shareholder William Wrigley, who shortly thereafter changed the name of the stadium from Weeghman Park to Cubs Park. In the midst of the sale, having exhausted his options and split with his lawyer, Cummings, Murphy dropped the legal proceedings.

During the fall of 1919 the saga of the West Side Grounds concluded in another windfall for Murphy. The state of Illinois wanted to expand the footprint of its growing medical sector. Murphy agreed to sell it the eight-acre property for $400,000, and the site became home to the expanding footprint of the Illinois Medical District.[22] Murphy made a tidy profit while removing a problematic piece of real estate from his portfolio.

On September 16, 1924, the city of Chicago awoke to sorrowful news. "Baseball can mourn," read the front page of the *Chicago Tribune*, "for the Peerless Leader is dead."[23] Frank Chance, who had just turned forty-seven, passed away in California following a protracted illness that had long made his reentrance into baseball problematic. Privately, Charlie Murphy authored a telegram expressing his condolences and sent it to Edythe, Frank's widow.

Publicly, neither quotes nor statements from Murphy appeared in the local press regarding Chance's death. Only silence. The perception that Murphy and Chance had operated collectively had long ago been shattered, and they were no longer linked together. Their relationship had never healed, which made it much easier to forget their early bond. The only mentions of Murphy in relation to Chance commented on their arguments. That narrative drowned out all memory of the good years when they worked together seamlessly and shared a modicum of personal friendship. Prior to Chance's death, Murphy had assessed how the dynastic Cubs had operated so effectively. "Chance was the architect and I was the builder, and Mr. Taft was the man who should get most of the credit because if he had not supplied the means neither Chance nor I might ever have had any place of note in baseball history."[24]

As he was out of the spotlight, tracking Charlie Murphy during the latter half of the 1920s is a challenging task. As he climbed into his fifties, Murphy's health eroded, which slowed him down, but he nonetheless continued to live a very active life. He enjoyed traveling with Louise. They spent a notable amount of time in Southern California and wintered in the South. He frequently took the train to Wilmington, where he visited his mother, Bridget, whom he had always adored, and the rest of his family. Of course, Murphy could still be spotted at the ballpark cheering on the Cubs from time to time. Those who thought it might be awkward for Murphy to root for the team that he no longer owned didn't know him very well. One thing had nothing to do with the other as far as he was concerned. Having become a millionaire, Murphy moved into the financial industry and got involved with the competitive world of the stock market. He also spent time adding his voice to baseball discussions through the occasional newspaper column, but they appeared with far less frequency than they once had.

He also remained heavily involved with the Murphy Theater. Changes in technology fascinated him, and he excitedly promoted the incorporation of talking pictures inside the playhouse, which his brother Frank had managed for over a decade. As they aged, the brothers realized they needed additional help with the theater so, in 1929, they asked Phil Chakeres, who operated a national theater chain, to assist them. The Murphys felt good about the new partnership. "I am very optimistic about the future of the venture," Charlie said before he hustled back to Chicago to watch the Cubs play the A's in the World Series at the recently rechristened Wrigley Field.[25]

Baseball underwent a transformation during the Roaring Twenties. On the field, the disappearance of the dead ball, the home run, and Babe Ruth's New York Yankees hailed a new era in the sport as the franchise values skyrocketed, and Wilmingtonians sought out Murphy to hear old stories and get his opinion on the condition of the game. He happily obliged them during his visits. Murphy openly pondered the state of baseball and reflected on his years in the sport. He was happy that broadcasts were expanding the reach of the games, but Murphy expressed his displeasure that the home run now played an outsized role in the outcome of baseball contests. He highly preferred the strategical style of his victorious Cubs teams. Murphy understood the value of sluggers like Babe Ruth and Hack Wilson, but he looked forward to the day when their style of slugging went out of vogue. "Then there will be a return to the machine-like play and the finer points of the game that characterized baseball in the old days," he said. His selection of the best players he had ever witnessed testified to his stylistic preference. "Well, as much as I hate to do it, I'll have to say Ty Cobb," Murphy answered reluctantly. "I hate to say it because I am a National Leaguer at heart. But Ty had everything. In addition to his ability, he had a disastrous effect on the psychology of the opposing team. They tightened up, got worried, and as a result Cobb was even more dangerous.

"But a National Leaguer comes next in my list of great players. Honus Wagner was almost his equal. Wagner was a wonderful player, and had unusual versatility," Murphy recalled.

That said, Murphy derided the insinuation by Deadball Era stars that they remained superior to the new crop of athletes. "That is hooey. Players are just as good as they ever were, or better."[26]

Murphy loved being Uncle Charlie to his four nephews, including Frank's son Charles, who spent years studying philosophy and theology in preparation for a life dedicated to religious leadership. On May 30, 1931, Charles F. Murphy became the first person in the history of

Wilmington to be ordained into the Catholic priesthood. His proud uncle made sure to attend the youngster's first mass at St. Columbkille Church.

Young Charles's service drew 650 enthusiastic parishioners, who packed out the pews, and the family beamed with pride at Reverend Murphy's accomplishment.[27] However, many members of the community immediately recognized that the typically boisterous elder Charlie Murphy appeared less vigorous than usual. The truth was Murphy had suffered a physical ailment the previous spring and, while he had recovered, he remained weakened.

Murphy returned to Chicago following the weekend celebration with his family, but he suffered a serious stroke six days later.[28] Charlie Murphy remained bedridden, in critical condition, for nearly three weeks before he showed signs of improvement. Murphy received care from several attending physicians, who—following another positive week of recovery—told him that he could again spend the winter in the warmer climate of the South, where he had sojourned for several years, if his condition continued to improve. However, on Friday, October 16, everything stopped in its tracks. Murphy suffered a second, catastrophic, paralytic stroke. Charlie's brother, Jim, and nephew, the newly appointed Reverend Murphy, received word of Charlie's deteriorating condition and rushed to the home on Sheridan Road, but there was nothing they could do. Charles Webb Murphy had died.

Charles F. Murphy helped officiate his uncle's funeral at St. Columbkille Church, on the morning of October 20, in front of family and friends. Murphy was laid to rest in Sugar Grove Cemetery alongside his little sister, Katie, father, P. J., and mother, Bridget, the heroic matriarch of the family, who had passed away in 1923. Murphy's gravestone matched those that accompanied his family members' graves: a small, simple plaque that read, "Charles W Murphy 1868–1931." The marker would have pleased Murphy. He always trusted that the theater on Main Street would serve as the real Murphy monument.

Probate court revealed the extent of Murphy's financial success. The teenage drug store clerk, who worked to support his mother and siblings, had grown into a prosperous multimillionaire. Murphy bequeathed many of his holdings to his wife. He split his largest holding, the Baker Bowl, with half going to her and the remaining 50 percent to his four nephews. Seven years later, the family struck a deal that allowed the Phillies to move to Shibe Park. Murphy gave the theater to his brothers and provided financial gifts to several friends.

Charlie Murphy's death resonated in Wilmington but to a lesser extent in Chicago. The death of Charles Comiskey, the longtime owner of the Chicago White Sox, ten days later, created front-page headlines in the Windy City, whereas news of Murphy's passing was confined to the sports page. National baseball writers, particularly those old enough to have experienced Murphy's impact on the sport, took note of his passing, but the overall reaction, the initial forays into legacy creation, were mixed. Some reporters still recoiled at Murphy's flippant attitude toward decorum, but the truth is only a few people fully understood him. Their interest in Murphy had limits, and his struggle to let down his façade and be vulnerable during his time in baseball curbed the possibilities of his friendships. Baseball insiders continued to hang the millstone of his mistakes around his neck for all to see, amid tepid praise, as demonstrated by an obituary that appeared in the *Sporting News*: "He did not build up the Cubs; the team was there, lacking the assistance of a competent third baseman," it read. He dealt for Harry Steinfeldt, and the Cubs went on to achieve great heights. "Yet he could not be satisfied with success; he wanted to assert his radical ideas and opinions against those of more conservative owners who would not hold with him that baseball was a show . . . Like a meteor that flashes across the horizon to meet the earth and burst, Murphy flashed across the horizon of the National League."[29]

However, local writers, who had interacted much more frequently with Murphy, put his personality in a more appropriate context. Irving Vaughan of the *Chicago Tribune*, who had become friends with the former Cubs president, noted that a blustery Murphy would call for a sportswriter's firing one day and stuff his pockets full of cigars the next. "Murphy's grudges were just part of his showmanship."[30]

The next generation of owners included members who now recognized that Murphy's incredible career could never be repeated. Clark Griffith, owner of the Washington Senators, who had once questioned the allegiance of Murphy's soul following a botched trade negotiation, now argued that Murphy's knack for understanding the business of baseball was ahead of its time. "To make baseball pay today, good, sound, common-sense business methods must be practiced, and the club owner who resorts to them, who will spend big money to make big money, will get more than a whale of a lot of fun out of his undertaking. Charles W. Murphy, who formerly owned the Chicago Cubs, realized all this 24 years ago," Griffith said.[31]

For Cubs fans, a new generation of players had already created new winning memories at Wrigley Field. The franchise had won two pennants since Murphy sold the team, including its World Series appearance in October 1929, just as the stock market crash began. Much had changed for the Cubs organization, and it enabled the memory of Murphy's career to be distilled into several bullet points that failed to convey the complexity of the man and his mission to make a winning club a championship team and first-rate business enterprise. However, not all of the newspapermen had forgotten the nuances of Murphy's personality.

Veteran New York sportswriter Joe Vila recalled a felicitous story from Charlie's younger days that exemplified his iconoclastic ways. The grumpy John T. Brush, amused by Murphy's high-spirited ways, had recently hired the energetic reporter to work as the New York Giants' press agent. During his first weeks on the job, Murphy wrote several informative pieces that garnered the Giants some off-season attention. He followed those up with a few more articles that were more fiction than fact. Several baseball reporters around town read those accounts with deep offense, and they harshly criticized the newbie from out west for making up stories. Word of their annoyance got back to Murphy, but he pressed on, undeterred.

One day, as he was walking in Manhattan, Murphy unexpectedly encountered one of the writers who had made fun of him. The guilty scribe felt sheepish and anticipated that Murphy would want to fight him because of his spiteful comments. Murphy, spotting him, desired nothing of the sort. Rather, Murphy walked right up to him, removed the pink flower situated on his own jacket, and promptly pinned it to the rude sportswriter's lapel.

"Keep up the good work, old boy," the young Murphy cried enthusiastically. "I don't care how much you roast me so long as you keep the Giants in the paper. If you leave me out, Brush will think that I'm not earning my coin. You know John T. is a businessman."[32] And, with that, Murphy cheerfully continued his way down Broadway into the New York afternoon.

EPILOGUE

I took my first trip to Wilmington in July of 2018 to experience the commemorative hundred-year celebration of the Murphy Theater. Rain dampened the opening event: Bike Night at the Murphy, a large gathering of motorcyclists, who could peruse antique choppers before taking in a screening of Peter Fonda's *Easy Rider*. The weather softened its tone and cooperated the rest of the week.

During my visit, it struck me that no one walking down Main Street could not be aware of Charlie Murphy's influence. His theater rises above the boulevard like the largest mountain in an otherwise plateaued range. Its window displays featured large photographs of Murphy as well as theater memorabilia from throughout the decades. It stood in stark contrast to Chicago, where Murphy's ghost has nowhere to haunt. The West Side Grounds is long gone in favor of the Illinois Medical District expansion. Charlie and Louise's house on Sheridan Road was toppled years ago to make way for crude apartment buildings along the lake. Wrigley Field? It would be just like Murphy to want to preside there, but there is no sign of him anywhere.

Murphy's theater indeed stands as the monument to him and his family, a testimony to their tribulations and triumphs. In my years of research, I kept asking myself, "Has Charlie Murphy really been forgotten?" No, not by many people in Wilmington, and Murphy would be perfectly content with that. The celebration's souvenir program featured a prominent picture of him wearing a dapper suit and bowler hat and pinching a cigar between his thumb and pointer finger. "A special thank you to the memory of Charles Webb Murphy for the love of your hometown where your monument stands tall with twinkling lights on Main Street for all to enjoy," it read.

The week-long celebration featured tours of the recently refurbished theater, a showing of the silent films patrons originally saw during the grand opening, and special musical performances. On the tour, guide Jennifer Hollon explained to visitors how Hollywood had discovered the theater's original flooring in 1992. A film version of *Lost in Yonkers* was shot on location in Wilmington, and the studio decided to hold the premiere of the film at the theater. The work crew pulled up the old carpet in the foyer, and they surprisingly discovered the original black and white tile. She also explained how Murphy coyly built the theater to seat fewer than a thousand patrons to avoid paying a tax on new buildings with a capacity over that number.

The birthday bash celebrating the Murphy Theater occurred on July 24, 2018, exactly one hundred years after its original Opening Day. A musical performance by Barry Campbell's Big Band called "A Century of America's Best Music" emphasized not only the theater's centennial anniversary but also the patriotic verve infused into the original event. A special appearance by "Charlie Murphy" during the birthday "party" shone the spotlight on the theater's founder. The bit fell a bit flat with a corny joke about the Cubs playing the Arizona Diamondbacks, a franchise unfamiliar to Murphy but, nevertheless, the physical presence of a costumed Murphy represented another act of homage. The week concluded with a well-attended concert featuring eighties cover bands.

Once the commemoration of the theater concluded, a more sobering reality settled in. During recent years, rural Wilmington has had to fight for its economic survival, and the COVID-19 pandemic devastated the theater. The odds seem unfairly stacked against the place, yet it steadfastly endures. It's no surprise a gritty place like that honors Charlie Murphy, an unfairly forgotten figure who was independence personified with audacity to spare.

ACKNOWLEDGMENTS

It took the kind help of quite a few people to put together this project, and I am incredibly grateful to all of them for their many contributions. The idea for this book germinated from a smaller bit of research about pitcher Orval Overall. During my first NINE Conference, Gary Mitchem introduced me to John Thorn, and the three of us energetically talked about Overall and the Deadball Era Cubs in the hotel lobby of the Doubletree Hotel in Tempe, Arizona. That conversation sparked my imagination and determination. I am forever grateful for the kindness that they showed me.

Much of what has been written about Charlie Murphy is anecdotal and, for that reason, I submerged myself in primary sources and, for the most part, remained there. Archivists and librarians around the country made that possible, and I am heavily indebted to them, especially considering the impact the COVID-19 pandemic had on their places of work.

Thank you, Jonathan Waltmire, and the other kind folks at the Annie Mitchell History Room, housed inside the Tulare County Library, who assisted me during this project's early stages, as I gathered information on the youthful origins of Frank Chance and Orval Overall.

The staff members at the Clinton County Historical Society and the Wilmington Public Library guided me through their archival materials as I learned about Charlie Murphy's hometown. A special thank you goes out to both Shelby Boatman and Jennifer Hollon.

The Ohio History Connection generously provided consequential documents that enlightened me on the state's hospital system.

The Taft family remains an important pillar of Cincinnati's political and cultural history. Thank you to the staffs of the Cincinnati History

Museum and Cincinnati Public Library for wheeling out a lot of large ledgers and fragile newspapers during my visits. A special thank you to Sarah Staples at the museum, who sent me the pages in Annie Taft's journal that detailed the sale of the Chicago Cubs to Charlie Weeghman.

The archive at the National Baseball Hall of Fame is a special place, and the chance to conduct research in wintertime Cooperstown, amidst the tall trees and frozen Otsego Lake, was an extraordinary experience. Cassidy Lent kindly provided crucial documents and patiently answered all my questions over the years. Thank you, Cassidy.

I really appreciate a pair of very helpful staffs in the Windy City: at the Chicago History Museum and the Chicago Public Library.

The supportive archivists at the Library of Congress guided me through any and all questions I had related to the William Howard Taft papers.

Five web resources provided me with detailed accounts of ballgames and the players who played them: retrosheet.com, newspapers.com, baseball-reference.com, the SABR Biography Project, and the LA84 Foundation Digital Library. They are astounding archives whose praise I cannot sing highly enough.

To everyone at the University of Nebraska Press who had a hand in this project, I would like to express my appreciation for your dedication and professionalism. I am very grateful to Rob Taylor for believing in this book and taking a chance on me. Thank you to Abby Goodwin and Courtney Ochsner for the roles they played in guiding me through this process. I appreciate all of the hard work by copyeditor Stephanie Ward, who patiently corrected a bevy of my errors. I especially want to show my appreciation to the anonymous reviewer, whose valuable critique of the manuscript made it better.

Everyone at the NINE Spring Training Conference has been incredibly supportive since I started attending it, as a sheepish graduate student, back in 2015. I want to thank Dan Levitt, who sent me one of Charlie Murphy's letters about Joe Tinker signing with the Federal League. Levitt's outstanding book *The Outlaw League and the Battle That Forged Modern Baseball* proved to be an invaluable resource as I studied the Federal League. A special thank you to Willie Steele for his support and belief in my work as well as all he does for NINE. I also want to thank Trey Strecker, Justin Turner, Lindsay Bell, Mitch Nathanson, and Paul Hensler, who generously provided me with support and advice at various stages of this process.

A very special thank you to my friend Jack Bales for his feedback on the manuscript and buoying my spirits every time I got bogged down in the mire. This book is better because of your influence.

John Ibson has believed in me from the start. Thank you, John, for your guidance over the years and, more importantly, for your friendship.

My conversations with Charlie Murphy's grandniece, the incredibly talented Amy Yasbeck, were a true highlight of working on this project. Her passion for family history enlightened me and broadened the scope of this book. Thank you, Amy, for all your help and support.

Thank you as well to Deborah Williams, who spoke to me on several occasions about her great-uncle Charlie Williams, the essential longtime front office member of the Cubs organization.

Aimee Tucker procured articles from the Chicago Public Library that greatly contributed to the book's final chapter. Thank you, Aimee!

Thanks to the fellas who help keep me on point in all pursuits: Amen, Ant, Jayson, Joel, Jon, and Scott, whose group text message about Orval Overall in 2016 started it all.

My mother and father read the book line by line, chapter by chapter, as it was built. They provided invaluable feedback. Mom sat on the phone with me for hours editing, among other things, my brutal punctuation errors. Love to you both.

Most importantly, thank you to my own family, who I love very much. Thank you to my wife, Reagan, whose love and support never waver, and to our old pup, Gervin, whose does depending on his hunger level. Scout: I love and miss you every day. Any and all has been made possible for me by God, who loves me, sustains me, and forgives me. What else could I possibly ask for?

I sincerely hope that I have not forgotten to thank anyone. Everyone worked diligently to ensure that this project would be error-free. All mistakes in the book are of my own doing.

NOTES

Abbreviations

AGHP August "Garry" Herrmann Papers, BA MSS 12, National Baseball Hall of Fame Library, Cooperstown NY.

HOF NL Meetings, Minutes, Conferences & Financial Ledgers, BA MSS 55, National Baseball Hall of Fame Library, Cooperstown NY.

WHTP William H. Taft Papers, Manuscript Division, Library of Congress, Washington DC.

Introduction

1. Hugh Fullerton, "Murphy Central Figure in Major League Ball," *Wilmington (OH) News-Journal*, October 23, 1931, 6.
2. Fullerton, "Murphy Central Figure in Major League Ball," 6.
3. Fullerton, "Murphy Central Figure in Major League Ball," 6.
4. Johnson to Herrmann, December 23, 1911, AGHP, Box 96, Folder 33.
5. Quote from Charles Ebbets appears in confidential meeting minutes sent by National League president Thomas Lynch to Garry Herrmann on December 19, 1911, AGHP, Box 96, Folder 33.
6. Hugh Fullerton, "Charles Webb Murphy Has Made His Base Ball Quarrels Pay Him in Handsome Dividends," *Fort Wayne (IN) Sentinel*, February 17, 1914, 8.
7. Fullerton, "Murphy Central Figure in Major League Ball," 6.
8. Fullerton, "Murphy Central Figure in Major League Ball," 6.
9. Fullerton, "Murphy Central Figure in Major League Ball," 6.
10. "Fullerton Springs One on Charles W. Murphy," *Wilmington (OH) News-Journal*, January 20, 1931, 6.
11. Shea, *Wrigley Field*, 14; Golenbock, *Wrigleyville*, 159; Rapp, *Tinker to Evers to Chance*, 144.
12. Fullerton, "Murphy Central Figure in Major League Ball," 6.

1. Wilmington

1. For more on the role of Catholicism in nineteenth-century Cincinnati see Roger Fortin, *Faith and Action: A History of the Archdiocese of Cincinnati, 1821-1906* (Columbus: The Ohio State University Press, 2002).
2. Brown, *History of Clinton County, Ohio*, 586.
3. Nolan, "The Great Famine and Women's Emigration from Ireland," 63. Irish immigration to the United States commenced earlier in the nineteenth century due to deteriorating economic circumstances, but those who left Ireland prior to the Great Famine mostly consisted of skilled artisans and small farmers from the northern and eastern parts of the country.
4. Laxton, *The Famine Ships*, 217.
5. Laxton, *The Famine Ships*, 113. According to Laxton, a Dr. Custis, of Dublin, wrote a series of newspaper articles about his experience on several voyages carrying Irish immigrants during the 1840s.
6. 1860 United States Census, Cincinnati, Hamilton County, Ohio, digital image s.v. "Patrick Murphy," Ancestry.com.
7. Legal document is from Clinton County Probate Court, Affidavit, Box S, No. 23. The medical report written by Dr. George Hill provides additional evidence. He listed "Cincinnati, Ohio" as Murphy's previous place of residence, prior to Wilmington.
8. Brown, *History of Clinton County, Ohio*, 81.
9. Brown, *History of Clinton County, Ohio*, 91-92.
10. Brown, *History of Clinton County, Ohio*, 95.
11. *St. Columbkille Catholic Church*, 7. It is impossible to know for sure where the wedding took place, but a church history publication states that the congregation used Preston's Hall for gatherings. Father O'Donoghue purchased a lot at the corner of Mulberry and Locust Streets for the purpose of constructing St. Columbkille Church, but ground was not broken on the project until June 6, 1866.
12. 1860 United States Census, Wilmington, Clinton County, Ohio, digital image s.v. "Ellen Murray," Ancestry.com.
13. "Passenger and Crew Lists (including Castle Garden and Ellis Island), 1820-1957," digital image s.v. "Michael Murray," Ancestry.com.
14. Patrick J. Murphy and Ellen Murray, certificate of marriage, September 11, 1864, Clinton County Recorder's Office, Wilmington, Ohio, copy in possession of author. The other marriage license on the same page of the registry does not have any edits pertaining to familial relation, suggest-

ing the change on Patrick and Ellen's document was not the product of a
newly enacted law.

15. 1870 United States Census, Wilmington, Clinton County, Ohio, digital
image s.v. "William Murphy," Ancestry.com. Five-year-old William is
listed in the census records as a member of both the Murray and Murphy
families.

16. Patrick J. Murphy and Bridget O'Donold, certificate of marriage, November 29, 1866, Clinton County Recorder's Office, Wilmington, Ohio, copy
in possession of author. The Murphys' marriage license exemplifies the
frequent misspellings of Bridget Murphy's maiden name. The document's top section is an affidavit, and it lists the groom as P. J. Murphy
and the bride as Bridget O'Donold. However, in the certification section
located just beneath the affidavit, Father O'Donoghue attested to marry-
ing Patrick J Murphy and Briget ODonnel.

17. Brown, *History of Clinton County, Ohio*, 587. The biographical sketch of
Frank Murphy states, "Mrs. Patrick Murphy is still living in the house
on South Mulberry street, in Wilmington, to which she and her husband
moved after they were married in 1866." Legal document is from the
Clinton County Recorder's Office, Deed Book No. 11, 386-87. Two local
notaries, along with Harry Hale, signed the deed signaling the real estate
sale to Murphy, for $500, on July 25, 1866. Hale does not appear to be
connected with Hale's Grocery, a store on Main Street operated by John
Hale.

18. Legal document is from the Clinton County Recorder's Office, Deed
Book No. 12, 413. The notary signed and filed the deed on May 10, 1867.

19. Bridget Murphy, death certificate, March 3, 1923, File No. 16531, State of
Ohio Bureau of Vital Statistics, copy in possession of author.

20. "Passenger and Crew Lists (including Castle Garden and Ellis Island),
1820-1957," digital image s.v. "Bridget Odonnell," Ancestry.com.

21. Nolan, "The Great Famine and Women's Emigration from Ireland," 61.

22. Nolan, "The Great Famine and Women's Emigration from Ireland," 65.

23. 1870 United States Census, Wilmington, Clinton County, Ohio, digital
image s.v. "Patrick Murphy," Ancestry.com. Census data suggests the
little ones grew up in a crowded household. The 1870 census lists twelve
residents living in the Murphy home, including the family, four laborers, another plasterer, a domestic servant, and a member of the driving
team.

24. January 22, 1868, is Murphy's generally accepted date of birth, but it
should be noted that his death certificate lists it as February 22, 1869.

25. Legal document is from the Clinton County Recorder's Office, Deed Book No. 14, 546–47.

26. Brown, *History of Clinton County, Ohio*, 338.

27. "Forty Days Fasting," *Wilmington (OH) Journal*, January 28, 1880, 3.

28. "Forty Days Fasting," 3. See also State and Local Archives: The Ohio Historical Society, Dayton State Hospital, Index to Series 153 (Admissions Register, 1855–1902), Series 1717, Box 1.

29. "Plastering," *Wilmington (OH) Journal*, October 24, 1872, 3.

30. Legal document is from the Clinton County Recorder's Office, Deed Book No. 18, 512–13.

31. Legal document is from the Clinton County Recorder's Office, Deed Book No. 19, 610–11. They sold "lot No two (2)" to Anna Showalter for $300 on October 7, 1872. Clinton County Recorder, Deed Book 18, 512–13. In an incomplete entry, the Murphys sold "Lot No three (3)" for "the sum of _____ dollars" to Charles Showalter.

32. Legal document is from the Clinton County Probate Court, Assignment of Patrick J. Murphy to S. W. Doan & R. E. Doan, filed on December 10, 1873.

33. Legal document is from the Clinton County Probate Court, Assignment of Patrick J. Murphy to S. W. Doan & R. E. Doan, filed on December 10, 1873.

34. Legal document is from the Clinton County Probate Court, Assignment of Patrick J. Murphy to S. W. Doan & R. E. Doan, filed on December 10, 1873. Lot 4 sold for $100 and lot 5 sold for $85.

35. "Notice to School Directors," *Wilmington (OH) Journal*, June 5, 1878, 3.

36. "A Serious Accident," *Wilmington (OH) Journal*, September 10, 1879, 3.

37. 1880 United States Census, Wilmington, Clinton County, Ohio, digital image s.v. "Patrick Murphy," Ancestry.com.

38. "School Entertainment," *Wilmington (OH) Journal*, March 9, 1881, 3.

39. "School Entertainment," 3.

40. "Roller Skating," *Wilmington (OH) Journal*, March 23, 1881, 3.

41. "Roller Skating," 3. "He is a very courteous gentleman and though young, shows no partiality whatever in teaching the ladies to skate. No matter what may be their social position, all receive the same attention at his hands."

42. "The Skaters," *Wilmington (OH) Journal*, March 30, 1881, 3.

43. Thomas Murphy, "Life of Charles W. Murphy," *The Wilmingtonian* 11, no. 3 (1910): 36.

44. Charles W. Murphy, "Taft, the Fan," *Baseball Magazine* 9, no. 3 (1912): 3–4. In particular, Murphy praised the baseball clubs organized in the city of Cleveland.

45. Bridget Murphy v. Patrick Murphy, Clinton County Court of Common Pleas, No. 4931 (1883). "Toward this plaintiff been guilty of habitual drunkenness for more than three years."

46. Legal document is from the Clinton County Probate Court, Affidavit, Box S, No. 23.

47. Murphy v. Murphy, No. 4931 (1883).

48. Murphy to Herrmann, January 26, 1905, AGHP, Box 48, Folder 13.

49. Murphy v. Murphy, No. 4931 (1883).

50. Legal document is from the Clinton County Probate Court, Affidavit, Box S, No. 23.

51. Ziff, *Asylum on the Hill*, 16.

52. Legal document is from the Clinton County Probate Court, Affidavit, Box S, No. 23.

53. Legal document is from the Clinton County Probate Court, Affidavit, Box S, No. 23.

54. Legal document is from the Clinton County Probate Court. C. W. King to John Matthews, December 27, 1884, Affidavit, Box S, No. 23.

55. State and Local Archives: The Ohio Historical Society, Dayton State Hospital, Index to Series 153 (Admissions Register, 1855–1902), Series 1717, Box 1.

56. "Court-House News," *Wilmington (OH) Journal*, July 8, 1885, 3.

57. The State of Ohio v. Harvey A. Murphy, No. 1891 (1886). In a subsection, the indictment is titled, in part, "The State of Ohio vs. Patrick Murphy alias Harvey A. Murphy."

58. "Local Matters," *Wilmington (OH) Journal*, June 16, 1866, 5. "Court-House News," *Wilmington (OH) Journal*, June 16, 1866, 8. There are two brief paragraphs noting the outcome of the case in the same edition of the paper. Readers were informed on page five that Sheriff Smith took Murphy to jail, and the outcome of the trial appears on page eight.

59. "Town Lots," *Wilmington (OH) Journal*, January 5, 1887, 2.

60. "Local Matters," *Wilmington (OH) Journal*, February 15, 1888, 5.

2. On to Cincinnati

1. Cincinnati City Directory, 1890, digital image s.v. "Chas. W Murphy," fold3.com.

2. Bill Bailey, "Bailey Tells of Charles W. Murphy's Rise: From Village Drug Clerk to Millionaire He Turns $105,000 Into a Vast Fortune." Charles W. Murphy File Folder. National Baseball Hall of Fame Library. Chicago defeated the Reds, 5–4, on Opening Day, April 19, 1890. Murphy was listed as a drug clerk in the Cincinnati City Directory in 1890 and 1891. Differing addresses suggest Murphy's employer did indeed change, lending credence to his story.

3. Charles W. Murphy, "Murphy Tells of the Many Troubles of Big League Ball Owner," *Chicago Evening American,* April 1, 1916.

4. "Baseball," *Cincinnati Enquirer,* October 25, 1931, 40.

5. "New Infirmary Druggist," *Cincinnati Enquirer,* April 2, 1891, 1.

6. "The Charter Bill," *Cincinnati Enquirer,* March 20, 1891, 4; "Six Officers," *Cincinnati Enquirer,* May 6, 1891, 8.

7. Zeigler, "When Store," 1424–25. See also Bill Lamb, "The Brush Family Women," SABR, https://sabr.org/bioproj/person/the-brush-family-women/.

8. John Saccoman, "John T. Brush," SABR, accessed May 1, 2020, https://sabr.org/bioproj/person/a46ef165.

9. "Base Ball," *Cincinnati Commercial Gazette,* January 4, 1891, 3.

10. "Mysterious Brush," *Cincinnati Commercial Gazette,* February 11, 1891, 8.

11. Cincinnati City Directory, 1892, digital image s.v. "Chas. W. Murphy," fold3 .com. Murphy listed himself as a reporter for the *Cincinnati Enquirer* in the 1892 city directory. It is possible he began working at the paper in late 1891.

12. "John R. McLean," Ohio History Central, accessed September 17, 2019, https://ohiohistorycentral.org/index.php?title=John_R._McLean& redirect=no. Circulation increased from sixteen thousand to ninety thousand papers.

13. Riess, *Touching Base,* 55.

14. "Thousands," *Cincinnati Enquirer,* April 25, 1892, 2.

15. Seymour, *Baseball,* 307–8. See also Joe Santry and Cindy Thomson, "Ban Johnson," SABR, https://sabr.org/bioproj/person/dabf79f8.

16. *Cincinnati Commercial Gazette,* July 12, 1893, 5. The story doesn't have a byline. Perhaps Ban Johnson didn't write it, but maybe he did.

17. "Danny Dalton," *Cincinnati Enquirer,* June 5, 1894, 8.

18. 1900 United States Census, Cincinnati, Hamilton County, Ohio, digital image s.v. "Chas. Murphy," Ancestry.com. The document states Charlie and Louise had been married for five years.

19. Cincinnati City Directory, 1871, digital image s.v. "Henry Krumdick," fold3.com; Cincinnati City Directory, 1871, digital image s.v. "Ernest Kenker," fold3.com.

20. "Patrick J. Murphy," *Cincinnati Enquirer*, August 6, 1896, 8.

21. For example, see Jack Ryder, "Griff," *Cincinnati Enquirer*, November 7, 1908, 3. Interestingly, Jack Ryder states that Bridget Murphy was born in Ireland but P. J. was born in Cincinnati, which again suggests Charlie may either have not known or been disingenuous about his father's birthplace.

22. "Administrator's Notice," *Wilmington (OH) Journal*, August 12, 1896, 5.

23. Document is from the Athens Mental Health Center, Mahn Center for Archives and Special Collections, Ohio University Libraries, Female Admissions, Nos. 2967-68.

24. "Probate Court," *Wilmington (OH) Journal*, January 27, 1897, 5.

25. Ziff, *Asylum on the Hill*, 1.

26. Ziff, *Asylum on the Hill*, 10. Ziff explains, "Compassionate, supportive treatment of those with mental illness was a sea change, a manifestation of the great Victorian impulse to provide systematic, decent public care for vulnerable individuals—those with mental illness, orphans, the poor, and persons in need of medical care."

27. *Wilmington (OH) Journal*, September 16, 1896, 5.

28. *Wilmington (OH) Journal*, April 21, 1897, 5.

29. "The Dewey Program," *Cincinnati Commercial Tribune*, September 21, 1899, 10.

30. For more on Bum: "Bum is Run Over Twice in One Night," *Cincinnati Commercial Tribune*, June 13, 1901, 5; "Looking," *Cincinnati Enquirer*, June 17, 1901, 5; "Bum, the Police Dog, Gone to Join Canine Majority," *Cincinnati Commercial Tribune*, June 17, 1901, 5.

31. 1900 United States Census, Lake, Cook County, Illinois, digital image s.v. "Louisa Murphy," Ancestry.com.

32. "Shocked," *Cincinnati Enquirer*, January 29, 1902, 4.

33. Charles W. Murphy, "Is Baseball Writing Overdone?" *Baseball Magazine* 22, no. 6 (1919): 355.

34. Richter, "The Press and Sport," 570.

35. Richter, "The Press and Sport," 571.

36. Charles W. Murphy, "Busy," *Cincinnati Enquirer*, December 11, 1900, 4.

37. Joseph Vila, "Vila Recalls Roles Played by Murphy," *Sporting News* 92, no. 9 (1931): 3.

38. Murphy, "Busy," 4.

39. Cincinnati City Directory, 1902, digital image s.v. "Chas. W. Murphy," fold3.com; Cincinnati City Directory, 1903, digital image s.v. "Chas. W. Murphy," fold3.com.

40. "Murphy's Enterprise," *Sporting Life* 53, no. 26 (1909): 15.

41. Ross, *An American Family*, 7.

42. Ross, *An American Family*, 12.

43. Ross, *An American Family*, 52. According to Ross, the Taft brothers played with boys from the Reading Road and Little Bethlehem neighborhoods.

44. Goss, *Cincinnati*, 316.

45. Ross, *An American Family*, 49.

46. Ross, *An American Family*, 58.

47. "Times-Star, Century Old, Recalls History from Time of First Issue on April 25th, 1840, to the Present Day," *Cincinnati Times-Star*, April 25, 1940, 2–3.

48. "Times-Star, Century Old, Recalls History," 2–3.

49. "New York's New Baseball Official," *New York Times*, February 2, 1905, 10.

50. "Answer," *Cincinnati Enquirer*, December 12, 1902, 4.

51. "Local Newspaper Man Gets Good Baseball Position," *Cincinnati Commercial Tribune*, January 26, 1905, 7.

52. Charles W. Murphy, "The Guiding Genius of the National League: John T. Brush, a Dominant Personality in Organized Baseball," *Baseball Magazine* 8, no. 4 (1912): 34.

53. Saccoman, "John T. Brush."

54. Alexander, *John McGraw*, Kindle edition, chap. 5. The original quote appeared in the *Sporting News* on October 29, 1904.

55. "New Field," *Cincinnati Enquirer*, January 26, 1905, 4.

56. "Local Newspaper Man Gets Good Baseball Position," 7.

57. "New Baseball Official in Town," *New York Times*, February 3, 1905, 8.

3. "A Real Wonder-Story"

1. Murphy to Herrmann, January 26, 1905, AGHP, Box 48, Folder 13.

2. "Joe Jackson Honored," *Buffalo Times*, March 7, 1905, 8.

3. Alexander, *John McGraw*, Kindle edition, chap. 3.

4. Bozeman C. Bulger, "McGraw Had Poker Party 'Raided,' and It Cost Secretary Murphy $100 to 'Square It' with Constables," *New York Evening World*, March 27, 1905, 8.

5. Charles W. Murphy, "Lack of Left-Handed Hitters," *Wilmington (OH) News-Journal*, July 16, 1929, 6.

6. "Giants Cheered on Parade," *New York Times*, April 15, 1905, 13.

7. Allen Sangree, "Baseball Season Opens with Great Victory for the Giants," *New York Evening World*, April 14, 1905, 1, 16.

8. "Baseball Season On." *New York Daily Tribune*, April 15, 1905, 7.

9. Fred Barber, "Herrmann Made Murphy Pay in the Fraser-Gessler Deal," AGHP, Box 48, Folder 15.

10. Charles W. Murphy, "Murphy Tells of the Many Troubles of Big League Ball Owner," *Chicago Evening American*, April 1, 1916.

11. J. Ed Grillo, "Brush Sells Cincinnati Ball Club to the Local Syndicate," *Cincinnati Commercial Tribune*, August 10, 1902, 9.

12. Charles W. Murphy, "Busy," *Cincinnati Enquirer*, December 11, 1900, 4.

13. "Baseball," *Cincinnati Enquirer*, October 25, 1931, 38.

14. "Charles W. Murphy Appointed," *Brooklyn Daily Eagle*, January 25, 1905, 15.

15. "Taft Visits the Press Club," *Cincinnati Commercial Tribune*, April 28, 1907, 2.

16. "Murphy Takes Up Hart's Burden," *Chicago Sunday Tribune*, July 16, 1905, B1.

17. Murphy to Herrmann, July 7, 1905, AGHP, Box 48, Folder 13.

18. Murphy to Herrmann, July 16, 1905, AGHP, Box 48, Folder 13.

19. "Murphy Takes Up Hart's Burden," B1.

20. Edward Mott Woolley, "The Business of Baseball," *McClure's Magazine* 39, no. 3 (1912): 245.

21. "Charles G. Williams, Secretary-Treasurer of the Chicago National League Club," *Sporting Life* 48, no. 5 (1906): 1.

22. Deborah Williams, conversation with author, December 6, 2020.

23. "How Squeeze Play Was Originated Here," *Daily Journal-Gazette (IL)*, October 11, 1913, 3.

24. "Murphy Banters Commy to Battle," Chicago *Inter Ocean*, July 27, 1905, 4.

25. "Notes of the Game," Chicago *Inter Ocean*, September 15, 1905, 4.

26. "Manager Selee is on Sick List," *Chicago Tribune*, July 1, 1905, 10; "Selee Confined to House," Chicago *Inter Ocean*, July 1, 1905, 4.

27. "Selee is Forced to Quit the Game," *Chicago Daily Tribune*, July 29, 1905, 4.

28. "Selee is Forced to Quit the Game," 4.

29. "Big Sales for Selee Benefit," *Chicago Daily Tribune*, September 24, 1905, 7.

30. "To Attend Selee Benefit," Chicago *Inter Ocean*, September 15, 1905, 4.

31. "Chicago's Debt to Frank G. Selee," *Chicago Daily Tribune*, September 17, 1905, 9.

32. "Pay Tribute to Manager Selee," *Chicago Daily Tribune*, September 29, 1905, 10.

33. "Hart Criticizes Work of Umpire," *Chicago Daily Tribune*, October 17, 1905, 6.

34. "Selee Thanks His Admirers," Chicago *Inter Ocean*, October 24, 1905, 4.

35. Harry W. Ford, "Evers' Errors Present Game to the Phillies," Chicago *Inter Ocean*, July 30, 1905, 9.

36. "Talk of the Baseball Men," *Chicago Daily Tribune*, October 24, 1905, 10.

37. "Comiskey and Hart in Accord," Chicago *Inter Ocean*, September 15, 1905, 4.

38. "Wild Cubs Take Deciding Game from White Sox," Chicago *Inter Ocean*, October 16, 1905, 7.

39. "Celebration by Nationals as Result of the Victory," *Chicago Daily Tribune*, October 16, 1905, 3.

40. "Hart Criticizes Work of Umpire," 6.

41. Bales, *Before They Were the Cubs*, 199.

42. "General Ledger, No. 10 Anna S. Taft. December 31, 1906–October 14, 1913," Series 2, Box 3, Volume 1, Taft Family Papers, 1817–1959, n.d., MSS 647, Cincinnati Museum Center; "Private Day Book Journal," Box 11, Folder 32, Anna Sinton Taft, 1870–1934, MSS T1241, Cincinnati Museum Center.

43. "Selee Thanks His Admirers," 4.

44. Murphy to Herrmann, November 2, 1905, AGHP, Box 48, Folder 13.

45. "James Hart, One Time Owner of Cubs, Dies After Long Illness," *Chicago Daily Tribune*, July 19, 1919, 11.

46. Bales, *Before They Were the Cubs*, 182–85.

47. "Final Summons to Frank Selee," *Chicago Daily Tribune*, July 6, 1909, 16.

4. "He Is One of Us"

1. "Murphy Takes Up Hart's Burden," *Chicago Daily Tribune*, July 16, 1905, B1.

2. "Baseball Magnate," *Oak Leaves*, August 25, 1906, 24. "Mr. Murphy has lived in Oak Park about twelve months and is an enthusiastic admirer of its people and its homes."

3. Reynolds, *The Young Hemingway*, 5.

4. C. H. F., "A Lesson from Hephzibah Home," *Oak Leaves*, August 25, 1906, 15.

5. Reynolds, *The Young Hemingway*, 4.

6. "Baseball Magnate," 24.

7. Harvey T. Woodruff, "'Chance Day' Made Possible by Scotch Strain in Blood of Peerless Leader," *Chicago Daily Tribune*, May 18, 1913, C2. See also Charles W. Murphy, "Is Baseball Writing Overdone?" *Baseball Magazine* 22, no. 6 (1919): 356.

8. Murphy to Herrmann, August 1, 1905, AGHP, Box 48, Folder 13.

9. Murphy to Herrmann, October 2, 1905, AGHP, Box 48, Folder 13.

10. Evers and Fullerton, *Touching Second*, 70–71.

11. Murphy to Herrmann, October 2, 1905, AGHP, Box 48, Folder 13.

12. Murphy to Herrmann, November 8, 1905, AGHP, Box 48, Folder 13.

13. Robert Peyton Wiggins, "Jimmy Sebring," SABR *Biography Project*, https://sabr.org/bioproj/person/77650ebd.

14. Quoted in Francis Richter, "National League Meeting Results," *Sporting Life* 46, no. 15 (1905): 4.

15. Murphy to Herrmann, August 7, 1905, AGHP, Box 48, Folder 13; Richter, "National League Meeting Results," 4.

16. "President Murphy Expects Cubs to Capture Pennant," Chicago *Inter Ocean*, December 18, 1905, 9.

17. "Murphy Pleased with New Men," *Chicago Daily Tribune*, December 18, 1905, 12.

18. "Cubs Move on Pennant of 1906," Chicago *Inter Ocean*, January 5, 1906, 4.

19. "President Murphy Expects Cubs to Capture Pennant," 9.

20. "Local Baseball News Notes," *Chicago Daily Tribune*, December 30, 1905, 10.

21. "Murphy Pleased with New Men," 12.

22. "Murphy Pleased with New Men," 12.

23. "Chicago Gleanings," *Sporting Life* 47, no. 4 (1906): 14.

24. Grantland Rice, "Tinker to Evers to Chance," *Collier's*, November 29, 1930, 11.

25. "Cubs Get a Great Outfielder," *Rochester (NY) Democrat and Chronicle*, December 18, 1905, 17.

26. J. C. Morse, "Trades Order of the Day," *Pittsburgh Press*, December 31, 1905, 24.

27. W. A. Phelon, "Chicago Gleanings," *Sporting Life* 46, no. 16 (1905): 7.

28. "Chat of the Diamond," *Decatur (IL) Herald*, January 14, 1906, 5.

29. "Great Times Here When Ball Begins," *Cincinnati Commercial Gazette*, April 8, 1894.

30. "Murphy Pleased with New Men," 12.

31. W. A. Phelon, "Chicago Gleanings," *Sporting Life* 47, no. 5 (1906): 13.

32. Phelon, "Chicago Gleanings," 13.

33. Phelon, "Chicago Gleanings," 14; Johnson to Herrmann, March 27, 1906, AGHP, Box 71, Folder 7.

34. W. A. Phelon, "Chicago Gleanings," *Sporting Life* 47, no. 12 (1906): 9.

35. "National League," *Sporting Life* 47, no. 12 (1906): 4.

36. Phelon, "Chicago Gleanings," 9; "Giant Killers Down Giants; 28,000 Cheer," Chicago *Inter Ocean*, May 21, 1906, 1; "New York Downed in First Game," *Chicago Daily Tribune*, May 21, 1906, 8.

37. "Last Game with New York Today," *Chicago Daily Tribune*, May 24, 1906, 10.

38. Phelon, "Chicago Gleanings," 9.
39. Johnson to Herrmann, July 6, 1906, AGHP, Box 71, Folder 7.
40. "Wise Sayings of Great Men," *Sporting Life* 47, no. 11 (1906): 3.
41. "Chicago Lands League Pennant," *Chicago Daily Tribune*, September 20, 1906, 6.
42. "Nearly Everybody in Chicago is Crazy About Baseball," *Chicago Daily Tribune*, September 9, 1906, G1.
43. "Nearly Everybody in Chicago is Crazy About Baseball," G1.
44. "Giant Killers and Sox Ready for the Battle," Chicago *Inter Ocean*, October 9, 1906, 4.
45. "Giant Killers and Sox Ready for the Battle," 4.
46. "Moving Pictures of Base Ball Game," *Sporting Life* 48, no. 4 (1906): 19.
47. "Modest Champions," *Sporting Life* 48, no. 5 (1906): 8.
48. Weisberger, *When Chicago Ruled Baseball*, 25.
49. "Frantic Rooters Crowd the Field," *Chicago Daily Tribune*, October 15, 1906, 3.
50. "'Fairly Won,' Says Chance," *Chicago Daily Tribune*, October 15, 1906, 3.
51. "Frantic Rooters Crowd the Field," 3.
52. "Makes Sox $15,000 Present," *Chicago Daily Tribune*, October 15, 1906, 2.
53. "Fans Frantic in Streets," *Chicago Daily Tribune*, October 15, 1906, 3.
54. "'Fairly Won,' Says Chance," 3.

5. Champions

1. "Baseball Magnate," *Oak Leaves*, August 25, 1906, 24.
2. "A Lucky Deal," *Sporting Life* 48, no. 4 (1906): 11.
3. "Modest Champions," *Sporting Life* 48, no. 4 (1906): 12.
4. Ren Mulford Jr., "Red Velvet Gone," *Sporting Life* 48, no. 5 (1906): 12.
5. "A Tribute to the Pulliam Regime," *Sporting Life* 48, no. 5 (1906): 6.
6. "Season's Baseball Crowds," *New York Times*, October 14, 1906, 12.
7. "Private Day Book Journal," Box 11, Folder 32, Anna Sinton Taft Papers, 1870-1934, n.d., MSS T1241, Cincinnati Museum Center.
8. "Nationals Have Made $100,000," *Chicago Daily Tribune*, October 15, 1906, 3.
9. "Local Matters," *Wilmington (OH) Journal*, September 5, 1906, 5.
10. "Pulliam Certain of Re-election to League Presidency," Chicago *Inter Ocean*, December 12, 1906, 4.
11. A. R. Cratty, "Pittsburg Points," *Sporting Life* 48, no. 5 (1906): 9.
12. "Gessler's Name on List," *Chicago Daily Tribune*, February 23, 1907, 10.
13. Dreyfuss to Herrmann, November 29, 1906, AGHP, Box 96, Folder 29.

14. Murphy to Herrmann, January 14, 1907, AGHP, Box 48, Folder 15.

15. "Herrmann Surprised at Story of Trade," AGHP, Box 48, Folder 15.

16. Murphy to Herrmann, January 15, 1907, AGHP, Box 48, Folder 15.

17. W. A. Phelon, "Chicago Gleanings," *Sporting Life* 48, no. 16 (1906): 6.

18. The Reading Red Roses of the Atlantic League were the first recorded team to use numbered uniforms, in 1907. The Cleveland Indians were the first Major League Baseball franchise to put numbers on player uniforms, on June 26, 1916, although they only wore them for a few weeks before the digits were removed from their sleeves.

19. "White Sox Will Hold on to Owen," *Chicago Daily Tribune*, February 28, 1907, 10.

20. "Chance Confers with Murphy," *Chicago Daily Tribune*, March 1, 1907, 10.

21. "Chance Confers with Murphy," 10.

22. Charles Dryden, "Spuds Rehearse on Cycle Track," *Chicago Daily Tribune*, March 5, 1907, 10. See also Charles Dryden, "Spring Exercise for the Spuds," *Chicago Daily Tribune*, March 4, 1907, 10.

23. I. E. Sanborn, "Rude Cubs Trim Memphis Team," *Chicago Daily Tribune*, March 25, 1907, 12.

24. I. E. Sanborn, "Cubs Beaten by a Muff," *Chicago Daily Tribune*, April 19, 1907, 10.

25. Frank Hutchinson, "Rain, Snow, Sleet, and Hail Prevent West Side Contest," Chicago *Inter Ocean*, April 13, 1907, 4.

26. "Double Page of Sports in The Tribune Every Day Beginning Monday," *Chicago Daily Tribune*, June 2, 1907, 9.

27. Charles Dryden, "Cubs Take First from Giants, 8–2," *Chicago Daily Tribune*, June 6, 1907, 7.

28. Dryden, "Cubs Take First from Giants, 8–2," 7.

29. Attendance numbers are taken from the box scores in the *Chicago Daily Tribune*.

30. "National League News," *Sporting Life* 49, no. 14 (1907): 9.

31. "Notes of the Cubs," *Chicago Daily Tribune*, July 3, 1907, 11.

32. I. E. Sanborn, "Cubs Drive Two Pennant Spikes," *Chicago Daily Tribune*, July 5, 1907, 16.

33. "Notes of the Cubs," *Chicago Daily Tribune*, July 5, 1907, 16.

34. "Notes of the Cubs," *Chicago Daily Tribune*, July 4, 1907, 7.

35. I. E. Sanborn, "Giants Maul Taylor, 12 to 4," *Chicago Daily Tribune*, August 22, 1907, 6.

36. "The 'Black Hand,'" *Sporting Life* 49, no. 24 (1907): 2.

37. W. A. Phelon, "Chicago Gleanings," *Sporting Life* 49, no. 25 (1907): 2.

38. Charles Dryden, "E-Yah and A-Las for Tiger," *Chicago Daily Tribune,* October 13, 1907, A2.

39. Dryden, "E-Yah and A-Las for Tiger," A2.

40. Ark., "Bad Taste Left in Mouth of Americans," *Indianapolis Star,* October 13, 1907, E2.

41. Dryden, "E-Yah and A-Las for Tiger," A2.

42. "Gift of $15,000 Made the Tigers," *Indianapolis Star,* October 13, 1907, F1.

43. "Hughey Censured," *Rochester (NY) Democrat and Chronicle,* October 13, 1907, 20.

44. "The Aftermath," *Sporting Life* 50, no. 6 (1907): 7.

45. "Gift of $15,000 Made the Tigers," F1.

46. "The Financial Result," *Sporting Life* 50, no. 6 (1907): 6.

47. W. A. Phelon, "Chicago Cheer," *Sporting Life* 50, no. 6 (1907): 8.

48. I. E. Sanborn, "Champion Cubs Feast with Fans," *Chicago Daily Tribune,* October 18, 1907, 10.

6. Supremacy Again

1. "Quest for Manager Fails; Griffith Comes for Kelley," *Chicago Daily Tribune,* October 23, 1907, 10.

2. "Johnny Evers Breaks into Journalism in the East," *Chicago Daily Tribune,* October 25, 1907, 10.

3. "Wise Sayings of Great Men," *Sporting Life* 50, no. 9 (1907): 4.

4. Ren Mulford, Jr., "Red Lights," *Sporting Life* 50, no. 7 (1907): 2.

5. "Murphy to Speak," *Oak Leaves,* November 16, 1907, 28.

6. William Jennings Bryan, "An Honest Game," *The Commoner,* October 25, 1907, 3.

7. "The Financial Result," *Sporting Life* 50, no. 6 (1907): 6. "Had any more games been played the receipts entire would have been shared by the clubs alone."

8. "Cubs Send Pass to Bryan," *Chicago Daily Tribune,* November 3, 1907, C1.

9. I. E. Sanborn, "Big Improvement for League Park," *Chicago Daily Tribune,* December 5, 1907, 8.

10. "National League Solons Gather," *Chicago Daily Tribune,* December 10, 1907, 12.

11. "Pulliam for Another Team," *Boston Globe,* December 12, 1907, 5.

12. Ray C. Pearson, "Murphy Predicts Close 1908 Race," *Chicago Daily Tribune,* December 16, 1907, 12.

13. "Charles Murphy Host at Banquet," *Chicago Daily Tribune,* December 12, 1907, 10.

14. I. E. Sanborn, "Advance is Made by Baseball Men," *Chicago Daily Tribune*, December 15, 1907, C1.

15. Pearson, "Murphy Predicts Close 1908 Race," 12.

16. "Notes of the Cubs' Victory," *Chicago Daily Tribune*, April 15, 1908, 11.

17. Charles Dryden, "Home Opening of Cubs is At Hand," *Chicago Daily Tribune*, April 22, 1908, 12.

18. W. A. Phelon, "Chicago Points," *Sporting Life* 51, no. 9 (1908): 2.

19. Charles Dryden, "Cubs Take Game by Clever Work," *Chicago Daily Tribune*, April 23, 1908, 8.

20. Frank Hutchinson, "Cubs Raise League Pennant and Defeat Cincinnati, 7–3," Chicago *Inter Ocean*, April 23, 1908, 4.

21. Charles Dryden, "Cubs Beat Reds in Lively Game," *Chicago Daily Tribune*, April 24, 1908, 8. Dryden noted Lobert's gifts, and that he didn't smoke, in his game story.

22. Charles Dryden, "Rain Stops Reds and Cubs," *Chicago Daily Tribune*, April 26, 1908, C1.

23. Dryden, "Rain Stops Reds and Cubs," C1.

24. Pulliam to Murphy, May 6, 1908, AGHP, Box 70, Folder 1.

25. Pulliam to Murphy, May 6, 1908, AGHP, Box 70, Folder 1.

26. "An Innovation," *Sporting Life* 51, no. 8 (1908): 2

27. I. E. Sanborn, "Camp of Pirates in Swamp Class," *Chicago Daily Tribune*, May 8, 1908, 10.

28. John H. Gruber, "Another Game Lost Through Bad Weather," *Pittsburgh Post-Gazette*, May 8, 1908, 9.

29. 1910 United States Census, Village of Oak Park, Cook County, Illinois, digital image s.v. "Miriam Pannell," Ancestry.com.

30. Lois Virginia Pannell, "How We Can Be Immortal," *Chicago Sunday Tribune*, November 25, 1956, H42.

31. "Death of Miss Helen Pannell," *Oak Leaves*, January 31, 1920, 17.

32. Pannell, "How We Can Be Immortal," H42.

33. I. E. Sanborn, "Doves Heartless in Abusing Cubs," *Chicago Daily Tribune*, May 22, 1908, 12; "Notes of the Cubs," *Chicago Daily Tribune*, May 22, 1908, 12; "Murphy's Men," *Sporting Life* 51, no. 13 (1908): 6.

34. "Cubs are Not Pulling Together, Say Giants," *Moline (IL) Daily Dispatch*, July 25, 1908, 6; Golenbock, *Wrigleyville*, 128–29.

35. I. E. Sanborn, "Brilliant Game Ends in a Draw," *Chicago Daily Tribune*, June 5, 1908, 13.

36. I. E. Sanborn, "Cubs' Game Needs a Disinfectant?" *Chicago Daily Tribune*, June 3, 1908, 12.

37. "Latest News," *Sporting Life* 51, no. 13 (1908): 1.

38. Rapp, *Tinker to Evers to Chance*, 210.

39. "Inquisitive Fans," *Chicago Daily Tribune*, July 19, 1908, C2.

40. I. E. Sanborn, "Cubs Will File Protest," *Chicago Daily Tribune*, September 5, 1908, 10.

41. Carmichael, *My Greatest Day in Baseball*, 68.

42. Charles Dryden, "Ghoulish Glee in Cub Camp," *Chicago Daily Tribune*, September 22, 1908, 8.

43. Bozeman Bulger, "Giants Outplayed in Both Chicago Games," *New York Evening World*, September 22, 1908, 1.

44. Bozeman Bulger, "Bridwell's Hit Wins for Giants; Riot Follows at Polo Grounds," *New York Evening World*, September 23, 1908, 1.

45. "Detail of the Squabble," *Chicago Daily Tribune*, September 24, 1908, 12.

46. "Notes of the Cubs," *Chicago Daily Tribune*, September 24, 1908, 12.

47. Charles Dryden, "Game Ends in Tie May Go to Cubs," *Chicago Daily Tribune*, September 24, 1908, 12.

48. HOF, Box 2, Folder 21.

49. Carmichael, *My Greatest Day in Baseball*, 24.

50. Carmichael, *My Greatest Day in Baseball*, 27.

51. Carmichael, *My Greatest Day in Baseball*, 27.

52. Carmichael, *My Greatest Day in Baseball*, 28.

53. "Statements of the Leaders," *Chicago Daily Tribune*, October 9, 1908, 2.

54. Pulliam to Herrmann, June 22, 1908, AGHP, Box 70, Folder 1.

55. "Major League Baseball Writers Form Association," *Chicago Daily Tribune*, October 15, 1908, 2.

56. "Scalpers' Power Angers Fans," *Chicago Daily Tribune*, October 13, 1908, 3.

57. "Scalpers' Power Angers Fans," 3.

58. "Scalpers' Power Angers Fans," 3.

59. "Scalpers' Power Angers Fans," 3.

60. "Answer to Scalping Charge," *Chicago Daily Tribune*, October 21, 1908, 10.

61. "Answer to Scalping Charge," 10.

62. Charles W. Murphy, "Murphy Answers His Critics; Brands Charges as Absurd," *Chicago Daily Tribune*, October 17, 1908, 6.

63. Murphy, "Murphy Answers His Critics," 6.

64. "Stinging Reply to Murphy," *Chicago Daily Tribune*, December 22, 1908, 12.

65. Hugh Fullerton, "Murphy's Rule of Cubs Succession of Scandals; His Tactics Injure the Prestige of Baseball," *Chicago Examiner*, January 24, 1911.

66. "The American Game!" *Chicago Daily Tribune*, February 13, 1909, 12.

7. The War of 1908–9

1. "Short Stop Has House Warming," *Oak Leaves*, August 29, 1908, 15.
2. Pulliam to Chance, December 26, 1908, AGHP, Box 70, Folder 2.
3. "Tilt on Between Leaders of Cubs," *Chicago Sunday Tribune*, November 1, 1908, C1.
4. I. E. Sanborn, "Breach in Cubs' Ranks Unhealed," *Chicago Daily Tribune*, November 3, 1908, 10.
5. "Tilt on Between Leaders of Cubs," C1.
6. Sanborn, "Breach in Cubs' Ranks Unhealed," 10.
7. "Cat," *Cincinnati Enquirer*, November 3, 1908, 4.
8. "Tilt on Between Leaders of Cubs," C1.
9. Jack Ryder, "Garry," *Cincinnati Enquirer*, November 4, 1908, 8.
10. W. A. Phelon, "Chicago Gleanings," *Sporting Life* 52, no. 9 (1908): 6.
11. Harvey Woodruff, "Hip! Hip! Hooray! Chance Will Play," *Chicago Sunday Tribune*, February 7, 1909, C1-2.
12. "Cubs Will Not Lose the P. L.," *Chicago Daily Tribune*, November 5, 1908, 14.
13. Jack Ryder, "Old Fox," *Cincinnati Enquirer*, November 6, 1908, 4.
14. HOF, Box 2, Folder 21.
15. HOF, Box 2, Folder 21.
16. Pulliam to Thomas, January 14, 1909, AGHP, Box 70, Folder 2.
17. Pulliam to Chance, December 26, 1908, AGHP, Box 70, Folder 2.
18. "Murphy is Grilled by Garry Herrmann and Harry Pulliam," Chicago *Inter Ocean*, February 9, 1909, 4.
19. Pulliam to Herrmann, January 14, 1909, AGHP, Box 70, Folder 2.
20. "Murphy is Grilled by Garry Herrmann and Harry Pulliam," 4.
21. Woodruff, "Hip! Hip! Hooray! Chance Will Play," C1-2. Woodruff relayed the price of the orange grove as "$38,500 in real money."
22. "Doubtfuls of Big League Clubs Disclose Their Plans for 1909," *Chicago Sunday Tribune*, January 3, 1909, C1.
23. "No Change in Cub Dispute," *Chicago Daily Tribune*, January 26, 1909, 10.
24. "Comiskey Buys Player Altizer," *Chicago Sunday Tribune*, January 10, 1909, C1.
25. Harvey T. Woodruff, "Reward of $10,000 Sure to 'Champs,'" *Chicago Daily Tribune*, January 11, 1909, 12.
26. Pulliam to Herrmann, January 14, 1909, AGHP, Box 70, Folder 2.
27. "Harvey Woodruff, Ex-Sports Editor," *New York Times*, June 3, 1937, 25.
28. Woodruff, "Hip! Hip! Hooray! Chance Will Play," C1-2.
29. Frank Graham, "Setting the Pace," *New York Sun*, February 6, 1940, 24.
30. Woodruff, "Hip! Hip! Hooray! Chance Will Play," C1-2.

31. Woodruff, "Hip! Hip! Hooray! Chance Will Play," C1-2.

32. Woodruff, "Hip! Hip! Hooray! Chance Will Play," C1-2.

33. "World's Champion Manager and Magnate Settle Differences," *Chicago Sunday Tribune*, February 7, 1909, C1.

34. HOF, Box 3, Folder 6.

35. Woodruff, "Hip! Hip! Hooray! Chance Will Play," C1-2.

36. Harvey Woodruff, "Chance Here for League Meeting," *Chicago Daily Tribune*, February 8, 1909, 14.

37. "Condensed Dispatches," *Sporting Life* 52, no. 6 (1909): 2.

38. "Peerless Leader Due This Noon," *Chicago Daily Tribune*, February 13, 1909, 12.

39. "Cub Squad No. 2 Departs," *Chicago Daily Tribune*, March 9, 1909, 6.

40. *Troy (NY) Northern Budget*, March 14, 1909.

41. Frank Graham, "Setting the Pace," Johnny Evers Player File, National Baseball Hall of Fame Library.

42. Woodruff, "Chance Here for League Meeting," C1-2.

43. *Troy (NY) Times*, March 27, 1909.

44. "National League Notes," *Sporting Life* 54, no. 26 (1910): 8.

45. "Kling May Get Franchise of the Kansas City Club," *Chicago Daily Tribune*, October 21, 1908, 10.

46. "Griffith Has Futile Talk with Murphy on Trades," *Chicago Daily Tribune*, December 17, 1908, 12.

47. "Chance is Home; Tells Cub Plans," *Chicago Sunday Tribune*, February 14, 1909, C1.

48. "John Kling Quits World's Champs," *Chicago Sunday Tribune*, March 21, 1909, C1.

49. "John Kling Quits World's Champs," C1.

50. "Kling to Become Magnate," *Chicago Daily Tribune*, March 22, 1909, 14.

51. "John Kling Quits World's Champs," C1.

52. "John Kling Quits World's Champs," C1.

53. "But Kling is Still Here," *Kansas City Times*, April 8, 1909, 10.

54. R. W. Lardner, "Chicago Fans After Kling; Cries of Distress by Mail," *Chicago Daily Tribune*, April 7, 1909, 14.

55. "J. Kling Rolled in the Double," *Kansas City Times*, April 8, 1909, 10.

56. I. E. Sanborn, "Two Pennants for Local Ball Fans," *Chicago Daily Tribune*, April 2, 1909, 6.

8. A Pair of Presidents

1. Pulliam to Herrmann, March 30, 1908, AGHP, Box 70, Folder 1.

2. Harry Pulliam, "Pulliam Denies Giving Out Personal Letters," *Chicago Daily Tribune*, February 12, 1909, 10.

3. "Pulliam Shuns Magnates' War," *Chicago Daily Tribune*, February 15, 1909, 10.

4. "Pulliam Shuns Magnates' War," 10.

5. Frank B. Hutchinson Jr., "Pulliam's Newspaper Banquet is Quiet," Chicago *Inter Ocean*, February 17, 1909, 4.

6. HOF, Box 3, Folder 1.

7. HOF, Box 3, Folder 1.

8. R. W. Lardner, "Chance Cancels Last Dayton Tilt," *Chicago Daily Tribune*, April 13, 1909, 8.

9. "Champion Leader Views of the 1909 Races: By Chance, of Chicago," *Sporting Life* 53, no. 6, (1909): 1.

10. See "Sunday Baseball as Viewed by Liquor Men," *Chicago Sunday Tribune*, March 7, 1909, C1; "Minister After Millers," *Chicago Sunday Tribune*, March 7, 1909, C2; "Death for Sunday Baseball," *Chicago Daily Tribune*, April 15, 1909, 8; "Oil for Troubled Waters," *Chicago Daily Tribune*, April 15, 1909, 8.

11. Riess, *Touching Base*, 136.

12. Riess, *Touching Base*, 136–37.

13. "Police Arrest Players," *New York Times*, April 10, 1905, 7.

14. "A Free Pass: Given by Murphy to Preacher Who Boosted the National Game," *Sporting Life* 53, no. 6 (1909): 3.

15. "'Ladies' Day' for West Side," *Chicago Daily Tribune*, March 28, 1908, 10.

16. Seymour, *Baseball*, 328–29.

17. HOF, Box 3, Folder 6.

18. "Mrs. Chance A 'Rooter,'" *New York Times*, April 13, 1909, 11.

19. HOF, Box 3, Folder 6.

20. R. W. Lardner, "Walsh and Evers Drop Bat for Pen," *Chicago Sunday Tribune*, May 2, 1909, B1.

21. I. E. Sanborn, "Cubs Beat Reds, 5-2. Sox on Top in Uphill Fight, 6-5. Evers Ineligible," *Chicago Daily Tribune*, May 6, 1909, 12.

22. Murphy to WHT, March 12, 1907, WHTP, reel 64.

23. WHT to Murphy, March 14, 1907, WHTP, reel 468.

24. Murphy to WHT, February 7, 1908, WHTP, reel 75.

25. Murphy to WHT, April 2, 1908, WHTP, reel 78.

26. CPT to Herrmann, July 24, 1907, WHTP, reel 21.

27. CPT to Herrmann, July 23, 1907, WHTP, reel 21.

28. Murphy to WHT, June 18, 1908, WHTP, reel 82.

29. Chance to WHT, June 18, 1908, WHTP, reel 82.

30. WHT to Chance, March 6, 1909, WHTP, reel 495.

31. "Taft Guest of Yale Men and City Today," *Pittsburgh Post-Gazette*, May 29, 1909, 1, 6.

32. "Taft Guest of Yale Men and City Today," 6.

33. "Taft Roots for Pirate Success," *Pittsburgh Post-Gazette*, May 30, 1909, 1.

34. R. W. Lardner, "Notes of the Cubs," *Chicago Daily Tribune*, May 30, 1909, 20. Lardner noted that Murphy spent time during the game chatting with Barney Dreyfuss.

35. "Taft Roots for Pirates," *Pittsburgh Post-Gazette*, May 30, 1909, 6. See also "Taft Roots for the Pirates," *Chicago Sunday Tribune*, May 30, 1909, 20. According to the story in the *Chicago Sunday Tribune*, Taft "arose from his three seats and stretched with the rest of the bugs" in the seventh inning.

36. "Taft Roots for Pirate Success," 1.

37. Charles W. Murphy, "Taft, the Fan," *Baseball Magazine* 9, no. 3 (1912): 2.

38. "New Home of Pirates Taxed to Utmost by Enthusiastic Crowd," *Pittsburgh Post-Gazette*, July 1, 1909, 1.

39. "Pitt Breaks Record," *Pittsburgh Post-Gazette*, July 1, 1909, 8.

40. Francis C. Richter, "Passing of Pulliam!" *Sporting Life* 53, no. 22 (1909): 1.

41. "Harry Pulliam Shoots Self," *Chicago Daily Tribune*, July 29, 1909, 1.

42. Richter, "Passing of Pulliam!" 1.

43. "Pres. Harry C. Pulliam Ends Life with A Bullet," *Brooklyn Daily Eagle*, July 29, 1909, 3.

44. "Chance-Griffith Confab Still Remains a Mystery," *Chicago Daily Tribune*, July 31, 1909, 10.

45. "Last Rites for Harry C. Pulliam," *Chicago Daily Tribune*, August 3, 1909, 8.

46. Richter, "Passing of Pulliam!" 1.

47. Stanley D. Solvick, "William Howard Taft and the Payne-Aldrich Tariff," *The Mississippi Valley Historical Review* 50, no 3. (1963): 440.

48. "Greatest Pilgrimage Ever Undertaken by the Head of a Nation," *Chicago Daily Tribune*, September 16, 1909, 18.

49. "Chicago Awaits President Today," *Chicago Daily Tribune*, September 16, 1909, 1.

50. R. W. Lardner, "Mud Halts Cubs; Pirates Climb," *Chicago Daily Tribune*, June 10, 1909, 8.

51. I. E. Sanborn, "Giants Shatter 'Big Ed's' Streak," *Chicago Daily Tribune*, August 15, 1909, 25.

52. "Notes of the Cubs," *Chicago Daily Tribune*, August 15, 1909, 25.

53. "All Chicago Host to Taft for Day," *Chicago Daily Tribune*, September 17, 1909, 1.

54. WHT to HHT, September 16, 1909, WHTP, reel 26.

55. "Taft, A Loyal Fan, Sees Cubs Beaten," *Chicago Daily Tribune*, September 17, 1909, 5.

56. I. E. Sanborn, "Rooter Taft Sees Cubs Take Fall," *Chicago Daily Tribune*, September 17, 1909, 14.

57. "Taft, A Loyal Fan, Sees Cubs Beaten," 5.

58. "Taft, A Loyal Fan, Sees Cubs Beaten," 5.

59. "Taft, A Loyal Fan, Sees Cubs Beaten," 5. See also "Taft as Fan Sees Cubs Lose Game," Chicago *Inter Ocean*, September 17, 1909, 3. The anecdote is relayed by articles in both newspapers, but the *Inter Ocean* story identifies Wilson as the responder to Taft. Puzzlingly, the *Inter Ocean* article mentions Wilson but fails to mention Murphy once.

60. Sanborn, "Rooter Taft Sees Cubs Take Fall," 14.

61. Richard G. Tobin, "President Taft Sees Giants Beat Cubs in Exciting Game," Chicago *Inter Ocean*, September 17, 1909, 13.

62. Sanborn, "Rooter Taft Sees Cubs Take Fall," 14.

63. "Ticket Scalpers Beaten at Their Own Little Game," *Chicago Daily Tribune*, September 18, 1909, 12.

64. Sanborn, "Rooter Taft Sees Cubs Take Fall," 14.

65. "Cub Troubles," *Sporting Life* 54, no. 3 (1909): 3.

66. Murphy to CPT, December 6, 1909, WHTP, reel 333.

67. Frank Schulte and R. W. Lardner, "Carr's Hoosiers Blanked by Cubs," *Chicago Daily Tribune*, April 8, 1910, 6.

9. The Final Pennant

1. Hemingway and Hotchner, *Dear Papa, Dear Hotch*, 30.

2. Reynolds, *The Young Hemingway*, 49.

3. Reynolds, *The Young Hemingway*, 26–27.

4. Hemingway and Hotchner, *Dear Papa, Dear Hotch*, 30.

5. Grantland Rice, "Tinker to Evers to Chance," *Collier's*, November 29, 1930, 11.

6. Hemingway and Hotchner, *Dear Papa, Dear Hotch*, 30.

7. "Protest Way Tickets Are Sold," *Chicago Sunday Tribune*, October 17, 1909, C2.

8. "City Champs Win from Lelands, 4–1," *Chicago Daily Tribune*, October 19, 1909, 8.

9. "Cubs Happy; Receive Coin," *Chicago Daily Tribune*, October 22, 1909, 12.

10. R. W. Lardner, "Foster Argues; Schulte Scores," *Chicago Daily Tribune*, October 22, 1909, 12.

11. Harvey T. Woodruff, "Owners Put Ban on Barnstorming," *Chicago Daily Tribune*, January 12, 1910, 12.

12. "Oak Park Club Notes," *Oak Leaves*, October 30, 1909, 8.

13. W. A. Phelon, "Chicago Chat," *Sporting Life* 54, no. 11 (1909): 5.

14. "Not in Any Plot," *Sporting Life* 54, no. 11 (1909): 6.

15. I. E. Sanborn, "Johnson Defies Baseball Foes," *Chicago Daily Tribune*, December 14, 1909, 14.

16. "Phillies Pass into Hands of New Owners," *Philadelphia Inquirer*, November 27, 1909, 1.

17. R. W. Lardner, "Williams Slated as N. L. Secretary," *Chicago Daily Tribune*, December 8, 1909, 20.

18. "Dreyfuss Will Stand Pat," *Chicago Daily Tribune*, December 8, 1909, 20.

19. "Blow to Heydler's Chances," *Chicago Daily Tribune*, December 8, 1909, 20.

20. R. W. Lardner, "Johnson Courts War with Rivals," *Chicago Sunday Tribune*, December 12, 1909, C1.

21. "Another Case of 'Finnegan,'" *Chicago Sunday Tribune*, January 9, 1910, C3.

22. "General Ledger, No. 10, Anna S. Taft, December 31, 1906–October 14, 1913," Series 2, Box 3, Volume 1, Taft Family Papers, 1817–1959, n.d., MSS 647, Cincinnati Museum Center.

23. "Taft Buys Phillies' Park," *Chicago Daily Tribune*, December 31, 1909, 10.

24. "Phillies Pass into Hands of New Owners," *Philadelphia Inquirer*, November 27, 1909, 1, 10.

25. Harvey T. Woodruff, "Cubs Boss Spikes Two Club Story," *Chicago Daily Tribune*, January 4, 1910, 12.

26. "Taft Hopes Soon to Own Stock in Phila. Ball Club," *Philadelphia Inquirer*, January 1, 1910, 6.

27. W. A. Phelon, "Chicago Chat," *Sporting Life* 54, no. 13 (1909): 10.

28. "Hippodrome to Follow Game," *Chicago Daily Tribune*, December 11, 1909, 10.

29. Phelon, "Chicago Chat," 10.

30. "Dooin Not Slated for Job?" *Chicago Daily Tribune*, January 14, 1910, 10.

31. "Bill to Legalize Sunday Baseball," *Chicago Daily Tribune*, January 17, 1910, 10.

32. Katie Murphy, death certificate, January 4, 1910, File No. 193, State of Ohio Bureau of Vital Statistics, copy in possession of author. Katie's last name is spelled incorrectly on the certificate as "Murphey." Her age at death is recorded as "32?" The document lists her date of birth as

"unknown." See also 1880 United States Census, Wilmington, Clinton County, Ohio, digital image s.v. "Kate Murphy," Ancestry.com. Her earliest suggested birth year appears in the 1880 census, which lists her as being five years of age. That would imply she was born in 1875 and would have been, at most, thirty-five years of age upon her death.

33. "Taft's 'Ould Sod' Safe on Way Here," *Chicago Daily Tribune*, March 11, 1910, 1.
34. "Murphy Goes to New Orleans," *Chicago Daily Tribune*, March 12, 1910, 12.
35. "Taft Wins Way to Erin's Heart," *Chicago Daily Tribune*, March 18, 1910, 1.
36. R. W. Lardner, "Cubs are Idle as J. Pluvius Pours," *Chicago Daily Tribune*, March 11, 1910, 14.
37. "Cubs Get M'Intyre in Trade," *Chicago Sunday Tribune*, April 10, 1910, C1.
38. "Chance Blames Ban Johnson," *Chicago Daily Tribune*, March 26, 1910, 14.
39. "Kling Decision Officially Out," *Chicago Daily Tribune*, March 31, 1910, 9.
40. "Tinker Hero in Kling Case," *Chicago Sunday Tribune*, April 3, 1910, C1.
41. Murphy to WHT, April 1, 1912, WHTP, reel 456.
42. R. W. Lardner, "Taft Sees Cubs Lose to Pirates," *Chicago Daily Tribune*, May 3, 1910, 12; "Taft Greeted by Thousands at Forbes Field," *Pittsburgh Post-Gazette*, May 3, 1910, 1, 6.
43. "Evers' Auto Hit; Writer Crushed," *Chicago Daily Tribune*, May 21, 1910, 1. See also "Fatally Injured in Evers' Automobile," Chicago *Inter Ocean*, May 21, 1910, 1–2.
44. "Evers and Chance to Give up Autos?" *Chicago Sunday Tribune*, May 22, 1910, A7.
45. Charles W. Murphy, "Murphy Praises Chance and Men," *Chicago Daily Tribune*, October 3, 1910, 21.
46. Frank Chance, "Pennant Verifies Chance's Prophecy," *Chicago Daily Tribune*, October 3, 1910, 21.
47. "Evers Gives 'Zim' a Boost," *Chicago Daily Tribune*, October 3, 1910, 21.
48. I. E. Sanborn, "Athletics Take Third Straight from Cubs, 12–5," *Chicago Daily Tribune*, October 21, 1910, 1.
49. "Rivals' Signs," *Sporting Life* 56, no. 26 (1911): 3.
50. Artie Hofman, "'Beaten Fairly' Declares Artie," *Chicago Daily Tribune*, October 24, 1910, 21.
51. "The Athletics' Signal Tipping Pitching System and Inside Ball Made Cubs Look Foolish in the World's Series," *Sporting Life* 57, no. 3 (1911): 5.

10. "Murphy Alone Is My Enemy"

1. "Growth of Baseball," *Sporting Life* 57, no. 2 (1911): 1.

2. "Scalpers' Work," *Sporting Life* 56, no. 12 (1910): 9.

3. "Chance's Apology," *Sporting Life* 56, no. 16 (1910): 17.

4. "Timely Topics," *Sporting Life* 56, no. 14 (1910): 4.

5. "Umpire Eye Test," *Sporting Life* 56, no. 17 (1910): 4.

6. "Umpires' Eyes Tested!" *Sporting Life* 57, no. 5 (1911): 1.

7. "Something to This," *Sporting Life* 56, no. 12 (1910): 3.

8. "National League Notes," *Sporting Life* 56, no. 26 (1911): 8.

9. "20,000 Strikers in West Side Parade," Chicago *Inter Ocean*, December 8, 1910, 3.

10. "Strikers Parade to Show Number," *Chicago Daily Tribune*, December 8, 1910, 3; "Union Calls Off Garment Strike; Yields Claims," *Chicago Daily Tribune*, February 4, 1911, 1.

11. Snelling, *Johnny Evers*, 101.

12. Handy Andy, "Kling to Boston in Player Swap," *Chicago Sunday Tribune*, June 11, 1911, C1.

13. "Local Bear Trainer," *Cincinnati Enquirer*, July 3, 1911, 2.

14. Jack Ryder, "Killed Off," *Cincinnati Enquirer*, July 1, 1911, 8.

15. "Frank Chance, 'Peerless Leader,' Deposed by President Murphy," *San Francisco Call*, September 29, 1912.

16. Jack Ryder, "Chance," *Cincinnati Enquirer*, July 2, 1911, A14.

17. "New 'Tribune' Sign at Cub Grounds Largest at Any Baseball Park in Country," *Chicago Daily Tribune*, July 3, 1911, 10.

18. I. E. Sanborn, "Chance Through as a Playing Cub, Official Edict," *Chicago Sunday Tribune*, April 14, 1912, C1.

19. Sam Weller, "I've Not Resigned, Declares Chance," *Chicago Daily Tribune*, September 30, 1912, 15.

20. "Murphy's Mind," *Sporting Life* 60, no. 5 (1912): 4.

21. "Operate on Manager Chance for Removal of Blood Clot," *Chicago Daily Tribune*, September 18, 1912, 11.

22. "Murphy's Mind," 4.

23. Frank Chance, "Chance Answers Murphy's Charge With 'Hot Fire,'" *Chicago Daily Tribune*, September 27, 1912, 15.

24. "Chance Gives Lie to Murphy, Defending Cubs," Chicago *Inter Ocean*, September 27, 1912, 1, 4.

25. "'Booze' Not Cause of Cubs' Defeat," *Chicago Daily Tribune*, September 26, 1912, 15.

26. Sam Weller, "Chance's Career as Cub Manager Ends This Year," *Chicago Sunday Tribune*, September 29, 1912, C1–2.

27. Weller, "Chance's Career as Cub Manager Ends This Year," C1–2.

28. Weller, "I've Not Resigned, Declares Chance," 15.

29. Harvey T. Woodruff, "F. L. Chance Sells Baseball Stock for $40,000 Cash," *Chicago Daily Tribune*, October 4, 1912, 13.

30. Frank L. Chance, "Chance Tells Why He Thinks the Cubs Will Win; First Story on Series as a 'Tribune' Reporter," *Chicago Sunday Tribune*, October 6, 1912, C1.

31. "Chance's Agreement to Sell Cub Stock," *Chicago Daily Tribune*, October 4, 1912, 13.

32. I. E. Sanborn, "Murphy Whets Ax for Waning Cubs," *Chicago Daily Tribune*, October 21, 1912, 13.

33. O. K. Lientz, "Murphy to Stay in Game: Frank Chance Claims Chicago Man Has Done Most to Injure Sport," *Los Angeles Evening Express*, February 12, 1914, 1.

34. "Grayson Starts Exposé of Game," *Louisville Courier-Journal*, August 22, 1913, 6.

35. F. C. Lane, "Shall Certain Magnates Defy the Public?" *Baseball Magazine* 10, no. 7 (1913): 25.

36. Lane, "Shall Certain Magnates Defy the Public?" 32.

37. Sanborn, "Murphy Whets Ax for Waning Cubs," 13

38. Harvey T. Woodruff, "Chance in Reply Lashes Cub Boss," *Chicago Daily Tribune*, October 21, 1912, 13.

39. "Cub Job for 'Red' Dooin—Not!" *Chicago Daily Tribune*, October 22, 1912, 15.

40. Harvey T. Woodruff, "Frank L. Chance, the Peerless Leader," *Chicago Sunday Tribune*, September 29, 1912, C1.

41. Frank L. Chance, "Chance's Farewell to Chicago Fans," *Chicago Sunday Tribune*, October 27, 1912, C1.

42. Handy Andy, "Chance Departs for California," *Chicago Sunday Tribune*, October 27, 1912, C1.

43. "Evers' Elevation," *Sporting Life* 60, no. 12 (1912): 3

44. Sam Weller, "Tinker Up in Air on Manager's Job," *Chicago Daily Tribune*, October 31, 1912, 11.

45. I. E. Sanborn, "Cardinal Hurler Sought by Cubs," *Chicago Daily Tribune*, December 16, 1912, 18.

46. "Deal for Tinker Finally Closed," *Chicago Daily Tribune*, December 12, 1912, 16.

47. Murphy to Herrmann, November 9, 1912, AGHP, Box 48, Folder 19.

48. Joseph Vila, "Chance Right," *Sporting Life* 60, no. 17 (1912): 3.

49. Farrell to Herrmann, January 11, 1913, AGHP, Box 53, Folder 18.

50. Sam Weller, "Chance Departs for Coast Today," *Chicago Daily Tribune*, January 10, 1913, 10.

11. "All Is Fair in Love and War"

1. "Bob Thayer's Sporting Gossip," *Washington Times*, August 13, 1912, 10.
2. HOF, Box 3, Folder 11.
3. HOF, Box 3, Folder 11.
4. HOF, Box 3, Folder 11.
5. "Fogel Fancies," *Sporting Life* 60, no. 5 (1912): 3.
6. "Fogel Fancies," 3.
7. "Philadelphia Points," *Sporting Life* 60, no. 9 (1912): 7.
8. "Cub Boss Declares He Was Not Aware of Part He Played," *Chicago Evening Post*, November 27, 1912.
9. HOF, Box 3, Folder 11.
10. "Cub Boss Declares He Was Not Aware of Part He Played."
11. "Murphy Approved Story," *Cincinnati Enquirer*, November 27, 1912, 6.
12. Jack Ryder, "Wee Hours," *Cincinnati Enquirer*, November 27, 1912, 6.
13. "Locke Finally Secures Phila. Baseball [C]lub," *Philadelphia Inquirer*, January 16, 1913, 1, 10.
14. "Doc Semmens Joins the Reds," *Chicago Daily Tribune*, April 11, 1913, 15.
15. Murphy to Herrmann, May 7, 1913, AGHP, Box 48, Folder 20.
16. I. E. Sanborn, "'Frank Chance Day' Brings Out 35,000, But White Sox Win," *Chicago Sunday Tribune*, May 18, 1913, C1–2.
17. Handy Andy, "Motorists Parade to Park," *Chicago Sunday Tribune*, May 18, 1913, C2.
18. HOF, Box 4, Folder 2.
19. Hugh S. Fullerton, "Federal League Organizes Today," *Chicago Daily Tribune*, March 8, 1913, 10.
20. "Federal League Threatens to Retaliate on Majors," *Chicago Daily Tribune*, June 14, 1913, 15.
21. R. W. Lardner, "In the Wake of the News," *Chicago Daily Tribune*, November 7, 1913, 17.
22. "Cub Boss Makes Bid for Tinker," *Chicago Daily Tribune*, December 11, 1913, 10.
23. Frank Menke, "Herman Blamed for New League," AGHP, Box 111, Folder 18.
24. "Tinker Sold for Cash to Dodgers," *Chicago Daily Tribune*, December 13, 1913, 13.

25. I. E. Sanborn, "Sale of Tinker Stops Cub Boss," *Chicago Sunday Tribune*, December 14, 1913, C1.

26. Johnson to Herrmann, December 17, 1913, AGHP, Box 110, Folder 5.

27. Herrmann to Ebbets, December 15, 1913, AGHP, Box 110, Folder 5.

28. I. E. Sanborn, "Deal for Tinker Starts Big Row," *Chicago Daily Tribune*, December 16, 1913, 16.

29. "Wires to Murphy: Hands Off," *Chicago Daily Tribune*, December 19, 1913, 14.

30. Herrmann to Ebbets, December 15, 1913, AGHP, Box 110, Folder 5.

31. Levitt, *The Outlaw League and the Battle That Forged Modern Baseball*, 9.

32. HOF, Box 4, Folder 2.

33. HOF, Box 4, Folder 2.

34. HOF, Box 4, Folder 2.

35. Levitt, *The Outlaw League and the Battle That Forged Modern Baseball*, 10.

36. Herrmann to Ebbets, May 14, 1915, AGHP, Box 110, Folder 5.

37. Murphy to Herrmann, December 31, 1913, AGHP, Box 112, Folder 12.

38. HOF, Box 4, Folder 2.

39. I. E. Sanborn, "Cubs are Warned Against Federal," *Chicago Daily Tribune*, January 3, 1914, 14.

40. Murphy to Herrmann, January 14, 1914, AGHP, Box 112, Folder 12.

41. Murphy to Herrmann, January 10, 1914, AGHP, Box 112, Folder 12.

42. Murphy to Herrmann, January 27, 1914, AGHP, Box 112, Folder 12.

43. Copy of the letter located in AGHP, Box 111, Folder 18.

44. Levitt, *The Outlaw League and the Battle That Forged Modern Baseball*, 78.

45. Levitt, *The Outlaw League and the Battle That Forged Modern Baseball*, 80.

46. Johnson to Herrmann, January 24, 1914, AGHP, Box 111, Folder 18.

47. Ebbets to Herrmann, January 29, 1914, AGHP, Box 110, Folder 33.

48. Murphy to Herrmann, January 23, 1914, AGHP, Box 112, Folder 12.

49. Levitt, *The Outlaw League and the Battle That Forged Modern Baseball*, 80.

50. Ebbets to Herrmann, January 28, 1914, AGHP, Box 110, Folder 33.

51. Johnson to Herrmann, December 19, 1913, AGHP, Box 73, Folder 31.

52. HOF, Box 4, Folder 2.

53. HOF, Box 4, Folder 2.

54. HOF, Box 4, Folder 2.

55. "Notes of City Series," *Chicago Sunday Tribune*, October 12, 1913, C2.

56. Deborah Williams, conversation with author, December 6, 2020.

57. Sam Weller, "Williams Jumps to Chicago 'Feds'; Club Secretary," *Chicago Sunday Tribune*, February 1, 1914, C1-2.

58. "West Side Fans Boost 'Feds,'" *Chicago Daily Tribune*, February 2, 1914, 14.

59. "Saves Federals," *Washington Post*, May 3, 1914, C2.

12. "The Malicious Mistake of Mr. Murphy"

1. HOF, Box 4, Folder 2.
2. HOF, Box 4, Folder 3.
3. HOF, Box 4, Folder 1.
4. HOF, Box 4, Folder 1.
5. HOF, Box 4, Folder 2.
6. HOF, Box 4, Folder 2.
7. HOF, Box 4, Folder 2.
8. HOF, Box 4, Folder 2.
9. HOF, Box 4, Folder 2.
10. HOF, Box 4, Folder 2.
11. HOF, Box 4, Folder 2.
12. HOF, Box 4, Folder 2.
13. HOF, Box 4, Folder 2.
14. HOF, Box 4, Folder 2.
15. HOF, Box 4, Folder 2.
16. HOF, Box 4, Folder 2.
17. HOF, Box 4, Folder 2.
18. HOF, Box 4, Folder 2.
19. HOF, Box 4, Folder 2.
20. HOF, Box 4, Folder 2.
21. HOF, Box 4, Folder 2.
22. Sam Weller, "Evers Deposed as Cub Leader; O'Day Gets Job," *Chicago Daily Tribune*, February 11, 1914, 1–2.
23. "Magnates Asked to Force Murphy Out of Baseball," *Chicago Daily Tribune*, February 12, 1914, 11.
24. "Federals on Evers' Trail; Seek Influence of Tinker," *Chicago Daily Tribune*, February 12, 1914, 11.
25. HOF, Box 4, Folder 2.
26. "Cub Owner Loses Evers Outright," *Chicago Daily Tribune*, February 13, 1914, 15.
27. Sam Weller, "Murphy to Start Suit for Slander Against Johnson," *Chicago Daily Tribune*, February 14, 1914, 14.
28. "'Get-Away' Week for Chicago's Ball Teams," *Los Angeles Evening Express*, February 16, 1914, 8.
29. Handy Andy, "Murphy Must Go, Johnson States," *Chicago Sunday Tribune*, February 15, 1914, C1.

30. Andy, "Murphy Must Go, Johnson States," C1.

31. Hugh Fullerton, "Charles Webb Murphy Has Made His Base Ball Quarrels Pay Him in Handsome Dividends," *Fort Wayne (IN) Sentinel*, February 17, 1914, 8.

32. "Taft to Uphold C. W. Murphy," *Chicago Daily Tribune*, February 21, 1914, 15.

33. Sam Weller, "N. L. Meets Today; Murphy Sick Man," *Chicago Daily Tribune*, February 21, 1914, 15.

34. HOF, Box 4, Folder 3.

35. "Murphy Out; Taft Now Owns His Cub Stock," *Chicago Sunday Tribune*, February 22, 1914, A1–2.

36. "Day Book Journal F," Box 21, Volume 64, 266, Anna Sinton Taft Papers, 1870–1934, MSS T1241, Cincinnati Museum Center.

37. HOF, Box 4, Folder 3.

38. Handy Andy, "Evers Returns for Moving," *Chicago Daily Tribune*, February 25, 1914, 15.

39. "Chance in Field for Evers," *Chicago Daily Tribune*, February 12, 1914, 11.

40. "Murphy Out; Taft Now Owns His Cub Stock," A1–2.

13. Show Business

1. "Murphy Retires from Game," *Cincinnati Enquirer*, February 22, 1914, A18.

2. Sam Weller, "C. W. Murphy Rich, Finds Happiness in Quitting Game," *Chicago Daily Tribune*, February 23, 1914, 10.

3. "National League Buys Out Murphy," *The Gazette* (Montreal), February 23, 1914, 14; "Baseball hat Charles W. Murphy zun Millionär gemacht," *Tagliches Cincinnatier Volksblatt*, February 23, 1914, 1.

4. Weller, "C. W. Murphy Rich, Finds Happiness in Quitting Game," 10.

5. Weller, "C. W. Murphy Rich, Finds Happiness in Quitting Game," 10.

6. Damon Runyon, "When They Throw Murphy Out Some One Else Must be Baseball Bugaboo," *Dayton (OH) Daily News*, November 26, 1914, 10.

7. HOF, Box 4, Folder 3.

8. Levitt, *The Outlaw League and the Battle That Forged Modern Baseball*, 154–55.

9. I. E. Sanborn, "Must Consult Murphy First in Cubs' Sale," *Chicago Daily Tribune*, November 12, 1914, 14.

10. "Murphy Meets C. P. Taft Today," *Chicago Daily Tribune*, November 16, 1914, 16.

11. James Crusinberry, "Murphy's 'No' Blocks Feds; Cubs to Stick," *Chicago Daily Tribune*, November 19, 1914, 9.

12. Crusinberry, "Murphy's 'No' Blocks Feds," 9.

13. I. E. Sanborn, "Roger Named Cub Manager; Feds Hostile," *Chicago Daily Tribune*, November 20, 1914, 14.

14. Levitt, *The Outlaw League and the Battle That Forged Modern Baseball*, 248.

15. Frank McDonald, "O Tempora! O Mores!" *Chicago Daily Tribune*, November 20, 1914, 14.

16. "Court Enjoins Cubs' Chief," *Chicago Daily Tribune*, May 1, 1909, 3.

17. "Raiders Wreck Seized Theater," *Chicago Daily Tribune*, July 11, 1910, 1.

18. "Splendid Isolation of Wilmington to be Disturbed," *Dayton (OH) Daily News*, January 23, 1916, 14.

19. "Nearing the Century Mark," *Wilmington (OH) Daily News*, February 8, 1916, 1.

20. "C. W. Murphy Buys Site," *Wilmington (OH) Daily News*, November 26, 1915, 5.

21. "C. W. Murphy Buys Site," 5.

22. "Nearing the Century Mark," 1.

23. "Commence on Theatre Soon," *Wilmington (OH) Daily News*, March 1, 1916, 8.

24. "Some Busy 'Burg' This!" *Wilmington (OH) Daily News*, March 2, 1916, 8.

25. "Architect is Now at Work," *Wilmington (OH) Daily News*, July 18, 1916, 8; "Building Laps Theatre Site," *Wilmington (OH) Daily News*, August 17, 1916, 1; "New Theatre Site Free of Buildings," *Wilmington (OH) Daily News*, August 26, 1916, 1.

26. *Wilmington (OH) Daily News*, November 27, 1916, 5.

27. "Schofield Property Obtained by Clinton Theater Owner," *Wilmington (OH) Daily News*, April 4, 1917, 6.

28. "Real Estate Transfers," *Wilmington (OH) Daily News*, April 17, 1917, 5.

29. "Theatre Plans Are Enlarged," *Wilmington (OH) Daily News*, April 6, 1917, 6.

30. "Schofield Property Obtained by Clinton Theater Owner," 6.

31. Charles W. Murphy, "Letters to the Editor," *Wilmington (OH) Daily News*, December 11, 1917, 2.

32. "Biographical Dictionary of Cincinnati Architects," Architectural Foundation of Cincinnati, accessed May 10, 2020, https://www.architecturecincy.org/programs/biographical-dictionary-of-cincinnati-architects/f/.

33. Murphy, "Letters to the Editor," 2.

34. Murphy, "Letters to the Editor," 2.

35. "No Gloom to be in Murphy Theater Says the Builder," *Wilmington (OH) Daily News*, June 25, 1918, 1.

36. "Wilmington's Beauty Lauded by Chicago Woman Visiting Here," *Wilmington (OH) News-Journal*, July 13, 1929, 3.

37. "Eleven Rooms for Business," *Wilmington (OH) Daily News*, July 12, 1917, 1.

38. "Make Change in The Plans," *Wilmington (OH) Daily News*, August 14, 1917, 4.

39. Charles W. Murphy, "Variety of Current Talkies," *Wilmington (OH) News-Journal*, October 3, 1929, 10.

40. Murphy, "Letters to the Editor," 2.

41. Murphy, "Letters to the Editor," 2.

42. "In Blaze of Glory and With Pat(r)iotic Ceremonies the Murphy Theater is Formally Opened and Dedicated," *Wilmington (OH) Daily News*, July 25, 1918, 6.

43. "In Blaze of Glory and With Pat(r)iotic Ceremonies the Murphy Theater is Formally Opened and Dedicated," 6.

44. "In Blaze of Glory and With Pat(r)iotic Ceremonies the Murphy Theater is Formally Opened and Dedicated," 6.

45. "Murphy Talks," *Wilmington (OH) Daily News*, July 25, 1918, 6–7.

46. W. J. Galvin, "C. W. Murphy," *Wilmington (OH) Daily News*, July 25, 1918, 6.

47. Galvin, "C. W. Murphy," 6.

48. "In Blaze of Glory and With Pat(r)iotic Ceremonies the Murphy Theater is Formally Opened and Dedicated," 6.

49. *Western Architect* 28, no. 11 (1919): plates 7–10.

14. Narratives

1. F. C. Lane, "Editorials," *Baseball Magazine* 16, no. 4 (1916): 13.

2. Charles W. Murphy, "Editorials," *Baseball Magazine* 16, no. 5 (1916): 16.

3. Charles W. Murphy, "Murphy Borrows $105,000, Buys Cubs and Makes Fortune," *Chicago Evening American*, March 4, 1916.

4. Charles W. Murphy, "Murphy Tells How He Became Part Owner of the Philly Park," *Chicago Evening American*, April 8, 1916.

5. Charles W. Murphy, "Murphy Tells of the Many Troubles of Big League Ball Owner," *Chicago Evening American*, April 1, 1916.

6. Murphy, "Murphy Tells of the Many Troubles of Big League Ball Owner."

7. Jim Collins is frequently cited as having developed the flywheel effect in his book *Good to Great: Why Some Companies Make the Leap and Others Don't*, first published in 2001. In his example, Collins's flywheel is a large metal disk, while Charlie Murphy cites a water wheel.

8. Charles W. Murphy, "My Idea of a Magnate's Popularity," *Baseball Magazine* 22, no. 5 (1919): 294.

9. Murphy, "My Idea of a Magnate's Popularity," 294.

10. Charles W. Murphy, "The Gambling Spirit an Evil Influence in Baseball," *Baseball Magazine* 25, no. 1 (1920): 348, 356.

11. Anna Sinton Taft, 1870–1934, MSS T1241, Cincinnati Museum Center.

12. James Crusinberry, "Ackerland to Keep His Shares in Cubs as Good Investment," *Chicago Daily Tribune*, January 6, 1916, 17.

13. "Murphy Sends His Regards," *Los Angeles Times*, January 8, 1916, 6.

14. "Chicago Feds Buy Cub Team from C. P. Taft," *Chicago Daily Tribune*, January 6, 1916, 17.

15. Harvey T. Woodruff, "The Chicago Situation," *Sporting Life* 66, no. 20 (1916): 2.

16. James Crusinberry, "Even Million Now Value of Chicago Cubs," *Chicago Daily Tribune*, January 7, 1916, 13.

17. "49,165 Souls and $56,000, Billy's Score," *Chicago Daily Tribune*, May 20, 1918, 1, 4.

18. "Public Schools Will Train Men for Army Work," *Chicago Daily Tribune*, September 20, 1918, 11.

19. HOF, Box 5, Folder 8.

20. Harvey T. Woodruff, "Former Boss of Chance Machine Secures Shares," *Chicago Daily Tribune*, February 14, 1919, 16.

21. Woodruff, "Former Boss of Chance Machine Secures Shares," 16.

22. Al Chase, "It's a Sad Tale to Cub Fans, but Not to Murphy," *Chicago Daily Tribune*, October 24, 1919, 26.

23. George Shaffer, "Great Leader Gave Chicago Four Pennants," *Chicago Daily Tribune*, September 16, 1924, 1, 3.

24. Murphy, "Murphy Tells of the Many Troubles of Big League Ball Owner."

25. Charles W. Murphy, "Murphy Theatre to Present Variety of Current Talkies," *Wilmington News-Journal*, October 3, 1929, 10.

26. "Baseball Lacks Science Charles W. Murphy Says," *Wilmington (OH) News-Journal*, May 29, 1931, 2.

27. "Rev. Charles F. Murphy Celebrates First Mass," *Wilmington (OH) News-Journal*, June 1, 1931, 1.

28. "C. W. Murphy is Seriously Ill," *Wilmington (OH) News-Journal*, June 15, 1931, 3.

29. "Charles Webb Murphy," *Sporting News* 92, no. 9 (1931): 4.

30. Kroger Babb, "Sport Honey from the Bumblebee," *Wilmington (OH) News-Journal*, October 29, 1931, 8.

31. Clark Griffith, "Baseball! A Summer Business," *Bulletin* (Pomona CA), July 29, 1924, 7.

32. Joseph Vila, "Vila Recalls Roles Played by Murphy," *Sporting News* 92, no. 9 (1931): 3.

BIBLIOGRAPHY

Alexander, Charles. *John McGraw: A Giant in His Time*. Kindle edition. South Orange NJ: Summer Game Books, 1988.

Bales, Jack. *Before They Were the Cubs: The Early Years of Chicago's First Professional Baseball Team*. Jefferson NC: McFarland, 2019.

Barth, Gunther. *City People: The Rise of Modern City Culture in Nineteenth-Century America*. Oxford: Oxford University Press, 1982.

Brown, Albert J., ed. *History of Clinton County, Ohio: Its People, Industries and Institutions*. Indianapolis: Bowen & Company, 1915.

Carmichael, John P. *My Greatest Day in Baseball: 47 Dramatic Stories by 47 Famous Stars*. New York: Grosset & Dunlap, 1951.

Cronon, William. *Nature's Metropolis: Chicago and the Great West*. New York: Norton, 1992.

Evers, John J., and Hugh Fullerton. *Touching Second: The Science of Baseball*. Chicago: Reilly & Britton Company, 1910.

Golenbock, Peter. *Wrigleyville: A Magical History Tour of the Chicago Cubs*. New York: St. Martin's Press, 1996.

Goss, Charles Frederick. *Cincinnati: The Queen City, 1788-1912*. Chicago: Clarke Publishing Company, 1912.

Hemingway, Ernest, and A. E. Hotchner. *Dear Papa, Dear Hotch: The Correspondence of Ernest Hemingway and A. E. Hotchner*, edited by Albert J. DeFazio III. Columbia: University of Missouri Press, 2005.

Laxton, Edward. *The Famine Ships: The Irish Exodus to America, 1846-1851*. London: Bloomsbury, 1996.

Levitt, Daniel R. *The Outlaw League and the Battle That Forged Modern Baseball*. Lanham MD: Taylor Trade Publishing, 2014.

Miller, Donald L. *City of the Century: The Epic of Chicago and the Making of America*. New York: Simon & Schuster, 2003.

Murphy, Cait. *Crazy '08: How a Cast of Cranks, Rogues, Boneheads, and Magnates Created the Greatest Year in Baseball History*. New York: HarperCollins, 2007.

Nolan, Janet. "The Great Famine and Women's Emigration from Ireland." In *The Hungry Stream: Essays on Emigration and Famine*, edited by E. Margaret Crawford, 61–70. Belfast: Nicholson & Bass, 1997.

Pierce, Bessie Louise. *A History of Chicago*. Vol. 3, *The Rise of a Modern City, 1871–1893*. Chicago: University of Chicago Press, 2007.

Rapp, David. *Tinker to Evers to Chance: The Chicago Cubs and the Dawn of Modern America*. Chicago: University of Chicago Press, 2018.

Reynolds, Michael. *The Young Hemingway*. New York: Norton, 1998.

Richter, Francis. "The Press and Sport." In *Athletic Sports in America, England, and Australia: Comprising History, Characteristics, Sketches of Famous Leaders, Organization and Great Contests of Baseball, Cricket, Football, La Crosse, Tennis, Rowing and Cycling*, edited by Harry Clay Palmer, James Austin Fynes, Francis C. Richter, and William Ingraham Harris, 569–74, Philadelphia: Hubbard Brothers, 1889.

Riess, Steven A. *Touching Base: Professional Baseball and American Culture in the Progressive Era*. rev. ed. Urbana: University of Illinois Press, 1999.

Ross, Ishbel. *An American Family: The Tafts, 1678 to 1964*. Cleveland: World Publishing Company, 1964.

Seymour, Harold. *Baseball: The Early Years*. New York: Oxford University Press, 1960.

Shea, Stuart. *Wrigley Field: The Long Life and Contentious Times of the Friendly Confines*. Chicago: University of Chicago Press, 2014.

Snelling, Dennis. *Johnny Evers: A Baseball Life*. Jefferson NC: McFarland, 2014.

St. Columbkille Catholic Church. *St. Columbkille Catholic Church: A History of the Parish, 1866–2016*. Wilmington OH: St. Columbkille Church, 2016.

Thomson, Cindy and Scott Brown. *Three Finger: The Mordecai Brown Story*. Lincoln: University of Nebraska Press, 2006.

Weisberger, Bernard A. *When Chicago Ruled Baseball: The Cubs-White Sox World Series of 1906*. New York: Harper, 2007.

Zeigler, Connie J. "When Store." In *The Encyclopedia of Indianapolis*, edited by David J. Bodenhamer and Robert G. Barrows, 1424–25. Bloomington: Indiana University Press, 1994.

Ziff, Katherine. *Asylum on the Hill: History of a Healing Landscape*. Athens: Ohio University Press, 2012.

INDEX